ENGLISCH

für Physiker

Lehrmaterial
für die Sprachkundigenausbildung
Stufe II b

VEB Verlag Enzyklopädie
Leipzig

Als Lehrbuch für die Ausbildung an Universitäten und Hochschulen der DDR anerkannt.

Berlin, Februar 1988 · Minister für Hoch- und Fachschulwesen

Autoren:

Hans Heidrich	Humboldt-Universität zu Berlin
Prof. Dr. sc. Hans Joachim Meyer	Humboldt-Universität zu Berlin
unter Mitarbeit von	
Hildegard Timm	Humboldt-Universität zu Berlin

Die Lieferung der zu diesem Lehrbuch entwickelten *technischen Unterrichtsmittel* (31 Tonbänder MB-H 344, 18 c/sw Dias HR 377, 60 c Folien und ein Beiheft) erfolgt über das Institut für Film, Bild und Ton, Krausenstraße 9—10, Berlin, DDR - 1080.

Heidrich, Hans:
Englisch für Physiker : Lehrmaterial für d. Sprachkundigenausbildung
Stufe IIb / [Autoren: Hans Heidrich ; Hans Joachim Meyer unter Mitarb. von Hildegard Timm]. — 4., unveränd. Aufl. — Leipzig : Verlag Enzyklopädie, 1989. — 280 S.

ISBN 3-324-00419-5

NE: Meyer, Hans Joachim: ; HST

ISBN 3-324-00419-5

4., unveränderte Auflage
© VEB Verlag Enzyklopädie Leipzig, 1989
Verlagslizenz 434-130/167/89
Printed in the German Democratic Republic
Grundschrift: 9p Times
Satz: Interdruck, Graphischer Großbetrieb
Leipzig—III/18/97
Druck und Einband: VEB Druckerei „Gottfried Wilhelm Leibniz",
4450 Gräfenhainichen · 7143
Einbandgestaltung: Rolf Kunze
LSV 0834
Bestell-Nr. 576 439 7
01500

Vorwort

Das Lehrbuch "Englisch für Physiker" ist sowohl für den fachsprachlichen Teil der Sprachkundigenausbildung der Stufe II b als auch für die fachsprachliche Ausbildung an Universitäten und Hochschulen bestimmt. Entsprechend der Zielsetzung der SKA II b ist es primär lese- und übersetzungsorientiert und dient daneben der Entwicklung der Fähigkeit, Sachverhalte in der Fremdsprache zu formulieren ("Sinnübertragung") sowie der Entwicklung von Hör- und Sprechfertigkeiten. Das Lehrbuch besteht aus dem hier vorliegenden graphischen Teil sowie aus einem Tonbandteil und visuellen Hilfen, die im Institut für Film, Bild und Ton erscheinen. Voraussetzung für die Arbeit mit dem Lehrmaterial sind die grammatischen und lexikalischen Kenntnisse, die bis zum Abitur an der Oberschule vermittelt werden.

Das Lehrbuch "Englisch für Physiker" verwirklicht in modifizierter Weise Prinzipien, die von Prof. Dr. Reinecke, Doz. Dr. Krampitz und A. Franz im "Modell der Sprachkundigenausbildung der DDR, II a und II b (Russisch)", Leipzig 1971 dargelegt wurden. Ferner konnten wir uns auf zahlreiche Anregungen stützen, die wir auf den Leipziger Kolloquien zur Problematik der SKA II b, auf Beratungen und Kolloquien der Sektion Fremdsprachen an der Humboldt-Universität zu Berlin und von den Autoren der anderen für die SKA II b bestimmten Englischlehrbücher erhielten. Außerdem konnten wir Hinweise von künftigen Benutzern verwerten, denen das Lehrmaterial auf einem besonderen Kolloquium vorgestellt wurde.

Die Auswahl des Lernwortschatzes erfolgte unter Berücksichtigung des von Prof. Dr. L. Hoffmann herausgegebenen Häufigkeitswörterbuches "Fachwortschatz Physik: Russisch / Englisch / Französisch", Leipzig 1973 und von Hans Heidrich, "Allgemeinwissenschaftlicher Wortschatz. Englisch" Leipzig 1974. Für die Erarbeitung der Abschnitte zur Wortbildung konnten Ergebnisse der Dissertation unserer Kollegin Dr. Ragna Sprigade, "Strukturelle Mittel der Terminusbildung in der englischen Fachsprache der Atom- und Kernphysik und ihre deutschen Äquivalente", Berlin 1973 genutzt werden.

Zuerst möchten wir unserer Kollegin Frau Dipl. Phil. Hildegard Timm Dank sagen für ihre Unterstützung bei der Erarbeitung des Lehrbuches.

Unser besonderer Dank gilt Mr. Keith Ebbutt, B.Sc., Dip. Ed., F.R.I.C. und Mr. Vincent Edwards, M. A., für ihre wertvollen Ratschläge und Hinweise zur sprachlichen Gestaltung des Lehrbuches sowie Herrn Dr. sc. nat. Kurt Peuker, Humboldt-

Universität Berlin, der uns bei physikalischen Problemen mit seinem sachkundigen Rat in verständnisvoller Weise unterstützte und das gesamte Material unter fachwissenschaftlichen Gesichtspunkten überprüfte, und Herrn Dipl. Phil. Roland Schreyer, Martin-Luther-Universität Halle-Wittenberg, für seine kritische Durchsicht des Lehrbuches und für seine wichtigen Hinweise. Nicht zuletzt möchten wir den Studenten der Erprobungsgruppen aus den Studienjahren 1973/74 und 1974/75 für ihr kritisches Interesse danken.

Berlin, im Juli 1976   Dr. phil. *Hans Joachim Meyer*
                                                                    Dipl. Phil. *Hans Heidrich*

Inhaltsverzeichnis

Einleitung   6

Hinweise für den Benutzer   10

Symbole und Abkürzungen   11

Übersicht über die Programmkomplexe   12

    1. Elements   19
    2. Atomic Structure and Isotopes   36
    3. Electricity   53
    4. Waves and Particles   73
    5. Solids and Semiconductors   94
    6. Bond Structure and Energy Levels   114
    7. Radioactivity and Nuclear Energy   135
    8. Spectroscopy and Optical Properties of Materials   155
    9. Phenomena of Magnetism and the Magnetic Field   175
    10. Mechanics   197
    11. Trends in Modern Physics   218
    12. University Courses and Co-operation in Research   238

Schlüssel   255

Wörterverzeichnis   266

Quellenverzeichnis   280

Einleitung

Das vorliegende Lehrbuch besteht aus den zwölf *Programmkomplexen* (PK):
Elements; Atomic Structure and Isotopes; Electricity; Waves and Particles; Solids
and Semiconductors; Bond Structure and Energy Levels; Radioactivity and Nuclear
Energy; Spectroscopy and Optical Properties of Materials; Phenomena of Magnetism and the Magnetic Field; Mechanics; Trends in Modern Physics und University
Courses and Co-operation in Research. Jeder Programmkomplex untergliedert sich
wiederum in je vier *Programmabschnitte* (PA), die ihrerseits aus Sequenzen (SQ)
bestehen. Eine Sequenz faßt jeweils eine Anzahl von Lehreinheiten (LE) zusammen.
Ein Teil der Lehreinheiten ist mit einem Lösungsschlüssel versehen.

Die Programmkomplexe bestehen aus *graphischen Teilen*, die in diesem Buch enthalten sind, und *Tonbandteilen*, die die Sequenzen A, B und D der Programmabschnitte 2 und 4 umfassen. Sie erscheinen — wie auch die visuellen Hilfen — im
Institut für Film, Bild und Ton und sind hier nur durch Listen, Übungsanweisungen
und Muster, Wortschatz- und Strukturelemente sowie durch die Ablaufschemata
der (Bild)Tonvorträge vertreten. Graphische, auditive und visuelle Elemente ergänzen sich gegenseitig. So ist der Wortschatz im graphischen Teil des Lehrbuches
lediglich in Listenform, unterteilt nach Wortschatz zur Wiederholung, neue Lexik
und Internationalismen, aufgeführt. Dagegen wird der neue Wortschatz im Tonbandteil schrittweise eingeführt und geübt.

Das gesamte Lehrbuch ist für 60 Stunden *Unterricht* und für etwa die gleiche Zeit
selbständiger Arbeit des Studierenden gedacht. Für die Abarbeitung der Programmkomplexe gehen wir von folgendem Modell aus:

Programmabschnitt 4 bzw. 2		
Sequenz D	(Bild)Tonvortrag; Sprechen oder Leistungs- kontrolle im Programmabschnitt 4 der Programmkomplexe 2, 5 und 8	— Unterricht
Programmabschnitt 1 bzw. 3		
Sequenz A:	Lexikvermittlung und -übung (Wortbildung, Gebrauch wichtiger Verben u. a.)	— Unterricht
Sequenz B:	Grammatikvermittlung und -übung	— Unterricht
Sequenz C:	Herübersetzen; Hinübersetzen und/oder Sinnübertragung	— Unterricht bzw. selbst. Arbeit
Programmabschnitt 2 bzw. 4		
Sequenz A:	Wortschatzeinführung (Tonband); Tonbandübungen zur Lexik	— selbst. Arbeit — selbst. Arbeit
Sequenz B:	Tonbandübungen zur Grammatik	— selbst. Arbeit
Sequenz C:	Verstehendes Lesen	— selbst. Arbeit bzw. Unterricht

Man beachte, *daß nach diesem Modell die Unterrichtsstunde mit der Sequenz D beginnt*, weil der (Bild)Tonvortrag und die Sprechaufgaben einerseits auf der vorher vermittelten Lexik und Grammatik basieren und andererseits vom Lernenden eine besonders hohe Aufmerksamkeit verlangen.

Der Lehrer hat in diesem Rahmen folgende *Variationsmöglichkeit en*:

(1) Er muß in den meisten Fällen entscheiden, ob die Hinübersetzung, die Vorbereitungsübungen zur Sinnübertragung, die Sinnübertragung selbst und die Aufgaben zum Lesetext schriftlich oder mündlich durchzuführen sind.

(2) Er kann entscheiden, ob diese soeben genannten Aufgaben unter seiner Anleitung im Unterricht oder selbständig zu lösen sind.

(3) Er kann ferner diejenigen Lexik- und Grammatikübungen der Sequenzen A und B in den Programmabschnitten 1 bzw. 3, die mit einem Schlüssel versehen sind, der selbständigen Arbeit zuweisen, um stattdessen mehr Zeit für die Sinnübertragung oder den Lesetext zu gewinnen.

Es sollte jedoch bei solchen Entscheidungen bedacht werden, daß das Lehrbuch auf einer klaren Schrittfolge beruht, die nur begrenzt ohne Schaden für den Lernerfolg verändert werden kann.

Im *Schlüssel* finden sich die Lösungen zu allen Transformations-, Formations-, Substitutions- und Komplettierungsaufgaben, allen Übungen zur Auswahl von Bedeutungsvarianten und zur Zuordnung von Äquivalenten, allen Aufgaben zur Hinübersetzung sowie einigen schwierigen Aufgaben zur Herübersetzung. Ferner sind mit Ausnahme einiger Sprechmusterübungen in den Programmkomplexen 11 und 12, die an reale Gesprächssituationen heranführen sollen, und einiger weniger Nachsprechaufgaben alle Tonbandübungen als 3- oder 4-Phasen-Übungen gestaltet. Da die Sinnübertragung den Gestaltungsmöglichkeiten des Lernenden freien Raum läßt, wurden nur einige Beispiele in den Schlüssel aufgenommen, die naturgemäß stark textorientiert sind und nur als eine der vielen möglichen Varianten angesehen werden dürfen. Dem Lehrer wird daher empfohlen, wenigstens einen Teil der Sinnübertragungsaufgaben als selbständige Arbeit schriftlich durchführen zu lassen und diese dann in Abhängigkeit von seinen zeitlichen Möglichkeiten und der Größe der Gruppe alle oder in Auswahl außerhalb des Unterrichts zu korrigieren bzw. zu kommentieren. Dies trifft natürlich vor allem für Kurse mit dem Ziel der Sprachkundigenprüfung zu. Für die Mehrzahl der mit einem Schlüssel versehenen Aufgaben gilt, daß sie mit geringem Aufwand gelöst und kontrolliert werden können, z. B. wenn man bei Komplettierungs- oder Substitutionsübungen lediglich das geforderte Element oder das entsprechende Symbol hinter der Satznummer notieren läßt.

Für die im Programmabschnitt 4, Sequenz D der Programmkomplexe 2, 5 und 8 vorgesehenen Leistungskontrollen liegen auf Tonband Kontrollübungen vor, die der Lernende zur Wiederholung und Vorbereitung durcharbeiten kann. Dem Lehrer wird empfohlen, auf der Grundlage dieser Kontrollübungen in Auswahl übersichtliche Arbeitsblätter für die Leistungstests zusammenzustellen. Der Lehrer kann diese Zeit auch für andere Kontrollen, etwa für einen Lesetext, für die Wiederholung eines schwierigen Übersetzungstextes oder einer schwierigen Übung oder für die Besprechung einer schriftlich angefertigten Sinnübertragungsaufgabe nutzen, Es wird darauf hingewiesen, daß die *Tonbandkontrollübungen nicht mit den* durch die Lehrprogramme vorgesehenen *obligatorischen Leistungsüberprüfungen* bestimmter Fertigkeiten *identisch sind.* Da diese Leistungsüberprüfungen z. T. nicht die gesamte Dauer einer Doppelstunde beanspruchen, kann die restliche Zeit der dafür verwendeten Unterrichtseinheit ebenfalls in der soeben beschriebenen Weise genutzt werden.

Die Programmkomplexe 1 und 2 und die Programmkomplexe 11 und 12 haben einen etwas anderen Charakter. Der Programmkomplex 1 beginnt mit einer Wortschatzeinführung im Unterricht und behandelt in der ersten B-Sequenz Lexikprobleme nach der Einführung des Grammatikstoffes. Beide Programmkomplexe haben noch keine obligatorischen Lesetexte, sondern die C-Sequenzen der Programmabschnitte 2 und 4 enthalten Hinübersetzungs- und Komplettierungsaufgaben für die selbständige Arbeit. Das ist durch den noch geringen Umfang an grammatischen und lexikalischen Kenntnissen bedingt.

Auf der anderen Seite sind die Programmkomplexe 11 und 12 stärker hör- und sprechorientiert als die übrigen Programmkomplexe. Nachdem mit dem Programmkomplex 10 die Vermittlung bzw. vertiefende Wiederholung der fachsprachlich relevanten Grammatikthemen abgeschlossen ist, dienen die Programmkomplexe 11 und 12 der Zusammenfassung unter übergreifendem kommunikativen Aspekt, wobei der Programmkomplex 12 zugleich thematisch zu den nichtfachsprachlichen Themenkomplexen der Sprachkundigenausbildung der Stufe II b überleiten soll. Die Tonvorträge werden hier nicht mehr visuell gestützt und die produktiven Fertigkeiten stärker entwickelt; daneben stellt der Programmkomplex 11 besondere Ansprüche an die Fertigkeit zur Herübersetzung. Naturgemäß sind diese beiden Programmkomplexe besonders für jene Kurse gedacht, die zur Sprachkundigenprüfung führen sollen.

Die in den A-Sequenzen der Programmabschnitte 2 und 4 enthaltenen *Wortschatzeinführungen* unterteilen sich in ihrem Aufbau in drei Typen: In den ersten vier Wortschatzeinführungen werden die neuen lexikalischen Einheiten zusammen mit dem deutschen Äquivalent und in Verbindung mit bekanntem Wortmaterial präsentiert und sodann in einem kurzen Satz verwendet, der ins Deutsche zu übersetzen ist. In den folgenden Wortschatzeinführungen werden jeweils 5 bis 7 lexikalische Einheiten, ebenfalls meist in Verbindung mit einem bekannten Element und zusammen mit dem deutschen Äquivalent, präsentiert und vom Lernenden wiederholt. Der Lernende hört dann einen kurzen Text, in dem diese neue Lexik verwendet wird. Abschließend hört er noch einmal die lexikalischen Einheiten, nennt ihr deutsches Äquivalent und vergleicht dies dann mit der Kontrolle vom Band. In den Wortschatzeinführungen ab Programmkomplex 8 werden schließlich die monologischen Kurztexte durch dialogische Kurztexte ersetzt. Im Lehrbuch erscheint die neue Lexik lediglich in Listenform, wobei die Abfolge in der Regel dem Auftreten der neuen lexikalischen Einheit im folgenden Übersetzungstext entspricht.

Die Tonbandübungen der Sequenzen A und B in den Programmabschnitten 2 und 4 dienen der weiteren Festigung und Wiederholung bereits vermittelter grammatischer und lexikalischer Kenntnisse und sind — wie die Wortschatzeinführungen — für die selbständige Arbeit bestimmt. Dagegen sollen die (Bild)Tonvorträge, die jeweils zwei Programmabschnitte abschließen, im Unterricht abgearbeitet werden.

Sie beginnen stets mit einer kurzen Einführung, um dem Hörer zu ermöglichen, sich auf das Thema einzustellen.

Auswahl und Abfolge der Grammatikstrukturen entspricht ihrer relativen Häufigkeit und kommunikativen Relevanz in Fachtexten. Daher werden auch Erscheinungen wie das Gerundium und das Partizip nicht als geschlossene Komplexe dargestellt, sondern unter funktionalem Aspekt behandelt und miteinander verglichen. Ein besonders schwieriges Problem war die Behandlung der *Lexik* im Lehrbuch, da der voraussetzbare Wortschatz nicht genügend gesichert ist. Aus diesem Grunde werden (1) der überwiegende Teil des vorausgesetzten Wortschatzes zur Wiederholung aufgeführt und (2) diejenigen lexikalischen Einheiten, die mit einer speziellen semantischen Variante in Fachtexten auftreten, in den Lernwortschatz aufgenommen, auch dann, wenn diese Bedeutungsvariante zunächst für rezeptive Aufgaben bei dem zu wiederholenden Wortschatz bereits aufgeführt wird. In Ergänzung der Wortschatzeinführungen werden weitere lexikalische Einheiten in Lehreinheiten zur Wortbildung und zum Gebrauch wichtiger Wörter eingeführt. Auch solche lexikalischen Einheiten erscheinen in einigen Fällen noch einmal in einer Wortschatzeinführung. Ferner muß beachtet werden, daß bei der Verwendung der Lexik in Übungen streng zwischen *rezeptiven* und *produktiven* Aufgaben unterschieden wurde. Während im ersteren Falle auch im Kontext erschließbare lexikalische Einheiten, vor allem Internationalismen, verwendet wurden, basieren die letzteren ausschließlich auf dem Lernwortschatz. Ein Teil der zunächst nur für rezeptive Aufgaben verwendeten Lexik tritt später in Wortschatzeinführungen auf. Schließlich enthalten die Lesetexte einige kommentierte lexikalische Einheiten, deren Kenntnis jedoch im weiteren Verlauf nicht vorausgesetzt wird.

Das Lehrbuch schließt mit einem längeren *Lesetext* ab, der in die verschiedenen Arten physikalischer Literatur einführen will und damit zugleich der Vorbereitung auf das Sprachpraktikum dient. In diesem Zusammenhang sei ausdrücklich darauf hingewiesen, daß das Lehrbuch den Lernenden systematisch auf die Beschäftigung mit fremdsprachiger Originalliteratur im Studien- und Arbeitsprozeß vorbereiten soll und daher erst die selbständige Durcharbeitung einer größeren Menge englischsprachiger Fachliteratur als Abschlußetappe der Ausbildung (wie dies in den gesetzlichen Ausbildungsdokumenten vorgesehen ist) einen stabilen Lernerfolg ermöglicht.

Hinweise für den Benutzer

Das Lehrbuch besteht aus zwölf Programmkomplexen, die folgenden Aufbau haben:

Programmabschnitt 1 des Programmkomplexes:
Sequenz A: Vermittlung und Übung von Lexik
Sequenz B: Vermittlung und Übung von Grammatik
Sequenz C: Herübersetzen / Hinübersetzen / Sinnübertragung

Programmabschnitt 2 des Programmkomplexes:
Sequenz A: Wortschatzeinführung und Lexikübungen (Tonband)
Sequenz B: Grammatikübungen (Tonband)
Sequenz C: Verstehendes Lesen
Sequenz D: (Bild)Tonvortrag / Sprechaufgaben
bzw. Leistungskontrolle

Die Programmabschnitte 3 und 4 setzen diesen Rhythmus fort. Die Programmkomplexe 1 und 2 sowie 11 und 12 weisen einige Besonderheiten auf (s. S. 8).

Bei der Arbeit mit dem Lehrbuch empfiehlt es sich, die Abfolge der Vermittlungs- und Übungsschritte einzuhalten, da die Anordnung der Lehreinheiten zugleich den Lernweg festlegen soll. Die aus dem Oberschulstoff vorausgesetzte Lexik ist jeweils als Lehreinheit 0 am Beginn einer neuen Lernwortschatzeinführung aufgeführt und sollte vor der Arbeit mit der neuen Lexik wiederholt werden. Besondere Übungen sind dafür im Lehrbuch nicht vorgesehen.

Im graphischen Teil ist der Lernwortschatz nur in Listenform aufgeführt. Desgleichen sind die Tonbandübungen nur durch die Übungsanweisung, die gelegentlich mit einer kurzen Einführung versehen ist, und durch das Übungsmuster vertreten. Im Muster bezeichnet T die Aufgabenstellung vom Tonband, während S das Beispiel für die Reaktion des Studenten kennzeichnet. Dieses ist in einer Reihe von Fällen durch Wortschatz- und Strukturelemente ergänzt, die für die Abarbeitung der Übungen notwendig sind bzw. diese erleichtern. Daher ist es zweckmäßig, den graphischen Teil für die Arbeit mit dem Tonband heranzuziehen. Die (Bild)-Tonvorträge (BTV) sind im Lehrbuch ebenfalls nur durch das methodische Ablaufschema und einige wenige lexikalische Stützen vertreten. Die Untergliederung des Lehrbuches in Programmkomplexe (PK), Programmabschnitte (PA), Sequenzen (SQ) und Lehreinheiten (LE) erlaubt Querverweise mit Hilfe vierstelliger Angaben. So verweist z. B. 4.1.A.–2. auf Programmkomplex 4, Programmabschnitt 1, Sequenz A, Lehreinheit 2. In gleicher Weise wird im Alphabetischen Wörterverzeichnis angegeben, wann eine lexikalische Einheit zuerst eingeführt wird.

Symbole und Abkürzungen

Nebenstrecke

Schlüssel

Tonband

Bildwerfer

Kontrollübung

Adj.	Adjektiv	PK	Programmkomplex
Adv.	Adverb(ial)	Pl.	Plural(isch)
Attr.	Attribut(iv)	Präp./Prep	Präposition
BTV	Bildtonvortrag	S	Student
chem.	chemisch	sb.	somebody
Dt./dt.	Deutsch	Sg.	Singular(isch)
el.	elektrisch	SQ	Sequenz
Engl.	Englisch	sth.	something
HerÜ	Herübersetzung	Subj.	Subjekt
HinÜ	Hinübersetzung	Subst.	Substantiv
Inf.	Infinitiv(isch)	SÜ	Sinnübertragung
LE	Lehreinheit	T	Tonband
math.	mathematisch	techn.	technisch
N	Nomen	TV	Tonvortrag
Obj.	Objekt	V	Verb
PA	Programmabschnitt	WB	Wörterbuch
phys.	physikalisch		

Übersicht über die Programmkomplexe

Seite	PA	Sequenz A	Sequenz B	Sequenz C	Sequenz D
		1. Elements			
19	1	T: Wortschatzeinf.	Pass. v. Verben m. einem Obj.; differ, distinguish, vary	HerÜ: Elements (I)	
23	2	T: Wortschatzeinf.; differ, distinguish, vary; dt. Verben mit 'sich'	T: Pass. v. Verben m. einem Obj. u. m. Modalverben	Pass.; different, various; differ, distinguish, vary	BTV: Elementary Particles; Definitionen in Engl.
28	3	relation, proportion, ratio	Pass. u. Stat.; Pass. v. Verben m. zwei Obj. u. v. Verben m. Präp.	HerÜ: Elements (II); Zusatztext: Hydrogen	
32	4	T: Wortschatzeinf.; Adj. v. Typ 'all', 'half'	T: 'sich lassen'; Pass. m. Modalverben, Pass. v. Vb. m. Präp.	relation, proportion, ratio; HinÜ zum Pass.	BTV: Isotopes; Definitionen in Engl.
		2. Atomic Structure and Isotopes			
36	1	up / down to; consider; same, equal, similar	unpers. pass. Satzeinl.; Subj. + Pass. + Inf.	HerÜ: Isotopes; Zusatztext; Radioactive Isotopes	
41	2	T: Wortschatzeinf.; assume, suppose	T: Subj. + Pass. + Inf.	obtain; HinÜ zum Pass.	BTV: Binding Energy and Mass Defect; Beantw. v. Fragen in Engl.
45	3	particular; assume	Subj. + Pass. + Inf. in Relativsätzen, m. Verben d. Veranlassens u. Zulassens u. m. 'to be'	HerÜ: The Separation Factor; Zusatztext: Pions and Muons	
49	4	T: Wortschatzeinf.; suggest	T: Pass.; Subj. + Pass. + Inf.	establish; HinÜ zum Pass.	Leistungskontrolle

3. Electricity

53	1	Substantivierung durch Nullelement, Akzentwechsel, -(a)tion u. -ment; evidence	Attrib. Partizipien der Gleichzeitigkeit	HerÜ: Insulators and Conductors; HinÜ zu d. attrib. Partizipien; Engl. Erkl. v. Begriffen auf d. Basis eines dt. Textes	BTV: Electricity; Beantwortung v. Fragen in Engl.
58	2	T: Wortschatzeinf.; Substantivierung	T: Attrib. Partizipien d. Gleichzeitigkeit	Lesetext: Ionisation	
62	3	in terms of; magnitude, quantity, amount	Attrib. Partizipien d. Nichtgleichzeitigkeit; nachgest. attrib. Adj.	HerÜ: Electrostatic Field; HinÜ zu d. attrib. Part.; Engl. Erkl. v. Begriffen auf d. Basis eines dt. Textes	
68	4	T: Wortschatzeinf.; unregelm. engl. Plurale	T: Attrib. Partizipien u. Adj.	Lesetext: Magnetic Effect of the Electric Current	BTV: Dielectrics; Beantwortung einer Komplexfrage in Engl. m. Wortgeländer

4. Waves and Particles

73	1	Substantivierung durch -(s)sion; will; rather (than)	Nachgest. nichterweit. attrib. Part.; vorangest. erweit. attribut. Part.	HerÜ: The Dual Nature of Matter and Waves; HinÜ z. d. attribut. Strukturen; SÜ eines dt. Textes m. Themenstellung	
79	2	T: Wortschatzeinf.; Substantivierung auf -(s)sion; any	T: Emphat. 'it'; attribut. Part.	Lesetext: Waves and Particles	BTV: Lines of Force; Sprechen in Engl. zu vorgegeb. Thema auf d. Basis engl. Sachverhalte

Seite	PA	Sequenz A	Sequenz B	Sequenz C	Sequenz D
83	3	Termini der Strukt. "N+N"; show, exhibit, display, reveal	Relativsätze beim Besitz- u. Teilungsverhältnis	HerÜ: The Diffraction of Electrons and Atoms; HinÜ zu attrib. Strukt.; SÜ eines dt. Textes m. Themenstellung	BTV: The Photon and the Compton Effect; Sprechen in Engl. zu vorgeg. Thema auf d. Basis engl. Sachverhalte
89	4	T: Wortschatzeinf.; Termini d. Struktur "N+N"; some	T: Relativsätze beim Besitz- u. Teilungsverhältnis	Lesetext: Aspects of Quantum Mechanics	

5. Solids and Semiconductors

Seite	PA	Sequenz A	Sequenz B	Sequenz C	Sequenz D
94	1	due to; easy, ready, slight	"Kontaktkonstruktion"; that / those + attrib. Struktur	HerÜ: The Crystal Lattice; HinÜ zu that / those + attrib. Strukt. u. due to; SÜ eines dt. Textes	
99	2	T: Wortschatzeinf.; due to; fail	T: "Kontaktkonstruktion"	Lesetext: Solid-State Physics	BTV: Crystals; Beantwortung einer Komplexfrage m. Unterfragen in Engl.
103	3	involve; Termini d. Struktur "Adj + N"	Zusammenfass. d. attrib. Strukturen; nichtersetzb. Relativsätze	HerÜ: The Structure of Semiconductors; HinÜ zu that / those + attrib. Struktur, 'sich lassen'; SÜ eines dt. Textes	
109	4	T: Wortschatzeinf.; Bildung v. Nominalgruppen	T: Zus. fass. d. attrib. Strukturen	Lesetext: Free Electron Theory	Leistungskontrolle

6. Bond Structure and Energy Levels

Seite	PA	Sequenz A	Sequenz B	Sequenz C	Sequenz D
114	1	Termini d. Struktur "N+N+N", Funktionen von '-ing'	Adv. Gerundien nach by, for, without, instead of	HerÜ: Types of Bonding; HinÜ zu Gerundien nach by, for, without; SÜ eines dt. Textes nach Fragen	

121	2	T: Wortschatzeinf.; attempt, experiment	T: Gerundien nach by, for, without	Lesetext: Classification of Crystal Binding	BTV: Semiconductors; Beantworten einer Komplexfrage mit Unterfragen in Engl.
124	3	Negationspräfixe	Adv. Gerundien nach after, before, in, on	HerÜ: Energy Levels; HinÜ zu Gerundien nach after, before, in, on; SÜ eines dt. Textes	
130	4	T: Wortschatzeinf.; the—the; Gerundium u. Subst.	T: Adv. Gerundien	Lesetext: Atomic Spectra and Energy Levels	BTV: Characteristic X-Rays; Sprechen in Engl. nach vorgeg. Thema mit Hinweisen

7. Radioactivity and Nuclear Energy

135	1	Präfix 're-'	"Verbundenes" adv. Partizip	HerÜ: Nuclear Radiation; SÜ dt. Sachverhalte nach Fragen	
140	2	T: Wortschatzeinf.; both — and, as well as	T: "Verbundenes" adv. Part.	Lesetext: Radioactivity	BTV: Comparison of Radiations; Sprechen zu einem Thema mit Komplexfragen in Engl.
144	3	Suffixe '-able /-ible'; Subst. auf '-a /-ibility'	"Unverbundenes" adv. Partizip; with-Phrase; stereotype Satzkerne	HerÜ: Nuclear Fission; Zusammenfass. SÜ eines dt. Textes	
150	4	T: Wortschatz.; '-able /-ible', '-a /-ibility'	T: Stereotype Satzkerne	Lesetext: Nuclear Fission	BTV: Nuclear Reactions; Sprechen zu einem Thema m. Komplexfragen in Engl.

8. Spectroscopy and Optical Properties of Materials

Seite	PA	Sequenz A	Sequenz B	Sequenz C	Sequenz D
155	1	appear; 'as' + Perfektpartizip	Attrib. Gerundium; "Verbalsubstantiv"	HerÜ: Spectroscopy; SÜ eines dt. Textes	BTV: Spectroscopy; engl. Zusammenfass.d. Lesetextes n. engl. Fragen u. Stichpunkten
160	2	T: Wortschatzeinf.; dependent on; independent of, as the result of	Attrib. Gerundium	Lesetext: Crystal Optics	
164	3	'as' + Präsenspartizip	Gerundium als Subj. u. (Präpositional)Obj.	HerÜ: Optical Properties of Materials; SÜ eines dt. Textes nach vorber. Übung	
171	4	T: Wortschatzeinf.; verbale Ausdrücke (Satzkerne)	T: Gerundium als Präpositionalobj.	Lesetext: Excitons	Leistungskontrolle

9. Phenomena of Magnetism and the Magnetic Field

Seite	PA	Sequenz A	Sequenz B	Sequenz C	Sequenz D
175	1	Termini der Struktur "N's N"	Obj.+Inf.; Adj.+Inf.	HerÜ: Magnetism; SÜ eines dt. Textes n. vorber. Übung	BTV: The Magnetic Field; Sprechen in Engl. zu einem Thema auf d. Basis eines dt. Textes
181	2	T: Wortschatzeinf.; "N+Präp.+N"	T: Obj.+Inf.	Lesetext: Ferromagnetism; Engl. Zusfassg. nach Schema	
185	3	Termini der Struktur "N's N"; acquire, achieve, obtain	for-Obj.+Inf.; so that / as to; Attrib. Inf.	HerÜ: The Galvanometer; SÜ eines dt. Textes nach vorber. Übung ('man')	
192	4	T: Wortschatzeinf.	T: Attrib. Inf.; how+Inf.; for-Obj.+Inf.; so as to	Lesetext: Particle Accelerators; engl. Zusammenfass. nach Schema	BTV: Magnetic Properties; Sprechen in Engl. zu einem Thema auf d. Basis eines dt. Textes

10. Mechanics

197	1	Dreigliedrige Termini (1); would, should	Konditional	HerÜ: The Coordinates of a Dynamical System; Engl. Formulierung im Dt. vorgeg. Sachverhalte (Bedingung, Voraussetzung, Annahme)	BTV: The Reference System; Erläuterung v. Sachverhalten in Engl.
203	2	T: Wortschatzeinf.; in turn	T: Konditional	Lesetext: Definition and Description of Particles; engl. Zusfass. n. engl. Fragen	
207	3	Dreigliedrige Termini (2)	Adverbien	HerÜ: The Laws of Motion; SÜ eines dt. Textes nach vorbereitender Übung	
214	4	T: Wortschatzeinf.	T: Adverbien	Lesetext zu Problemen d. Beschleunigung; engl. Zus.-fass. nach Instruktion	BTV: Gravitation; Erläuterung eines Sachverhaltes in Engl.

11. Trends in Modern Physics

218	1	Zustandsänderung v. Stoffen	Angabe d. Zwecks u. d. Durchführung einer Analyse bzw. eines Verfahrens mit SÜ dt. Texte	HerÜ (WB): Aspects of the X-Ray Spectroscopy of Solids	
222	2	T: Wortschatzeinf.; math. Ausdrücke (1)	T: Dialogübungen	Lesetext (WB): Laser; engl. Inhaltsreferat	TV: Physics and other Sciences; Sprechen in Engl. zu vorgegebenem Thema
227	3	Mathemat. Verfahren; Nachweisverfahren mit SÜ dt. Texte	Angabe d. Grundes u. d. Folge bzw. Schlußfolgerung	HerÜ (WB): Plasma Physics	
232	4	T: Wortschatzeinf.; mathemat. Ausdrücke (2)	T: Dialogübungen	Lesetext (WB): Superconductors; engl. Inhaltsreferat	TV: Physics and Technology; Sprechen in Engl. zu einem vorgegebenen Thema

12. University Course and Co-operation in Research

238	1	dt. 'bei' m. SÜ dt. Texte nach Beispiel	Probleme d. Physikstudiums (Übung d. Tempora)	HerÜ (WB): University Course of Physics Studies; Beantw. eines engl. Briefes in Engl.
243	2	T: Wortschatzeinf.; engl. Präp. für dt. 'bei'	T: Dialogübungen	Lesetext (WB): Joint Institute for Nuclear Research	TV: John Bernal; Bericht über einen Physiker in Engl.
247	3	Quantitative Angaben m. SÜ eines dt. Textes	Internationale wissenschaftliche Zusammenarbeit	HerÜ (WB): The Position of Theoretical Physics	
251	4	T: while, during, whereas	T: Dialogübungen	Lesetext (WB): Classification of Physics Literature	

Elements

PK 1 · PA 1 · SQ A

LE 0   Wortschatz zur Wiederholung

to arrange: anordnen / to attend: (Schule) besuchen / to call: nennen / to carry out: durchführen / to cause: verursachen / to change: (ver)ändern / to combine: (sich) verbinden / to compare: vergleichen / condition: Bedingung / to consist of: bestehen aus / to continue: (sich) fortsetzen / to control: steuern, kontrollieren / co-operation: Zusammenarbeit / to develop: (sich) entwickeln / distance: Entfernung / to divide: teilen / to find, found, found: finden / to get: bekommen / group: Gruppe / to grow: (an)wachsen / however: jedoch / idea: Vorstellung / to increase: (sich) erhöhen / for instance: zum Beispiel / letter: Buchstabe / light: leicht / number: Zahl / power-station: Kraftwerk / plant: Fabrik, Werk / to prepare: vorbereiten / to produce: erzeugen / to provide: geben, liefern / result: Ergebnis / science: (Natur)Wissenschaft / scientist: (Natur)Wissenschaftler / since: seit; weil, da / society: Gesellschaft / source: Quelle / to study: untersuchen / therefore: deshalb / together: zusammen / to use: benutzen

LE 1   ⊕ ⊕   Neue Lexik

material	[məˈtiəriəl]	materiell
universe	[ˈjuːnivəːs]	Universum, Weltall, Kosmos
about	[əˈbaut]	(bei Zahlenangaben) etwa, ungefähr
either — or	[ˈaiðə — ɔː]	entweder — oder
pure	[ˈpjuə]	rein
chemical	[ˈkemikəl]	chemisch
combination	[ˌkɔmbiˈneiʃən]	Verbindung, Vereinigung, Kombination
definite	[ˈdefinit]	bestimmt; eindeutig, genau
proportion	[prəˈpɔːʃən]	Verhältnis, Proportion; Menge, Anteil
compound	[ˈkɔmpaund]	(chem.) Verbindung
to form	[fɔːm]	bilden; sich bilden
to differ (from)	[ˈdifə]	sich unterscheiden (von)
nucleus	[ˈnjuːkliəs]	(Atom)Kern
Pl.: nuclei	[ˈnjuːkliai]	
atomic	[əˈtɔmik]	atomar, Atom-
to be made up of	[ˈmeid ˈʌp‿əv]	bestehen aus, gebildet werden aus
integral number	[ˈintigrəl …]	ganze Zahl

atomic number		Ordnungszahl (eines Elements)
to determine	[di'tə:min]	bestimmen
total	['toutl]	ganz, gesamt, total
weight	[weit]	Gewicht
rough(ly)	['rʌf(li)]	ungefähr, etwa
thus	[ðʌs]	so, somit, demzufolge
given	['givn]	bestimmt, gegeben, beliebig
to vary	['vɛəri]	schwanken, variieren
oxygen	['ɔksidʒən]	Sauerstoff
stable	['steibl]	stabil, beständig, fest
mass	[mæs]	Masse

LE 2 ⊕ ⊕ Internationalismen

element	['elimənt]	(chem., phys.) Element
structure	['strʌktʃə]	Struktur, Aufbau
atom	['ætəm]	Atom
proton	['proutɔn]	Proton
neutron	['nju:trɔn]	Neutron
gold	[gould]	Gold
isotope	['aisoutoup]	Isotop

PK 1 · PA 1 · SQ B

LE 1 Die Verben können unterschieden werden nach der Zahl ihrer notwendigen nominalen Satzpartner (N).

1. Das Verb hat nur das Subjekt N^1:

$$N^1 \qquad + V \qquad (+ \ldots)$$
The student   comes   (into the room).

Diese Verben werden als intransitiv bezeichnet.

2. Das Verb hat das Subjekt N^1 und das Objekt N^2:

$$N^1 \qquad + V \qquad + N^2$$
The professor   publishes   a book.

Diese Verben werden als transitiv bezeichnet.

LE 2 Bilden Sie acht Sätze, indem Sie zunächst ein V, dann ein geeignetes N^2 und dann ein N^1 auswählen:

N^1	V		N^2	
student	attend	get	college	lesson
scientist	compare	use	result	cause
team	control		experiment	idea
book	prepare		information	job
specialist	provide		thermometer	
teacher	find		energy source	

LE 3 Zwischen "N + V" und "N + V + N" können unterschiedliche Beziehungen bestehen:

1. Das Obj. N^2 kann ohne Bedeutungsänderung entfallen:
   $N^1 + V\,(+N^2)$
   He writes (a letter).
2. N^2 tritt als Subj. an die Stelle von N^1:
   $N^1 + V + N^2$ $N^2 + V$
   He begins the lesson. → The lesson begins.

LE 4 Bilden Sie Sätze nach den Mustern *change – temperature*. Vergleichen Sie dann die engl. und dt. Sätze:

1. They change the temperature.	Sie verändern die Temperatur.
2. They change.	Sie verändern sich.
3. The temperature changes.	Die Temperatur (ver)ändert sich.

change – condition / read – book / combine – substances / continue – lesson
develop – society / increase – distance / study – problem

LE 5 Das Passiv wird gebildet aus *be* und dem Perfektpartizip V-*ed*, wobei *be* = *am* / *is* / *are*; *was* / *were*; *has* / *have* / *had been*; *shall* / *will be* sein kann:

N	+ *be*	+ V-*ed*
Radium	was	discovered (in 1896).
Radium	wurde	(1896) entdeckt.

LE 6 ⊸ Setzen Sie ins Passiv nach diesen Mustern:

$N^1 + V + N^2 \rightarrow$	N^2 + *be* + V-*ed*
Scientists studied the compounds.	The compounds were studied.
Die Wissenschaftler untersuchten die Verbindungen.	Die Verbindungen wurden untersucht.
$N^1 + V + N^2 \rightarrow$	N^2 + *be* + V-*ed* + *by* + N^1
Chadwick discovered the neutron.	The neutron was discovered by Chadwick.
Chadwick entdeckte das Neutron.	Das Neutron wurde von Chadwick entdeckt.

Beachten Sie, daß nur notwendige Handlungsträger bzw. Handlungsursachen mit *by* hinzugefügt werden.

1. Mendeleyev arranged the elements in eight groups. 2. Scientists have studied the chemical properties of plutonium. 3. The total number of protons and neutrons determine the mass number of the element. 4. Power-stations produce electrical energy. 5. Science did not find the transuranic elements in nature. 6. Scientists have studied the atomic structure since about 1900.

LE 7   Wir üben *differ, distinguish* und *vary*.

1. to differ: sich unterscheiden, verschieden sein
to differ in: sich unterscheiden in / nach
  The isotopes of an element differ in the number of their neutrons.
to differ by: sich unterscheiden, differieren um
  The temperatures differed by 10°.
to differ from: sich unterscheiden von
  Hydrogen differs from its isotopes deuterium and tritium in its mass.

2. to distinguish sth.: etwas unterscheiden
  We distinguish the isotopes of a given element by their mass numbers.
  The isotopes of a given element are distinguished by their mass numbers.

3. to vary: sich unterscheiden, abweichen
to vary from – to: schwanken, variieren, sich erstrecken von – bis
  The temperatures vary from 40° to 45°
to vary between: schwanken, variieren zwischen
  The temperature varies between 40° and 45°.
to vary with: sich verändern mit
  The atomic number varies with the number of protons.
to vary from: abweichen von, sich unterscheiden von, nicht übereinstimmen mit.
  The nucleus of deuterium varies from that of the hydrogen atom.

PK 1 · PA 1 · SQ C

LE 1   Übersetzen Sie:

Elements (I)

The material universe consists of about one hundred elements, either pure or in chemical combination. Two or more elements often combine in definite proportions and form chemical compounds. The elements consist of atoms which differ from one another in the structure of the nucleus of the atom. These nuclei are made up of an integral number of protons and neutrons. The number of protons determines the atomic number of the element, and the total number of protons and neutrons together determine the mass number, which is equal to the rough atomic weight. For instance, the nucleus of the gold atom is made up of 79 protons and 118 neutrons. It is thus given an atomic number of 79 and an atomic weight of 197.

The number of protons in the nucleus is the same for all atoms of a given element, but the number of neutrons may vary. These atoms, with a different number of neutrons, but the same number of protons, are called isotopes. For instance, all oxygen atoms have 8 protons in the nucleus. However, they may have either 8, 9, or 10 neutrons in the nucleus and, therefore, it is said that oxygen consists of three stable isotopes.

PK 1 · PA 2 · SQ A

LE 0   Wortschatz zur Wiederholung

actual(ly): tatsächlich / also: auch / action: Wirkung / always: immer / as well as: sowohl − als auch / because: weil / to become: werden / to build: bauen / careful(ly): sorgfältig / case: Fall / to create: schaffen / to depend on: abhängen von / to destroy: zerstören / in detail: gründlich / difference: Unterschied / early: früh(zeitig) / earth: Erde / even: sogar / example: Beispiel / to explain: erklären / fact: Tatsache / famous: berühmt / to follow: (ver)folgen / foreign: ausländisch, Fremd- / former: frühere / free: frei / further: weitere / future: Zukunft / to give, gave, given: geben / great: groß / to heat: erwärmen / high: hoch / to hold, held, held: halten / important: wichtig / interesting: interessant / late: spät / to learn: lernen / less: weniger / long: lang / main: hauptsächlich / to make, made, made: machen / matter: Materie / to mean: bedeuten / method: Verfahren / to move: (sich) bewegen / natural: natürlich, Natur- / near(by): nahe (gelegen) / never: niemals / next: nächster / now: jetzt / to offer: (an)bieten / opportunity: Gelegenheit / orbit: Kreisbahn / in order to: um zu / other: anderer / outside: außerhalb / part: Teil / possible: möglich / quality: Eigenschaft / quite: ganz / scientific: wissenschaftlich / several: einige / to show: zeigen / single: einzeln / small: klein / though: obwohl / time: Zeit / to-day: heute / true: richtig / type: Art, Typ / to understand, understood, understood: verstehen / useful: nützlich, zweckmäßig / while: während / wide(ly): weitgehend / whole: ganz / work: Arbeit / year: Jahr / young: jung

LE 1 ⊕ ⊕ Neue Lexik

ratio [ˈreiʃiou] (quantitatives) Verhältnis, Zahlenverhältnis

gradual(ly) [ˈgrædjuəl(i)] allmählich

to decrease [diːˈkriːs] abnehmen, sich verringern, fallen; senken, erniedrigen

hydrogen	[ˈhaidridʒən]	Wasserstoff
abundance	[əˈbʌndəns]	(Vorkommens)Häufigkeit
abundant	[əˈbʌndənt]	häufig (vorkommend)
as	[æz]	wenn; in dem Maße, wie; da
earth's crust	[ˈɪːθs ˈkrʌs t]	Erdrinde
even number	[ˈːəən ...]	gerade Zahl
odd number	[ˈɔdv...]	ungerade Zahl
all the rest	[ɔl ð ə ˈrest]	alle übrigen, der Rest
vice versa	[ˈvaisi ˈvɔːsə]	umgekehrt
usual(ly)	[ˈjuːʒʊəl(i)]	gewöhnlich; meistens
lead	[led]	Blei
above	[əˈbʌv]	über, oberhalb
some	[sʌm]	(bei Zahlwörtern) ungefähr, etwa; einige
billion	[ˈbiljən]	(US Engl.) Milliarde
heavy	[ˈhevi]	(Gewicht) schwer
to occur	[əˈkɔː]	vorkommen
nature	[ˈneitʃə]	Natur
artificial	[ˈaːtifiʃəl]	künstlich; synthetisch
to obtain	[əbˈtein]	erhalten, bekommen, erzielen
transuranic elements	[ˈtrænsjuəˈrænik ...]	Transurane
on the basis of	[ˈɔn ðə ˈbeisis‿əv]	auf der Grundlage von, auf Grund von, ausgehend von, entsprechend, nach
common	[ˈkɔmən]	gemeinsam; häufig; üblich
property	[ˈprɔpəti]	Eigenschaft
to discover	[disˈkʌvə]	entdecken; feststellen

LE 2 | ⊕ ⊕ | Internationalismen

radioactive	[ˈreidiouˈæktiv]	radioaktiv
relative	[ˈrelətiv]	relativ; verhältnismäßig

LE 3 | ⊕ ⊕ | Wir üben das Verb *to differ*. Bilden Sie Sätze nach dem Muster:

T: compounds − structure
S: The compounds differ in their structure.

LE 4 | ⊕ ⊕ | Wir üben das Verb *to distinguish*. Beantworten Sie die Fragen nach dem Muster:

T: By what can compounds be distinguished? − elements
S: Compounds can be distinguished by their elements.

LE 5 ⊕ ⊕ Wir üben das Verb *to vary*. Beantworten Sie Fragen nach dem Muster:

T: Is the number of neutrons of an element always the same?
S: No, the number of neutrons varies.

LE 6 ⊕ ⊕ Übersetzen Sie mit Hilfe von *differ*, *distinguish* oder *vary* ins Engl.!

LE 7 ⊕ ⊕ Wir üben engl. Verben ohne Obj. und dt. Verben mit 'sich'. Übersetzen Sie ins Dt. nach dem Muster:

T: The number of energy sources has increased.
S: Die Zahl der Energiequellen hat sich erhöht.

LE 8 ⊕ ⊕ Übersetzen Sie ins Engl. nach dem Muster:

T: Die Zahl der Energiequellen hat sich erhöht.
S: The number of energy sources has increased.

PK 1 · PA 2 · SQ B

LE 1 ⊕ ⊕ Beantworten Sie die Fragen nach dem Muster:

T: Did they study a number of compounds?
S: A number of compounds were studied.

Wenn Sie diese Übung ohne Schwierigkeit gelöst haben, dann können Sie die drei folgenden Übungen auslassen.

LE 1a ◤ ⊕ ⊕ Beantworten Sie die Fragen nach dem Muster:

T: Do they study the weight of the material?
S: The weight of the material is studied.
Achten Sie auf Singular und Plural!

LE 1b ◤ ⊕ ⊕ Beantworten Sie die Fragen nach dem Muster:

T: Did they discover new compounds of this element?
S: New compounds of this element were discovered.
Achten Sie auf Singular und Plural!

LE 1c ◣ ⊕ ⊕ Siehe LE 1

LE 2 ⊕ ⊕ Übersetzen Sie ins Engl. mit Hilfe der Passivkonstruktion nach dem Muster:

T: Wir untersuchten die Isotope dieses Elements.
S: The isotopes of this element were studied.

LE 3 ⊕ ⊕ Wir üben das Passiv nach Modalverben. Reagieren Sie nach dem Muster:

T: I was told we must read the book.
S: Yes, the book must be read.

LE 4 ⊕ ⊕ Wir üben das Passiv nach Modalverben. Übersetzen Sie ins Engl. nach dem Muster:

T: Die Elemente können in Gruppen angeordnet werden.
S: The elements can be arranged in groups.

PK 1 · PA 2 · SQ C

LE 1 ⊼—0 Ergänzen Sie die passiven Verbformen unter Verwendung von *to use, to find, to obtain, to determine, to create, to call, to discover*:

1. The properties of the atoms ... by the number of their outer electrons. 2. Energy can ... from the radioactive elements uranium and plutonium. 3. About twelve elements can now ... artificially. 4. In 1932 the positron ... by the American scientist C. Anderson. 5. Atoms with a different number of neutrons but the same of protons ... isotopes. 6. Radioactive isotopes ... in industry for years. 7. New elements may ... in the near future.

LE 2 Die engl. Adj. *different* und *various* können wie folgt unterschieden werden:

different = not the same: unterschiedlich
    The isotopes of oxygen have masses of 8, 9 and 10. →
    The isotopes of oxygen have different masses.
various = a number of different ...: verschiedene
    This element occurs in a number of compounds. →
    This element occurs in various compounds.

LE 3 ⊓—0 Übersetzen Sie ins Engl.:

1. Die Isotope eines Elements haben unterschiedliche Massenzahlen. 2. Dieses Element kommt in einer Reihe von Verbindungen vor. 3. Es gibt viele Verbindungen gleicher Elemente mit unterschiedlichen Eigenschaften. 4. Die unterschiedlichen Eigenschaften der Elemente hängen von ihrer Struktur ab. 5. Sauerstoff bildet Verbindungen mit verschiedenen Elementen.

LE 4 ⊓—0 Ergänzen Sie durch Zeitformen von *differ, distinguish* oder *vary*:

1. Aston ... the two isotopes of chlorine (Cl) by means of a mass spectrograph. 2. Gram-molecules of various substances, though they ... in relative atomic mass, have equal numbers of molecules. 3. Each chemical element has its own spectrum, which ... from those of other elements. 4. The elements ... in their relative abundance. 5. The number of neutrons in the isotopes of oxygen ... between 16 and 18. 6. The radius of the atoms ... from 0.5 Å for the hydrogen atom to 2.6 Å for the caesium atom. 7. Protons and neutrons can be ... on the basis of their electrical properties. 8. In order to ... between the three isotopes of hydrogen, their chemical symbols are written as $_1^1H$, $_1^2H$ and $_1^3H$.

Bereiten Sie die Übersetzung des Textes *"Elements (II)"* (1.3.C. − 1.) vor!

PK 1 · PA 2 · SQ D

LE 1 ⊕ ⊕ Einführender Dialog: Nucleons

LE 2 ⊕ ⊕ ⊃▷ Hören Sie den gesamten BTV *"Elementary Particles"* und machen Sie sich Notizen!

LE 3 ⊃▷ Vergleichen Sie Ihre Notizen mit dem Schema auf dem Bild!

LE 4 ⊕ ⊕ ⊃▷ Hören Sie noch einmal den Text, der jetzt in zwei Teilen präsentiert wird. Ergänzen Sie Ihre Notizen und beantworten Sie nach jedem Teil die Fragen in Dt.!

LE 5 Give a short definition of protons, neutrons and electrons.

What is their charge? / What is their mass? / Where do we find them in the atom? In which way do they determine the atomic number and the mass number?

PK 1 · PA 3 · SQ A

LE 1   Wir üben *relation, proportion* und *ratio*

relation: Beziehung oder Verhältnis zwischen zwei oder mehr Größen

There is a simple relation between the number of atoms in equal volumes of gases.

Es gibt eine einfache Beziehung zwischen der Zahl der Atome in gleich großen Gasvolumina.

proportion: 1. Verhältnis zwischen Mengen

Elements combine in simple proportions by volume and by atoms.

Elemente verbinden sich in einfachen Volumenverhältnissen und Atomverhältnissen.

2. mengenmäßiger Anteil

A certain proportion of the electrons in metals is free to move through the atoms.

In Metallen kann sich ein bestimmter Teil der Elektronen frei zwischen den Atomen bewegen.

ratio: zahlenmäßiges quantitatives Verhältnis

The ratios of 1 to 5 and 20 to 100 are the same.

Das Verhältnis von 1 zu 5 ist gleich dem von 20 zu 100.

LE 2   Übersetzen Sie den folgenden Text und beachten Sie die Verwendung der drei Begriffe:

The British scientist John Dalton studied the relations between different forms of matter. He discovered a simple relation between the different proportions in which elements combine: When an element combines with another element in more than one proportion, the different proportions are in the ratio of whole numbers. Thus, copper (Cu) combines with chlorine (Cl) in the proportions 63.56 to 2 ×35.46 and 63.56 to 35.46, that is, the proportions of chlorine are in the ratio of 2 : 1.

PK 1 · PA 3 · SQ B

LE 1   In Sätzen der Struktur N + *be* + V-*ed* entspricht *be* Formen von dt. 'sein' oder dt. 'werden'.

1. The term "isotope" is widely known.

Der Begriff "Isotop" ist weithin bekannt.

2. Elements with the same number of protons but a different number of neutrons are called isotopes.

Elemente mit der gleichen Protonenzahl aber einer unterschiedlichen Neutronenzahl werden Isotope genannt.

Hier informiert 1. über einen Zustand von N ("Stativ"), 2. dagegen über einen Vorgang ("Passiv"). Der Unterschied zwischen Stativ und Passiv ergibt sich aus der Bedeutung der beteiligten "V".

LE 2   Übersetzen Sie ins Dt.:

1. The next experiment must be better prepared. 2. The atoms in a molecule are held together through their electrons. 3. Scientists must learn foreign languages because many books are written in English, Russian, French etc. 4. A new book on these problems will be published in the near future. 5. In the Periodic Table the elements are arranged in eight main groups. 6. One of the most abundant elements, helium, was discovered on the sun before it was known on the earth. 7. When a new compound is discovered, its physical and chemical properties must be determined in detail. 8. The first transuranic element was discovered in 1940 in a study of the effect of neutrons on uranium.

LE 3   Wird *being* vor V-*ed* eingeschoben, so handelt es sich eindeutig um das Passiv: N + *be* + *being* + V-*ed*. Diese Form gibt es nur im Präsens (*am / is / are*) und im Präteritum (*was / were*).

LE 4   Übersetzen Sie ins Dt.:

1. Hydrogen is being produced on the earth. 2. Nuclear reactors are being built to obtain energy for industry. 3. Most elements with unstable isotopes would no longer be found on the earth if they were not being formed from uranium and thorium.

LE 5   Andere Möglichkeiten, den Passivcharakter deutlich zu machen, sind der Anschluß des Handlungsträgers mit *by* und die Verwendung von *become* oder *get* statt *be*.

> The water was heated by the sun.
> The water becomes / gets heated.

LE 6   Verben mit zwei Objekten lassen im Engl. zwei Passivstrukturen zu:

> N^1 + V + N^3 + N^2
> The teacher gives the student / him a book.

1. N^2 + *be* + V-*ed* + *to* + N^3
     The book is given to the student / him.
     Das Buch wird ihm gegeben.

2. N^3 + *be* + V-*ed* + N^2
     The student / He is given a book.
     Ihm wird ein Buch gegeben. / Man gibt ihm ein Buch.

Die zweite Passivstruktur wird häufig als "Persönliches Passiv" bezeichnet. Sie wird im Engl. häufiger benutzt als die erste Passivstruktur.

LE 7 ⊼—0 Wandeln Sie die vorgegebenen aktiven Sätze in die folgende Passivstruktur um:

N^3 + *be* + V-*ed* + N^2

He is given the book.

Meist entspricht nur die Passivform dieser Sätze dem engl. Sprachgebrauch. Wie lautet die dt. Entsprechung?

1. They offered the young scientist an opportunity for interesting work. 2. His teacher showed him an article with useful information. 3. They gave the new element the name of a famous scientist. 4. Scientists often give newly produced substances names that show their properties. 5. They showed the students the difference between the two methods. 6. They showed us a number of experiments that demonstrate the action of high-energy electrons.

LE 8 Im Engl. kann auch die Einheit "Verb (+ Nomen) + Präposition" als Ganzes ins Passiv gesetzt werden:

N^1 + V + Prep + N^2 → N^2 + *be* + V-*ed* + Prep
they speak of the book   the book is spoken of

Die dt. Entsprechungen dieser Passivsätze stellen die Präposition an die Spitze oder beginnen mit 'man': Über dieses Buch wird gesprochen. Man spricht über dieses Buch.

Übersetzen Sie nach diesen Mustern:

1. The old method is still often made use of in experiments in schools. 2. The results of our scientific work were spoken of at the conference.

LE 9 Folgende Verbindungen von Verb und Präposition treten relativ häufig in physikalischen Fachtexten auf, wobei die Verwendung im Passiv überwiegt:

to account for [əˈkaunt]: erklären
    The change in mass when atomic nuclei are formed is accounted for by the mass-energy relation $E = m c^2$.

to allow for [əˈlau]: berücksichtigen
    This factor must be allowed for in our hypothesis.

to deal with [diːl]: behandeln, sich beschäftigen mit
    Problems of atomic structure are dealt with under various aspects.

to look upon as [ˈluk əˈpɔn æz]: ansehen, betrachten als
    This technique may be looked upon as out of date.

to refer to [riˈfəː]: verweisen auf
    This book was referred to by our professor.

to refer t o as: bezeichnen als
    Protons and neutrons are together referred to as nucleons.

to think of as: sich denken / ansehen als, halten für
    In former times water was thought of as an element.

PK 1 · PA 3 · SQ C

LE 1 Übersetzen Sie:

Elements (II)

The first twenty elements have roughly equal numbers of protons and neutrons in the nucleus. From these on, the ratio of protons to neutrons gradually increases so that the element of atomic number 100 has roughly 150 neutrons in the nucleus. The relative abundance of chemical elements decreases as the atomic number increases. Hydrogen is the most abundant element in the universe followed by helium etc. About 80% of the earth's crust is made up of elements with even numbers of protons and neutrons in the nucleus. Nearly all the rest have an odd number of protons and an even number of neutrons, or vice versa. Elements of even atomic number usually have several isotopes while elements of odd atomic number never have more than two stable isotopes.

　　All elements above lead (Pb), atomic number 82, are unstable and radioactive. Thus, in some billions of years there will be no element that is heavier than lead. There are now 105 elements known. All elements with an atomic mass higher than 238 (uranium) are called "transuranic elements" − they do not occur in nature but can be obtained artificially. The elements are arranged into eight groups on the basis of their common properties. This fact was discovered by Mendeleyev, a Russian scientist.

LE 2 Diesen Text können Sie zusätzlich lesen oder übersetzen:

Hydrogen

Ordinary (gewöhnlich) hydrogen is a mixture of three kinds of atoms which are called isotopes. Ordinary hydrogen consists of a single proton and a single electron. In addition to (zusätzlich) the atoms of ordinary hydrogen one finds atoms of "heavy hydrogen" or deuterium and also atoms of tritium. The concentration of deuterium in ordinary hydrogen is only about one part in 5000, and that of tritium is even less. The nucleus of a deuterium atom which is called a deuteron consists of one proton and one neutron. The nucleus of a tritium atom consists of one proton and two neutrons. In deuterium as well as in tritium there is one electron outside the nucleus. Of these three isotopes of hydrogen two are stable and one is radioactive. The stable isotopes are the light isotope of mass 1 and the heavy isotope of mass 2. The abundance of ordinary hydrogen in the naturally occurring compounds of hydrogen is 99.9844%, while the heavy isotope (deuterium) of mass 2 occurs to the extent of (im Umfang von) only 0.0156%.

PK 1 · PA 4 · SQ A

LE 0   Wortschatz zur Wiederholung

almost: fast / one another / each other: gegenseitig / at all: überhaupt / average:
Durchschnitt(s-) / to believe: glauben, annehmen / colour: Farbe / development:
Entwicklung / easy: leicht / to express: ausdrücken / few: wenige / forward: vor-
wärts / general: allgemein / half: halb / how: wie / line: Linie / to need: benötigen /
to occupy: besetzen / place: Ort, Stelle / pressure: Druck / process: Vorgang / to represent: darstellen / to rise: (an)wachsen / second: Sekunde / to see, saw, seen:
sehen / to serve: dienen / slow: langsam / step: Schritt / in this way: auf diese Weise,
so

LE 1   ⊕ ⊕   Neue Lexik

form	[fɔ:m]	Form, Gestalt
nuclear	[ˈnju:kliə]	nuklear, Kern-, Nuklear-
i.e. (id est)	[ai i:]	das heißt
meist: that is		
charge	[tʃa:dʒ]	(elektrische) Ladung
identical	[aiˈdentikəl]	(genau) gleich, identisch
extranuclear	[ˈekstraˈ —]	außerhalb des Kerns (befindl.)
to separate	[ˈsepəreit]	trennen, teilen
by chemical means		auf chemischen Wege, chemisch
chemist	[ˈkemist]	Chemiker
to consider	[kənˈsidə]	betrachten, ansehen (als)
distinct	[disˈtiŋkt]	eindeutig; charakteristisch, ausgeprägt
physicist	[ˈfizisist]	Physiker
periodic table	[ˌpiəriˈɔdik ˈteibl]	Periodensystem (der Elemente)
to recognize	[ˈrekəgnaiz]	erkennen
to contain	[kənˈtein]	enthalten
mixture	[ˈmikstʃə]	Mischung, Gemisch
quantity	[ˈkwɔntiti]	Menge, Masse, Betrag, Quantität
percentage	[pəˈsentidʒ]	Prozentsatz, Anteil
to note	[nout]	feststellen, bemerken
up to		bis zu
in addition to	[əˈdiʃən]	zusätzlich zu, außer
including	[inˈkludiŋ]	einschließlich, darunter
data (Pl.)	[ˈdeitə]	Daten, Angaben, Werte
ungebr.: datum (Sg.)	[ˈdeitəm]	
exception	[ikˈsepʃən]	Ausnahme
rule	[ru:l]	Regel, Normalfall
double	[ˈdʌbl]	doppelt, zweifach, Doppel-; das Doppelte, Zweifache

LE 2 ⊕ ⊕ Internationalismen

negative	['negətiv]	negativ, Negativ-
positive	['pɔzitiv]	positiv, Positiv-
isotopic	[ˌaisou'tɔpik]	Isotopen-

LE 3 ⊕ ⊕ Wir üben die Angabe von Mengen.

1. Hören Sie und sprechen Sie nach:

half the quantity	die halbe Menge
double the weight	das doppelte Gewicht
twice the mass	die zweifache Masse
two times the pressure	der zweifache Druck
three times the number	die dreifache Anzahl
four times the distance	die vierfache Entfernung /
	der vierfache Abstand
many times the energy	ein Vielfaches der Energie

2. Reagieren Sie nach dem Muster:

T: In our study we used the same quantity. − double
S: We used double the quantity.

LE 4 ⊕ ⊕ Übersetzen Sie nach dem Muster

T: die doppelte Menge
S: double the quantity

PK 1 · PA 4 · SQ B

LE 1 ⊕ ⊕ In vielen Fällen entspricht dem dt. Ausdruck "sich lassen + V" im Engl. "*can* + *be* + V-*ed*". Übersetzen Sie nach dem Muster:

T: The two elements can easily be separated.
S: Die beiden Elemente lassen sich leicht trennen.

LE 2 ⊕ ⊕ Wir üben Modalverben in Passivsätzen. Formen Sie die engl. Sätze nach diesem Muster um:

T: Many isotopes are produced artificially.
S: Many isotopes can be produced artificially.

LE 3 ⊕ ⊕ Wir üben Modalverben in Passivsätzen. Übersetzen Sie ins Engl. nach dem Muster:

T: Deuterium läßt sich aus natürlichem Wasser darstellen.
S: Deuterium can be obtained from natural water.

LE 4 ⊕ ⊕ Wir üben das Passiv von: *to refer to | to deal with | to look upon as | to account for | to think of as | to refer to as*! Übersetzen Sie ins Dt. nach dem Muster:

T: His new book on nuclear physics is often referred to.
S: Auf sein neues Buch über die Kernphysik wird oft verwiesen.

PK 1 · PA 4 · SQ C

LE 1 ⊼—0 Ergänzen Sie *relation, proportion* oder *ratio* (vgl. 1.3.A. – 1.):

1. Elements can combine in more than one ... to form two or more compounds. 2. The quantities of hydrogen (H) which combine with a given quantity of carbon (C) are in the ... of 2 to 1. 3. In elements such as copper (Cu) a definite ... of electrons is free to move through the atoms. 4. The ... of neutrons in the atoms of the same element may vary. 5. It has been found that the naturally occurring isotopes of a given element are obtained in a definite ... 6. It was shown that there was no definite ... between these two data. 7. The ... of a given isotope in any quantity of the naturally occurring element is called natural abundance. 8. There is a definite ... between the ... of protons to neutrons in the atomic nucleus and the atomic number.

LE 2 ⊼—0 Übersetzen Sie ins Engl. mit Hilfe der Struktur *"be + V-ed"*:

1. Das Neutron wurde 1932 von Chadwick entdeckt. 2. Der Kern des Deuteriums besteht aus einem Proton und einem Neutron (wird von einem Proton und einem Neutron gebildet). 3. Das radioaktive Isotop des Wasserstoffs wird Tritium genannt. 4. Isotope des gleichen chemischen Elements können nicht auf chemischem Wege getrennt werden. 5. Bis jetzt sind 105 chemische Elemente gefunden worden. 6. Fast die gesamte Masse eines Atoms ist im Atomkern enthalten. 7. Das Elektron wurde schon 1897 von J. J. Thomson entdeckt, während das Proton und Neutron viel später gefunden wurden. 8. In Kernreaktionen entstehen neue radioaktive Isotope chemischer Elemente.

Bereiten Sie die Übersetzung des Textes *"Isotopes"* (2.1.C. – 1.) vor.

PK 1 · PA 4 · SQ D

LE 1 ⊕ ⊕ Einführender Dialog

mass spectrograph: Massenspektrograf / spectrum, spectra: Spektrum, Spektren /
superscript: hochgestellter Index

LE 2 ⊕ ⊕ ▷☐ Hören Sie den gesamten BTV *"Isotopes"* und machen Sie
sich Notizen!

LE 3 ▷☐ Vergleichen Sie Ihre Notizen mit dem Schema auf dem Bild!

LE 4 ⊕ ⊕ ▷☐ Hören Sie noch einmal den Text, der jetzt in zwei Teilen
präsentiert wird. Ergänzen Sie Ihre Notizen und beantworten Sie nach
jedem Teil die Fragen in Dt.!

LE 5 Give a definition of isotopes.

What do you know about the true mass numbers of elements? / In which way can
isotopes be distinguished? / What do you know about the symbols for isotopes of
the same element? / Give an example of an element with isotopes.

Atomic Structure and Isotopes

PK 2 · PA 1 · SQ A

LE 1 Dt.'bis zu' wird bei Steigerung durch engl. *up to* und bei Minderung durch engl. *down to* wiedergegeben.

π—0 Formulieren Sie die Vorgaben nach folgenden Mustern:

a) pressure: $10 \rightarrow 12$ atm.
It was found that the pressure increased up to 12 atm.

b) pressure: $8 \leftarrow 10$ atm.
It was found that the pressure decreased down to 8 atm.

1. weight: $10 \rightarrow 20$ gram 2. number of protons: $1 \rightarrow 105$ 3. temperature: $70° \leftarrow 100°$
4. weight: $6 \leftarrow 10$ kg

LE 2 Wir vergleichen die Bedeutungsvarianten von *consider*.

1. *to consider* N: 1. berücksichtigen, in Rechnung stellen
When we compare the data for the two materials, we should consider their different weights.

2. betrachten, untersuchen
In this article we shall consider the physical properties of some elementary particles.

2. *to consider that* ...: annehmen, meinen, daß ...
The German scientist Döbereiner considered that the relationship he had found could serve as a basis for a system of classification of the elements.

3. *to consider* $N^1 \, ^{(as)}_{(to \, be)} \, N^2$ / Adj.: jmdn. / etw. ansehen als, halten für
Bohr's atomic theory must be considered (as) an important step forward in the development of atomic physics.

LE 3 Wir vergleichen *same, equal* und *similar*.

1. *same*: (völlig) gleich, identisch
Das Adj. *same* wird in folgenden Strukturen verwendet:

N^1 *is the same as* N^2
A hydrogen nucleus is the same as a proton.

N^1 *and* N^2 *are the same*
A helium nucleus and an alpha-particle are the same.

N^1 *and* N^2 *have the same* N^3
A proton and a neutron have almost the same mass.

N^2 *is the same for* (*all*) N^1
The number of protons is the same for all atoms of a given element.

2. *equal*: gleich (in bezug auf etw.), gleichartig

Das Adj. *equal* wird in folgenden Strukturen verwendet:

N^1 *is equal to* N^2 / *and* N^2 *are equal*
> Things which are equal to the same thing are equal to one another.

N^1 *and* N^2 *have equal* N^3-*s*
> The first twenty elements have roughly equal numbers of protons and neutrons in the nucleus.

3. In den folgenden Fällen kann der gleiche Tatbestand sowohl durch *same* als auch durch *equal* bezeichnet werden. Die strukturellen Unterschiede bleiben jedoch bestehen:
> Under high pressure these materials show the same properties / are equal in their properties.

> The mass of the neutron is almost the same as that of the proton / is almost equal to that of the proton.

4. Neben dem Adj. *equal* gibt es auch das Verb *equal*:

N^1 *equals* N^2 = N^1 *is equal to* N^2 : N^1 ist gleich N^2

> Übersetzen Sie:

1. The atomic nuclei of the lighter elements are stable if the number of neutrons equals the number of protons. 2. There are only 14 stable elements in which the number of neutrons exactly equals the number of protons. 3. The number of extranuclear orbital electrons equals the number of protons in the nucleus.

5. Von *same* und *equal* muß das Adj. *similar* unterschieden werden:

similar: (annähernd) gleich, ähnlich

> Übersetzen Sie:

1. Uranium, plutonium and neptunium are similar in their chemical properties. 2. In Rutherford's nuclear model of the atom, the atomic structure is similar to a planetary system. 3. In 1829 Döbereiner found that elements with similar properties form groups of three, which he called triads.

PK 2 · PA 1 · SQ B

LE 1 Im wissenschaftlichen Englisch werden Aussagen nicht selten mit einer unpersönlichen passiven Satzkonstruktion eingeleitet, der ein *that*-Nebensatz folgt:

$$It\ is \begin{cases} will\ be \\ \\ was \\ has\ been \end{cases} + \text{V-}ed + that + \ldots$$

It has been found that there are about 300 different stable isotopes in nature.
It was shown that isotopes are different forms of the same element.

1. Die Passivformen in unpersönlichen Satzeinleitungen werden vor allem im Präsens, Präteritum und Perfekt verwendet:

It is shown that ...	Es wird nachgewiesen, daß ...
	Man weist nach, daß ...
It was found that ...	Es wurde festgestellt, daß ...
	Man hat festgestellt, daß ...

2. Daneben sind andere Übersetzungsvarianten möglich:

It is known that ...	Es ist bekannt, daß ...
It is understood that ...	Man nimmt an, daß ...
It can be seen that ...	Man kann sehen, daß ...
	Man kann feststellen, daß ...

3. Die Satzeinleitung *"it + will + be + V-ed"* wird verwendet, um auf die Zwangsläufigkeit oder Regelmäßigkeit eines Vorganges unter bestimmten Bedingungen hinzuweisen:

It will be found that chemical elements often combine in definite proportions to form chemical compounds.

LE 2 Die beiden Vorgänge, die in Sätzen mit unpersönlichen passiven Satzeinleitungen genannt werden, können auch unmittelbar in einer Struktur miteinander verbunden werden. Diese wird als "Subjektkasus (+ Passiv) + Infinitiv", häufig aber auch traditionell als "NcI" (Nominativus cum Infinitivo) bezeichnet. Sätze dieser Struktur haben im Dt. keine eigentliche Entsprechung. Da beide engl. Satztypen die gleiche Situation bezeichnen und meist in gleicher Weise ins Dt. übersetzt werden, kann die neue Konstruktion aus den unpersönlichen passiven Satzeinleitungen abgeleitet werden:

1. Dem aktiven Prädikat des *that*-Satzes entspricht ein aktiver Infinitiv:

$it + be + V_a\text{-}ed + that + N + V_b + ...$

It was found that the nucleus of hydrogen consists of one proton.

$N + be + V_a\text{-}ed + to + V_b + ...$

The nucleus of hydrogen was found to consist of one proton.
Es wurde festgestellt, daß der Wasserstoffkern aus einem Proton besteht.

2. Dem Prädikat des *that*-Satzes mit einer Form von *be* entspricht ein Infinitiv mit *to be*:

$it + be + V_a\text{-}ed + that + N + be + V_b\text{-}ed + ...$

It was found that small quantities of helium 3 are contained in natural helium.

N + *be* + V$_a$-*ed* + *to* + *be* + V$_b$-*ed* + ...

Small quantities of helium 3 were found to be contained in natural helium.
Es wurde festgestellt, daß kleine Mengen von Helium 3 im natürlichen Helium enthalten sind.

3. Dem Prädikat des *that*-Satzes im Präteritum bzw. im Perfekt entspricht ein Infinitiv der Vorzeitigkeit *to have* V-*ed*:

it + *be* + V$_a$-*ed* + *that* + N (+ *have*) + V$_b$-*ed* + ...

It is known that Chadwick (has) discovered the neutron.

N + *be* + V$_a$-*ed* + *to* + *have* + V$_b$-*ed* + ...

Chadwick is known to have discovered the neutron.
Es ist bekannt, daß Chadwick das Neutron entdeckt hat.

4. Bei modalen oder verneinten Ausdrücken werden unpersönliche Satzeinleitungen verwendet:

It was recognized that the isotopic mixture can be separated into two distinct atom types.
It was shown that electrons are not contained in the nucleus

LE 3   ↼—0   Wandeln Sie die Sätze nach diesem Muster um:

It is known that elements combine in definite proportions. →
Elements are known to combine in definite proportions.

1. It was found that the mass number of radon is 222. 2. We know that Rutherford discovered the proton. 3. It is now known that the mass of the atom is mainly contained in the nucleus. 4. It has been found that most elements consist of two or more isotopes. 5. It is known that heavy hydrogen has the atomic number 1 and the mass number 2.

LE 4   ↼—0   Wandeln Sie die Sätze nach diesem Muster um:

Oxygen atoms are found to have mass numbers of 16, 17, and 18. →
It is found that oxygen atoms have mass numbers of 16, 17, and 18.

1. The universe is now believed to be made up of certain elementary particles.
2. The hydrogen isotope of mass number 3 could not be shown to occur in natural

hydrogen. 3. Lithium was found to be formed when deuterium is bombarded with deuterons. 4. In former years the nucleus in heavier atoms was believed also to contain electrons. 5. Isotopes were recognized to have the same chemical properties with the exception of those of hydrogen.

PK 2 · PA 1 · SQ C

LE 1   Übersetzen Sie:

Isotopes

It has been shown that isotopes are elements or different forms of the same chemical element, the atoms of which have the same atomic number. This means that they have the same number of nuclear protons, but different atomic weights or mass numbers, i.e. a different number of nuclear neutrons. Since the number of extranuclear electrons (negative charges) must always be equal to the number of protons (positive charges) in the nucleus, isotopes of the same chemical element have an identical electron structure. It is known that the chemical properties of all elements are determined by the extranuclear electron structure of their atoms. Therefore, isotopes of the same chemical element have identical chemical properties, i.e. they cannot be separated by chemical means. There are many isotopes which for the chemist are different forms of the same element but can be considered to represent distinct elements for the physicist, due to their different physical properties.

Thus ionium is a distinct radioactive element for the physicist but only an isotope of thorium ($^{230}_{90}$Th) for the chemist since its chemical properties are identical with those of thorium and it occupies the same place in the periodic table. It has been found that there are about 300 different stable isotopes in nature. While the chemist recognizes only 105 elements the nuclear physicist distinguishes three times as many. There are only 23 among the 105 known chemical elements which have no isotopic forms, i.e. they contain only atoms of one atomic mass. All the other elements occur in nature as mixtures of two or more isotopes. Their proportion in any given quantity of the natural element is called "natural abundance" and is expressed in percentages. It is interesting to note that elements with even atomic number may have up to 10 naturally occurring isotopes. Elements with odd atomic number have not more than three natural isotopes. In addition to the natural stable isotopes there are more than 500 radioactive elements including the artificially produced radioactive isotopes. All isotopes with an atomic number above 82 are unstable and naturally radioactive, with the exception of the bismuth isotope $^{209}_{83}$Bi.

It was found that generally the atomic masses of the different isotopes of the same element differ from each other by about 10%. Data on the isotopes of hydrogen show that deuterium ($^{2}_{1}$H) is an exception to this general rule. Its mass number is double that of the normal hydrogen isotope ($^{1}_{1}$H).

LE 2 Diesen Test können Sie zusätzlich lesen oder übersetzen:

Radioactive Isotopes

Atoms which have the same nuclear charge but different masses are called isotopes. Isotopes were first discovered in 1909 in the course of (im Verlauf) a study of naturally occurring radioactive elements. Radioactive isotopes are found in the naturally occurring compounds of some elements. For instance, all the known isotopes of some of the heavy elements (Ra, Th, U etc.) are radioactive. The naturally occurring compounds of some other elements (K, Sb, Sm) contain stable isotopes and, in addition, small amounts of not quite stable, but usually long-lived (langlebig) isotopes. Frédéric and Irène Joliot-Curie, in 1934, discovered the phenomenon of artificial radioactivity. After 1934 a great number of new (artificial) isotopes were obtained. All these isotopes were found to be radioactive. As a result (im Ergebnis), the number of known isotopes of different elements has greatly increased. Thus, about 280 isotopes of different elements have been found since that time in naturally occurring compounds. If we add to (hinzufügen) this the artificial isotopes, the number rises to 1400. And this number is increasing with each year as more new isotopes are produced. Various isotopes have also been obtained of atoms with a nuclear charge higher than 92. These new artificial elements are known as the transuranic elements.

PK 2 · PA 2 · SQ A

LE 0 Wortschatz zur Wiederholung

according to: entsprechend / to achieve: erzielen / active: wirksam / to bring, brought, brought: bringen / centre: Mittelpunkt / to connect: verbinden / construction: (Auf)Bau / difficult: schwierig / difficulty: Schwierigkeit / to expect: erwarten / factory: Fabrik / field: Feld / to finish: beenden / industrial: industriell / to invite: einladen / light: Licht / low: niedrig / to measure: messen / to overcome: überwinden / to play: spielen / to repeat: wiederholen / to seem: scheinen / to solve: lösen / speed: Geschwindigkeit / state: Zustand / subject: Gegenstand, Fach / to take, took, taken: nehmen / view: Ansicht / wave: Welle

LE 1 ⊕ ⊕ Neue Lexik

separation	[ˌsepəˈreiʃən]	Trennung, Teilung
to enrich	[enˈritʃ]	anreichern, konzentrieren
certain	[ˈsəːtn]	gewiß, bestimmt
application	[ˌæpliˈkeiʃən]	Anwendung, Verwendung, Gebrauch; Verwendungszweck
considerable	[kənˈsidərəbl]	erheblich, beträchtlich, ziemlich

interest in	['intrist]	Interesse an
to attach to	[ə'tætʃ]	beimessen, zurechnen; befestigen an, verbinden mit
concept	['kɔnsept]	Begriff, Vorstellung
partial	['pa:ʃəl]	teilweise, partiell; Teil-, Partial-
such as	['sʌtʃ‿əz]	wie zum Beispiel
chlorine	['klɔri:n]	Chlor
spectacular	[spek'tækjulə]	groß(artig), hervorragend
purpose	['pə:pəs]	Zweck, Ziel
evidence	['evidəns]	Beweis, Nachweis; Beweismaterial
existence	[ig'zistəns]	Existenz, Vorhandensein
success	[sək'ses]	Erfolg
to result in	[ri'zʌlt]	führen zu, zur Folge haben
revival	[ri'vaivəl]	Wiederaufleben, Erneuerung
extent	[iks'tent]	Ausmaß, Umfang, Grad
by means of	[ˌbai 'mi:nz‿əv]	mittels, mit Hilfe von, durch
to define	[di'fain]	definieren, bestimmen
initial	[i'niʃəl]	anfänglich, Anfangs-, Ausgangs-
fraction	['frækʃən]	Anteil; Bruchteil; Fraktion
treatment	['tri:tmənt]	Bearbeitung(sverfahren); Behandlung
to be present	['preznt]	vorhanden sein, anwesend sein, vorliegen

LE 3 ⊕ ⊕ Internationalismen

concentration	[ˌkɔnsən'treiʃən]	Konzentration, Konzentrierung, Anreicherung
neon	['ni:ən]	Neon
zinc	[ziŋk]	Zink
factor	['fæktə]	Faktor, (mitwirkender) Umstand, Wirkgröße

LE 3 ⊕ ⊕ Wir üben das Verb to *assume* (1)

Beantworten Sie die Fragen nach dem Muster:
T: Will new elements be found?
S: It is assumed that new elements will be found.

LE 4 ⊕ ⊕ Wir üben das Verb to *assume* (2)

Beantworten Sie die Fragen nach dem Muster:
T: What do nuclei consist of? − protons and neutrons
S: They are assumed to consist of protons and neutrons.

nuclei and electrons / in orbits / in different concentrations / particle and wave properties / the same elements as the earth

LE 5 ⊕ ⊕ Wir üben das Verb *to suppose*

Reagieren Sie nach dem Muster:

T: We do no longer believe that atoms are the smallest particles.
S: No, but it was supposed that they were the smallest particles.

PK 2 · PA 2 · SQ B

LE 1 ⊕ ⊕ Beantworten Sie die Fragen nach dem Muster:

T: Will the charge decrease during the process?
S: Well, it is expected to decrease during the process.

have a spectacular success / provide further evidence / find new applications / produce a concentration of the isotope / result in a better knowledge of this problem

LE 2 ⊕ ⊕ Beantworten Sie die Fragen nach dem Muster:

T: Do you know that his experiments were a great success?
S: Yes, they are known to have been a great success.

LE 3 ⊕ ⊕ Beantworten Sie die Fragen nach dem Muster:

T: Has the problem of isotopes been studied by Soddy and Aston?
S: Yes, they are known to have studied it.

PK 2 · PA 2 · SQ C

LE 1 ⊤—0 Für die Übersetzung von *to obtain* gibt es eine Vielzahl dt. Äquivalente: a) erhalten b) erzielen c) herstellen d) gewinnen e) erreichen f) darstellen (chem.)

Wählen Sie die geeignete(n) Variante(n):

1. A distinct concentration can only be obtained when the pressure is increased. 2. Separation may also be obtained in the case of other isotopes. 3. We need a considerable quantity of hydrogen to obtain a small fraction of deuterium. 4. Concentration of isotopes is obtained by means of various treatments. 5. These results can only be obtained at low pressure. 6. The data that were obtained in the last

experiment seem to be an exception to the general rule. 7. Hydrogen was obtained for the first time by the British chemist Cavendish. 8. The earliest information on the structure of atoms was obtained from the study of radioactive elements.

LE 2 🔲—0 Übersetzen Sie:

1. Man hat festgestellt, daß es in der Natur ungefähr 300 verschiedene stabile Isotope gibt. 2. Man weiß heute, daß die Ordnungszahl durch die Zahl der Protonen im Atomkern bestimmt wird. 3. In früheren Jahren wurde die Trennung von Isotopen nur als Beweis für ihre Existenz angesehen. 4. Um das Ausmaß der Trennung zu definieren, muß der Anfangszustand berücksichtigt werden. 5. Die Anwendung der Methode hatte in beiden Experimenten das gleiche Ergebnis. 6. Die Entdeckung dieses radioaktiven Elements kann als ein großer Erfolg angesehen werden. 7. Mit Ausnahme von 22 reinen Elementen sind alle anderen Elemente Gemische verschiedener Atomarten mit gleicher Ladung aber verschiedener Masse. 8. Es wurde festgestellt, daß der Prozentsatz eines bestimmten Isotops im Isotopengemisch allmählich auf 0,03 % sank.

Bereiten Sie die Übersetzung des Textes "*The Separation Factor*" (2.3.C. – 1.) vor!

PK 2 · PA 2 · SQ D

LE 1 ⊕ ⊕ Einführender Dialog

binding energy: Bindungsenergie / *mass defect*: Massendefekt

LE 2 ⊕ ⊕ ⊱▷☐ Hören Sie den gesamten BTV "*Binding Energy and Mass Defect*" und machen Sie sich Notizen!

LE 3 ⊱▷☐ Vergleichen Sie Ihre Notizen mit dem Schema!

LE 4 ⊕ ⊕ ⊱▷☐ Hören Sie noch einmal den Text, der jetzt in zwei Teilen präsentiert wird. Ergänzen Sie Ihre Notizen und beantworten Sie nach jedem Teil die Fragen in Dt.!

LE 5 What do you know about the atomic mass?

Why are the atomic masses always represented by integrar numbers? / Why do the mass numbers differ from the relative atomic masses (atomic weights)? / What is the relation between mass defect and binding energy?

PK 2 · PA 3 · SQ A

LE 1 ⊓─0 Das engl. Adj. *particular* kann durch verschiedene dt. Äquivalente wiedergegeben werden:

a) bestimmt, b) speziell, c) besondere(r, s), d) einzeln e) jeweilig
Wählen Sie die geeignete(n) Variante(n):

1. The chemical properties of a particular element are determined by its extranuclear electrons. 2. All elements have a particular "natural abundance". 3. The properties of this particular group of compounds have been studied for years. 4. Alpha particles and deuterons play a particular role in nuclear processes. 5. Some particular elements have as many as 10 isotopes. 6. A mass spectrometer can be used to distinguish particular groups of elements in chemical compounds. 7. Isotopes of particular elements cannot be distinguished on the basis of their chemical properties. 8. The atomic masses of isotopes of the same element generally differ by about 10 %; deuterium is a particular case as its mass is double that of the normal hydrogen isotope.

LE 2 Übersetzen Sie ins Dt. und beachten Sie den Gebrauch von *assume*:

Rutherford's theory of the nuclear atom

Rutherford published his theory of atomic structure in 1911 in order to explain the wide scattering (Streuung) of alpha particles by matter (Materie). He assumed the existence within the atom of an electric field. He further assumed that the alpha particle is deflected (ablenken) by a single atom. He assumed that the total positive charge which is present within the atom is concentrated in a very small nucleus and thus explained the existence of an electric field within the atom. All the rest of the atom, outside of the nucleus, is occupied by electrons. This theory was later developed by Bohr.

PK 2 · PA 3 · SQ B

LE 1 Wir haben gesehen, daß engl. Sätze der Struktur N + *be* + V-*ed* + *to* + V ("NcI") mit Hilfe eines kurzen, meist unpersönlichen Hauptsatzes als Einleitung und einem "daß-Satz" übersetzt werden:

This mixture was found to contain useful substances.
Es wurde festgestellt,
daß dieses Gemisch nützliche Stoffe enthält.

1. Ist der "NcI" jedoch als Relativsatz Bestandteil eines größeren Satzgefüges, so müssen wir von einem anderen Übersetzungsmuster ausgehen:

> The mixture *which was assumed to contain useful substances* was studied under the microscope.
> Das Gemisch, *von dem angenommen wurde, daß es nützliche Stoffe enthält*, wurde unter dem Mikroskop untersucht.

2. Oft liefert uns dieses Übersetzungsmuster jedoch nur eine Rohübersetzung, die in Abhängigkeit vom jeweiligen Satz verbessert werden muß. So kann das Passiv von Verben wie *know, assume, suppose, believe, think* mit Hilfe von 'bekanntlich', 'vermutlich' oder 'wahrscheinlich' übersetzt werden:

> This mixture which is supposed to contain useful substances will be carefully studied.
> Dieses Gemisch, das vermutlich nützliche Stoffe enthält, wird sorgfältig untersucht.

3. Ferner kann die Bezeichnung irgendeiner Zugehörigkeit durch den Infinitiv von Verben wie *have, show* und *contain* vielfach mit Hilfe von Präp. wie 'bei' oder 'in' vor dem Relativpronomen wiedergegeben werden:

> This compound which has been found to have useful properties should be carefully studied.
> Diese Verbindung, bei der nützliche Eigenschaften festgestellt worden sind, sollte gründlich untersucht werden.

LE 2   Übersetzen Sie:

1. The Curies separated the uranium compound U_3O_8 (pitchblende), which was assumed to contain further radioactive elements, into fractions. 2. The compound which had been found to have interesting properties was studied by means of a mass spectrograph. 3. The scientist who is known to have taken an active part in the development of satellites was invited by our university. 4. Heavy water, which is known to occur in very small quantities only, was discovered by Urey in 1932.

LE 3   Ein weiteres Muster für die Übersetzung des "NcI" benötigen wir, wenn in der Struktur $N + be + V_a\text{-}ed + to\,V_b$ als V_a kein Verb des Wissens, Feststellens oder Vermutens wie *know, show, find, think, believe, expect, assume* oder *suppose* auftritt, sondern *make* als Ausdruck des Veranlassens oder *allow* bzw. *permit* als Ausdruck des Zulassens:

$$\text{Electrons were} \left\{ \begin{array}{l} \text{allowed} \\ \text{permitted} \\ \text{made} \end{array} \right\} \text{to pass through the structure.}$$

> Man ließ Elektronen durch die Struktur hindurchtreten.

Beachten Sie, daß dt. 'lassen' sowohl 'veranlassen' als auch 'zulassen' bedeuten kann.

1. Fungieren *allow* oder *permit* als V_a, so finden wir als V_b meist Verben der Ruhe oder Bewegung wie *to stand* 'stehen'; *to fall* 'fallen, auftreffen'; *to pass* 'hindurchgehen, -treten'; *to strike* 'auftreffen auf' u. a.

> The mixture was permitted to stand overnight.
> Man ließ das Gemisch über Nacht stehen.

2. Wird das Passiv "*be + V_a-ed*" mit *make* gebildet, so folgt oft ein Verb der gezielten Zustandsveränderung wie z. B. *to combine* 'vereinigen' oder *to bombard* 'beschießen':

> Neutrons were made to bombard uranium.
> Man ließ Neutronen Uran beschießen.

Auch hier liefert uns das Übersetzungsmuster vielfach nur eine Rohübersetzung, die in Abhängigkeit vom jeweiligen Satz verbessert werden muß:

> Neutrons were made to bombard uranium.
> Man benutzte Neutronen zum Beschuß von Uran. /
> Man beschoß Uran mit Neutronen.

LE 4   Übersetzen Sie:

1. In experiments on problems of atomic structure alpha particles from a radioactive source were allowed to fall on gold. 2. Nuclear particles can be made to provide important information about the nucleus and its structure. 3. In 1895 Perrin carried out experiments, in which electrons were allowed to fall on a Faraday cylinder which was connected with an electrometer to determine the electric charge. 4. When neutrons are permitted to strike uranium, we obtain two atoms, each of about half the atomic mass of uranium. 6. In 1933 it was discovered that positrons can be obtained when alpha-particles are allowed to fall on certain light elements.

LE 5   In der Struktur N + $\boxed{be + V\text{-}ed + to + be}$ + N / Adj. entspricht *to be known to be* 'angesehen werden', 'bekannt sein als'; *to be considered to be* 'betrachtet werden als'; *to be said to be* 'bezeichnet werden als'.

LE 6   Übersetzen Sie:

1. A body is said to be negatively charged when it contains more electrons than protons. 2. It is now known to be a general rule that the mass of an atomic nucleus is not the same as the total mass of the protons and neutrons of which it is made up. 3. Protons, neutrons and electrons are considered to be elementary particles. 4. The material is said to be technically pure when it contains not more than 5 % of foreign substances. 5. Nuclear power is considered to be the main source of energy in the future.

PK 2 · PA 3 · SQ C

LE 1 Übersetzen Sie:

The Separation Factor

Materials that have been enriched in particular isotopic forms of certain elements have found many applications. Thus considerable interest attaches to the subject of the separation of isotopes. In the years following the first development of the concept of isotopes partial concentrations had been achieved of the isotopes of a number of nonradioactive elements such as zinc, chlorine, neon and some others. The results were, however, not spectacular, and their main purpose was to provide further evidence for the existence of isotopes. The considerable success which was achieved in the concentration of deuterium, despite its very small abundance (one part in about 6500 of ordinary hydrogen) and the useful scientific applications which were found for it resulted in a revival of interest in the general problem of the separation of isotopes. The extent to which separation of isotopes is, or can be, achieved in a particular process is represented by means of a separation factor. This separation factor is defined as the ratio of the abundance of a given isotope in the enriched state to that in the initial state. For example, if an isotopic mixture contains a fraction (or percentage) f of a given isotope before treatment and f^1 is the fraction or percentage that is present in the system after treatment, the separation factor s for the particular treatment is given by $s = \dfrac{f^1}{f}$.

LE 2 Diesen Text können Sie zusätzlich lesen oder übersetzen:

Pions and Muons

In an attempt (Versuch) to account for the forces (Kraft) which hold together the nucleus of an atom the Japanese physicist H. Yukawa, in 1935, postulated the existence of a charged particle, which he assumed to have a mass about 200 times that of an electron. This particle would thus have a mass between an electron (or positron) and a proton. At that time there was no experimental evidence for such a particle. But during the years 1936 and 1937 American scientists demonstrated the existence of charged particles, which had roughly the mass of the Yukawa particle. During the ten years after the discovery (Entdeckung) of this particle, which is now called a meson, its properties were studied. However, these studies resulted in a difficult problem. It was found that the interaction (Wechselwirkung) of mesons with atoms was much less frequent than was expected from the Yukawa theory. In order to overcome this difficulty it was suggested in 1947 that there were two kinds of mesons which differed in mass. A few weeks after publication British scientists obtained evidence for the existence of these two kinds of mesons. The heavier type, which is now known to have a mass 273 times that of the electron (or positron), is called a pi-meson, or pion. The lighter type, which is 207 times as heavy as an electron, is referred to as a mu-meson, or muon. Positively as well as negatively charged pions and muons have been found in cosmic rays (Strahl) and have also been produced in the laboratory.

PK 2 · PA 4 · SQ A

LE 0 Wortschatz zur Wiederholung

able: fähig, in der Lage / cloud: Wolke / direction: Richtung / direct(ly): unmittelbar / effective: wirksam / to enter: eintreten / little: klein; wenig / to lose: verlieren / necessary: notwendig / neighbour: Nachbar / pair: Paar / practical: praktisch / to raise: steigern, erhöhen / readily: leicht / to replace: ersetzen / right: rechts / role: Rolle / salt: Salz / to set up: aufstellen / set up: (Versuchs)Anordnung, Anlage / sign: (Vor)Zeichen / technique: Verfahren / unknown: unbekannt / whether: ob

LE 1 ⊕ ⊕ Neue Lexik

insulator	[ˈinsjuleitə]	Isolator, Nichtleiter
conductor	[kənˈdʌktə]	(el.) Leiter
to charge	[tʃaːdʒ]	laden (Batterie etc.)
excess	[ikˈses]	Überschuß; Übermaß
sign	[sain]	(el.) Vorzeichen
liquid	[ˈlikwid]	Subst. Flüssigkeit; Adj. flüssig
in response to	[in riˈspɔns tə]	als Reaktion auf
force	[fɔːs]	Kraft; Stärke
motion	[ˈmouʃən]	Bewegung
to apply (to)	[əˈplai]	anwenden (auf), verwenden (für); anlegen (an); ausüben (auf); gelten (für)
collision	[kəˈliʒən]	Zusammenstoß, Stoß, Zusammenprall
matter	[ˈmætə]	Materie, Stoff
to classify	[ˈklæsifai]	(ein)ordnen, einteilen, klassifizieren
to ionize	[ˈaiənaiz]	ionisieren
to act (on)	[ækt]	(ein)wirken (auf); angreifen
solid	[ˈsɔlid]	Subst. Festkörper; Adj. fest
close	[klous]	nahe, dicht, benachbart
exchange	[iksˈtʃeindʒ]	Austausch
rare	[rɛə]	selten

present	[ˈpreznt]	vorliegend; zur Debatte stehend
conduction	[kənˈdʌkʃən]	(Strom)Leitung
to conduct	[kənˈdʌkt]	leiten (Strom)
to bind,	[baind,	(ver)binden; zusammenfügen
bound, bound	baund, baund]	
wire	[ˈwaiə]	Draht; Leitung
ciruit	[ˈsəːkit]	Stromkreis; Kreislauf
to flow	[flou]	fließen (Strom, Flüssigkeit); strömen

LE 2 ⊕ ⊕ Internationalismen

neutral	[ˈnjuːtrəl]	neutral (el. etc.)
molecule	[ˈmɔlikjuːl]	Molekül
metal	[ˈmetl]	Metall
ion	[ˈaiən]	Ion

LE 3 ⊕ ⊕ Wir üben das Verb *to suggest* (1)

Das Verb *suggest* hat in der Fachsprache zwei Grundbedeutungen:

1. Mit einem Personalsubj. hat *suggest* vorwiegend die Bedeutung 'vorschlagen', 'anregen'; '(als sicher) annehmen'.

Rutherford suggested a new atomic theory.   Rutherford schlug eine neue Atomtheorie vor.

2. Mit einem Sachsubj. hat das Verb *suggest* die Bedeutung 'andeuten', 'auf etw. hindeuten'; 'auf etw. schließen lassen', 'vermuten lassen'. Häufig folgt ein *that*-Nebensatz.

This fact suggests that ...   Diese Tatsache läßt vermuten, daß ...

   Reagieren Sie nach dem Muster:
   T: Formerly scientists did not assume that the mass of the atom is contained in the nucleus.
   S: No, but later experiments suggested that it is contained in the nucleus.

move in different orbits / at various distances / the properties of a wave / particular spin / consist of isotopes

LE 4 ⊕ ⊕ Wir üben das Verb *to suggest* (2)

   Beantworten Sie die Fragen nach dem Muster:
   T: Who suggested the existence of the meson? – Yukawa
   S: It was Yukawa who suggested the existence of the meson.

system of elements / new model of the hydrogen atom / new atomic theory / new method / structure of this compound

PK 2 · PA 4 · SQ B

LE 1   ⊕_⊕   Beantworten Sie die Fragen nach dem Muster:

T: Is it right that the number of protons determines the atomic number?
S: Yes, the atomic number is actually determined by the number of protons.

deuterium — water / nucleus — protons and neutrons / chemical properties — extranuclear electrons / mass number — number of protons and neutrons

LE 2   ⊕_⊕   Beantworten Sie die Fragen nach dem Muster:

T: Do you know whether we can enrich a particular isotopic form in a given material?
S: Yes, a particular isotopic form can be enriched in a given material.

LE 3   ⊕_⊕   Beantworten Sie die Fragen nach dem Muster:

T: Does oxygen consist of three stable isotopes?
S: It is known to consist of three stable isotopes.

PK 2 · PA 4 · SQ C

LE 1   π—0   Wir üben den Gebrauch des Verbs *to establish*, das in naturwissenschaftl. Texten hauptsächlich in drei Grundbedeutungen vorkommt:

a) to establish a fact etc.: eine Tatsache etc. feststellen
b) to establish a theory, a model etc.: eine Theorie, ein Modell etc. aufstellen
c) to establish a theory experimentally: eine Theorie experimentell beweisen

    Wählen Sie die geeignete Variante:

1. Einstein established his theory of relativity in 1905. 2. In 1776 the British chemist Cavendish established the properties of hydrogen. 3. Mendeleyev arranged the elements into the periodic table and thus established the relationships that exist between the different elements. 4. In 1913 the physicist Niels Bohr established the fact that under certain conditions electrons and atomic nuclei may have wave properties. 5. In 1935 Yukawa suggested the existence of a new charged particle, the meson; 12 years later British scientists established the existence of even two kinds of mesons.

LE 2 ☛─0 Übersetzen Sie:

1. Wenn man Neutronen auf bestimmte Elemente auftreffen läßt, können radioaktive Isotope erzeugt werden. 2. Rutherford hat bekanntlich im Jahre 1920 das Proton entdeckt. 3. Isotope können auf Grund ihrer unterschiedlichen Masse unterschieden werden. 4. Das künstliche Uranisotop 239 wird gebildet, wenn man langsame Neutronen auf Uran 238 (auf)treffen läßt. 5. Vor etwa 200 Jahren ist festgestellt worden, daß Wasser aus Wasserstoff und Sauerstoff besteht und demzufolge eine Verbindung und kein Element ist. 6. Elemente und Verbindungen können auf der Grundlage ihrer elektrischen Eigenschaften in Leiter und Isolatoren unterteilt (als Leiter und Isolatoren klassifiziert) werden. 7. Da die Metalle freie Elektronen enthalten, sind sie gute Leiter und können als Material für Drähte benutzt werden. 8. Leitungsvorgänge in ionisierten Gasen und Flüssigkeiten unterschieden sich von der Leitung in Festkörpern.

Bereiten Sie die Übersetzung des Textes *"Insulators and Conductors"* (3.1.C. – 1.) vor!

PK 2 · PA 4 · SQ D

⊕─⊕ Leistungskontrolle

Electricity

PK 3 · PA 1 · SQ A

LE 1 Das engl. Substantiv hat nur eine Singularendung und, in den meisten Fällen, die Pluralform -*s* bzw. -*es*.

condition — conditions / process — processes

Neben dem "Einheitskasus" gibt es nur noch für bestimmte Substantive bzw. in bestimmten Wendungen den "Besitzkasus", der durch die Endung -'*s* charakterisiert ist:

Rutherford's experiments

Die Funktion des Substantivs im Satz wird gekennzeichnet

a) durch die Stellung im Satz (vor oder nach dem Verb): Every atom contains a nucleus.

b) durch vorangestellte Funktionswörter, insbesondere durch Präpositionen (*of*, *to*, *for*, u. a.)

LE 2 In der Wortform ist das Substantiv in einer Reihe von Fällen nicht vom Verb zu unterscheiden:

change [tʃeindʒ]:   a) Veränderung   b) verändern
flow [flou]:   a) Fluß, Strömung   b) fließen, strömen

Bei zweisilbigen Wörtern kann in der Schriftsprache die Wortform von Substantiv und Verb gleich, die Betonung aber unterschiedlich sein:

Erste Silbe betont = Substantiv   Zweite Silbe betont = Verb
increase ['inkri:s]:Anstieg,Erhöhung   increase [in'kri:s]: ansteigen, (sich) erhöhen
decrease ['di:kri:s]: Verringerung,   decrease [di:'kri:s]: (sich) verringern, senken,
　　　　　　　Senkung, Abfall　　　　　　　　　　sinken

LE 3 Viele Substantive sind aus Verben entstanden durch Anfügen eines formalen Elements — des Suffix. Dieses unterscheidet das Substantiv vom Verb und kann ihm eine zusätzliche Bedeutungskomponente verleihen, z. B.

conduct	[kən'dʌkt]	leiten
conduction	[kən'dʌkʃən]	Leitung
conductor	[kən'dʌktə]	Leiter
amplify	['æmplifai]	verstärken
amplification	[ˌæmplifi'keiʃən]	Verstärkung
amplifier	['æmplifaiə]	Verstärker

Das Suffix -(a)*tion* bezeichnet hier einen Vorgang, das Suffix *-or* (*-er*) einen Handlungsträger oder ein Instrument.

LE 4   Bei der Ableitung von Verben sind besonders häufig *-ation* und *-ment* = dt. meist '*-ung*'.

Das Substantiv entsteht aus dem Verb

1. durch einfaches Anfügen des Suffixes *-ation* oder *-ment*:

	form	[fɔ:m]	(sich) bilden
→	formation	[fɔ:'meiʃən]	Bildung
	transform	[træns'fɔ:m]	umformen
→	transformation	[ˌtrænsfə'meiʃən]	Umformung
	consider	[kən'sidə]	betrachten, darstellen
→	consideration	[kənˌsidə'reiʃən]	Betrachtung, Darstellung
	treat	[tri:t]	behandeln
→	treatment	['tri:tmənt]	Behandlung

2. unter Ausfall des stummen End-*e* beim Anfügen von *-ation*:

	combin*e*	[kəm'bain]	verbinden
→	combination	[ˌkɔmbi'neiʃən]	Verbindung

aber:

	measur*e*	['meʒə]	messen
→	measur*e*ment	['meʒəmənt]	Messung

3. bei vokalisch auslautenden Verben durch Anfügen von *-ation* nach Einschub von *-c-* [*k*]. Dabei wird *-y* im Inlaut zu *-i-*:

	apply	[ə'plai]	anwenden, verwenden
→	appl*i*cation	[ˌæpli'keiʃən]	Anwendung, Verwendung
	classif*y*	['klæsifai]	(ein)ordnen, klassifizieren
→	classif*i*cation	[ˌklæsifi'keiʃən]	(Ein)Ordnung, Klassifizierung

LE 5   Wir üben das Substantiv *evidence*

Im fachsprachlichen Gebrauch hat *evidence* die Bedeutungen: a) 'Beweis(e)', 'Nachweis' b) 'Hinweis(e)', c) 'Beweismaterial'. Das Substantiv hat hier den Charakter eines Sammelbegriffs und wird zusammen mit dem nachfolgenden verbalen Prädikat im Sg. gebraucht. Dabei tritt es häufig in festen Wendungen auf:

There is no evidence (that) ...	Es gibt keinen Beweis (dafür), (daß) ... Es gibt keine(n) Hinweis(e) (dafür), (daß) ...
There is little evidence (that) ...	Es gibt kaum einen Beweis / Beweise (dafür), (daß) ...
to provide / produce evidence (that) ...	den Beweis / Nachweis liefern / erbringen (dafür), (daß); beweisen, nachweisen
to obtain evidence (for) ...	den Beweis / Nachweis erhalten; beweisen, nachweisen

LE 6   Übersetzen Sie:

1. Evidence has been provided for the existence of a new elementary particle.
2. Evidence has been obtained for the fact that generally masses of different isotopes of the same element differ from each other by about 10%. 3. More evidence
will be necessary to explain why the results of our experiment differ so widely.
4. There is little evidence that this technique can easily be used under practical
conditions. 5. The problem cannot be solved on the basis of the existing evidence
6. There is little evidence that classical methods will be effective in this case.

PK 3 · PA 1 · SQ B

LE 1   Zu den nominalen Gliedern eines Satzes kann eine eingrenzende Bestimmung oder eine Erläuterung ("Attribut") in Form eines Relativsatzes der Struktur
... + *that* / *which* / *who* + *be* + V-*ed* + ... hinzutreten, z. B.:

> Water is a compound that is made up of hydrogen and oxygen.

Streicht man *that*, *which* bzw. *who* und die Form von *be*, so bleibt das Partizip
"V-*ed*" als Attribut:

> Water is a compound made up of hydrogen and oxygen.

Beide engl. Sätze können mit Hilfe eines Relativsatzes ins Dt. übersetzt werden:

> Wasser ist eine Verbindung,
> die aus Wasserstoff und Sauerstoff gebildet wird /
> die aus Wasserstoff und Sauerstoff besteht.

Hauptsatz und Relativsatz weisen die gleiche Zeit auf.

LE 2   🔴 Wandeln Sie die passiven Relativsätze in nachgestellte erweiterte
Perfektpartizipien nach diesem Muster um:

> One coulomb represents the charge
> that is carried by 6×10^{18} electrons.
> →   carried by 6×10^{18} electrons.

1. Most elements are mixtures of different kinds of atoms which are called isotopes.
2. "Natural abundance" is the proportion of a natural isotope that is contained in
any quantity of the element. 3. The nucleus of a deuterium atom which is called
a deuteron consists of one proton and one neutron. 4. The two isotopes that are
contained in neon have the mass numbers 20 and 22. 5. The charge that is carried
by a single electron was determined by the American scientist Millikan.

3.1.

LE 3   Relativsätze können jedoch auch die Struktur
... that | which | who + V(-*s | ed*) + ... haben:

A substance that contains atoms of the same kind is called an element.

Relativsätze dieser Art können in ein attributives Partizip umgewandelt werden, indem man das Relativpronomen streicht und für die aktive Verbform ein Präsenspartizip "V-ing" setzt:

A substance containing atoms of the same kind is called an element.

Beide engl. Sätze können mit Hilfe eines Relativsatzes ins Dt. übersetzt werden:

Eine Substanz, die Atome des gleichen Typs enthält, wird Element genannt.

Hauptsatz und Relativsatz weisen die gleiche Zeit auf.

LE 4   🔲 Wandeln Sie die aktiven Relativsätze in nachgestellte erweiterte Präsenspartizipien nach diesem Muster um:

Substances that contain   an excess of electrons
→   containing an excess of electrons
are said to be negatively charged.

1. A small number of the nuclei which occur in nature are radioactive. 2. Dalton produced the first table of atomic weights which consisted of 14 elements. 3. Electrical forces that act on ions in gases or liquids will produce a motion of these charged particles. 4. A substance that contains free electrons is a conductor. 5. Alpha-particles that move through gases will produce ions by their collisions with atoms or molecules.

LE 5   🔲 Wandeln Sie nach den unter LE 2 und LE 4 geübten Mustern die Relativsätze in nachgestellte erweiterte Perfekt- oder Präsenspartizipien um, je nachdem, ob der Relativsatz eine passive oder eine aktive Verbform aufweist.

1. Atomic nuclei which contain roughly the same number of protons and neutrons have been shown to be the most stable. 2. The properties which distinguish hydrogen from other gases were discovered in 1776. 3. The first transuranic element which was called neptunium was discovered in 1940. 4. The motion of alpha-particles through gases can be shown by means of the ions that are formed by their collision with atoms of gases. 5. The hydrogen atom easily loses its electron and becomes a positively charged hydrogen ion which consists only of a proton.

LE 6   🔲 Wandeln Sie jetzt bei Umkehrung der unter LE 2 und LE 4 geübten Muster die Präsens- und Perfektpartizipien in aktive oder passive Relativsätze um:

1. A gas made up of neutral atoms is normally a non-conductor. 2. Nuclei containing 20, 50, 82 and 126 protons or neutrons are particularly stable. 3. Any system con-

sisting of equal numbers of protons and electrons has no charge. 4. The free electrons moving about in a metal flow in a definite direction as soon as an electrical potential is applied. 5. The mass of a particle is usually defined as the quantity of matter contained in the particle.

LE 7 ╼O Kombinieren Sie die beiden Sätze, indem Sie den zweiten in eine attributive Partizipialkonstruktion umwandeln und hinter dem Bezugswort in den ersten eingliedern:

The materials are used for wires. –
The materials contain free electrons. →
The materials containing free electrons are used for wires.
The materials must contain free electrons. –
The materials are used for wires. →
The materials used for wires must contain free electrons.

Beachten Sie, daß das Bezugswort an unterschiedlichen Stellen des Satzes stehen kann!

1. Only atoms of non-metals can become negative ions. – These atoms contain more than five electrons in their outer orbit. 2. The charge of the electron is the smallest quantity of electricity. – It was determined by Millikan in 1906/07. 3. The electrical properties of metals are determined by their structure. – These structures are formed by positively charged ions and free electrons. 4. Urey suggested that the concentration of deuterium could be increased by the heating of liquid hydrogen. – Deuterium has mass number 2.

PK 3 · PA 1 · SQ C

LE 1 Übersetzen Sie:

Insulators and Conductors

At the centre of an atom is a very small positively charged nucleus. Around atomic nuclei there is a cloud of electrons. In electrically neutral atoms the negative charge of the electrons is equal to the positive charge of the nucleus. Atoms and molecules need not be electrically neutral. If there is an excess of charge of one sign, the particle is called an ion. Ions in a gas or liquid will move in response to electrical forces. The details of the motion will depend on the applied force and on the collisions between the ions and their neighbours.

Matter may be classified electrically into two categories, according to whether electrical forces will produce moving charges or not. Ionized gases or liquids are examples of electrical conductors, because electrical forces that act on charged particles will produce motion. Gases and most liquids when they contain only neutral atoms are non-conductors. In solids, atoms are so close to each other that it is difficult for two atoms to change places. Such exchanges occur, but they are so rare that for the present purpose we shall suppose that ions in a solid do not move in response to electrical forces. Therefore the process of electrical conduction in solids is different from that in gases or liquids. Metals are electrical conductors, and they conduct because they contain free electrons. In an insulator, the electrons of an atom may be thought of as a cloud around its nucleus. In a metal, in addition to these bound electrons, there are some free electrons that can move about. If a wire is connected into an electrical circuit, the free electrons flow out at one end and are replaced by other free electrons that enter the wire at the other end.

LE 2 ▾—0 Übersetzen Sie ins Engl. Verwenden Sie, soweit dies nach den beiden geübten Mustern möglich, attributive Partizipien der Gleichzeitigkeit:

1. In vielen chemischen Verbindungen gibt es Atome, die miteinander durch ein Elektronenpaar verbunden sind. 2. Zur Trennung von Substanzen wird in der Industrie häufig ein Verfahren verwendet, das als Ionenaustausch bezeichnet wird. 3. Metalle sind Festkörper, in denen die Atome sehr dicht nebeneinander liegen (= sind). 4. Es gibt Metalle, die in der Natur selten vorkommen, aber wichtige technische Verwendungszwecke haben. 5. In einem Draht, der an einen Stromkreis angeschlossen ist, fließen die Elektronen in einer Richtung.

LE 3 Dieser Text beschreibt folgende physikalische Begriffe: Nichtleiter (Gase, Flüssigkeiten), Leiter (Metalle, Gase, Flüssigkeiten), Ionen, Ionenbewegung (Gase, Flüssigkeiten). Geben Sie in dieser Reihenfolge eine Beschreibung der genannten Begriffe in Engl. auf der Grundlage des Textes:

Gase und Flüssigkeiten, die nur neutrale Atome enthalten, sind Nichtleiter. Leiter sind Stoffe, die freie elektrisch geladene Teilchen enthalten. Metalle, die freie Elektronen enthalten, sind deshalb gute elektrische Leiter. Gase und Flüssigkeiten können auch freie Elektronen enthalten und sind dann elektrische Leiter. Ionen sind Atome oder Moleküle, in denen ein Überschuß an positiver oder negativer Ladung vorhanden ist. Diese Ionen erhalten dann ein positives oder negatives Vorzeichen. Ionen in Gasen und Flüssigkeiten bewegen sich auf Grund der elektrischen Kräfte, die auf sie einwirken.

PK 3 · PA 2 · SQ A

LE 0 Wortschatz zur Wiederholung

along: entlang, an / both — and —: sowohl — als auch / branch: Zweig / to break, broke, broken: (unter)brechen / circle: Kreis / clear: klar, eindeutig / com-

plete: vollständig / connection: Verbindung / to direct: führen / engineering:
Subst. Maschinenbau; Adj. technisch / to found: gründen / indeed: tatsächlich /
influence: Einfluß / to influence: beeinflussen / inside: innerhalb / iron: Eisen /
large: groß / largely: größtenteils, im wesentlichen / law: Gesetz / to lead, led, led:
führen / at least: zumindestens / to lie, lay, lain: liegen / movement: Bewegung /
progress: Fortschritt / short: kurz / solution: Lösung / sometimes: manchmal /
strength: Stärke, Intensität / to turn: drehen / turn: Drehung

LE 1   ⊕ ⊕   Neue Lexik

well-established	[ˈwelisˈtæbliʃt]	gut bewiesen, eindeutig festgestellt
in vacuo	[in ˈvækjuou]	im Vakuum
to exert (on)	[igˈzə:t]	ausüben (auf)
to imagine	[iˈmædʒin]	sich vorstellen
to surround	[səˈraund]	umgeben
field	[fi:ld]	(phys.) Feld
theoretical	[θiəˈretikəl]	theoretisch
to extend	[iksˈtend]	sich erstrecken, sich ausdehnen, reichen
infinity	[inˈfiniti]	unendliche Menge oder Größe; das Unendliche
to infinity		bis ins Unendliche
to place	[pleis]	anordnen; setzen, stellen, legen; bringen
to experience	[iksˈpiəriəns]	erfahren
to detect	[diˈtekt]	nachweisen; feststellen
to infer (from)	[inˈfə:]	schließen, folgern, herleiten (aus)
to specify	[ˈspesifai]	(genau) angeben, bestimmen, spezifizieren
intensity	[inˈtensiti]	Stärke; Intensität
point	[pɔint]	Punkt
to calculate	[ˈkælkjuleit]	berechnen
unit	[ˈju:nit]	(Maß)Einheit
in terms of	[in ˈtə:mz ͜ əv]	mit Hilfe (von), durch
standard	[ˈstændəd]	Standard-, Normal-; typisch
convenient	[kənˈvi:njənt]	zweckmäßig, praktisch, geeignet
to choose	[tʃu:z]	wählen
chose, chosen	[tʃouz, ˈtʃouzn]	
numerical	[nju(:)ˈmerikəl]	zahlenmäßig, numerisch (phys. oder math.)
quantity	[ˈkwɔntiti]	Größe; Menge, Betrag, Quantität
magnitude	[ˈmægnitju:d]	Betrag, (zahlenmäßig ausdrückbare) Größe
opposite	[ˈɔpəzit]	entgegengesetzt

LE 2 ⊕ ⊕ Internationalismen

vacuum	['vækjuəm]	Vakuum
electrostatic	[i'lektrou'stætik]	elektrostatisch
electrostatics	[i'lektrou'stætiks]	Elektrostatik
definition	[ˌdefi'niʃən]	Definition
dyne	[dain]	Dyn
vector	['vektə]	Vektor

LE 3 ⊕ ⊕ Bilden Sie Substantive aus den vorgegebenen Verben nach den Mustern:

a) T: determine → S: determination
b) T: treat → S: treatment

LE 4 ⊕ ⊕ Bilden Sie Substantive aus den vorgegebenen Verben nach den Mustern:

a) T: to determine the weight S: determination of the weight
b) T: to combine elements S: combination of elements

LE 5 ⊕ ⊕ Beantworten Sie die Fragen nach dem Muster:
T: Does the charge increase?
S: Yes, there is an increase in charge.

PK 3 · PA 2 · SQ B

LE 1 ⊕ ⊕ Beantworten Sie die Fragen nach dem Muster:

T: What kind of a particle is a proton?
  contained in the nucleus
S: It is a particle contained in the nucleus.

contained in the nucleus / made up of two elements / formed by ions and free electrons / made up of large atoms / experienced by a standard electric charge

LE 2 ⊕ ⊕ Beantworten Sie die Fragen nach dem Muster:

T: Is the proton a particle carrying a positive or a negative charge?
S: It is a particle carrying a positive charge.

positive or negative charge / positive or negative ions / free or bound electrons / mass or charge

LE 3 ⊕ ⊕ Beantworten Sie die Fragen nach dem Muster:

T: Are there substances containing ions?
S: Yes, there are substances containing ions.

LE 4 ⊕ ⊕ Beantworten Sie die Fragen nach den Mustern:

T: Heavy water is a natural substances.
Does it contain deuterium?
S: Yes, it is a natural substance containing deuterium.
T: Heavy water is a deuterium compound.
Is it found in ordinary water?
S: Yes, it is a deuterium compound found in ordinary water.

PK 3 · PA 2 · SQ C

LE 1 Lesen Sie den Text und beantworten Sie die folgenden Fragen:

1. Welche Typen der Ionisierung gibt es?
2. Wieviel Energie ist notwendig zur Ablösung eines Elektrons oder mehrerer Elektronen vom Atom oder Molekül?
3. Woher kommt diese Energie?

Ionisation

The process in which an atom or molecule is separated into two parts (ions) which have opposite electrical charge is called ionisation. Two general types can be distinguished. First there is that which occurs when a salt is dissolved (auflösen) in water and which results in the formation of two atomic or molecular ions. Second, there is that which occurs when one or more electrons becomes detached (ablösen) from an atom or molecule. The second process is very important in atomic physics, because it occurs when a charged nuclear particle passes through matter. For the ionisation of an atom or molecule it is necessary that one or more electrons in the atom or molecule is raised from a bound to an unbound state. In order to detach an electron, a very small amount (Betrag) of energy which is equal to the electron's binding energy, has to be transferred (übertragen) to the atom or molecule. This energy increases from element to element. It varies from 5 eV (electron volt) for the alkali metals to about 20 eV for the rare gases. Greater energies have to be transferred in order to release (freisetzen) more than one electron from an atom. The energy that is needed to produce ionisation can be supplied (liefern) when collisions of other particles with the atom or molecule occur. Among these particles are other ions and all the charged elementary particles. They must disturb (stören) in some way the electric field in the atom or molecule. When a charged particle of this kind passes through a material it loses energy. Almost all this energy is used to produce the ionisation of the atoms or molecules in this material.

Bereiten Sie die Übersetzung des Textes *"Electrostatic Field"* (3.3.C. −1.) vor!

PK 3 · PA 2 · SQ D

LE 1 ⊞_⊞ Einführender Dialog:

attractive force: Anziehungskraft / repulsive force: Abstoßungskraft / current: Strom / potential difference: Potentialdifferenz

LE 2 ⊞ ⊞ ⇥ Hören Sie den gesamten BTV *"Electricity"* und machen Sie sich Notizen!

LE 3 ⊞ ⊞ ⇥ Hören Sie noch einmal den Text, der jetzt in zwei Teilen präsentiert wird. Ergänzen Sie Ihre Notizen!

LE 4 ⊞ ⊞ Beantworten Sie die Fragen zum Gesamttext in Dt.!

LE 5 What are electrostatic forces?

charged particles in the atoms / atoms − normally neutral / parts of bodies − excess of protons or electrons / two types of electrostatic forces: repulsive and attractive

What are the conditions under which an electric current will flow?

different electrical charges of two bodies / different potentials / two bodies connected to a conductor / motion of electrical charges

PK 3 · PA 3 · SQ A

LE 1 Ein häufiger Ausdruck der engl. Wissenschaftssprache ist *in terms of*. Für die Übersetzung stehen uns mehrere Varianten zur Verfügung:

1. Im Kontext mit

account for, explain; *explanation*:   erklären; Erklärung
define; *definition*:   definieren; Definition
specify; *specification*:   angeben, bestimmen; Angabe, Bestimmung

wird *in terms of* durch 'mit Hilfe', 'vermittels' oder 'durch' übersetzt:

> This effect can only be explained in terms of the nuclear structure.
> Diese Wirkung kann nur mit Hilfe der Kernstruktur erklärt werden.

2. Im Kontext mit

measure: messen; *give, express*: angeben u. a. und nachfolgenden Maßangaben wird *in terms of* durch 'in' übersetzt:

> The data are given in terms of the S.I. system.
> Die Werte sind im S.I.-System angegeben.

LE 2   Übersetzen Sie

1. It is usual in nuclear physics to express energy in terms of electron volts. 2. Physical quantities specified in terms of one number only are known as scalars; examples are mass and electric charge. 3. Differences in the chemical and physical properties of the elements in Mendeleyev's periodic table can be explained in terms of their atomic structure. 4. If the magnitude of the Planck constant h is given in terms of the centimetre-gram-second system, the energy unit is the *erg*. 5. On the basis of the concept of the magnetic field we define the forces that two magnets exert on each other in terms of the fields of one magnet and the magnetization of the other. 6. The motion of electric charge through a conductor such as a metal wire can be accounted for in terms of the atomic structure of the conducting material.

LE 3   Beim Gebrauch der engl. Bezeichnungen für dt. 'Größe', 'Menge' und 'Betrag' sind folgende Unterschiede zu beachten:

a) *magnitude*: zahlenmäßig ausdrückbarer Betrag einer physikalischen oder mathematischen Größe

> magnitude of the charge: Betrag der Ladung
> magnitude of the vector: Betrag des Vektors

b) *quantity*: physikalische oder mathematische Größe

> The physical quantity represented   Die durch das Symbol $\vec{B}$ repräsen-
> by the symbol $\vec{B}$ is called the   tierte physikalische Größe wird als
> magnetic induction.   magnetische Induktion bezeichnet.

c) *quantity*: Menge, Betrag, Quantität

> quantity of electricity: Strommenge
> quantity of heat: Wärmemenge

d) *amount*: Betrag, Menge; Aufwand

> amount of energy: Energiebetrag
> amount of heat: Wärmemenge
> amount of information: Datenmenge
> amount of work: Arbeitsaufwand, Aufwand an Arbeit

Beachten Sie: Auf die Frage *What is the quantity*? erfolgt eine Zahlenangabe, auf die Frage *What is the amount*? erfolgt eine allgemeine Mengenangabe (z. B. *much / little*)!

LE 4   ⊼—0   Ergänzen Sie durch a) *magnitude*, b) c) *quantity* oder d) *amount*:

1. The artificial radioactive elements are obtained in very small ... 2. Experiments were made to investigate the ... of the force exerted on a conductor in a magnetic field. 3. We can find by experiment how the force between two point charges depends on (1) the ... of the charges, and (2) their distance. 4. In electrical problems the electrostatic potential energy is an important ... 5. If we form the work done per unit positive charge, we shall have a ... which only depends on the initial and final positions and the source of the field. 6. Biot and Savart carried out the first experiments to determine the ... of a magnetic field produced by a conductor through which electric charges are flowing.

PK 3 · PA 3 · SQ B

LE 1   Wir haben gesehen, daß zu den nominalen Gliedern eines Satzes statt eines Relativsatzes ein attributives Partizip der Form "V-*ed*" mit seinen Ergänzungen hinzutreten kann:

> The electric field can only be detected by the force (that is) exerted on a charge.
> Das elektrische Feld kann nur durch die Kraft festgestellt werden, die auf eine Ladung ausgeübt wird.

Hauptsatz und Relativsatz weisen die gleiche Zeit auf. Das attributive Partizip "V-*ed*" kann aber auch das Resultat einer Handlung bezeichnen, die nicht gleichzeitig mit der Handlung des Hauptsatzes stattfindet. Meistens gibt das Partizip das Resultat einer Handlung wieder, die vor der des Hauptsatzes liegt ("Vorzeitigkeit"):

> In nuclear research we often need materials
> that have been enriched in a particular isotope /
> →   enriched in a particular isotope.
> In der Kernforschung benötigt man häufig Materialien, die mit einem bestimmten Isotop angereichert wurden / worden sind.

Da "Gleichzeitigkeit" und "Vorzeitigkeit" formal nicht gekennzeichnet sind, ergibt sich der Unterschied bei der Übersetzung mit einem dt. Relativsatz allein aus dem Kontext.

LE 2 π—0 Wandeln Sie die Relativsätze in attributive Partizipialkonstruktionen nach diesem Muster um:

The success
which had been achieved in the concentration of deuterium
→ achieved in the concentration of deuterium
led to a revival of interest in the separation of isotopes.

1. The extent of isotope separation that has been achieved by a particular treatment can be defined by the separation factor. 2. The signs of electrical charge which were chosen by Franklin about 200 years ago are opposite to the directions in which electrons actually flow. 3. The alpha-particles which had been discovered by Rutherford were found to be identical with helium nuclei. 4. Uranium that has been enriched in the isotope 235 is necessary to obtain atomic energy. 5. According to the atomic theory that was established by Heisenberg in 1934, the atomic nucleus consists of nucleons which may be protons or neutrons.

LE 3 π—0 Wandeln Sie die Partizipien in Relativsätze um und achten Sie auf Gleich- und Vorzeitigkeit:
The methods referred to in this book play an important role in solid-state physics.
→ that are referred to in this book
The methods referred to by the professor in his last lesson play an important role in solid-state physics
→ that were referred to by the professor …

1. The charge carried by an electron was determined by Thomson in 1898 and by Millikan in 1911. 2. The positron, a positively charged particle discovered by C. D. Anderson in 1932, is equal to an electron in mass and energy and magnitude of charge. 3. The total number of different types of atoms found in nature or obtained artificially is about 800. 4. The force exerted by one charge on another charge is explained by means of the electric field. 5. Many students attended the lesson of the British scientist invited by our university. 6. The magnitude and direction of the electric force that would act on a unit positive charge placed at any point in space is specified by the electric field, which is a vector quantity.

LE 4 Es ist auch möglich, daß die im Partizip mitgeteilte Handlung nach der des Hauptsatzes liegt ("Nachzeitigkeit"):

The hydrogen isotope deuterium, sometimes also referred to as heavy hydrogen, was discovered by Urey, Murphy and Brickwedde in 1931.
The hydrogen isotope deuterium, which is sometimes also referred to as heavy hydrogen, was discovered by Urey, Murphy and Brickwedde in 1931.

LE 5 Die attributive Konstruktion, die sich auf ein vorangehendes nominales Satzglied bezieht, kann auch von einem Adjektiv und seinen Ergänzungen gebildet werden. Das erweiterte attributive Adjektiv entspricht einem Relativsatz der

3.3.

Struktur ... *that | which | who* + *be* + Adj + ... und kann aus diesem durch Weg-streichen von *that, which* bzw. *who* und der Form von *be* gebildet werden:

> The positive charge that is present in the atom
> →   present in the atom
> is concentrated in a very small nucleus.

LE 6   π—0   Wandeln Sie die Relativsätze nach dem Muster in LE 5 um:

1. The mass spectrograph method produces a separation factor that is much higher than can be obtained with the other methods used for the separation of isotopes. 2. The electric strength which is due to a single charge can be calculated from Coulomb's law. 3. The difference of potential between two points is the work that is necessary to move unit charge from one point to the other. 4. A helium nucleus carries a positive charge that is equal to twice the charge of an electron. 5. Mesons are highly unstable particles of a mass that is less than that of a proton but greater than that of an electron. 6. The potential that is due to many charges is much easier to find than is the electric field that is due to many charges.

LE 7   π—0   Verbinden Sie die Sätze durch ein attributives Perfektpartizip oder ein Adjektiv nach dem Muster:

> The strength of a magnetic field is defined in terms of a force. – The force is exerted on a unit magnetic pole. → The strength of a magnetic field is defined in terms of the force exerted on a unit magnetic pole.

1. The number of neutrons is given by the symbol N. – The neutrons are present in the nucleus. 2. The positive charge is equal in magnitude to Z × the charge of the electron. – The positive charge is carried by the nucleus. 3. The theory of the hydrogen atom is still used for teaching purposes. – The theory was established by Niels Bohr. 4. One method for the separation of isotopes depends on the difference of gases in weight. – The method was developed by Gustav Hertz. 5. In 1865 Loschmidt found a method to determine the number of molecules. The molecules are contained in a definite gas volume.

LE 8   Im Dt. ist die Stellung von erweiterten attributiven Perfektpartizipien vor dem nominalen Bezugswort insbesondere für die wissenschaftliche Darlegungs-weise charakteristisch:

> | die | auf eine negative Ladung ausgeübte | Kraft |

Dagegen sahen wir, daß im Engl. das erweiterte attributive Perfektpartizip hinter sein nominales Bezugswort tritt:

> | the force | exerted on a negative charge |

Gelegentlich beobachten wir den Gegensatz auch bei Präsenspartizipien und bei bestimmten Adjektiven:

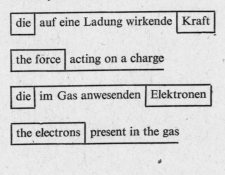

PK 3 · PA 3 · SQ C

LE 1   Übersetzen Sie:

Electrostatic Field

It is a well-established fact that two charges in vacuo exert forces on each other. It is difficult to imagine how one charge can exert a force on another when there is nothing between them. Faraday therefore suggested that every charge is surrounded by an electrostatic (or electric) field which, at least theoretically, extends to infinity in all directions. The electric field due to a charge has the property that all other charges placed in it experience a force. We should, however, note that an electric field can only be detected by the force experienced by a charge placed in it; i.e. we can demonstrate the existence of the force by experiment but we can only infer the existence of the field.

Before we can use the idea of the electric field for the solution of problems in electrostatics we must be able to specify the strength, or intensity, of the electric field at a point in such a way that we can then calculate the force which would act on any charge placed at that point. To do this, it is necessary to define a unit of electric field strength. It should be clear that we must define strength in terms of the force which would be experienced by a standard electric charge; for this purpose, it is convenient to choose a charge of 1 electrostatic unit (e.s.u.).

Definition of the Unit of Electric Field Strength: The unit electric field is such that a unit charge placed in it experiences a force of 1 dyne.

It follows that the strength of the electric field at a point is numerically equal to the force in dynes experienced by a unit charge at that point. Thus, if a unit charge experiences a force of 5 dynes, the strength of the electric field at that point is 5 e.s.u. of electric field strength.

Since electric field strength is defined in terms of a force it should be clear that it is, like force, a vector quantity. Thus, in order to specify it completely we need both its magnitude and direction.

Definition of the Direction of an Electric Field: The direction of the electric field at a point is the same as the direction of the force experienced by a positive charge placed at that point. The force experienced by a negative charge will be in the opposite direction.

LE 2 ⚲—0 Übersetzen Sie:

1. Elektrische Kräfte wirken zwischen den Körpern, die einen Überschuß von Elektronen oder Protonen haben. 2. Elektronen, die in positiver Richtung fließen, bilden einen negativen Strom. 3. Der Kern trägt die im Atom enthaltene positive Ladung. 4. Physikalische Größen wie Masse und Ladung sind Skalare, die mit Hilfe nur einer Zahl definiert werden. 5. Auf Grund ihrer wichtigen Rolle in Kernreaktionen werden Alphateilchen und Deuteronen oft als Elementarteilchen angesehen.

LE 3 ⚲—0 Erklären Sie in Engl. die Begriffe 'Feld' und 'Feldstärke' auf der Grundlage dieses Textes:

Jede Ladung ist von einem Feld umgeben, das sich theoretisch ins Unendliche erstreckt. Jede in solch ein Feld gebrachte elektrische Ladung erfährt eine Kraft. Die elektrische Feldstärke kann mit Hilfe der Kraft definiert werden, die eine elektrische Einheitsladung in diesem Feld erfährt. Die auf eine positive Ladung ausgeübte Kraft wirkt in der Richtung des elektrischen Feldes. Die durch eine einzelne Ladung bewirkte elektrische Feldstärke wird auf der Grundlage des Coulombschen Gesetzes berechnet.

PK 3 · PA 4 · SQ A

LE 0 Wortschatz zur Wiederholung

to accept: an-, aufnehmen / ball: Ball / beginning: Beginn, Anfang / to drive: fahren; (an)treiben / correct: genau; richtig / independent: unabhängig / list: Liste / literature: Literatur / majority: Mehrheit / neither − nor: weder − noch / reference: Hinweise, Verweis / to save: sparen / side: Seite / surface: Oberfläche / zero: Null(punkt)

LE 1 ⊕ ⊕ Neue Lexik

dual	[ˈdjuːəl]	zweifach; doppelt; Doppel-
nature	[ˈneitʃə]	Natur, Charakter, (Eigen)Art
momentum	[mouˈmentəm]	(phys.) Impuls, Bewegungsgröße

corpuscle	[ˈkɔ:pʌsl]	Korpuskel, klein(st)es Teilchen
to be true (of)	[tru:]	gelten, richtig sein (für)
ray	[rei]	(phys.) Strahl
to diffract	[diˈfrækt]	(phys.) beugen
to force (to)	[fɔ:s]	zwingen (zu)
conclusion	[kənˈklu:ʒən]	(logischer) Schluß, Schlußfolgerung
to devise	[diˈvaiz]	(Versuchsanordnung) entwickeln; ausdenken, erfinden
to behave	[biˈheiv]	sich verhalten; funktionieren
entire	[inˈtaiə]	gesamt, ganz, vollständig; Gesamt-
converse	[ˈkɔnvəːs]	gegenseitig, umgekehrt
equation	[iˈkweiʃən]	Gleichung
frequency	[ˈfri:kwənsi]	(phys.) Frequenz, Schwingungszahl; (math.) Häufigkeit
kinetic	[kiˈnetik]	kinetisch
to attempt	[əˈtempt]	(abstr.) versuchen
wave-packet	[ˈweivˌpækit]	Wellenpaket
formula	[ˈfɔ:mjulə]	(math., chem.) Formel
to support	[səˈpɔ:t]	(unter)stützen, aufrecht(er)halten
to dissipate	[ˈdisipeit]	(sich) zerstreuen; verlorengehen, dissipieren
to avoid	[əˈvɔid]	(ver)meiden; (Schwierigkeit) umgehen
carrier	[ˈkæriə]	(el.) Träger; Trägerwelle
transmission	[trænzˈmiʃən]	Übertragung
to transmit	[trænzˈmit]	übertragen
to correspond (to)	[ˌkɔrisˈpɔnd]	(etw.) entsprechen, äquivalent sein
length	[leŋθ]	Länge; z. B. in wavelength
to interpret	[inˈtə:prit]	interpretieren, auffassen als
probability	[ˌprɔbəˈbiliti]	Wahrscheinlichkeit
density	[ˈdensiti]	Dichte

LE 2 ⊕ ⊕ Internationalismen

experimental	[eksˌperiˈmentl]	experimentell; Experimental-, Versuchs-
molecular	[mouˈlekjulə]	molekular; Molekular-
crystal	[ˈkristl]	Kristall
aspect	[ˈæspekt]	Aspekt, Gesichtspunkt, Hinsicht
constant	[ˈkɔnstənt]	Subst. Konstante; Adj. konstant
mechanics	[miˈkæniks]	Mechanik
interpretation	[inˌtə:priˈteiʃən]	Interpretation, (Aus)Deutung, Erklärung
differentiation	[ˌdifərenʃiˈeiʃən]	Differenzierung
volume	[ˈvɔljum]	Volumen
term	[tə:m]	Term

LE 3   ⊕ ⊕   Hören Sie die folgenden dt. Wörter und ihre engl. Entsprechungen im Sg. und Pl.! Wiederholen Sie beiden Formen der engl. Wörter:

Atomkern	nucleus	nuclei	[ˈnjuːkliəs, -iai]
Radius	radius	radii	[ˈreidjəs, -iai]
Phänomen	phenomenon	phenomena	[fiˈnɔminən, -ə]
Kriterium	criterion	criteria	[kraiˈtiəriən, -ə]
Minimum	minimum	minima	[ˈminiməm, -ə]
Maximum	maximum	maxima	[ˈmæksiməm, -ə]
Spektrum	spectrum	spectra	[spektrəm, -ə]
Vakuum	vacuum	vacua	[ˈvækjuəm, -ə]
Medium	medium	media	[ˈmiːdjəm, -ə]
Doktorarbeit	thesis	theses	[ˈθiːsis, -iːz]
Analyse	analysis	analyses	[əˈnæləsis, -iːz]
Hypothese	hypothesis	hypotheses	[haiˈpɔθisis, -iːz]
Index	index	indices	[ˈindeks, -isiːz]
Formel	formula	formulae / formulas	[ˈfɔːmjulə, -iː]

LE 4   ⊕ ⊕   Beantworten Sie die Fragen nach dem Muster:

T: Where did you find the values for this nucleus?
S: The values of all the nuclei are given in this handbook.

LE 5   ⊕ ⊕   Beantworten Sie die Fragen nach dem Muster:

T: Is this the only thesis of this kind?
S: No, there are several theses of this kind.

PK 3 · PA 4 · SQ B

LE 1   ⊕ ⊕   Übersetzen Sie ins Dt. nach dem Muster:

T: the isotope separation achieved by this treatment
S: die durch dieses Verfahren erzielte Isotopentrennung

LE 2   ⊕ ⊕   Übersetzen Sie ins Dt. nach dem Muster:

T: the particles determining the mass number
S: die die Massenzahl bestimmenden Teilchen

LE 3   ⊕ ⊕   Übersetzen Sie ins Engl. nach den Mustern:

T: der von Elektronen umgebene Kern
S: the nucleus surrounded by electrons
T: die den Kern umgebenden Elektronen
S: the electrons surrounding the nucleus

LE 4   ⊕ ⊕   Beantworten Sie die Fragen nach dem Muster:

T: These materials are enriched in particular isotopes. Where are they used?
S: Materials enriched in particular isotopes are used in nuclear research.

LE 5   ⊕ ⊕   Stellen Sie Fragen nach dem Muster:

T: Neutrons are present in the nucleus.
S: Can we determine the number of neutrons present in the nucleus?

PK 3 · PA 4 · SQ C

LE 1   Lesen Sie den Text und beantworten Sie folgende Fragen:

1. Welche Wirkung hat ein magnetisches Feld auf einen stromdurchflossenen feinen Draht? 2. Wie kann dieser Effekt für die Messung der Stromstärke benutzt werden? 3. Welche Entdeckung machte Faraday im Jahre 1831?

Magnetic Effect of the Electric Current

The electric charge and the magnetic field of force had been known for a long time before it was assumed that there was any connection between them. In 1820 Oerstedt demonstrated the fact that a wire carrying a current exerts a force on a magnet parallel to the current. Faraday explained that this was due to the magnetic force produced by the current, acting in circles with their centres on the wire and lying in a plane (Ebene) at right angles (Winkel) to the wire.

A consequence of the fact that a current produces a magnetic field is that a very fine wire, which can move freely, will move sideways in a magnetic field if a current flows through it. This is the basis of an instrument for the measuring of an electric current, or galvanometer, as it is called. Another form of galvanometer consists of a light coil (Spule) between the poles of a magnet that are opposite to one another: when a current flows through the coil, this coil acts as a magnet and turns in the magnetic field. In 1831 Faraday made a discovery (Entdeckung) that is very important for electromagnetic theory and is also the basis of practically all electrical engineering. He found that when a steady (stetig) current was flowing in one coil, no current flowed in the other coil, but that the breaking and making of the current in one coil was the cause of a short current in the other coil. This is called electromagnetic induction. Modern dynamos which are machines for the production of large currents, are all founded on electromagnetic induction.

Bereiten Sie die Übersetzung des Textes *"The Dual Nature of Matter and Waves"* (4.1.C. – 1.) vor!

PK 3 · PA 4 · SQ D

LE 1   ⊕ ⊕   Einführender Dialog

dielectric: Dielektrikum / *dielectric strength*: Durchschlagsfestigkeit / *dielectric breakdown*: Durchschlag

LE 2   ⊕ ⊕ ⊳   Hören Sie den gesamten BTV *"Dielectrics"* und machen Sie sich Notizen!

LE 3   ⊕ ⊕ ⊳   Hören Sie noch einmal den Text, der jetzt in zwei Teilen präsentiert wird. Ergänzen Sie Ihre Notizen!

LE 4   ⊕ ⊕   Beantworten Sie die Fragen zum Gesamttext in Dt.!

LE 5   What do you understand by "conductors" and "non-conductors"?

basic difference between conductors and non-conductors: existence of free electrons or ions / metals – free electrons: conductors / ionized gases and liquids: also conductors / neutral gases or liquids: non-conductors or dielectrics / dielectric breakdown under the influence of a strong electric field: gas no longer dielectric or non-conductor

Waves and Particles

PK 4 · PA 1 · SQ A

LE 1 Es gibt im Engl. eine Anzahl von Nomen, die von Verben abgeleitet sind mit Hilfe der Suffixe -*sion* oder -*ssion*.

1. Das Suffix -*sion* wird vor allem bei Ableitung aus Verben, die auf -*de* oder -*se* enden, verwendet:

  collide → collision
  disperse → dispersion

2. Das Suffix -*ssion* dient zur Ableitung von Nomen aus Verben, die auf Vokal + *ss* oder Vokal + *t* enden:

  discuss → discussion
  emit → emission

3. Die dt. Äquivalente der Nomen können das gleiche Suffix haben, besonders in der Fachsprache:

  division = Division

Vielfach entsprechen den engl. Wörtern mit dem Suffix -(*s*)*sion* dt. Wörter auf '-ung':

  division = Teilung
  transmission = Übertragung
  conclusion = Schlußfolgerung

LE 2 Zum Ausdruck der Gesetzmäßigkeit oder Notwendigkeit eines Tatbestandes oder eines Vorgangs als Folge einer vorher genannten Bedingung wird in engl. wissenschaftlichen Texten häufig das Modalverb *will* verwendet. Daher kann *will* hier meist nicht durch dt. 'wird' übersetzt werden. Vielmehr wird die gleiche Mitteilung oft durch Adv. wie 'stets', 'immer', 'gesetzmäßig' oder 'regelmäßig' übernommen. Nicht selten steht der entsprechende dt. Satz auch nur im Präsens, d. h. ohne ein Adv.

LE 3 Übersetzen Sie ins Dt. unter Beachtung dieser Hinweise:

Consider a point, P, placed near to a positive charge. The electric field at P will be directed from the charge towards infinity; thus the field will be opposite to the motion of a unit positive charge from infinity to P, and mechanical work will have to be done on this charge to move it from infinity to P. Therefore, the potential energy of the unit positive charge at P will be greater than zero and the potential of P will be positive. If P is placed near to a negative charge, the field will be in the same direction as the motion of a positive charge from infinity. Therefore, the field will do work on the charge as it moves to P, just as the gravitational field of the earth does work on a falling ball. Thus, the potential energy of the unit positive charge at P will be negative. It follows that movement against the field takes us to points of higher potential while movement in the direction of the field takes us to points of lower potential.

LE 4   Beim Gebrauch von *rather* müssen in Fachtexten drei Bedeutungen unterschieden werden:

a) *rather* gibt an, daß eine Größe (Eigenschaft oder Tatsache) in größerem Ausmaß vorhanden ist. Das dt. Äquivalent ist in der Regel 'ziemlich':

His new book on problems of solid-state physics was rather a success.
Sein neues Buch über Probleme der Festkörperphysik war ein ziemlicher Erfolg.

b) Enthält der Kontext zwei gegensätzliche Möglichkeiten, so bringt *rather* zum Ausdruck, daß eine davon überwiegt. Das dt. Äquivalent ist in der Regel 'eher', 'vielmehr':

There is actually no clear difference between the electromagnetic waves, but rather a gradual change from one type to another.
In Wirklichkeit gibt es keinen klaren Unterschied zwischen den elektromagnetischen Wellen, sondern eher einen allmählichen Übergang von einer Form zur anderen.

c) Enthält der Satz einen klaren Gegensatz, so gibt *rather (than)* an, daß nur eine Möglichkeit richtig ist. Das dt. Äquivalent von *rather than* ist '(an)statt', 'und nicht' und von *rather* allein 'stattdessen'.

The relative atomic mass of hydrogen is now known to be 1.0080, *rather than* exactly 1.
Es ist jetzt bekannt, daß die relative Atommasse von Wasserstoff 1,0080 beträgt *und nicht genau* 1.

Beachten Sie: Gelegentlich sind die Grenzen zwischen b) und c) fließend. Für Fachtexte ist es jedoch charakteristisch, daß meist nur '(an)statt' bzw. 'und nicht' richtig, 'eher' dagegen sachlich falsch ist.

🔄 Wählen Sie die geeignete(n) Variante(n):

1. Up to now most of the problems solved have been of a rather elementary nature. 2. Today there is so much evidence for the atomic structure of matter that the concept is generally accepted as an established fact rather than a theory. 3. When the reflection of a beam of electrons in a nickel crystal was studied, it was found that the electrons behave like waves rather than like particles. 4. It is more useful to distinguish between particle properties and wave properties rather than between particle and wave. 5. The wavelength of a 1-ev neutron is 2.87×10^{-9} cm, and such a neutron can no longer be considered as a point colliding with a nucleus, but rather as a wave which can surround many nuclei. 6. The methods for the determi-

nation of a nuclear radius do not involve the approach of particles to the nucleus or the emission of particles. They depend, rather, on electrical forces of one kind or another.

PK 4 · PA 1 · SQ B

LE 1   Bisher waren die nachgestellten attributiven Perfektpartizipien "V-*ed*" stets durch weitere Bestimmungen erweitert:

> the rays emitted by radioactive elements
> die von radioaktiven Elementen emittierten Strahlen

In bestimmten Fällen kann auch ein nichterweitertes Perfektpartizip oder ein Adj. hinter das nominale Bezugswort treten. Oft handelt es sich dabei um das Perfektpartizip von Verben, die einen belebten Handlungsträger haben, dessen ausdrückliche Nennung meist überflüssig ist:

> They obtained results. → the results obtained (by them):
> the results obtained   = die erzielten Ergebnisse

Vor der Struktur "N + V-*ed*" kann ein Superlativ stehen:

> the best conductor known = der beste der bekannten Leiter

LE 2   Übersetzen Sie:

1. Gases are among the best insulators known. 2. Work can be changed into heat in such a way that all the work done is turned into heat. 3. In 1842 Mayer suggested that there was a close relation between the work done and the heat produced. 4. Electrons are smaller than the smallest atom known. 5. The potential difference between two points is the work done when a coulomb of positive charge is moved from one point to the other. 6. For the majority of elements studied the relative abundances of their isotopes have been found to be independent of the source of the material.

LE 3   Während einerseits auch nichterweiterte Perfektpartizipien hinter das nominale Bezugswort treten können, finden wir andererseits durch ein Nomen erweiterte Präsenspartizipien in Frontstellung:

> The cathode is an electron-emitting electrode.
> Die Katode ist eine elektronenemittierende Elektrode.

Das allgemeine Schema solcher Bildungen ist $N^1 + V + N^2 \rightarrow N^2 + V\text{-}ing + N^1$

> The electrode emits electrons: An electron-emitting electrode

Oft haben solche Bildungen, die man mit und ohne Bindestrich geschrieben findet, terminologischen Charakter.

> energy-absorbing material
>> The material absorbs energy.
>>> energieabsorbierendes Material

> current multiplying factor
>> The factor multiplies the current.
>>> Stromvervielfachungsfaktor

> time varying field
>> The field varies with time.
>>> zeitabhängiges Feld

Beachten Sie beim letzten Beispiel den Fortfall der Präposition.

LE 4   Analysieren Sie die Ausdrücke nach dem Schema:
$$N^2 + V\text{-}ing + N^1 \rightarrow N^1 + V + N^2$$

current-carrying conductor	current-measuring instrument
heat conducting element	ion conducting substance
nitrogen-containing compound	emission measuring instrument
heat-dissipating element	power saving machine

LE 5   In einigen Fällen tritt auch ein Perfektpartizip oder ein Adj. mit einer nominalen Ergänzung vor das Bezugswort:

> valency-controlled element
>> The element is controlled by its valency.
>>> valenzgesteuertes Element

LE 6   ⚡   Ordnen Sie den Ausdrücken der Struktur "N + V-*ed* / Adj" ihre dt. Bedeutung zu:

a) charge-controlled b) charge-independent c) time-dependent d) field-independent e) earth-connected f) ion-heated g) power-driven
(a) zeitabhängig (b) motorbetrieben (c) geerdet (d) ladungsunabhängig (e) feldunabhängig (f) ionenbeheizt (g) ladungsgesteuert

PK 4 · PA 1 · SQ C

LE 1 Übersetzen Sie:

The Dual Nature of Matter and Waves

It has been established experimentally that electrons have the properties of waves. At the same time they have the properties of particles since they have mass and momentum which can be thought of as typical properties of corpuscles. This is true of the electron but it is also true of atoms and molecules. Stern showed in 1932 that atomic and molecular rays were diffracted at crystal surfaces in the same way as electrons so that he was forced to the conclusion that all matter has a wave aspect as well as a particle aspect. Thus both matter and electromagnetic waves have a dual nature. It can be shown that if an experiment is devised to test the wave properties of matter then the matter behaves entirely as waves. Conversely, if an experiment is devised, e.g. to measure the momentum of a particle then the material side of matter only will be in evidence. If we consider wavelength as the property of the waves we are thinking of, and momentum as the property of the particles, the two are then connected by the de Broglie equation

$$\frac{\lambda}{2\pi} = \frac{\hbar}{mv} \tag{1}$$

where mv is the momentum. Thus, the connecting factor is $\hbar$, Planck's constant.

The de Broglie equation can also be used to connect frequency ω with energy ($\frac{1}{2} mv^2$) since the wavelength $\lambda = \dfrac{2\pi v}{\omega}$. The corresponding equation would be:

$$\omega = \frac{mv^2}{\hbar} = \frac{\frac{1}{2} mv^2}{\dfrac{\hbar}{2}} \tag{2}$$

We see again that the factor connecting frequency (a wave property) with kinetic energy (a particle property) is Planck's constant $\hbar$.

The system of wave mechanics attempts to explain this dual nature of matter. In order to avoid theoretical difficulties Schrödinger suggested that electrons should be considered as wave-packets. This interpretation cannot be supported since wave-packets would, in the course of time, be dissipated, but the formulae established on this basis are correct. According to de Broglie's theory a freely moving particle should be represented by a wave of the form

$$\psi(x, t) = A \exp\left[2\pi i\left(\frac{x}{\lambda} - vt\right)\right] \tag{3}$$

Differentiation shows that

$$\frac{d^2}{dx^2} = -\frac{p^2}{\hbar^2}\psi \tag{4}$$

However, the energy of the particle is

$$E = \frac{p^2}{2m} + V, \tag{5}$$

where the first term on the right side is the kinetic energy and the second term is the potential energy, which is constant if the particle is moving under no forces. Equation (4) thus becomes

$$\frac{d^2\psi}{dx^2} + \frac{2m}{\hbar^2}(E - V)\psi = 0 \tag{6}$$

Although this equation has been established only for a free particle, Schrödinger assumed that it also applies to a particle moving under a force, so that the potential energy V is a function of x. It is known as the Schrödinger equation or the wave equation for a particle moving in one dimension, and the function $\psi(x)$ is called the wave function.

It was suggested by Bohr, in 1926, that $|\psi|^2$ may be interpreted as a probability density, such that

$$|\psi(x, y, z)|^2 \, dx \, dy \, dz$$

is the probability that the particle is found in the small volume element dx, dy, dz at the point (x, y, z).

LE 2 ☛―0 Übersetzen Sie ins Engl.:

1. Die von de Broglie aufgestellte Gleichung konnte experimentell gestützt werden. 2. Durch Mayer ist gezeigt worden, daß eine bestimmte Beziehung zwischen der verrichteten Arbeit und der erzeugten Wärme besteht. 3. Die 1927 durchgeführten Experimente haben erstmalig gezeigt, daß sich Elektronen wie Wellen verhalten. 4. Die erzielten Ergebnisse zeigen, daß diese Formel nicht den experimentellen Daten entspricht. 5. Kristalle können benutzt werden, um Strahlen zu beugen, die aus Atomen oder Molekülen bestehen.

LE 3 ☛―0 Übertragen Sie die Information des Textes unter Berücksichtigung der unten aufgeführten Fragen ins Engl.:

Die Quantenmechanik ist eine von Heisenberg und Born einerseits und von Schrödinger andererseits 1925/26 auf zwei verschiedenen Wegen gefundene Mechanik atomarer Erscheinungen, die sowohl die Wellen- als auch die Teilcheneigenschaften der Elektronen in einer widerspruchsfreien (consistent) Theorie beschreibt. Bereits, im Jahre 1924 hatte de Broglie die Vermutung geäußert, daß der für das Licht festgestellte Doppelcharakter eine Grundeigenschaft der gesamten Materie sein könnte. Die von Davisson und Germer im Jahre 1927 durchgeführten Experimente bewiesen dann erstmalig, daß sich Elektronen wie Wellen verhalten können. Durch Experimente, die im Jahre 1932 durchgeführt wurden, erhielt man auch den Nachweis der Welleneigenschaften atomarer und molekularer Strahlen.

- Wer entwickelte die Quantenmechanik?
- Was wird durch die Quantenmechanik beschrieben?
- Wer sprach als erster die Vermutung aus, daß nicht nur das Licht Teilchen- und Welleneigenschaften aufweist?
- Wann wurden die Welleneigenschaften der Elektronen experimentell nachgewiesen?
- Wann wurden auch für atomare und molekulare Strahlen Welleneigenschaften festgestellt?

PK 4 · PA 2 · SQ A

LE 0 Wortschatz zur Wiederholung

agreement: Übereinstimmung; Übereinkunft / already: schon / approach: Näherkommen, Annäherung; Herangehen, Methode / area: Gebiet / to associate: (sich) verbinden, zuordnen / to award: (akad. Grad, Preis) verleihen / to be based (on): basieren (auf) / to cross: kreuzen, über-, durchqueren / department: Abteilung, Institut / fast: schnell / to instruct: unterrichten / to introduce: einführen; vorstellen / to leave: verlassen, (in einem Zustand) zurücklassen / to be left: (in einen Zustand) übergehen; erzeugt werden / to mention: erwähnen / order: (Größen-) Ordnung / special: besondere(r,s) / to start: anfangen, beginnen / to tell: mitteilen

LE 1 ⊕ ⊖ Neue Lexik

diffraction	[di'frækʃən]	(phys.) Beugung, Diffraktion
proof	[pru:f]	Beweis, Nachweis
consequently	['kɔnsikwəntli]	daher, deshalb, infolgedessen, folglich
to exhibit	[ig'zibit]	zeigen, aufweisen
reflection	[ri'flekʃən]	(phys.) Reflexion, Reflektierung
scatter(ing)	['skætə(riŋ)]	Streuung; Streubereich
beam	[bi:m]	(Leit / Richt)Strahl, Strahlenbündel
velocity	[vi'lɔsiti]	Geschwindigkeit
rather (than)	['ra:ðə]	anstatt, und nicht
to accelerate	[ək'seləreit]	beschleunigen
value	['vælju:]	Wert; Betrag
to pass	[pa:s]	hindurchtreten (lassen); hindurchschicken

stream	[stri:m]	Strom, Strahl
thin	[θin]	dünn
sheet	[ʃi:t]	Platte; Scheibe
resulting	[ri'zʌltiŋ]	resultierend, sich ergebend, entstehend
pattern	['pætən]	Muster; Struktur; Schema; System
to indicate	['indikeit]	(an)zeigen, angeben; hinweisen, hindeuten (auf)
to distort	[dis'tɔ:t]	verzerren
X-ray(s)	['eks'rei(z)]	Röntgenstrahl(en)
examination	[ig,zæmi'neiʃən]	Untersuchung, Prüfung
visible	['vizibl]	sichtbar
behaviour	[bi'heivjə]	Verhalten
to involve	[in'vɔlv]	einbeziehen, einschließen, von Bedeutung sein, eine Rolle spielen
to observe	[əb'zə:v]	beobachten, verfolgen; feststellen
apparent	[ə'pærənt]	offenbar, offensichtlich; scheinbar, anscheinend

LE 2 ⊕ ⊕ Internationalismen

nickel	['nikl]	Nickel
potential	[pə'tenʃəl]	Subst. Potential; Adj. potentiell
volt	[voult]	Volt
equivalent	[i'kwivələnt]	Subst. Äquivalent, gleichwertiger Betrag, gleichwertige Menge; Adj. äquivalent, gleichwertig; Äquivalent-
magnet	['mægnit]	Magnet
effect	[i'fekt]	Effekt, Einwirkung, Einfluß; Effekt, Ergebnis, Resultat

LE 3 ⊕ ⊕ Wir üben die Bildung von Substantiven aus Verben. Bilden Sie Substantive nach den Mustern:

T: divide → S: division − Teilung (1)
T: emit → S: emission − Emission (2)
T: invert → S: inversion − Inversion (3)

LE 4 ⊕ ⊕ Beachten Sie den Gebrauch von *any* in der Bedeutung 'beliebig, jede(r,s)'! Beantworten Sie die Fragen nach dem Muster:

T: Do I find the periodic table only in this book?
S: No, you can find it in any elementary textbook.

LE 5 ⊕ ⊕　Beachten Sie den Gebrauch von *any* in der Bedeutung 'keine(r,s)'. Beantworten Sie die Fragen nach dem Muster:

> T: Did they use one of these methods?
> S: No, they didn't use any of these methods.

PK 4 · PA 2 · SQ B

LE 1 ⊕ ⊕　Beantworten Sie die Fragen nach dem Muster:

> T: What is Moseley famous for? Didn't he improve Mendeleyev's Periodic Table?
> S: That's right. It was Moseley who improved Mendeleyev's Periodic Table.

Die Satzeinleitung mit *it* dient der Hervorhebung.

LE 2 ⊕ ⊕　Beantworten Sie die Fragen nach dem Muster:

> T: Does copper conduct current?
> S: Yes, it is a current-conducting element.

LE 3 ⊕ ⊕　Reagieren Sie nach dem Muster:

> T: At this institute they obtained new results.
> S: I've heard the results obtained are interesting.

LE 4 ⊕ ⊕　Reagieren Sie nach dem Muster:

> T: They obtained new values at this institute. I think they are interesting.
> S: The values obtained at this institute are really interesting.

PK 4 · PA 2 · SQ C

LE 1　Lesen Sie den Text und beantworten Sie folgende Fragen:

1. Wie wird das Photon charakterisiert? 2. Durch welche Experimente werden Welleneigenschaften festgestellt? 3. Wie wurde die Annahme de Broglies durch Schrödinger weiterentwickelt?

Waves and Particles

The work of Planck, in 1900, and the work of Einstein, in 1905, suggested that light must, for some purposes, be assumed to consist of particles called light quanta or photons. The energy of a photon is given by $E = h\nu$ and its momentum by $p = h/\lambda$, where ν is the frequency and λ the wavelength of the light, and h is Planck's constant, which has the value 6.624×10^{-27} erg sec. On the other hand, diffraction phenomena, for example, can only be explained if we assume that light consists of waves so that neither the corpuscular nor the wave theory is entirely satisfactory (ausreichend). In fact, it must be accepted that light can behave either as particles or as waves. The nature of a given experiment will emphasize (hervorheben) one aspect or the other, and the relation between the two aspects are given by the equations

$$E = h\nu \quad \text{and} \quad p = h/\lambda$$

In 1924 de Broglie went further and suggested that any moving particle, with mass m and speed ν will, in some experiments, show wave-like properties; the wavelength is then given by the equation $p = h/\lambda$, with $p = mv$. This theoretical concept received experimental confirmation (Bestätigung) in 1927, when Davisson and Germer observed that a beam of electrons was diffracted by a crystal of nickel; similar results have since been obtained with beams of other kinds of particles including atoms and molecules. De Broglie's theory was the beginning of wave mechanics, but its further development was due to Schrödinger who showed, in 1926, how the theory could be used to account for the existence of stationary states (stationärer Zustand) of atoms.

Bereiten Sie die Übersetzung des Textes "*Diffraction of Electrons and Atoms*" (4.3.C. – 1.) vor!

PK 4 · PA 2 · SQ D

LE 1 ⊕ ⊕ Einführender Dialog

continuous: kontinuierlich, stetig / isolated: isoliert / straight: gerade / curve: Kurve

LE 2 ⊕ ⊕ ⊳☐ Hören Sie den BTV "*Lines of Force*" und machen Sie sich Notizen!

LE 3 ⊕ ⊕ ⊳☐ Hören Sie noch einmal den gesamten Text und ergänzen Sie Ihre Notizen!

LE 4   ⊕ ⊕   Beantworten Sie die Fragen in Dt.!

LE 5   Speak about the electric field on the basis of the following facts:

— Electrically charged bodies exert forces on each other.
— Each electrically charged body is surrounded by an electric field.
— A definite electrostatic force is found for each point in an electric field.
— There is only one line of force passing through any point in an electric field.
— Lines of Force start at the positive charge and end at the negative charge.

PK 4 · PA 3 · SQ A

LE 1   In der engl. Fachsprache können zwei Nomen zu einem Mehrwortterminus verschmelzen, dem vielfach im Dt. eines der folgenden drei zusammengesetzten Subst. entspricht:

wave length   — Wellenlänge
atom model   — Atommodell
charge exchange   — Ladungsaustausch

Das ist ein produktiver Typ der Wortbildung im Engl. Die beiden Nomen werden gelegentlich durch Bindestrich verbunden oder, seltener, in einem Wort zusammengeschrieben:

wave length — wave-length — wavelength

(Im angeführten Beispiel ist von den 3 möglichen Formen *wavelength* die gebräuchlichste.)
Dadurch wird die Vorstellung einer festgefügten Bedeutungseinheit noch verstärkt.

LE 2   Kombinieren Sie mögliche Zweiworttermini!

Bilden Sie auch Wortkombinationen in umgekehrter Reihenfolge:

atom	hydrogen	quantity	intensity
wave	charge	X-ray	concentration
energy	electron	model	element
metal	vector	factor	isotope
field	unit	length	exchange
mass	separation	wire	number
ion		potential	

6*

LE 3 Das engl. Verb *to show* verfügt über mehrere Bedeutungsvarianten. Sie können z. T. durch andere Verben ersetzt werden, die ebenfalls für das wissenschaftliche Engl. charakteristisch sind:

1. Eine Bedeutungsvariante von *to show* beinhaltet, daß eine Größe N^1 die Eigenschaft N^2 hat:

N^1 *shows* $N^2 \rightarrow N^1$ *has* $N^2 \rightarrow N^2$ *of* N^1

In dieser Bedeutungsvariante kann für *show* das Verb *to exhibit* verwendet werden:

Particles show / have / exhibit wave-like properties.

2. Bezeichnet N^2 eine mehrgliedrige Größe (z. B. durch den Plural), so finden wir statt *show* auch das Verb *to display*:

Neptunium and plutonium display valencies of 3, 4, 5 and 6.

Die dt. Entsprechungen von show, exhibit und display sind: zeigen, aufweisen, zum Ausdruck kommen u. a.

3. Eine dritte Variante von *show* bezeichnet einen Vorgang, durch den N^1 eine Beziehung zwischen N^2 und N^3 aufdeckt. Hier kann *show* nicht auf *have* zurückgeführt werden:

N^1 *shows that* N^2 *has* N^3 / N^1 *shows* N^3 *of* N^2

In dieser Variante kann *reveal* für *show* verwendet werden. Als N^1 finden wir *method, experiment, study* u. a.:

The investigation showed / revealed that atoms may have ...

Die dt. Entsprechungen von *show* und *reveal* sind hier: zeigen, aufdecken, sichtbar machen u. a.

LE 4 ▼—0 Ersetzen Sie *to show* durch andere Verben:

1. The rare earth elements show similar properties dependent on their extranuclear structure. 2. The earliest determination of the charge of an electron made by Kaufmann in 1900 showed that the mass of an electron varies with its velocity. 3. It is assumed that even heavier atoms and molecules show the diffraction effects characteristic of wave motion. 4. The usual methods do not show the existence of more than one substance. 5. The photographic pictures of positive rays obtained by Thomson from neon-gas showed two lines indicating different atomic weights. 6. Experiments showed that atoms having small numbers of electrons (under four) in their outer orbit can only lose electrons.

PK 4 · PA 3 · SQ B

LE 1 Bisher haben wir uns mit attributiven Strukturen beschäftigt, die an die Stelle notwendiger Relativsätze treten können, das Präsenspartizip "V-*ing*":

the nucleus containing particles

das Perfektpartizip "V-*ed*":

the particles contained in the nucleus.

Im folgenden wollen wir uns mit Relativsätzen beschäftigen, die nicht durch andere attributive Strukturen ersetzt werden können. Generell gilt dies für alle Relativsätze, die durch eine Präp. mit Orts- oder Richtungsbedeutung eingeleitet werden.

LE 2 Übersetzen Sie:

1. Enriched materials are substances in which the proportion of a certain isotope has been artificially raised above its natural abundance. 2. Absolute zero is the temperature at which all molecular motion comes to an end. 3. The anode is the positively charged electrode toward which the main electron stream is flowing.

LE 3 Wir benötigen Relativsätze zum Ausdruck attributiv zugeordneter Besitz- oder Zugehörigkeitsverhältnisse.

1. Ist das Bezugswort im Hauptsatz "belebt", so wird der Relativsatz stets mit "*whose* + N" eingeleitet:

Einstein was one of the leading physicists of our time.
His name is known to many people. →
Einstein, whose name is known to many people, was one of the leading physicists of our time.
Einstein, dessen Namen viele Menschen kennen, war einer der führenden Physiker unserer Zeit.

2. Ist das Bezugswort im Hauptsatz "unbelebt", so wird der Relativsatz durch "N + *of* + *which*", daneben auch durch "*whose* + N" eingeleitet:

Hydrogen is the most abundant element.
Its atoms consist of one proton and one electron. →
Hydrogen the atoms of which / whose atoms consist of one proton and one electron, is the most abundant element.
Wasserstoff, dessen Atome aus einem Proton und einem Elektron bestehen, ist das häufigste Element.

LE 4 Übersetzen Sie:

1. Chlorine, the atoms of which have a mass of 35.46 units, is a mixture of atoms of mass 35 and atoms of mass 37 units. 2. Niels Bohr, whose atomic theory combined Rutherford's model of the nuclear atom and Planck's quantum theory, was awarded the Nobel Prize in 1922. 3. Nickel, a metallic element in Group VIII of the periodic table, the atomic weight of which is 58.69, was discovered by Cronstedt in 1751. 4. Thomson's discovery of the electron in 1897 may be said to be the starting point of the branch of science known as atomic physics, the study of which has transformed our ideas about the nature of matter. 5. Anti-electron was the name suggested by Dirac for a "positively charged electron", the existence of which he assumed and which was later discovered by Anderson in 1932 and is now called positron.

LE 5 π—0 Verbinden Sie die Sätze in Abhängigkeit von der "Belebtheit" oder "Unbelebtheit" des Bezugswortes nach einem der beiden Muster:

a) Aston devised the first mass spectrograph. – His isotopic studies are well-known. →
Aston, whose isotopic studies are well-known, devised the first mass spectrograph.

b) With molecules, atoms, protons and electrons there is associated some wave motion. – Its wavelength is determined by the de Broglie equation. →
With molecules, atoms, protons and electrons there is associated some wave motion, the wavelength of which is determined by the de Broglie equation.

1. The separation of isotopes is a very difficult problem. – Their chemical properties are practically identical. 2. Electrons are the smallest quantities of electricity. – Their mass was determined by Thomson. 3. X-rays were discovered by Röntgen. – Their properties could at first not be explained. 4. In a lesson the name of Goldstein was mentioned. – His book on classical mechanics is well-known. 5. Most elements occur in nature as mixtures of two or more isotopes. – Their proportion in any given quantity of the natural element is called natural abundance.

LE 6 Wir benötigen Relativsätze auch zum Ausdruck des Teilungsverhältnisses.

1. Ist das Bezugswort im Hauptsatz "belebt", so wird der Relativsatz mit "(Pro)N + of + whom" eingeleitet:

A number of nuclear physicists left Germany in 1933. – Many of them had worked in Göttingen. →
A number of nuclear physicists, many of whom had worked in Göttingen, left Germany in 1933.
Eine Reihe von Kernphysikern, von denen viele in Göttingen gearbeitet hatten, verließen Deutschland im Jahre 1933.

2. Ist das Bezugswort im Hauptsatz "unbelebt", so wird der Relativsatz mit
"(Pro)N + *of* + *which*" eingeleitet:

Scientists have artificially obtained a number of elements. – All of them
are radioactive. →
Scientists have artificially obtained a number of elements, all of which are
radioactive.
Wissenschaftler haben eine Reihe von Elementen künstlich hergestellt, die
alle radioaktiv sind.

LE 7   Übersetzen Sie:

1. In oxygen, nitrogen and hydrogen, each of which is an element, the molecules
consist of two atoms that are closely bound together. 2. In metals the current is
caused by the motion of electrons, a certain proportion of which is free to move
through their atoms. 3. There are 49 known naturally occurring radioactive
isotopes, almost all of which have an atomic number above 80. 4. The atomic nuclei
consist of protons and neutrons, both of which have been found to exhibit the
wave property of diffraction. 5. In the course of his study of radioelements, the
first part of which was published in 1912, Fleck found that radium B, radium D,
thorium B and actinium B were chemically identical with lead (Pb).

LE 8   🔲 Verbinden Sie die Sätze in Abhängigkeit von der "Belebtheit" oder
"Unbelebtheit" des Bezugswortes nach einem der beiden Muster:

a) The physics department of this university gives instruction to an in
creasing number of students. – Most of them will later work in industry. →
The physics department of this university gives instruction to an increasing
number of students, most of whom will later work in industry.

b) Common salt is sodium chloride (NaCl). – Each molecule of it is made
up of one atom of sodium and one atom of chloride. →
Common salt is sodium chloride (NaCl), each molecule of which is made
up of one atom of sodium and one atom of chlorine.

1. Hydrogen has three isotopes. – Two of these are stable. 2. These students study
physics. – Some of them I know from school. 3. It is often difficult to study the
behaviour of radioactive elements. – Some of them occur in nature in small
quantities only. 4. Elements can be distinguished in various ways. – The simplest
way is the division into metals and nonmetals. 5. There are almost fifty naturally
occurring radioactive isotopes. – Only five of them have an atomic number less
than 80.

PK 4 · PA 3 · SQ C

LE 1 Übersetzen Sie:

The Diffraction of Electrons and Atoms

The first proof that electrons can be diffracted and consequently exhibit wave as well as particle properties was obtained by J. C. Davisson and H. L. Germer in 1927. When Davisson and Germer studied the reflection and scattering, by a nickel crystal, of a beam of electrons that had been given a definite velocity they found that the electrons behaved like waves rather than like particles. When electrons were used which had been accelerated by a potential of 54 volts, the experimental results were found to be equivalent to those expected from radiation of wave length 1.65 Å. This was in good agreement with the value of 1.67 Å calculated by means of the de Broglie equation $\lambda = \dfrac{h}{mv}$.

Further evidence for the existence of electron waves was obtained independently in 1927 by the British physicist G. P. Thomson, son of J. J. Thomson. He passed a stream of fast moving electrons through a very thin sheet of metal. The resulting beam was then allowed to fall on a photographic plate. Upon development the plate showed a diffraction pattern indicating that the electrons were exhibiting wave properties. It is of special interest to mention that the diffraction pattern could be distorted by means of a magnet. This showed that the diffraction pattern was actually produced by electrons and not by radiations from outside such as X-rays, which might have been present. The electron microscope which is used for the examination of particles much too small to be visible in the best optical instruments depends on the behaviour of electrons as waves, although diffraction is not involved. Diffraction effects have been observed with streams of hydrogen and helium atoms, and even with neutrons. Actually ions, i.e. protons and alpha particles, were used since they could be accelerated by means of an electric field. It is thus apparent that these particles also have wave properties.

LE 2 ⊼—0 Übersetzen Sie ins Engl.:

1. Das Element Blei hat neun Isotope, von denen fünf radioaktiv sind. 2. Protonen sind Elementarteilchen, die alle eine positive Ladung tragen. 3. Die experimentell ermittelten Werte stimmen gut mit den theoretischen Ergebnissen überein, die mit Hilfe der de Broglie-Gleichung berechnet wurden. 4. Der im Experiment beobachtete Beugungseffekt tritt nur unter bestimmten Bedingungen auf. 5. Einstein begründete die Photonentheorie, die im gewissen Sinne eine Wiederbelebung der Newtonschen Auffassung vom Licht darstellt.

LE 3 🔑—0 Erläutern Sie in Engl. auf der Basis dieses Textes die heutige Grundvorstellung von der Natur des Lichtes:

Das Licht ist eine elektromagnetische Strahlung bestimmter Wellenlängen, von denen nur ein Teil für das menschliche Auge sichtbar ist. Das Licht hat alle Merkmale und Eigenschaften, die auch alle anderen elektromagnetischen Wellen aufweisen. Die von Huygens und Fresnel begründete Theorie erklärt das Licht als einen Wellenvorgang. Maxwell, der die elektromagnetische Natur des Lichtes erkannte, schuf die elektromagnetische Wellentheorie des Lichtes. Die von Planck und Einstein begründete Auffassung, daß Licht aus kleinsten Teilchen — sogenannten Photonen oder Lichtquanten — besteht, ist in gewissem Sinne eine Wiederbelebung der Teilchentheorie, die von Newton schon 1704 aufgestellt wurde. Die moderne Theorie verbindet jedoch die typischen Welleneigenschaften mit der Emission und Absorption von Licht, die beide auf die Quantennatur des Lichtes hinweisen.

PK 4 · PA 4 · SQ A

LE 0 Wortschatz zur Wiederholung

air: Luft / ever: stets, immer / hard: schwer, mühevoll / hardly (ever): kaum (jemals) / introduction: Einführung / to join: verbinden; (sich) anschließen / local: örtlich / picture: Bild / proper: eigentlich / seat: Sitz, Platz, Stelle / towards: zu(m) ... hin

LE 1 ⊕ ⊕ Neue Lexik

lattice	[ˈlætis]	Gitter
to approximate	[əˈprɔksimeit]	sich nähern, nahekommen; nähern
regular	[ˈregjulə]	regelmäßig, gleichmäßig
array	[əˈrei]	Ordnung, Anordnung, Reihe
site	[sait]	Stelle, Ort, Lage, Platz (z. B. im Gitter)
specimen	[ˈspesimin]	Muster, Probe
ground state	[ˈgraund ˌsteit]	Grundzustand
idealized	[aiˈdiəlaizd]	idealisiert
real	[ˈriəl]	real, tatsächlich, wirklich
vacant	[ˈveikənt]	leer, unbesetzt, frei; Leer-
to fail + Inf.	[feil]	Ausdruck der Verneinung
to penetrate	[ˈpenitreit]	durchdringen, eindringen in
to oscillate	[ˈɔsileit]	oszillieren, schwingen
ideal	[aiˈdi(:)əl]	ideal, uneigentlich

sense	[sens]	Sinn, Bedeutung; Hinsicht
to discuss	[dis'kʌs]	diskutieren, besprechen, erörtern
actual	['æktjuəl]	wirklich, real; eigentlich
cell	[sel]	Zelle
coincidence	[kou'insidəns]	Übereinstimmung, Koinzidenz
simple	[simpl]	einfach, nicht zusammengesetzt
to belong to	[bi'lɔŋ]	gehören zu
set	[set]	(Zahlen)Reihe, System, (Zahlen)-Menge
range	[reindʒ]	Raum, Bereich, Gebiet
size	[saiz]	Größe, Format, Ausdehnung
shape	[ʃeip]	Gestalt, Form

LE 2 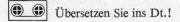 Internationalismen

geometric(al)	[ˌdʒiə'metrik(l)]	geometrisch
dimensional	[dai'menʃənl]	dimensional
analytical	[ˌænə'litikəl]	analytisch
translation	[træns'leiʃən]	Translation
dislocation	[ˌdislə'keiʃən]	Dislokation, Versetzung

LE 3   Wir üben Mehrworttermini vom Typ "wave-length". Sie hören zwei engl. Wörter. Nennen Sie deren dt. Bedeutung! Dann hören Sie ein zusammengesetztes dt. Substantiv. Nennen Sie die engl. Entsprechung:
T: *wave* S: Welle T: *length* S: Länge T: Wellenlänge S: *wave-length*

LE 4 Die Bedeutung von *some* hängt vom folgenden Subst. ab.

some particles (Pl.):   einige Teilchen
some particle (Sg.):   (irgend)ein Teilchen
some pressure (nur Sg.): etwas Druck, ein gewisser Druck

Beachten Sie den Unterschied!

 Übersetzen Sie ins Dt.!

PK 4 · PA 4 · SQ B

LE 1 ⊕ ⊕ Übersetzen Sie ins Engl. nach den Mustern:

T: der Kern, dessen Struktur (1)
S: the nucleus, the structure of which /
    the nucleus, whose structure

T: der Lehrer, dessen Buch (2)
S: the teacher, whose book

T: die radioaktiven Elemente, von denen viele (3)
S: the radioactive elements, many of which

T: die Physiker, von denen einige (4)
S: the physicists, some of whom

LE 2 ⊕ ⊕ Reagieren Sie nach dem Muster:

T: This is not true for particles with a negative charge.
S: But I didn't refer to particles whose charge is negative.

LE 3 ⊕ ⊕ Beantworten Sie die Fragen nach dem Muster:

T: Which elements did he refer to?   atomic mass, higher than 82
S: I think he referred to elements, the atomic mass of which is higher than
    82.

wavelength, very short / optical properties, today of special interest / method,
used for isotope separation / behaviour, dependent on temperature / structure,
still unknown

LE 4 ⊕ ⊕ Verbinden Sie die beiden Sätze nach einem der beiden Muster:

T: Oxygen has three stable isotopes. (1)

    Each of them has eight protons.

S: Oxygen has three stable isotopes, each of which has eight protons.

T: In our group there are fifteen students. (2)

    Two of them are from Africa.

S: In our group there are fifteen students, two of whom are from Africa.

PK 4 · PA 4 · SQ C

LE 1   Lesen Sie den Text und beantworten Sie folgende Fragen:

1. Was besagt die Gleichung $E = h\nu$?
2. Welche Tatbestände führten zur quantenmechanischen Beschreibung des elektromagnetischen Feldes?
3. Welche Schlußfolgerungen ergeben sich aus den Erkenntnissen der Quantenmechanik für physikalische Beobachtungen und Messungen?

Aspects of Quantum Mechanics

According to the fundamental equation of quantum mechanics — $E = h\nu$ — the energy of radiation stays concentrated in limited regions of space in amounts of $h\nu$ and, therefore, behaves like the energy of particles. On the other hand, this equation establishes a definite relationship between the frequency ν and the energy E of an electromagnetic wave. This dual behaviour of light corresponds, in one way, to experimental situations of the interference properties of radiation, for the description (Beschreibung) of which one uses the wave theory of light; in another way, it corresponds to the properties of exchange of energy and momentum between radiation and matter, which require (erfordern) for their definition the quantum description or quantization of the electromagnetic field. A new theory was formulated quantitatively by de Broglie, according to which all forms of energy and momentum will exhibit a dual behaviour, i.e. a wave or a particle property, depending on the type of experiment used.

Quantum theory has laid the foundations (Grundlage) of new physical concepts for the process of measurements in physics and the definition of physical reality. A dynamical theory is required for the description of the wave character of material particles. Furthermore, it was recognized in quantum mechanics that large changes in the state of a system being observed must be taking place in the act of observation. Thus, the complete determinism of classical theory is replaced by an indeterministic description, the extent of which is determined by the size of the universal constant h, Planck's constant.

Bereiten Sie die Übersetzung des Textes *"The Crystal Lattice"* (5.1.C. − 1.) vor!

PK 4 · PA 4 · SQ D

LE 1   ⊕ ⊕   Einführender Dialog

quantum, -a: Quant(en) / interaction: Wechselwirkung / to scatter: streuen / recoil: Rückstoß

LE 2   ⊕ ⊕ ▷   Hören Sie den BTV *"The Photon and the Compton Effect"* und machen Sie sich Notizen!

LE 3   ⊕ ⊕ ▷   Hören Sie noch einmal den ganzen Text und ergänzen Sie Ihre Notizen!

LE 4   ⊕ ⊕   Beantworten Sie die Fragen in Dt.!

LE 5   Speak about some basic properties of light:

- Light consists of electromagnetic waves.
- The properties of light depend on the frequency / wavelength.
- Light of a definite frequency exhibits a definite colour.
- White light is a mixture of all wavelengths of the visible light.
- Light displays wave properties (e.g. diffraction) as well as particle properties (e.g. absorption and emission).

Solids and Semiconductors

LE 1 In der Fachsprache wird häufig die Wortgruppe *to be due to* verwendet. Sie entspricht weitgehend als Synonym den Wortgruppen *to be caused by, to be the result of.*

Zweckmäßige Übersetzungen sind:

a) zurückzuführen sein auf   c) die Folge sein von
b) verursacht werden durch   d) zurückgehen auf

> Electrical conduction in metals is due to free electrons in them.

due to wird auch als nachgestelltes attributives Adjektiv gebraucht:

> The electrical field due to a charge has the property that all charges placed in it experience a force.

LE 2 In Fachtexten kann die Wortgruppe *due to* auch selbständig auftreten. Die Wortgruppe *due to* entspricht dann etwa den präpositionalen Wortgruppen *owing to, because of,* in der Übersetzung: 'auf Grund (von)', 'infolge', 'durch'.

> Isotopes of the same element are often considered to represent distinct elements for the physicist owing to / due to their physical properties.

✒—0 Finden Sie in den folgenden Sätzen ein geeignetes dt. Äquivalent für *due to*:

1. Mechanical energy is either kinetic energy, i.e. energy due to motion, or potential energy, i.e. energy due to position. 2. Alpha particles and the deuteron are compound particles which are often considered to be elementary particles due to the important role they play in nuclear reactions. 3. Electric currents are due to the movement of electrons in electric conductors. 4. Ionization may be due to the absorption of light or X-ray photons or due to a collision with an electron. 5. The Compton effect is the decrease in frequency and increase in wavelength of X-rays and gamma rays due to scattering by free electrons.

LE 3 Den Bedeutungsvarianten des dt. Adj. 'leicht' entsprechen unterschiedliche engl. Adj.:

a) *easy* (Adv. *easily*):   leicht, mühelos, ohne Schwierigkeit

> The third electron of the lithium atom may be easily detached.

Das Gegenteil von *easy* ist *difficult* (Adv. *with difficulty*).

b) *ready* (Adv. *readily*): leicht, schnell
> Valence electrons of metals are quite readily lifted into the conduction band.

Dieses Adj. bezeichnet ein im Wesen der Erscheinung begründetes Verhalten. Daher wird es in Fachtexten häufiger verwendet als *easy*, mit dessen Anwendung es z. T. übereinstimmt.

c) *slight* (Adv. *slightly*): leicht (geringfügig), etwas
> The reaction temperature was slightly increased in order to obtain this effect.

Das Gegenteil von *slight*(*ly*) ist *large*(*ly*). Beide bezeichnen einen Grad.

PK 5 · PA 1 · SQ B

LE 1 Wir wiederholen die "Kontaktkonstruktion".

1. Bisher kennen wir folgende Entsprechungen engl. Relativsätze, die notwendige Bestimmungen des Bezugswortes enthalten: Aktiven Relativsätzen entspricht eine Struktur mit den Präsenspartizip "V-*ing*":
> The space which surrounds a charge contains an electric field.
> The space surrounding   a charge contains an electric field.

Passiven Relativsätzen entspricht eine Struktur mit dem Perfektpartizip "V-*ed*":
> Oersted discovered the magnetic effect that is produced by an electric current.
> Oersted discovered the magnetic effect produced by an electric current.

2. Ist das Relativpronomen nicht Subj., sondern direktes bzw. präpositionales Obj., so gibt es eine dritte Möglichkeit der Relativsatzverkürzung:

Bei notwendigen Relativsätzen der Struktur *that / which / whom* + N + V (+ Prep) kann das Relativpronomen entfallen:
> a) The number of isotopes   increases.
>   (which) we know
>   b) I could not find the book
>   (which) I was looking for.

Dadurch entstehen Satzgefüge der folgenden Strukturen:

a) N + N + V + V

b) N + V + N + N + V

Verkürzte Relativsätze dieser Art werden meist als "Kontaktkonstruktion" bezeichnet.

LE 2   Übersetzen Sie ins Dt.:

1. The forces two particles exert on each other are equal and opposite and lie along the line joining them. 2. The mineral aluminium is obtained from is called "bauxite". 3. Priestley did not know that the gas he had obtained (which was later called oxygen) was contained in air. 4. The elements a substance consists of, and the proportions in which they are combined, must be determined before the structure of the substance can be represented by a formula. 5. Wave motion can be said to be the most common and most important type of motion we know.

LE 3   Die drei Verkürzungsmöglichkeiten notwendiger Relativsätze

Präsenspartizipien   "V-*ing* + ..."
Perfektpartizipien   "V-*ed* + ..."
Kontaktkonstruktionen "N + V + ..."

schließen sich in ihren Anwendungsbedingungen aus.

⊞─0 Prüfen Sie, in welcher Weise in den folgenden Satzgefügen die Relativsätze verkürzt werden können:

1. The existence of electric charges can only be detected by the forces which they exert. 2. The electric field intensity at a point is defined as the force which acts on a unit positive charge at that point. 3. A germanium crystal has an atomic structure which contains four valency electrons. 4. In wave mechanics, the frequency is identical with energy which is divided by Planck's constant, while wave number is momentum which is divided by Planck's constant. 5. The heaviest stable element which we know is lead (Pb). 6. Electromagnetism and optics can be explained by the wave theory which is based on Maxwell's equation.

LE 4   Das Demonstrativpronomen *that / those* mit nachfolgendem Attributivkomplex dient zur Gliederung eines Satzes, der einen Vergleich, eine Gegenüberstellung oder einen Gegensatz enthält. Auf *that / those* folgt:

1. ein Präsenspartizip, "*that / those* + V-*ing* + ..."
    The elements found in nature differ in their structure from those occurring only in compounds.

2. ein Perfektpartizip, "*that / those* + V-*ed* + ..."
    The diffraction patterns of neutrons are similar to those produced by X-rays.

3. ein Relativsatz, "*that / those* + *which* + ..."
    Under ordinary conditions most elements, at least those which are gases, form diatomic molecules.

4. ein nominales Gefüge, "*that / those* + Prep + N"
    The nuclei with an odd number of nuclear particles differ in stability from those with an even number.

LE 5 Übersetzen Sie ins Dt.! Beachten Sie dabei folgende Übersetzungsvarianten:

1. 'der' / 'die' / 'das' usw.:

The effect is different from that observed in earlier experiments.

Der Effekt unterscheidet sich von dem bei früheren Versuchen beobachteten.

2. 'der-' / 'die-' / 'dasjenige' usw.:

The values are different from those of the corresponding subgroup.

Die Werte unterscheiden sich von denjenigen der entsprechenden Untergruppe.

3. Im dt. Satz wird das Bezugswort wiederholt:

The best conductors, metals, have an electrical conductivity greater than that of the best insulators by a factor of more than 10^{24}.

Die besten Leiter, nämlich die Metalle, haben eine Leitfähigkeit, die um einen Faktor von mehr als 10^{24} über der Leitfähigkeit der besten Isolatoren liegt.

4. Im dt. Satz gibt es kein Äquivalent für *that / those*:

The absorption of gamma-rays is studied in a manner similar to that used for beta particles.

Die Absorption von Gamma-Strahlen wird ähnlich untersucht wie die der Beta-Strahlen.

1. Direct measurement of the wavelengths of gamma-rays gave values corresponding to those for very short gamma-rays. 2. The energy involved in nuclear processes may be a million times as great as that obtained from the same quantity of material taking part in a chemical change. 3. Anderson described mesons as highly unstable particles, of a mass less than that of a proton but higher than that of an electron. 4. The masses of a proton and a neutron are nearly equal, and the mass of each is about 1840 times as great as that of an electron. 5. The earliest current-measuring instrument based on the magnetic effect of an electric current was that devised towards the end of 1820 by J.S.C. Schweiger. 6. Nuclei with an odd number of protons and an even number of neutrons, and vice versa, are equally common, while those containing odd numbers of both protons and neutrons are rare.

PK 5 · PA 1 · SQ C

LE 1 Übersetzen Sie:

The Crystal Lattice

Any discussion of the properties of a solid must begin with a definition of the geometrical structure to which the arrangement of atoms is supposed to approximate. This is the crystal lattice, a regular array of sites, or points in a three-dimensional space, where the atoms are supposed to lie when the whole specimen is in its ground state. This picture is rather idealized. In a real crystal, there are always vacant sites in the structure, dislocations etc., so that even in the most carefully prepared single crystal, the pattern cannot be expected to repeat itself quite regularly. The definition also fails to account for the fact that the surrounding electron clouds can be penetrated or distorted and that the atom or ion is oscillating about its position in the zero-point motion.

It is more correct to say that the ideal lattice represents the structure of the solid in the sense that the local conditions are 'hardly ever' different at any two points in the crystal which are separated by the distance between two lattice sites. Some solids, such as glass, do not exhibit any proper crystal structure and it is often necessary to discuss their properties in the rather difficult language which has been developed for the theory of liquids. The actual analytical definition of a lattice is as follows. The structure is thought to consist of equal, geometrically similar unit cells, which can be brought into coincidence by simple translations with vectors all belonging to the set $\vec{l} = l_1\vec{a}_1 + l_2\vec{a}_2 + l_3\vec{a}_3$, where $\vec{a}_1, \vec{a}_2, \vec{a}_3$ are vectors of the lattice and l_1, l_2, l_3 are three integral numbers whose values lie inside some range determined by the size and the shape of the crystal as a whole. To make a picture of the lattice we draw all the points in the three-dimensional array defined by the equation and surround each point by the unit cell, in which the actual atoms are supposed to lie.

LE 2 ⊓—0 Übersetzen Sie ins Dt. unter Verwendung von *that / those* + attr. Struktur bzw. *due to*:

1. Die im vorliegenden Versuch durchgeführten Tests führten zu ähnlichen Ergebnissen wie frühere Untersuchungen. 2. Die Kristallstruktur der meisten anorganischen (inorganic) Stoffe unterscheidet sich von der anderer Stoffe. 3. Für die Kristallanalyse wird ein Verfahren verwendet, das auf M. von Laue zurückgeht. 4. Das Gittersystem natürlicher Kristalle ist niemals so regelmäßig aufgebaut wie das eines idealen Kristalls.

LE 3 ⊓—0 Geben Sie die Information des folgenden Textes in einer zusammenhängenden engl. Darstellung wieder:

Es konnte gezeigt werden, daß kristalline Stoffe ein Gitter aus Atomen, Molekülen oder Ionen aufweisen. Die Struktur fast aller anorganischer Stoffe unterscheidet sich von der anderer Stoffe, weil die Atome der ersteren keine Moleküle bilden. Ein Kristall besteht aus einer dreidimensionalen periodischen Anordnung atomarer Bausteine. Der Kristallgittertyp des jeweiligen Stoffes ist bedingt durch die Größe der atomaren Bausteine und der zwischen ihnen wirkenden Kräfte. Die Struktur der in der Natur vorkommenden Kristalle unterscheidet sich jedoch von der des idealen Kristalls, da sich deren Strukturmuster, bedingt durch Fehlstellen, Dislokationen etc. nicht völlig regelmäßig wiederholt.
Ein direkter Beweis für den Aufbau der Kristalle konnte erst 1912 mit Hilfe einer

Methode erbracht werden, die auf Max von Laue zurückgeht. Dieser schlug vor, die Kristallgitter mit Hilfe von Röntgenstrahlen zu untersuchen. Die dadurch erhaltenen Beugungsbilder zeigten die Wellennatur der Röntgenstrahlen und die Gitterstruktur der kristallinen Stoffe. Die später für Elektronen und langsame Neutronen erhaltenen Beugungsbilder ähnelten denen, die durch Röntgenstrahlen verursacht werden.

PK 5 · PA 2 · SQ A

LE 0 Wortschatz zur Wiederholung
progressive: progressiv / family: Familie / member: Mitglied / corner: Ecke / hole: Loch / enough: genug, genügend

LE 1 ⊕ ⊕ Neue Lexik

semiconductor	[ˈsemikənˈdʌktə]	Halbleiter
silicon	[ˈsilikən]	Silizium
diamond	[ˈdaiəmənd]	Diamant
cubic	[ˈkjubik]	kubisch; Kubik-, Raum-
cube	[kju:b]	Kubus, Würfel, Hexaeder; Kubus Kubikzahl
with respect to	[wið‿riˈspekt‿tə]	in bezug auf, hinsichtlich
to arise from	[əˈraiz]	entstehen aus, die Folge sein von, sich ergeben aus
to exist	[igˈzist]	existieren, vorhanden/da sein, sich finden
bond	[bɔnd]	(chem.) Bindung
to result from	[riˈzʌlt]	sich ergeben aus, resultieren aus, zurückzuführen sein auf
to share	[ʃɛə]	gemeinsam haben, anteilig besitzen
sharing		Subst. vom Verb to share
carbon	[ˈka:bən]	Kohlenstoff
perfect	[ˈpə:fikt]	vollkommen, perfekt, ideal, fehlerfrei
tight	[tait]	fest(gefügt); eng, dicht
conductivity	[ˌkɔndʌkˈtiviti]	Leitfähigkeit (el., Wärme)
significance	[sigˈnifikəns]	Bedeutung, Wichtigkeit; Bedeutung, Sinn
imperfection	[ˌimpəˈfekʃən]	Störstelle, Fehlstelle; Störung
to introduce into	[ˌintrəˈdju:s]	einführen, hineinbringen in
disturbance	[disˈtə:bəns]	Störung; Wellen-

7*

to deliver	[diˈlivə]	(Energie etc.) liefern; abgeben
to eject	[i(:)ˈdʒekt]	ausstoßen, emittieren
localized	[ˈloukəlaizd]	lokalisiert; ortsgebunden
to require	[riˈkwaiə]	erfordern, verlangen; nötig, erforderlich sein
level	[levl]	Niveau, Höhe, Ebene, Stufe
conduction band	[kənˈdʌkʃən ˈbænd]	Leitungsband
impurity	[imˈpjuəriti]	Verunreinigung; Störstelle
to substitute for	[ˈsʌbstitjuːt]	ersetzen durch, austauschen gegen

LE 2 ⊕ ⊕ Internationalismen

germanium	[dʒəˈmeiniəm]	Germanium
crystalline	[ˈkristəlain]	kristallin(isch); Kristall-
covalent	[ˈkouˈveilənt]	kovalent, Kovalenz-
valency (valence)	[ˈveiləns(i)]	Wertigkeit, Valenz
gallium	[ˈgæliəm]	Gallium

LE 3 ⊕ ⊕ Wir üben die Wortgruppe *due to*

Beantworten Sie die Fragen nach dem Muster:
T: The motion of electrical charges in a conductor —
What is it due to? — electrical force —
S: It is due to an electrical force.

LE 4 ⊕ ⊕ Beantworten Sie die Fragen nach dem Muster:

T: Is it possible to account for these facts on the basis of that theory?
S: No, that theory fails to account for these facts.

PK 5 · PA 2 · SQ B

LE 1 ⊕ ⊕ Übersetzen Sie ins Dt. nach dem Muster:

T: The isotopes Soddy discovered ...
S: Die Isotope, die Soddy entdeckte ...

LE 2 ⊕ ⊕ Übersetzen Sie ins Engl. nach dem Muster:

T: Das Gas, durch das die Teilchen hindurchtreten ...
S: The gas the particles pass through ...

LE 3   ⊕ ⊕   Reagieren Sie nach dem Muster:

T: Our new professor has written an interesting book.
S: I don't know the book he's written.

LE 4   ⊕ ⊕   Beantworten Sie die Fragen nach dem Muster:

T: Is this the book? I think he spoke of it.
S: Yes, this is the book he spoke of.

LE 5   ⊕ ⊕   Beantworten Sie die Fragen nach dem Muster:

T: We determined new data. Do you think they are interesting?
S: Yes, the data we determined are interesting.

PK 5 · PA 2 · SQ C

LE 1   Lesen Sie den Text und beantworten Sie in Stichpunkten die Fragen zu den Absätzen:

Solid State Physics

    1. Was ist Festkörperphysik?

Solid-state physics is the study of the electronic (Elektronen-) and lattice properties of solids, particularly of crystalline solids. It deals with both theoretical and experimental aspects of solids. Theorists attempt to apply both classical and quantum mechanical principles to the basic understanding of the nature of solids; experimentalists apply a wide range of experimental techniques to the study of the properties of solids.

    2. Womit können die Atome eines Festkörpers verglichen werden?

The atoms of which a given solid is made up can be considered, for many purposes, to be hard balls which form regular patterns called the crystal structure. Crystal structures have a wide range of symmetries. Most elements have structures of symmetries.

    3. In welcher Weise kann der Deformierbarkeit der Atome Rechnung getragen werden?

The hard-ball model (Modell) of solids just referred to is too simple to explain many properties of solids. That solids can be deformed (deformieren) by external (äußere) forces and that atoms in a solid have vibrational energy is accounted for in the model by the introduction of springs (Feder) to connect the atoms to their nearest neighbours. This ball-and-spring model has been very successful; one important use was by Einstein who devised a quantum mechanical theory of specific heats.

4. Wie kommt es zu Störstellen und wie werden sie definiert?

The perfect crystal, one with all atoms on well-defined lattice points, is nonexistent. By the way in which crystals are produced, either in the laboratory or by nature, defects in structure exist. These defects may be defined by their geometry and size.

Defects which extend along one dimension only are called line defects, the most important of which are the dislocations. Defects which extend to only about an atomic diameter (Durchmesser) also exist in crystals. They are called point defects.

5. Worin liegt die Bedeutung von Störstellen?

Defects are highly important for many properties of solids, in spite of (trotz) the relatively small number which exist in most solids. Among such properties are the behaviour of solids under mechanical stress (Druck), and mass, heat and charge transport; and a large number of electrical properties which may be influenced by the presence of particular kinds of defects.

6. In welcher Weise wird die Elektronenstruktur von Festkörpern untersucht?

The electronic structure of solids is determined, in principle, only by the electronic structure of the free atoms of which the solid is made up. When the crystalline structure of solids is studied, two steps are useful. First, the perfect electronic structure is defined; then irregularities (Störungen) in the structure, called defects, are characterised.

Bereiten Sie die Übersetzung des Textes "*The Structure of Semiconductors*" (5.3.C. – 1.) vor! Vgl. dazu die Varianten von *net*:

a) 'Rest-'	net loss factor	Restdämpfungsfaktor
b) 'Gesamt-', 'total'	net gain	Gesamtverstärkung
	net current	totaler Strom (vgl. Netto-)
c) 'Nutz-'	net load	Nutzlast
d) 'Netto-'	net transport	Nettotransport
	net current	Nettostrom (vgl. total).
e) 'effektiv, resultierend'	net energy gain	effektiver Energiegewinn
	net force	resultierende Kraft

Engl. *net* kann auch dt. 'Netz' entsprechen.

PK 5 · PA 2 · SQ D

LE 1 ⊕ ⊕ Einführung

symmetry: Symmetrie / bonding: Bindung(en) / defect: Fehlstelle

LE 2 ⊕ ⊕ ⊳□ Hören Sie den BTV *"Crystals"* und machen Sie sich Notizen!

LE 3 ⊕ ⊕ ⊳□ Hören Sie noch einmal den ganzen Text und ergänzen Sie Ihre Notizen!

LE 4 ⊕ ⊕ Beantworten Sie die Fragen in Dt.!

LE 5 What do you know about crystals?

— Describe the basic structure of an ideal crystal.
— In which way do natural crystals differ from the ideal crystals?
— In which way do lattice defects influence the properties of crystals?

PK 5 · PA 3 · SQ A

LE 1 Das Verb *to involve* teilt mit, daß Personen, Gegenstände oder Prozesse an einem Gesamtvorgang oder an einem Stadium des Gesamtvorganges beteiligt oder dafür von Bedeutung sind. Auf Grund dieser Bedeutungsbreite ist eine bedeutungsgerechte Übersetzung nur in engem Zusammenhang mit dem Kontext möglich. Folgende Bedeutungsgruppen führen oft zu einer adäquaten Übersetzung.

a) gehören zu, umfassen
b) von Bedeutung sein, wichtig sein
c) verbunden sein mit, zusammenhängen mit, beteiligt sein an
d) zur Folge haben, mit sich bringen, ermöglicht werden durch, möglich sein durch

LE 2 ■—0 Überprüfen Sie in den folgenden Sätzen die Übersetzungsmöglichkeiten von *to involve* in Abhängigkeit vom Kontext.

1. The production of an electric current involves the movement of electrons in electric conductors. 2. The faraday is the quantity of electricity (96.500 coulomb) necessary for an electrochemical reaction involving one chemical equivalent. 3. In

order to exhibit some of the concepts involved in the discussion of nuclear potentials and the quantum states of nuclei it is convenient to consider the deuteron. 4. The formation of positive ions involves the loss of one or more electrons. 5. Free electrons are involved in a process in which there is a decrease in frequency and an increase in wavelength of X-rays and gamma-rays. 6. Industrial application of this technique involves considerable difficulty.

LE 3 In der gleichen Weise wie zwei Substantive zu einer Bedeutungseinheit verschmelzen können, gibt es auch Kombinationen von Adjektiv + Nomen (Substantiv), die als Z w e i w o r t t e r m i n u s aufzufassen sind. Besonders wichtig ist eine Gruppe von Adjektiven, die nur attributiv in Verbindung mit einem Nomen (Substantiv) auftreten. Diese Adjektive selbst sind von anderen Substantiven abgeleitet mit Hilfe von Suffixen und stellen so eine Beziehung zwischen den Bedeutungen der beiden Substantive her. Im Dt. wird diese Bedeutungskombination häufig durch ein zusammengesetztes Substantiv, aber auch durch die Verbindung Adj. + Subst., wiedergegeben:

atomic	= Atom-, atomar
atomic model	= Atommodell
atomic hydrogen	= atomarer Wasserstoff

Zur Bildung solcher Adj. werden u. a. die Suffixe *-al*, *-ic*, *-ar*, *-ary*, *-ous*, *-ive* benutzt.

experiment	− experimental:	Versuchs-, Experimental-
electron	− electronic:	Elektronen-
nucleus	− nuclear:	Kern-, Nuklear-
element	− elementary:	Element-, Elementar-
nitrogen	− nitrogenous:	Stickstoff-
progress	− progressive:	progressiv, Folge-

LE 4 Bilden Sie aus den aufgeführten Substantiven mit Hilfe der Suffixe *-al*, *-ic*, *-ar*, *-ic*(*al*) das Bestimmungsadjektiv! Geben Sie ein Beispiel für eine Kombination Adj + N:

1. molecule   5. isotope   8. economy
2. structure   6. nature   9. microscope
3. theory   7. period   10. nation
4. industry

PK 5 · PA 3 · SQ B

LE 1 Wir wiederholen die attributiven Strukturen.
Als Ausgangspunkt bei der Behandlung der attributiven Strukturen dient uns stets der Relativsatz. In Abhängigkeit von diesem unterscheiden wir die folgenden Fälle:

1. Der aktive Relativsatz kann in ein erweitertes Präsenspartizip umgewandelt werden:

> The electron pairs which form the so-called covalent bonds ...
> The electron pairs forming the so-called covalent bonds ...

2. Der passive Relativsatz kann in ein erweitertes Perfektpartizip umgewandelt werden:

> The set of higher energy levels which is called the conduction band ...
> The set of higher energy levels called the conduction band ...

3. Der Relativsatz mit einem prädikativen Adj. kann in ein erweitertes Adj. umgewandelt werden:

> The free electrons which are present in metals ...
> The free electrons present in metals ...

4. Auch nichterweiterte Perfektpartizipien und Adjektive können an Stelle eines Relativsatzes nachgestellt werden:

> This depends on the work which is done.
> This depends on the work done.

5. Ist das Relativpronomen nicht Subj., sondern (Präpositional) Obj., so kann der Relativsatz nur durch Fortfall des Relativpronomens zu einer sogenannten Kontaktkonstruktion verkürzt werden:

> The elementary particles of which atoms consist ...
> The elementary particles the atoms consist of ...

Beachten Sie: Den unter 1. und 4. genannten Strukturen können im Dt. auch vorangestellte erweiterte Attribute entsprechen:

> die zwischen den Atomen wirkenden Kräfte ...
> the forces acting between the atoms ...
> die in die Struktur eingeführten Fremdatome ...
> the impurity atoms introduced into the structure ...

LE 2   Einige Relativsätze können nicht durch andere attributive Strukturen ersetzt werden. Es sind dies:

1. Relativsätze, die mit einer nicht fest mit dem Verb verbundenen Präposition beginnen:

> The extent to which separation is achieved ...
> (vgl. dagegen *consist of* unter LE 1.5.)

2. Verneinte Relativsätze:

> These electrons which do not enter the process of conduction ...

3. Relativsätze mit einem Modalverb:

> The imperfections which can be introduced into the crystal ...

4. Relativsätze, die ein Besitz- oder ein Teilungsverhältnis beinhalten:

Semiconductors $\begin{Bmatrix} \text{the conductivity of which} \\ \text{whose conductivity} \end{Bmatrix}$ depends on ...

Germanium and gallium both of which have four valence electrons ...

LE 3 ◼━O Wandeln Sie in den folgenden Beispielen diejenigen Relativsätze, die eine solche Umwandlung zulassen, in eine der unter LE 1. 1. bis 5. aufgeführten attributiven Strukturen um:

1. Current in metals and semiconductors is carried by electrons which move through a periodic lattice. 2. The potential difference between two points A and B in an electrostatic field is the mechanical work which is done to move a positive unit charge from B to A. 3. The separation of isotopes may be achieved by the use of any physical process in which the behaviour of the atoms depends on their mass. 4. The energy which is required to produce ionisation can be provided when another particle collides with the atom or molecule. 5. The amount of energy which is lost in the production of an ion pair varies from one material to another but it generally is a few tens of electron volts per ion pair. 6. The particles of the canal rays are positive ions of the substances of which the gas consists. 7. It was found that the elements could be arranged into families, whose members have similar chemical properties.

LE 4 ◼━O Verbinden Sie die folgenden Satzpaare mit Hilfe einer geeigneten attributiven Struktur:

1. Many scientific developments have occurred since 1900. − A number of them are due to the application of electric principles. 2. Ionization is the process in which an atom or molecule separates into two parts. − These parts have opposite electrical charges. 3. Several methods have been devised for the determination of nuclear spins. − They involve the behaviour of nuclei in magnetic fields. 4. Any elementary particle is a particle that up to the present time has not been shown to be made up of two or more simpler particles. − These simpler particles are held together by some type of force.

LE 5 ◼━O Bilden Sie aus den vorgegebenen Elementen Sätze nach folgenden Mustern:

a) The molecular weight of heavy water / the molecular weight of ordinary water
− to be different from −
The molecular weight of heavy water is different from that of ordinary water.

b) The properties of heavy water / the properties of ordinary water
− to be different from −
The properties of heavy water are different from those of ordinary water.

1. Calculations in the Bohr-Sommerfeld theory / calculations on the basis of wave mechanics — to be simpler than. 2. The energy involved in nuclear processes / the energy involved in chemical processes — to be larger than. 3. The diffraction pattern of electrons / the diffraction pattern obtained for X-rays — to be similar to. 4. The crystalline structure of germanium / the crystalline structure found for gallium — to be the same as. 5. The properties of glass / the properties of proper solids — to have to be distinguished from.

PK 5 · PA 3 · SQ C

LE 1   Übersetzen Sie:

The Structure of Semiconductors

Germanium and silicon, which are the most common semiconductors, have the well-known crystalline structure of diamond. In this cubic structure, each atom is surrounded by four other atoms. These four atoms are placed in the corners of the cube. An interesting geometrical property is associated with this arrangement: it is the only way in which four balls can be placed around a fifth so that all four balls are in completely equivalent positions with respect to each other. This structure arises from the nature of the chemical forces that exist between atoms. The atoms in most substances are held together largely by electron-pair bonds resulting from the sharing of electrons between atoms. These electron pairs form the so-called covalent bonds.

A carbon atom, a silicon atom, and a germanium atom all have four valence electrons and form sets of four bonds with their neighbours. In a perfect crystal, each covalent bond contains two electrons. Consequently, every electron is tightly bound and thus unable to enter into the process of electric conduction. However, conductivity can be produced in crystals of this type in a number of ways, all of which destroy the perfect covalent bond structure.

Various types of imperfections can be introduced in a semiconductor. For example, an electronic disturbance can be produced in germanium when a photon delivers its energy to an electron, which is ejected from one of the bonds. This ejected electron is a localized negative charge in the crystal, while the electron-pair bond structure was electrically neutral. Such an electron represents an excess over and above the number of electrons required. It can move around much like an electron in a metal, since it has been brought into a set of higher energy levels, which in semiconductors are called the "conduction band". A similar conduction process takes place in the crystal through the motion of the hole left in the bond when the electron was ejected. This hole is a net, localized, positive charge in the crystal. The conduction electrons and holes represent two types of imperfections, which can be introduced into the crystal by light. It is also possible to substitute an arsenic

5.3.

(As) atom, for example, for a germanium atom. The arsenic atom uses four of its five valence electrons to make four covalent bonds. Its fifth electron is free to wander about, which gives the crystal a conductivity by negative carriers. Similarly, if an impurity with three valence electrons (like gallium) is substituted for a germanium atom in the crystal structure, it does not have enough electrons to form the four covalent bonds. Consequently, a hole is formed which is free to move about the crystal; in this way, the crystal is given a conductivity by positive carriers.

LE 2   ⊶—0   Übersetzen Sie ins Engl. mit Hilfe von *due to, that / those* + Attr. und *"can be* + V-*ed"* = dt. 'sich lassen + V' (vgl. 1.4.B. – 1., 2., 3.):

1. Die Leitfähigkeit der Halbleiter beruht entweder auf Leitungselektronen oder auf Löchern. 2. Die Leitung in Metallen unterscheidet sich von der in Gasen. 3. Die Bewegung der freien Elektronen in Metallen ist der Bewegung von Teilchen in Gasen ähnlich. 4. Nach ihrem elektrischen Verhalten lassen sich Stoffe generell in zwei Gruppen unterteilen: die Leiter und die Nichtleiter. 5. Die Leitfähigkeit von Halbleitern läßt sich mit Hilfe des Bändermodells (band model) erklären.

LE 3   Geben Sie die Informationen des folgenden Textes in einer zusammenhängenden engl. Darstellung wieder:

Ein elektrischer Strom ist eine gerichtete Bewegung von Ladungsträger, deren Bewegung durch ein elektrisches Feld hervorgerufen wird. Dieses entsteht zwischen zwei Elektroden, an die eine Spannung angelegt wird, und übt eine Kraft auf alle Ladungsträger aus. Solche Ladungsträger sind die Elektronen und Ionen. Daher unterscheiden sich Stoffe, die keine freien Elektronen oder Ionen aufweisen, in ihrem Verhalten von den Stoffen, die solche Ladungsträger enthalten. So lassen sich die elektrischen Eigenschaften der Metalle aus dem kristallinen Aufbau und aus der metallischen Bindung erklären. Die metallische Bindung beruht auf der Tatsache, daß sich Valenzelektronen zwischen den positiven Ionen frei bewegen können. Diese freien Elektronen bilden das Elektronengas. Das Elektronengas ist ein Modell, mit dessen Hilfe sich physikalische Vorgänge leichter erklären lassen. Das Verhalten des Elektronengases unterscheidet sich von dem Verhalten anderer Gase durch die Tatsache, daß die Elektronen das Metall nur unter bestimmten Bedingungen verlassen können. Die gute elektrische Leitfähigkeit der Metalle ist bedingt durch die große Zahl freier Elektronen, die in metallischen Leitern vorhanden sind. Auch andere Eigenschaften der Metalle lassen sich mit Hilfe des Elektronenmodells erklären.

PK 5 · PA 4 · SQ A

LE 0   Wortschatz zur Wiederholung

reason: Grund / to fill: füllen / silver: Silber / to reach: reichen / arrangement: Anordnung / contact: Kontakt / to estimate: einschätzen / excellent: ausgezeichnet / instead of: anstelle, anstatt / to try: versuchen / to mix: mischen / crowd: (Menschen)Menge / to pick up: aufnehmen / to realize: sich vorstellen / below: unter(halb) / incomplete: unvollständig

LE 1   ⊕   ⊕   Neue Lexik

to retain	[riˈtein]	behalten, beibehalten, erhalten, halten
random	[ˈrændəm]	zufällig, Zufalls-; ungeordnet; regellos, wahllos
to favour	[ˈfeivə]	bevorzugen, begünstigen, erleichtern
attraction	[əˈtrækʃən]	Anziehung
tendency	[ˈtendənsi]	Tendenz, Neigung, Richtung
to close	[klouz]	(ab-, ein-, zu)schließen, verschließen
shell	[ʃel]	Schale; Hülle
sodium	[ˈsoudjəm]	Natrium
to detach	[diˈtætʃ]	ablösen, (ab-, los)trennen, loslösen
likewise	[ˈlaikwaiz]	auch, ebenfalls, gleichfalls
to tend (+ to + Inf.)	[tend]	tendieren, neigen, eine Tendenz (Neigung) haben, streben nach
to take up	[ˈteik ˈʌp]	aufnehmen
to complete	[kəmˈpliːt]	vervollständigen, ergänzen; auffüllen
outer	[ˈautə]	äußere(r,s), Außen-; äußerste(r,s)
predominant	[priˈdɔminənt]	vorwiegend, vorherrschend
repulsive	[riˈpʌlsiv]	abstoßend, Abstoßungs-
equilibrium	[ˌiːkwiˈlibriəm]	Gleichgewicht
directed	[diˈrektid]	gerichtet
spherical	[ˈsferikl]	kugelförmig, Kugel-
to relate to	[riˈleit]	in Zusammenhang (Beziehung) bringen, verbinden; sich beziehen, Bezug haben, in Verbindung (Beziehung) stehen (zu, mit)
weak	[wiːk]	schwach (Kraft etc.)
assumption	[əˈsʌmpʃən]	Annahme, Vermutung; Voraussetzung
manner	[ˈmænə]	Art (und) Weise
approximation	[əˌprɔksiˈmeiʃən]	Annäherung; Näherung

LE 2 ⊕ ⊕ Internationalismen

amorphous	[ə'mɔ:fəs]	amorph
alkali	['ælkəlai]	Alkali; Alkali-
electropositive	[i'lektrou'pɔzətiv]	elektropositiv
electronegative	[i'lektrou'negətiv]	elektronegativ
electronegativity	[i'lektrounegə'tiviti]	Elektronegativität
halogen	['hælədʒən]	Halogen
chloride	['klɔ:raid]	Chlorid

LE 3 ⊕ ⊕ Wandeln Sie die vorgegebenen Sätze in Nominalgruppen nach diesem Muster um:

T: Electrons are emitted.
S: The emission of electrons.

LE 4 ⊕ ⊕ Wandeln Sie die Nominalgruppen in kurze Sätze nach diesem Muster um:

T: The determination of the data.
S: The data were determined.

LE 5 ⊕ ⊕ Beantworten Sie die Fragen nach dem Muster:

T: Is it possible to determine the wavelength?
S: Yes, a determination of the wavelength is possible.

LE 6 ⊕ ⊕ Beantworten Sie die Fragen nach den Mustern:

T: Does the electrode emit electrons?
S: Yes, it is an electron-emitting electrode.

T: Is this transistor controlled by charge?
S: Yes, it is a charge-controlled transistor.

PK 5 · PA 4 · SQ B

LE 1 ⊕ ⊕ Wandeln Sie die vorgegebenen Relativsätze in Partizipialkonstruktionen nach diesen Mustern um:

T: The structure that was revealed in the mass spectrograph.
S: The structure revealed in the mass spectrograph.

T: The ions that move through the gas.
S: The ions moving through the gas.

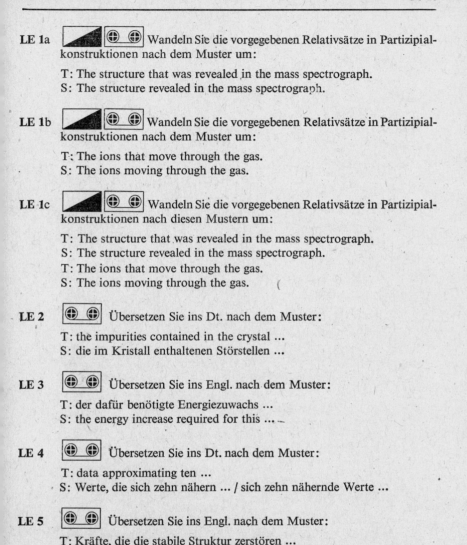

LE 1a   Wandeln Sie die vorgegebenen Relativsätze in Partizipial-konstruktionen nach dem Muster um:

T: The structure that was revealed in the mass spectrograph.
S: The structure revealed in the mass spectrograph.

LE 1b   Wandeln Sie die vorgegebenen Relativsätze in Partizipial-konstruktionen nach dem Muster um:

T: The ions that move through the gas.
S: The ions moving through the gas.

LE 1c   Wandeln Sie die vorgegebenen Relativsätze in Partizipial-konstruktionen nach diesen Mustern um:

T: The structure that was revealed in the mass spectrograph.
S: The structure revealed in the mass spectrograph.
T: The ions that move through the gas.
S: The ions moving through the gas.

LE 2   Übersetzen Sie ins Dt. nach dem Muster:

T: the impurities contained in the crystal ...
S: die im Kristall enthaltenen Störstellen ...

LE 3   Übersetzen Sie ins Engl. nach dem Muster:

T: der dafür benötigte Energiezuwachs ...
S: the energy increase required for this ...

LE 4   Übersetzen Sie ins Dt. nach dem Muster:

T: data approximating ten ...
S: Werte, die sich zehn nähern ... / sich zehn nähernde Werte ...

LE 5   Übersetzen Sie ins Engl. nach dem Muster:

T: Kräfte, die die stabile Struktur zerstören ...
S: forces destroying the stable structure ...

LE 6   Übersetzen Sie ins Dt. nach den Mustern:

T: the crystal containing impurities ...
S: der Kristall, der Störstellen aufweist ...
T: the impurities contained in the crystal ...
S: die im Kristall enthaltenen Störstellen / die Störstellen, die im Kristall enthalten sind ...

LE 7 | ⊕ ⊕ | Übersetzen Sie ins Engl. nach diesen Mustern:

T: die Kräfte, die im Kern wirken ...
S: the forces acting in the nucleus ...

T: die Kraft, die auf eine Ladung ausgeübt wird ...
S: the force exerted on a charge ...

PK 5 · PA 4 · SQ C

LE 1 Lesen Sie den folgenden Text und beantworten Sie die Fragen zu den Absätzen:

Free Electron Theory

- Was besagt die Theorie der freien Elektronen im Hinblick auf die Elektronenbewegung und den Leitungsvorgang?
- Welche Faktoren werden vernachlässigt?

It is possible to understand a number of important physical properties of some metals, in particular the monovalent metals, in terms of the free electron theory. According to this theory the valence electrons of the atoms of the metal are able to move freely through the volume of the specimen. The conduction of electricity by the metal is due to the valence electrons, and for this reason these electrons are called conduction electrons as distinguished from the electrons of the filled shells (Schale) of the iron cores (Ionenrumpf). The interaction of the conduction electrons with the ion cores of the atoms is neglected (vernachlässigt) in the free electron theory, and all values are calculated as if the conduction electrons were entirely free in the space bounded (begrenzt) by the surfaces of the specimen.

- Wird die Ladungsverteilung der Elektronen durch das elektrostatische Potential der Ionenrümpfe beeinflußt?
- Worin besteht der Wert der Theorie?

Even in the metals for which the free electron theory is most useful, such as sodium (Na), copper (Cu), and silver (Ag), it is not correct to imagine that the charge distribution (Verteilung) of the electrons is not influenced by the strong attractive electrostatic potential of the ion cores. The value of the free electron theory for the discussion of certain properties of metals depends on the fact that the energy of a conduction electron may depend on the square (Quadrat) of the velocity, just as for an electron in free space, which does not mean that the charge distribution should be that of a free electron.

- Worin bestand der Wert der Definition der Eigenschaften von Metallen mit Hilfe freier Elektronen?
- Wo versagte diese frühe Form der Theorie?

The concept that metallic properties may be defined in terms of free electrons was developed long before wave mechanics was introduced. The early theory had successes as well as failures (Mißerfolg). Among the successes were the derivation (Ableitung) of the functional form of Ohm's law connecting the electric current with the electric field and, in particular, the validity (Gültigkeit) of the Wiedemann-Franz relation between the electrical conductivity and the thermal conductivity. Failures were the discrepancies between observed and calculated values of the electronic heat capacity.

> Bereiten Sie die Übersetzung des Textes "Types of Bonding" (6.1.C. – 1.) vor!

PK 5 · PA 4 · SQ D

Leistungskontrolle

Bond Structure and Energy Levels

PK 6 · PA 1 · SQ A

LE 1 Fachtermini können aus bekannten Wortelementen aufgebaut sein. Ihre Bedeutung läßt sich vielfach erschließen, wenn man ihre Struktur erkennt und über Sachkenntnis verfügt. Das trägt zum schnellen Erfassen des Inhalts beim informatorischen Lesen bei, bedeutet jedoch nicht, daß damit in jedem Fall die exakte Fachwortbezeichnung im Dt. gefunden wird.

Häufig sind Mehrworttermini vom Typ

      1. high-speed press   2. high-speed particle

Umschreibung zur Verdeutlichung des Bedeutungsgehaltes:

1. high-speed press	= press	working at high speed
Adj N_2 N_1	N_1	(V-*ing*) Prep Adj N_2
2. high-speed particle	= particle moving at	high speed
Adj N_2 N_1	N_1	(V-*ing*) Prep Adj N_2
1. 'Schnellpresse'	2. 'schnelles Teilchen'	

Einige Termini lassen mehrere Umschreibungen zu, wobei auch Bedeutungsunterschiede deutlich werden können:

3. high-frequency wave	= wave	of high frequency / having a high frequency
4. high-frequency power	= power	obtained through high frequency / reached at high frequency
3. 'Kurzwelle'	4. 'Hochfrequenzleistung'	

LE 2 ⊶ Umschreiben Sie die folgenden Termini und ordnen Sie ihnen dt. Äquivalente zu:

a) high-energy electron   g) high-power motor
b) long-distance gas   h) long-distance control
c) long-range force   i) low-temperature physics
d) high-temperature stability   j) low-pressure test
e) slow-motion camera   k) low-frequency generator
f) high-energy radiation   l) high-frequency circuit

(a) Fernsteuerung, Fernlenkung (b) Ferngas (c) Tieftemperaturphysik (d) Zeitlupenkamera (e) Hitzebeständigkeit (f) Niederdruckversuch (g) NF Generator (h) Hochleistungsmotor (i) energiereiches Elektron (j) Fernwirkungskraft (k) Hochfrequenz(strom)Kreis (l) energiereiche Strahlung

LE 3   Die engl. Nachsilbe -*ing* erfüllt auch Funktionen im Bereich der Wortbildung:

1. Substantivisch verwendete *ing*-Formen können zu folgenden Bedeutungsgruppen gehören:

a) Die vom Verb abgeleitete *ing*-Form bezeichnet das Resultat eines Vorgangs:

    to bind = binding   = Bindung
    to find = finding(s) = Ergebnis(se), Erkenntnis(se)

b) Die von einem Substantiv abgeleitete *ing*-Form bezeichnet eine Kollektivgröße:

    the bonds   = bonding   = Bindung
    the contacts = contacting = Kontaktierung

2. In der Regel bezeichnen attributiv verwendete *ing*-Formen als Präsenspartizipien Handlungen, deren Träger vom nominalen Bezugswort bezeichnet wird:

    conducting crystal   = leitender Kristall
    isolating transformer = Trenntransformator

Gelegentlich wird aber auch ein Zustand bezeichnet:

    the neighbour − to be a neighbour − to neighbour → neighbouring atom
    = benachbartes Atom

LE 4   Charakterisieren Sie die verschiedenen *ing*-Formen:

It is useful to make a qualitative classification of crystals in terms of the predominant type of chemical binding displayed. The static forces binding atoms and molecules in solids are almost entirely electrostatic in nature. There are also important kinetic effects on the binding energy, arising from the motion of the atomic electrons. The important differences among the several types of crystal bonding are due to differences in the arrangement of electrons around the atoms and molecules.

PK 6 · PA 1 · SQ B

LE 1   Vergleichen Sie die beiden folgenden Sätze:

    We can reduce the electronic conductivity of heat.   (1)

    We apply a strong magnetic field.   (2)

Während Satz (1) einen Tatbestand mitteilt, informiert Satz (2) über das Mittel oder die Methode zur Erreichung dieses Tatbestandes. Die Handlungsträger beider Sätze sind identisch. In physikalischen Texten bleiben die Handlungsträger jedoch oft ungenannt. So kann auch für die beiden folgenden Sätze der gleiche Handlungs-träger angenommen werden:

> It is possible to reduce the electronic conductivity of heat. (3)

> A strong magnetic field is applied. (4)

Die Sätze (2) und (4) können beide auf die Struktur V + N zurückgeführt werden:

> to apply a strong magnetic field

1. Der Anschluß des Mittels oder der Methode erfolgt mit Hilfe der Präp. *by*, gelegentlich auch durch *through*. Um eine Präposition vor die Struktur V + N setzen zu können, muß *-ing* an das Verb angefügt werden:

> Prep + V-*ing* + N
> by applying a strong magnetic field

Hier vereinigt V-*ing* eine substantivische Eigenschaft (die Stellung hinter der Präposition) und eine verbale Eigenschaft (den direkten Objektanschluß). Diese *-ing*-Form wird als Gerundium bezeichnet.

2. Der englische Satz

> It is possible to reduce the electronic conductivity of heat by applying a strong magnetic field

hat folgende dt. Übersetzungsvarianten:

a) Es ist möglich, die Wärmeleitfähigkeit der Elektronen durch Anlegen eines starken magnetischen Feldes zu verringern.
b) Es ist möglich, die Wärmeleitfähigkeit der Elektronen dadurch zu verringern, daß man ein starkes magnetisches Feld anlegt.
c) Es ist möglich, die Wärmeleitfähigkeit der Elektronen zu verringern, indem man ein starkes magnetisches Feld anlegt.

3. Das Gerundium kann wie ein Verb durch Adverbien modifiziert werden:

> This effect can only be established by carefully observing the change in temperature.
> Dieser Effekt kann nur durch sorgfältige Beobachtung der Temperaturveränderung festgestellt werden.

4. Eine weitere verbale Eigenschaft ist die Passivform des Gerundiums. Vergleichen Sie die beiden Sätze:

> Currents are measured when they are passed through a calibrated galvanometer. (1)

> Currents are measured by being passed through a calibrated galvanometer. (2)

Das aktive Gerundium erfordert hier die Angabe des Obj. und damit eine Wiederholung:

> Currents are measured by passing them through a calibrated galvanometer. (3)

LE 2 Übersetzen Sie:

1. The electrical energy is calculated by multiplying together the potential and the charge. 2. The weight in grams of a single atom of any element is obtained by dividing its atomic weight by the Avogadro constant. 3. Since we cannot determine the potential of a point by measuring the potential difference between that point and a point at infinity, its theoretical definition cannot be used in practical work. 4. Molecular and atomic radii can be estimated by making use of Loschmidt's assumption that a solid may be treated as an arrangement of closely-packed spherical molecules or atoms. 5. The electric field $\vec{E}$ at any point may be determined through placing a test charge q at that point, measuring the magnitude and direction of the electrical force exerted on q, and then dividing the observed force $\vec{F}$ by q.

LE 3 Das Gerundium nach *for* drückt Zweck oder Absicht aus und erfüllt manchmal die gleiche Funktion wie der Infinitiv.

Übersetzen Sie nach diesen Mustern:

Radioactive isotopes are used for solving scientific problems.

a) Radioaktive Isotope werden benutzt, um wissenschaftliche Probleme zu lösen.

b) Radioaktive Isotope werden für die Lösung / zur Lösung wissenschaftlicher Probleme benutzt.

1. The mass spectrograph is used for determining the masses of positively charged ions. 2. Three methods can be used for determining the number of alpha-particles emitted from a radioactive source. 3. A transistor is an instrument in which semiconductors are used for amplifying electric signals. 4. For gamma-rays having energies in excess of 1.02 Mev, an excellent method for determining the energy is based on the formation of a positron-electron pair. 5. The Compton recoil electrons resulting from the collisions of the gamma-ray photons with electrons from a light element, such as aluminium, can be used for determining the energy of the photon.

LE 4 Das Gerundium nach *for* kann auch den Grund bezeichnen. Die Unterscheidung zum Ausdruck des Zweckes kann mit Hilfe der Vorzeitigkeit "*having* V-*ed*" erfolgen:

Millikan was awarded the Nobel Prize for having determined the electronic charge.

Daneben wird auch die einfache *ing*-Form verwendet. Die Unterscheidung erfolgt dann, ähnlich wie bei dt. 'für', nur durch den Kontext:

Millikan was awarded the Nobel Prize for determining the electronic charge.
Millikan wurde der Nobelpreis für die Bestimmung der Elektronenladung verliehen.

LE 5 Das Gerundium nach *without* drückt das Fehlen eines Umstandes aus. Das Gerundium nach *instead of* schließt darüber hinaus einen Gegensatz ein. Die beiden Gerundialkonstruktionen können in der folgenden Weise übersetzt werden:

1. Without trying to present the mathematical details, we shall discuss the application of quantum mechanics to the problem of the hydrogen atom.

> a) Ohne den Versuch zu machen, die mathematischen Einzelheiten darzulegen /
> b) Ohne daß wir versuchen, die mathematischen Einzelheiten darzulegen /
> c) Ohne den Versuch einer Darstellung der mathematischen Einzelheiten (zu machen) /
> werden wir die Anwendung der Quantenmechanik auf die Probleme des Wasserstoffatoms behandeln.

2. Instead of presenting the mathematical details, we shall discuss the physical concepts involved.

> (An)Statt die mathematischen Einzelheiten darzulegen, werden wir hier die wichtigsten physikalischen Begriffe erörtern.

1. The number of neutrons in the nucleus may vary without changing the charge number. 2. The basic idea of quantum theory is that we cannot imagine an isolated quantity of energy without associating with it a certain frequency. 3. In 1843, without knowing Mayer's paper, Joule tried to determine the mechanical work that must be done to produce a certain quantity of heat. 4. An isotope can be used like a detective who mixes with the crowd without being recognized. 5. Instead of measuring the forces acting on a magnet needle near a conductor carrying a current, it is possible to determine a current in a conductor by measuring the forces which a magnet will exert on a conductor.

LE 6 Das Gerundium kann gelegentlich einen eigenen Handlungsträger haben, der dann, wie das Subj. des Satzes, vor der verbalen *ing*-Form steht:

> The electrical and magnetic effects can be transmitted through space. + Material contact is not necessary. =
> The electrical and magnetic effects can be transmitted through space without material contact being necessary.

LE 7 ◄─O Verbinden Sie die Sätze nach dem Muster:
Fluorine tends to form a stable closed shell. + It picks up an extra electron to become a negative ion which then forms ionic compounds. →
Fluorine tends to form a stable closed shell by picking up an extra electron to become a negative ion which then forms ionic compounds.

1. Scientists have been able to make discoveries. − They used the electron theory. 2. They developed a new method. − They introduced impurities into semiconductors. 3. An electron can move indefinitely in one of its permitted orbitals. − It does

not emit energy. 4. Uranium changes into radium. − It emits alpha- and beta-particles. 5. Atoms may have equal atomic weights. − They do not have the same nuclear charge. 6. The neutral sodium atom becomes a sodium ion. − It loses an electron.

PK 6 · PA 1 · SQ C

LE 1 Übersetzen Sie:

Types of Bonding

A solid body is generally made up of one or more crystals, in each of which the atoms are arranged in a more or less regular lattice. An amorphous solid is an exception though it does retain some short-range order, i.e. any group of closely neighbouring atoms is not arranged in a completely random way. The particular crystal favoured by an element or compound depends largely on the way in which the atoms are bound to each other. One of the simplest types of bonding arises from the Coulomb attraction between ionized atoms with charges of opposite sign. The charging of the atoms arises from the tendency for the formation of filled electron shells. Thus, an alkali metal such as sodium has only one electron outside its full shells and this electron can easily be detached; the alkali metals are said to be strongly electropositive. Likewise the halogens are strongly electronegative, since neutral halogen atoms tend to take up the one electron that is needed to complete their outer shell. Ionic bonding is thus favoured in compounds between electropositive and electronegative elements. The alkali halides (Halogenide), e.g. sodium chloride, form cubic crystals in which each positive or negative ion is surrounded by six nearest neighbours with charges of the opposite sign. It will be realised, of course, that the Coulomb attraction between ions of opposite sign must change to a predominantly repulsive force as the distance between the ions decreases below that for the equilibrium position in the natural crystal. Bond formation in a non-metallic element such as diamond, or in a compound between two elements of similar electronegativity results from the sharing between neighbouring atoms of the electrons in the incomplete outer shells. A carbon atom in diamond has four outer electrons, each of which is shared with another atom; thus, in a diamond-type crystal each atom has four nearest neighbours. The very strong bonds that arise from the sharing of electrons are called covalent. In a covalent crystal the binding electrons are found close to the lines that join neighbouring atoms, i.e. the bonds are directed, whereas in ionic crystals the outer electrons tend to form spherical clouds around the electronegative atoms. Metallic binding is likewise due to the sharing of electrons, but in metals all the outer electrons are shared between all the atoms. Here it is unnecessary that the number of nearest neighbours should be related to the valency of the elements and it is found that many metals are made up of one of the two crystal structures in which there is a very close packing.

Atoms which are electrically neutral are held together by the rather weak van der Waals-type of bond.

The assumption that the atoms of a crystal are arranged in a perfectly regular manner is no more than a good approximation.

LE 2 ╦─0 Übersetzen Sie ins Engl. unter Verwendung von *by* + V-*ing*, *for* + V-*ing* und *without* + V-*ing*:

1. Die elektrische Leitfähigkeit der Metalle kann dadurch verringert werden, daß man ihre Temperatur erhöht. 2. Halbleiter werden für die Lösung vieler technischer Probleme verwendet. 3. Theoretische Probleme können nicht gelöst werden, ohne gewissen allgemeinen Regeln zu folgen. 4. Elektronegative Elemente können ihre Schale vervollständigen, indem sie ein Elektron aufnehmen. 5. Rutherford führte Versuche mit Alpha-Teilchen durch, um die Struktur des Atoms zu erforschen.

LE 3 ╦─0 Geben Sie die Informationen des Textes in einer zusammenhängenden engl. Darstellung wieder:

Berücksichtigen Sie dabei besonders folgende Fragen:

– Wodurch kann die Energie der Elektronen im Kristallgitter der Halbleiter erhöht werden?
– Wofür können Halbleiter auf Grund der Wirkung von Wärme und Licht auf ihre Leitfähigkeit besonders verwendet werden?
– Auf welche Weise entstehen freie Elektronen oder Löcher im Halbleiterkristall?
– Wofür können diese freien Elektronen und Löcher verwendet werden?

Halbleiter sind Stoffe, die sich in ihren elektrischen Eigenschaften von den Metallen und den Isolatoren unterscheiden. Im Gegensatz zu den Metallen erhöht sich ihre Leitfähigkeit durch Erhöhung der Temperatur. Ferner kann eine höhere Leitfähigkeit erzielt werden, indem man die Energie im Halbleiterkristall mit Hilfe von Licht- oder Röntgenstrahlen erhöht. Auf Grund dieses Effekts verwendet man Halbleiter in Thermometern und zur Messung von Licht. In einem Halbleiter sind alle Elektronen am Aufbau des Kristallgitters beteiligt. Durch die Zufuhr von Energie werden Elektronen aus ihren Bindungen gelöst. Eine besonders starke Erhöhung der Leitfähigkeit wird durch die Einführung von Fremdatomen mit einer ungeraden Zahl von Valenzelektronen erzielt. Die dadurch entstandenen freien Elektronen oder Löcher können für die Leitung verwendet werden.

PK 6 · PA 2 · SQ A

LE 0   Wortschatz zur Wiederholung

introduction: Einführung / stage: Stadium / to listen to: (zu)hören / to reach: erreichen / cold: kalt

LE 1   ⊕ ⊕   Neue Lexik

term	[tə:m]	Terminus, Begriff
discrete	[dis'kri:t]	(phys.) diskret
allowable	[ə'lauəbl]	erlaubt, zulässig
spectral	['spektrəl]	spektral, Spektral-
distribution	[ˌdistri'bju:ʃən]	Verteilung
radiation	[ˌreidi'eiʃən]	Strahlung, Strahlen
transition	[træn'siʒən]	Übergang
to gain	[gein]	gewinnen; aufnehmen
quantum	['kwɔntəm]	Quant, Teilchen
original	[ə'ridʒənl]	Original-, original, ursprünglich
angular	['æŋgjulə]	Dreh-; Winkel-
multiple	['mʌltipl]	Subst. (das) Vielfache Adj. Vielfach-, Mehrfach-, Mehr-
circular	['sə:kjulə]	rund, kreisförmig, Kreis-
quantization	[ˌkwɔnti'zeiʃən]	Quantelung
explanation	[ˌeksplə'neiʃən]	Erklärung, Erläuterung; Aufklärung
to modify	['mɔdifai]	modifizieren, abändern, abwandeln
stationary	['steiʃənri]	stationär; ruhend, Ruhe-; ortsfest
essential	[i'senʃəl]	(unbedingt) notwendig, erforderlich, wesentlich; wichtig, bedeutend
eo propose	[prə'pouz]	vorschlagen
txclusion	[iks'klu:ʒən]	Ausschließung, Ausschluß
to possess	[pə'zes]	besitzen, haben
axis	['æksis]	Achse
to excite	[ik'sait]	anregen, erregen
to accompany	[ə'kʌmpəni]	begleiten, eine Begleiterscheinung sein
probable	['prɔbəbl]	wahrscheinlich; vermutlich, mutmaßlich

LE 2   ⊕ ⊕   Internationalismen

absorption	[əb'sɔ:pʃən]	Absorption; Aufnahme
spectrum	['spektrəm]	Spektrum; Frequenzband
elliptic	[i'liptik]	elliptisch, Ellipsen-
spin	[spin]	Spin, Eigendrehimpuls

LE 3 ⊕ ⊕ Beantworten Sie die Fragen nach dem Muster:

T: Which tendency can be established for the electromotive force?
− to produce a current in a circuit −
S: It tends to produce a current in a circuit.

LE 4 ⊕ ⊕ Beachten Sie den Unterschied zwischen "attempt" und "experiment", die beide dt. "Versuch" entsprechen können! Stellen Sie Fragen nach dem Muster:

T: In this article a new attempt is made to explain this phenomenon.
S: Is the article based on new experimental evidence?
T: No, the author of this article attempts to give a new theoretical interpretation of this phenomenon.

PK 6 · PA 2 · SQ B

LE 1 ⊕ ⊕ Beantworten Sie die Fragen nach dem Muster:

T: How did Bohr develop the nuclear model of the atom?
− to apply Planck's quantum theory −
S: By applying Planck's quantum theory.

LE 2 ⊕ ⊕ Beantworten Sie die Fragen nach dem Muster:

T: What is this instrument used for?
− to determine the current strength −
S: It is used for determining the current strength.

LE 3 ⊕ ⊕ Beantworten Sie die Fragen nach dem Muster:

T: Why was Millikan awarded the Nobel Prize?
− to determine the electronic charge −
S: He got it for determining the electronic charge.

LE 4 ⊕ ⊕ Beantworten Sie die Fragen nach dem Muster:

T: Did he use this instrument when he made this experiment?
S: No, he did it without using this instrument.

know the book / increase the temperature / vary the field intensity / devise a new technique / apply a new method

PK 6 · PA 2 · SQ C

LE 1 Lesen Sie den folgenden Text, und beantworten Sie kurz die dt. Fragen am Ende des Textes:

Classification of Crystal Binding

In ionic crystals electrons are transferred (übertragen) from atoms of one type to atoms of a second type, so that the crystal is made up of positive and negative ions. The ions arrange themselves so that the Coulomb attraction between ions of opposite sign is stronger than the Coulomb repulsion between ions of the same sign. Thus, the ionic bond results from the electrostatic interaction of oppositely charged ions. The degree of ionization of the atoms of an ionic crystal is often such that the electronic configuration of all ions corresponds to filled electronic shells, as in the inert (Edel-) gas atoms.

When a covalent bond is formed we imagine that an electron from each atom is transferred to the region between the two atoms joined by the bond. The covalent bond is the normal electron-pair bond of chemistry. It is usually formed from two electrons, one from each atom. Metals are characterized by high electrical conductivity, and so a proportion of the electrons in a metal must be free to move about. These electrons are called conduction electrons. In some metals such as the alkali metals the interaction of the ion cores (Ionenrumpf) with the conduction electrons largely accounts for the binding energy. We may think of an alkali metal crystal as an array of positive ions in a sea of negative charge.

Inert gas atoms are bound together in the solid state by weak electrostatic forces known as van der Waals forces. These forces arise in the following way: even in an atom or molecule which has on the average an electric dipole moment of zero there will be a fluctuating dipole moment associated with the instantaneous (momentan) position of the electrons in the atom. The electric field associated with the moment will induce (induzieren) a dipole moment in neighbouring atoms. The interaction of the two moments causes an attractive force between the atoms. As neutral hydrogen has only one electron, it should form a covalent bond with only one other atom. It is known, however, that under certain conditions an atom of hydrogen is attracted by rather strong forces to two atoms and forms what is called a hydrogen bond between them. The hydrogen atom loses its electron to one of the other atoms in the molecule; the proton forms the hydrogen bond. Because of the small size of the proton there are only two nearest neighbour atoms. Thus the hydrogen bond connects only two atoms.

1. Was wird über die Ionenkristalle ausgesagt? 2. Wie entsteht eine kovalente Bindung? 3. Was erfahren wir über die Struktur metallischer Elemente? 4. Was sind van der Waalssche Kräfte? 5. Charakterisieren Sie die Wasserstoffbrückenbindung!

6.2.

Bereiten Sie die Übersetzung des Textes *"Energy Levels"* (6.3.C. – 1.) vor.
Beachten Sie den Unterschied zwischen: momentum: Impuls / angular momentum: Drehimpuls / torque: Drehmoment!

PK 6 · PA 2 · SQ D

LE 1   ⊕ ⊕   Einführung:

band theory: Bandtheorie / empty: leer / gap: (Energie)Lücke / forbid, forbade, forbidden: verbieten / forbidden gap: verbotene Zone

LE 2   ⊕ ⊕ ▷   Hören Sie den BTV *"Semiconductors"* und machen Sie sich Notizen!

LE 3   ⊕ ⊕ ▷   Hören Sie noch einmal den gesamten Text, und ergänzen Sie Ihre Notizen!

LE 4   Geben Sie eine kurze zusammenhängende Darstellung der wesentlichen Informationen in Dt.!

LE 5   Why are semiconductors so important for the development of industry?

– You may consider the difference between metallic conductors, non-conductors and semiconductors
– Give examples of semiconductors and of substances used for impurity additions
– Speak about the application of semiconductors, e.g. as transistors or in computers

PK 6 · PA 3 · SQ A

LE 1   Negationspräfixe (Vorsilben zum Ausdruck der Verneinung) haben im allgemeinen zwei Funktionen. Sie bezeichnen:

a) neutral das Bedeutungsgegenteil des negierten Wortes:

radioactive = radioaktiv
non-radioactive = 'nicht' radioaktiv, 'in'aktiv
metal = Metall
non-metal = 'Nicht'metall

b) das Bedeutungsgegenteil des negierten Wortes u n d zusätzlich abgeleitete neue
Bedeutung(en):

significant   = bedeutsam, wichtig
*in*significant = 1. unwichtig, bedeutungslos
                2. geringfügig, unerheblich

Die Möglichkeit der zusätzlichen Bedeutungsveränderung muß immer beachtet
werden.
Wichtige Negationspräfixe der engl. Fachsprache sind:

1. *non-* (bedeutungsneutral)

*non-*Adj	non-polar	= 'un'polar
	non-dimensional	= dimensions'los'
	non-mobile	= 'un'beweglich, stationär, ortsfest
*non-*Subst	non-metal	= 'Nicht'metall

2. *un-*

*un-*Adj	unsymmetrical	= 'nicht' symmetrisch, 'un'symme-trisch
	undistorted	= 'un'verzerrt, 'un'gestört
	uncoloured	= 1. farb'los'
		2. 'un'verfärbt
*un-*Verb	load	= beladen
	unload	= 'ent'laden

3. *in-* (*im-*)

in- (*im-*)Adj	inelastic	= 'nicht' elastisch, 'un'elastisch
	indefinite	= 1. 'un'bestimmt
		2. 'un'begrenzt
		3. 'un'bestimmt, vage
	effective	= 1. wirksam
		2. effektiv, tatsächlich
a b e r :	ineffective	= 1. 'un'wirksam, 'in'effektiv
		2. −
	inorganic	= 'an'organisch

Folgende Negationspräfixe tauchen nur gelegentlich in physikalischen Fachtexten auf:

4. *dis-*

*dis-*Adj	dissymmetrical	= 'a'symmetrisch, 'un'symmetrisch
*dis-*Verb	connect	= verbinden
	disconnect	= trennen

5. *a(n)-*

| *a(n)-*Adj | asymmetrical | = 'a'symmetrisch |
| | anhydrous | = wasser'frei', 'nicht' wäßrig |

B e a c h t e n S i e auch, daß in manchen Fällen zwei unterschiedliche Negationspräfixe benutzt werden, um Bedeutungsnuancierungen bei Negation des gleichen

Ausgangswortes auszudrücken:

> *non*-scientific: nicht wissenschaftlich, nicht zur Wissenschaft gehörend
> *un*scientific: unwissenschaftlich, die wissenschaftliche Darlegungsweise
> verfälschend oder verletzend

LE 2 Ersetzen Sie in den folgenden Sätzen das Negationspräfix durch *not*:
indirect → not direct
Prüfen Sie, ob das Negationspräfix lediglich das Bedeutungsgegenstück
der unverneinten Form ist oder ob eine neue Bedeutung entsteht:

1. There are three isotopes of hydrogen, two are radioactive, one is non-radioactive.
2. Atoms and molecules are indefinitely small. 3. The neutron is an uncharged
nuclear particle. 4. The molecular structure of this compound is unknown. 5. The
material showed an unusual behaviour. 6. We can determine the nature of light
only by indirect observation. 7. Nitrogen was discovered independently by C.
Scheele and D. Rutherford, a Scotsman. 8. This is a rather uninteresting article.
9. The number of organic compounds is in practice indefinite. 10. The table of data
given in the present paper is incomplete. 11. The halogens are typical non-metals.
12. Scientists of the 19th century had rather indefinite views of the structure of
matter.

PK 6 · PA 3 · SQ B

LE 1 Das Gerundium nach *after* und *before* drückt einen Zeitunterschied zum
Kernsatz aus:

> a) Before making any measurement we should know what it will be used
> for.
> Bevor wir eine Messung vornehmen, müssen wir wissen, wofür sie ver-
> wendet wird.
> b) After discovering (having discovered) the atomic nucleus, Rutherford
> established the planetary model of the atom.
> Nachdem Rutherford den Atomkern entdeckt hatte, stellte er das plane-
> tare Atommodell auf. / Nach der Entdeckung des Atomkerns stellte Ruther-
> ford das planetare Atommodell auf.

> Übersetzen Sie:

1. Before considering the energy of the hydrogen molecule-ion and the hydrogen
molecule we must discuss their wave functions. 2. Neutrons, after being reduced to
thermal energies, are easily absorbed by most materials. 3. Before considering the
value of the various hypotheses, we must know all the relevant facts. 4. It is convenient in the study of fast neutrons to make use of the ionization due to a light
nucleus after being struck by a high-energy neutron. 5. After discovering particles

which were smaller than the smallest atom known, scientists had to develop a new concept of the atom.

LE 2 Das Gerundium nach *in* gibt an, daß beiden Handlungen der Zeitraum gemeinsam ist. Wir finden folgende Übersetzungsvarianten:

a) There are practical difficulties in detecting the main parts of the conduction band in a metal.
Es gibt praktische Schwierigkeiten bei der Feststellung der Hauptteile des Leitungsbandes in Metallen / wenn man die Hauptteile des Leitungsbandes in Metallen feststellen will.

b) In der Vergangenheit tritt im Dt. 'als' an die Stelle von 'wenn':

Bohr was influenced by Planck's quantum theory of radiation in developing his ideas on the structure of the atom.
Bohr war von Plancks Quantentheorie der Strahlung beeinflußt, als er seine Vorstellungen hinsichtlich der Atomstruktur entwickelte.

c) In einigen Fällen ist auch die Übersetzung durch einen Infinitivsatz (Zweck) möglich:

Various methods may be used in studying the structure.
Verschiedene Methoden können benutzt werden, um die Struktur zu untersuchen.

Übersetzen Sie:

1. In raising the cathode temperature we increase the number of electrons emitted. 2. Heavy water is more effective in decreasing the velocity of neutrons than graphite. 3. Equilibrium is reached when the work done by the chemical forces in carrying unit positive charge from the negative to the positive side is just equal and opposite in sign to the work done by the electrical forces. 4. The potential difference between charged bodies is equal to work that must be done by mechanical or other nonelectrostatic forces in carrying a unit positive charge from the lower to the higher potential. 5. A lattice imperfection is very effective in scattering electrons because of the electric charge associated with most types of impurity.

LE 3 Beim Gerundium nach *in* u. a. kann man gelegentlich finden, daß ein anderes Satzglied des Kernsatzes (also nicht das Subjekt) Handlungsträger zum Gerundium ist.

Rutherford made a study of the scattering of alpha particles in passing through matter.

LE 4 Das Gerundium nach (*up*)*on* drückt aus, daß die Handlung des Kernsatzes zum Zeitpunkt der Handlung des Gerundiums beginnt. Auf Grund dieser engen zeitlichen Beziehung bezeichnet es gelegentlich auch das Mittel. Die Übersetzungsmöglichkeiten entsprechen meist denen unter LE 2 a) und b) genannten mit dt. 'bei' bzw. 'wenn' / 'als'.

Übersetzen Sie:

1. On losing an electron, a neutral atom becomes a positive ion. 2. On passing from the liquid to the solid state a substance emits heat. 3. On taking up a definite amount of energy, an atom may eject an electron. 4. In general, fast moving electrons will produce X-rays upon striking particular materials. 5. Upon comparing the mass of the electron with the mass of a hydrogen atom, it is seen that it would require 1837 electrons to have the same mass as an atom of hydrogen.

LE 5   🔾—0   Verwandeln Sie die gekennzeichneten Nebensätze und Infinitivkonstruktionen in Gerundialkonstruktionen nach dem Muster:

> *When a nucleus changes from one energy state to another*, it can emit a beta-particle.
> *On changing from one energy state to another* a nucleus can emit a beta-particle.

1. *When heat is applied to a material*, electrons are driven out of it. 2. Semiconductors may be used *in order to obtain heat and cold*. 3. *When neutral atoms lose or gain electrons*, they become ions. 4. Diffraction patterns of rays are distorted *when they pass through a magnetic field*. 5. *After Pauli had established the exclusion principle*, he was able to explain the Periodic System on the basis of the electron shells of atoms.

LE 6   🔾—0   Bilden Sie aus den aufgeführten Wörtern weiterführende Gerundialkonstruktionen! Wählen Sie dafür eine geeignete Präposition aus:

1. Various methods are used ...
     / to separate − isotope − element /
     / to determine − extent − ionization /
     / to establish − structure − unknown − substance /

2. An interesting phenomenon was discovered ...
     / to study − conductivity − liquid /
     / to increase − amount − heat − during − reaction /
     / to pass − X-rays − through − magnetic − field /

3. A new feature was established ...
     / to compare − data − various − experiment /
     / to pass − electron − through − crystal /
     / to study − effect − electric − current − magnet /

4. This result could not be obtained ...
     / to raise − temperature − substance /
     / to apply − low − potential difference − only /
     / to lose − some − energy − in the form − heat /

PK 6 · PA 3 · SQ C

LE 1　Übersetzen Sie:

Energy Levels

The term "energy level" is used in referring to discrete amounts of energy which atoms and molecules can have with respect to their electron or nuclear structure. The concept of allowable energy levels was first introduced by Planck in explaining the physical basis for the spectral distribution of black-body radiation. The second related principle due to Planck was that emission and absorption of radiation are associated with transition between these energy levels. The energy lost or gained in this process is equal to the energy $h\nu$ of the quantum of radiation. Here h is Planck's constant and ν is the frequency of the radiation.

　　　The first application of energy levels in the electron structure of atoms to explain optical spectra was made by Bohr. The original Bohr atom had as its basis that the only allowable states of an atom were those in which the electronic angular momentum was an integral multiple of $h/2$. Circular orbits suggested by Bohr were extended by Sommerfeld to include the quantization of momentum in elliptic orbits, and to provide an improved explanation of optical spectra. These early concepts were modified by the development of the theory of wave mechanics, in which it was shown that the allowable "stationary" states for the electrons in an atom represent solutions of the Schrödinger equation. These solutions are conveniently represented by a set of "quantum numbers" for each electron. On this basis the electron structure of an atom containing any number of electrons can be built up. Two further concepts which are essential to this picture, however, are electron spin proposed by Uhlenbeck and Goudsmit, and the exclusion principle due to Pauli. In addition to the angular momentum of the electron in its orbit, each electron possesses angular momentum due to spin about an axis. The Pauli exclusion principle specifies that no two electrons in an atom can exist in the same quantum state, corresponding to the same set of quantum numbers.

　　　An atom is stable when it exists in the state for which the quantum numbers of its electrons give the lowest total energy. The energy of the atom may be increased to a higher level by a different set of allowed quantum numbers. Transitions back again to the 'ground' state will be accompanied by the emission of radiation. Wave mechanics indicates, however, that only certain transitions from one quantum state to another can be probable.

LE 2　�O Übersetzen Sie ins Engl. unter Verwendung von *after / before* + V-*ing* und *on / in* + V-*ing*:

1. Nachdem Planck den Begriff des Energiequants eingeführt hatte, konnte er die Schwarzkörperstrahlung erklären. 2. Nach Einführung eines Fremdatoms weist der Halbleiterkristall ein Leitungselektron oder ein Loch auf. 3. Bevor man

sich mit speziellen Problemen von Halbleitern beschäftigt, muß man die wichtigsten Beziehungen zwischen Kristallstruktur und Leitfähigkeit kennen. 4. Bei der Bewegung durch Gase können Alphateilchen mit einem Atomkern zusammenstoßen. 5. Bei Anstieg der Temperatur erhöht sich die Leitfähigkeit der Halbleiter, während die der Metalle sinkt.

LE 3   Geben Sie die Informationen des Textes in einer zusammenhängenden engl. Darstellung wieder!

Berücksichtigen Sie dabei besonders folgende Fragen:
- Wann emittiert ein Atom Energie?
- Was geschieht nach der Absorption von Energie im Atom?
- Wann befindet sich ein Wasserstoffatom im Grundzustand?
- In welcher Weise kann das Wasserstoffatom aus dem Grundzustand in einen angeregten Zustand übergehen?
- Warum mußte das Bohrsche Atommodell durch eine kompliziertere Theorie ersetzt werden?

Im Jahre 1913 stellte Niels Bohr auf der Basis der Quantentheorie ein Atommodell auf, das auf zwei Annahmen beruhte:

1. Die Elektronen im Atom können sich nur auf bestimmten Bahnen bewegen. Bei der Bewegung auf diesen "erlaubten" Bahnen emittieren sie keine Energie.
2. Energie wird nur bei einem Sprung von Elektronen auf eine kernnähere Bahn emittiert. Nach der Absorption von Energie springt das Elektron auf eine Bahn, die vom Atomkern entfernter ist.

Das Wasserstoffatom weist die einfachste Struktur auf. Nach dem von Bohr entwickelten Modell befindet sich das Wasserstoffatom im Grundzustand, wenn das Elektron auf der kernnächsten Bahn kreist. Durch den Zusammenstoß mit Elektronen kann das Wasserstoffatom in einen angeregten Zustand versetzt werden. Beim Zurückspringen des zum Atom gehörenden Elektrons auf die kernnähere Bahn wird diese Energie als Licht oder elektromagnetische Strahlung emittiert. Die Struktur aller anderen Elemente ist komplizierter (complex) als die des Wasserstoffs. Durch Anwendung des Bohrschen Atommodells konnten viele Probleme des Atombaus gelöst werden, aber für die Erklärung der neuesten Forschungsergebnisse sind heute kompliziertere Gleichungen notwendig. Diese wurden nach der Aufstellung der Quantenmechanik entwickelt.

PK 6 · PA 4 · SQ A

LE 0   Wortschatz zur Wiederholung

to return: zurückkehren / house: Haus / to forget, forgot, forgotten: vergessen / to remember: sich erinnern / far: weit / husband: Ehemann

LE 1 ⊕ ⊕ Neue Lexik

chief	[tʃiːf]	hauptsächlich, Haupt-; Ober-, Höchst-
radioactivity	[ˈreidiouækˈtiviti]	Radioaktivität
constituent	[kənˈstitjuənt]	Subst. Bestandteil, Komponente Adj. einen Teil bildend oder ausmachend
rearrangement	[ˈriːəˈreindʒmənt]	Umlagerung, Umgruppierung, Umstellung
discovery	[disˈkʌvəri]	Entdeckung; Auffindung
respectively	[riˈspektivli]	(nachgestellt) beziehungsweise
latter	[ˈlætə]	letztere(r, s)
series	[ˈsiəriːz]	Reihe, Serie; Reihenfolge
to travel	[ˈtrævl]	sich fortbewegen, wandern
wave-like	[ˈweivlaik]	wellenähnlich
characteristics	[ˌkæriktəˈristiks]	Charakteristik; (phys., chem.) Kenndaten, -ziffern
the ... the	[ðə ... ðə]	je ... desto
pronounced	[prəˈnaunst]	ausgeprägt, deutlich, klar
individual	[ˌindiˈvidjuəl]	einzeln, Einzel-; verschieden
present-day	[ˈprezntˈdei]	gegenwärtig, heutig; modern
to deflect	[diˈflekt]	ablenken (Strahl etc.)
rest	[rest]	Subst. Ruhe; Rest Adj. Ruhe-; Rest-
massive	[ˈmæsiv]	massehaltig, Masse-
century	[ˈsentʃuri]	Jahrhundert
to identify	[aiˈdentifai]	identifizieren; nachweisen; bestimmen
recent	[ˈriːsnt]	vor kurzem, unlängst (entstanden, geschehen etc.); neueste(r, s), letzte(r, s); modern
then	[ðen]	damals
to induce	[inˈdjuːs]	induzieren; hervorrufen, bewirken, auslösen
(in)stability	[(in)stəˈbiliti]	(In)Stabilität, (Un)Beständigkeit
whereas	[wɛərˈæz]	wohingegen, während

LE 2 ⊕ ⊕ Internationalismen:

nuclide	[ˈnjuːklaid]	Nuklid
electromagnetic	[iˈlektrouməgˈnetik]	elektromagnetisch
mechanical	[miˈkænikəl]	mechanisch

LE 3 ⊕ ⊕ Formen Sie die Sätze nach diesem Muster um:

T: If the frequency is high the particle character is distinct.
S: The higher the frequency — the more distinct the particle character

ow atomic number — abundant element / short wavelength — high frequency / large binding energy — stable atoms / short distance — strong attraction / fast nuclear motion — warm body

LE 4 ⊕ ⊕ Übersetzen Sie nach dem Muster:

T: The shorter the distance — the stronger the attraction
S: Je kürzer der Abstand — desto größer die Anziehung

⊕ ⊕ Wandeln Sie die nominale Struktur nach diesem Muster in ein Gerundium um:

T: without the production of ionization
S: without producing ionization

PK 6 · PA 4 · SQ B

LE 1 ⊕ ⊕ Übersetzen Sie ins Dt. nach diesem Muster:

T: in absorbing energy
S: bei der Aufnahme von Energie

LE 2 ⊕ ⊕ Übersetzen Sie ins Engl. nach dem Muster:

T: durch Abgabe eines Elektrons
S: by detaching an electron

LE 3 ⊕ ⊕ Beantworten Sie die Fragen nach dem Muster:

T: Had he read the article when he began the experiment?
S: Yes, he began it after reading the article.

read the book / specify the term / modify the model / make new experiments / introduce a new factor

LE 4   🔄   Wählen Sie eine geeignete Präposition zur Vervollständigung der Sätze nach dem Muster:

> T: These data were found ... carrying out these experiments.
> S: These data were found by carrying out these experiments.
> Der zweite Teil des Satzes bleibt unverändert.

1. New knowledge was gained ... 2. These properties could not be explained ... 3. This concept could not be retained ... 4. Scientists did not know these properties ... 5. An explanation will not be possible ... 6. Various methods had to be used ... 7. A new hypothesis was suggested ...

PK 6 · PA 4 · SQ C

LE 1   Lesen Sie den folgenden Text, und beantworten Sie kurz die dt. Fragen am Ende des Textes:

Atomic Spectra and Energy Levels

Many spectral lines are found to exhibit a still finer structure of several lines very close together. This is called hyperfine structure and has been found to be due to two causes. One is the isotope effect in which atoms of different isotopes of the same element possess slightly different excited electron energy levels. The other cause of hyperfine structure has been determined to be due to the fact that the atomic nucleus also possesses angular momentum, which is vectorially added (hinzufügen) to the electronic angular momentum and then quantized. Differences in the resulting states of the atom correspond to very small differences in the energy levels and thus in the observed spectrum.

Another source of structure in spectra results when the atoms emitting the radiation are in a magnetic or electric field. In a field, space quantization in the direction of the field takes place. The values of the magnetic moment or electric moment of the atom, associated with the various possible components of angular momentum as quantized in the field direction, result in different energy levels. This splitting (Aufspaltung) of levels is referred to as the Zeeman effect in the case of an applied magnetic field, and the Stark effect in the case of an applied electric field. The amount of splitting increases with the intensity of the superimposed (überlagern) field. Any electron of an atom may be excited to some higher allowed energy level by absorption of the amount of energy specified by the difference in the energy levels involved. By absorption of a sufficient (genügend) amount of energy, any electron can be detached from an atom; this results in ionization. It is not necessary to consider only the outer electrons, because electrons from inner shells may also be excited. When they return to the 'ground' or lowest energy state, this process involves the emission of "characteristic" X-rays. They are characteristic in that the X-ray spectrum produced is typical of the particular atom producing the radiation.

1. Was wird als Hyperfeinstruktur eines Spektrums bezeichnet? 2. Was sind die beiden Ursachen der Hyperfeinstruktur? 3. Was wird als Zeeman-Effekt und was als Stark-Effekt bezeichnet? 4. Was sind charakteristische Röntgenstrahlen?

Bereiten Sie die Übersetzung des Textes *"Nuclear Radiation"* (7.1.C. − 1.) vor!

PK 6 · PA 4 · SQ D

LE 1 ⊕ ⊕ Einführung
to confirm: bestätigen, erhärten

LE 2 ⊕ ⊕ :▷▭ Hören Sie den BTV *"Characteristic X-Rays"*, und machen Sie sich Notizen!

LE 3 ⊕ ⊕ :▷▭ Hören Sie noch einmal den gesamten Text und ergänzen Sie Ihre Notizen!

LE 4 Geben Sie eine kurze, zusammenhängende Darstellung der wesentlichen Informationen des Textes in Dt.!

LE 5 Speak about the basic concepts of the atomic structure:

In this report you should give a short explanation of the terms "atomic nucleuse", "electron shell", "electron orbit" and "discrete energy level". In explaining the term "discrete energy level" you should consider the transition or jump from one quantum state to another which is accompanied by the emission or absorption of radiation.

Radioactivity and Nuclear Energy

PK 7 · PA 1 · SQ A

LE 1 Im Engl. kann das Präfix *re-* vor bestimmte Nomen bzw. Substantive oder Verben gesetzt werden.

> arrangement of atoms → rearrangement of atoms
> to charge a battery → to recharge a battery

Es verleiht dem Subst. oder Verb zusätzlich folgende Bedeutungen:

a) Das Präfix *re-* zeigt an, daß der vom Subst. oder Verb ausgedrückte Vorgang zu einer Veränderung eines Zustandes oder zu einem neuen Tatbestand führt.

> rearrangement of atoms in a molecule =
> Umgruppierung bzw. Umlagerung / Neuordnung von Atomen in einem Molekül

Dem engl. Präfix *re-* entsprechen hier oft die dt. Präfixe 'Um-' ('um-') oder 'Neu-' ('neu-').

b) Das Präfix *re-* zeigt an, daß der vom Subst. oder Verb ausgedrückte Vorgang einen früheren (Ausgangs-)Zustand oder Tatbestand wiederherstellt oder wiederherstellen soll.

> to recharge a battery =
> eine Batterie wiederaufladen, nachladen
> recombination of two particles =
> Rekombination / Wiedervereinigung von zwei Teilchen
> reconversion of (into) a compound =
> Rückumwandlung einer (in eine) Verbindung

Dem engl. Präfix *re-* entsprechen sehr oft die dt. Präfixe 'Wieder-' ('wieder-'), 'Re-' ('re-'), 'Nach-' ('nach-') und 'Rück-' ('rück-'). Beachten Sie, daß das Präfix *re-* in der gleichen Wortkombination zwei verschiedene Bedeutungen ausdrücken kann:

> to rebuild a house = (1) ein Haus umbauen
> (2) ein Haus wiederaufbauen

c) Das Präfix *re-* zeigt an, daß der vom Subst. oder Verb ausgedrückte Vorgang einfach wiederholt wird, ohne daß damit ein früherer Zustand wieder erreicht wird oder werden soll.

> to reheat a material = ein Material wiedererhitzen / nachheizen
> (tempern)
> redevelopment of a film = Nachentwicklung eines Films

Dem engl. Präfix *re-* entsprechen in diesem Fall oft die dt. Präfixe 'Wieder-' ('wieder-') und 'Nach-' ('nach-').

LE 2 ⊶O Geben Sie auf dieser Grundlage eine Übersetzung der folgenden engl. Wortkombinationen, und vergleichen Sie diese mit den vorgegebenen Übersetzungsvarianten:

a) regeneration of a material in a technical process b) to reconstruct a laboratory c) reintroduction of an old and nearly forgotten method d) to refill a tank e) reexamination of experimental data f) to rerun a computer programme g) reapplication of the same technique h) to regroup experimental data

> (a) umbauen, rekonstruieren (b) Nachprüfung, Überprüfung (c) Wiedereinführung (d) wiederholen (e) nachfüllen, wiederauffüllen (f) wiederholte Anwendung (g) umgruppieren, neuordnen (h) Wiedergewinnung, Regeneration

---

PK 7 · PA 1 · SQ B

LE 1 Begleitende Umstände unterschiedlicher Natur können durch das adverbiale Gerundium, d. h. durch die Struktur "Prep + V-*ing* + ..." an den Kernsatz angeschlossen werden. Diese adverbiale Funktion kann auch durch die beiden mit -*ing* und -*ed* gebildeten Partizipien übernommen werden. In diesem Fall fehlt die Präp., so daß sich die inhaltliche Beziehung zum Kernsatz allein aus dem Kontext ergibt.

> Developing the photographic plate, G. P. Thomson found a diffraction pattern.
> Als G. P. Thomson die photographische Platte entwickelte, stellte er ein Beugungsmuster fest.

> The static methods lead to more accurate values for the thermal conductivity than can be obtained, using dynamic methods.
> Die statischen Methoden führen zu genaueren Werten für die Wärmeleitfähigkeit als man mit Hilfe dynamischer Methoden ermitteln kann.

Da der Handlungsträger des Partizips mit dem Subj. bzw. mit dem nicht ausdrücklich genannten Handlungsträger des Kernsatzes identisch ist, wird diese Struktur meist als "verbundenes Partizip" bezeichnet. Ihr Gebrauch ist in der physikalischen Fachsprache auf bestimmte Fälle beschränkt.

Beachten Sie, daß meist: *having* + V-*ed* + ... = 'nachdem'
being + Adj/V-*ed* + ... = 'da'
using + ... = 'mit Hilfe'

LE 2 Übersetzen Sie:

1. Being electromagnetic in nature and having zero charge, gamma rays are not deflected by electric or magnetic fields. 2. Any problem in atomic structure can be

solved, at least in principle, using the methods of quantum mechanics. 3. Starting from the principles of the kinetic theory developed by Clausius and Maxwell, Boltzmann and Gibbs worked out systematic methods for the calculation of all the properties of gases. 4. There are a number of possible methods for the separation of isotopes, using electromagnetic principles. 5. It is believed that the hydrogen bond is largely ionic in character, being formed only with the most electronegative ions. 6. Statistical mechanics treats the average or statistical properties of a system consisting of a large number of particles, using standard mathematical techniques and the properties of the constituent particles.

LE 3 Die inhaltliche Funktion der "verbundenen Partizipien" kann durch die Konjunktionen *when* und *while* verdeutlicht werden:

Übersetzen Sie:
1. When excited in a definite way, atoms emit light of certain discrete wavelengths. 2. While retaining the general concept of oscillators, Planck assumed that the emission or absorption of energy occurs only in discrete amounts or quanta. 3. When trying to calculate the conductivity of a solid, we may follow a given photon and see how well it is scattered by the electrons.

LE 4 Die "verbundenen Partizipien" können eine Bedingung bezeichnen. Sie werden dann durch einen Konditionalsatz mit 'wenn' oder durch ein geeignetes dt. Partizip übersetzt:

Properly insulated a wire may be used as a conductor.
Wenn ein Draht richtig isoliert ist, kann er als elektrischer Leiter benutzt werden. / Richtig isoliert kann ein Draht als elektrischer Leiter benutzt werden.

Übersetzen Sie:
1. Being connected so that the current is not divided at any point, electrical devices are said to be connected in series. 2. Given the quantum numbers n, l and m_l, the wave function of the atom is completely determined.

LE 5 Bezeichnet das "verbundene Partizip" eine allgemeine Neben- oder Folgewirkung, so kann es in der dt. Übersetzung mit 'wobei', 'wodurch' oder 'und' an den Kernsatz angeschlossen werden:

The emission of an alpha-particle changes the emitting atom into an atom of a different element, reducing its atomic number by 2 and its mass number by 4.

Die Emission eines Alphateilchens wandelt das emittierende Atom in das Atom eines anderen Elements um, wobei die Ordnungszahl um 2 und die Massenzahl um 4 reduziert werden.

Beachten Sie, daß manchmal der Handlungsträger des Partizips mit dem Subj. eigentlich nicht identisch ist (vgl. Satz 5).

⚓—O Übersetzen Sie:

1. A hotter liquid will move through the colder liquid, carrying heat with it. 2. Free electrons attach themselves to neighbouring atoms, ionizing them by collision and turning them into negative ions. 3. The ionization potential is defined as the energy required to detach an electron from an atom or molecule in the ground state, leaving the resulting ion in its lowest state. 4. Certain radioactive atoms emit positrons, thus reducing their atomic number by 1 but leaving their mass number unchanged. 5. The classical free electron theory gave a value for the electrical conductivity, assuming the number of free electrons to be equal to the number of atoms.

LE 6 In einigen Fällen besteht folgende Beziehung:
A gas in the conducting state shows as a whole no electric charge, indicating / which indicates / This indicates that the positive and negative ions are equal in number.
Ein Gas im leitenden Zustand weist insgesamt keine elektrische Ladung auf, was darauf hindeutet, daß die positiven und negativen Ionen gleichzahlig sind. /
... Das deutet darauf hin, daß ...

Übersetzen Sie:

1. By absorption of a definite amount of energy, any electron can be detached from an atom, resulting in ionization. 2. It was found by Aston that neon exists in two forms (mass numbers 20 and 22) and that the proportions are 10 : 1, giving an average atomic weight of 20.2 to neon. 3. In diffraction experiments with electrons, the photographic plate showed a pattern just as might have been produced by X-rays, indicating that the electrons exhibit wave properties.

PK 7 · PA 1 · SQ C

LE 1 Übersetzen Sie:

Nuclear Radiation

Nuclear radiation results from the transitions of atomic nuclei. The two chief types of transition in natural radioactivity are those in which the number of constituent particles of a given nucleus (nuclide) are changed by the emission of one or more particles, and those in which there is a rearrangement of the particles of a given nuclide, without change in number, such that the nuclide passes from a state of higher energy to a state of lower energy. Soon after the discovery of radioactivity in 1896, it was found that naturally radioactive substances emit three kinds of radiation: alpha, beta and gamma rays. The first two consist of high-speed charged particles, alpha and beta particles respectively. They are called particle rays to distinguish them from the gamma rays discovered by Villard in 1900. The latter were shown by a series of experiments to be a form of high-frequency electromagnetic radiation travelling with the speed of light. However, in discussing the nature of these rays, it must be remembered that experiments clearly show that the so-called particles may exhibit distinctly wave-like characteristics, and conversely the higher the frequency of the gamma radiation the more pronounced becomes the particle-like character of its individual quanta or photons. From such considerations arises present-day quantum mechanical theory. Two of the most important differences between alpha rays and beta rays are: (1) they are deflected in opposite directions by a magnetic field indicating that they are oppositely charged, and (2) the alpha particle is far more massive than the beta particle. Early measurements indicated that alpha particles may be emitted with speeds up to 1/15 the speed of light, and beta rays with speeds up to 0.98 c. The rest masses of the two particles and their energy equivalents in millions of electron volts (MeV) are 6.645×10^{-27} kg $= 3727.2$ MeV for the alpha particle and 9.109×10^{-31} kg $= 0.511$ MeV for the beta particle. Thus the alpha particle is nearly 7 300 times more massive than the beta particle. The reason for such a difference in the masses was found early in this century. In experiments begun in 1903, Rutherford showed that an alpha particle is the doubly charged (positive) nucleus of a helium atom. Experiments of Becquerel and others identified the beta particle as the then recently discovered, negatively charged electron.

With the discovery of what has been called "artificial" or induced radioactivity by Irène Curie and her husband Frédérick Joliot in 1933, it was found that positive electron (positron) emission may occur in nuclides whose instability results from the nucleus possessing "too much charge for its mass". This is, of course, only another form of beta emission represented as β^+ whereas ordinary electron emission is represented as β^-.

LE 2   Teilen Sie in Engl. mit,

  1. was unter Radioaktivität zu verstehen ist;
  2. wodurch sich Alpha-, Beta- und Gamma-Strahlen unterscheiden;
  3. womit die Emission dieser Strahlenarten verbunden ist.

Stützen Sie sich dabei auf folgende Informationen:

1. Eine Reihe von Kernen, die als Radionuklide bezeichnet werden, sind von Natur aus instabil. Nach der Emission eines Teilchens aus dem Kern wandeln sich diese in andere Kerne um. Diese Erscheinung wird als Radioaktivität bezeichnet. Mit Hilfe der für den radioaktiven Prozeß benötigten Zeit können die Radionuklide charakterisiert werden.

2. Die Strahlen, die beim radioaktiven Prozeß auftreten, werden als Alpha-, Beta- und Gamma-Strahlen unterschieden. Die Alpha-Strahlen sind schnelle, positiv geladene Heliumkerne, die Beta-Strahlen sind Elektronen und die Gamma-Strahlen sind Photonen hoher Energie. Da die Gamma-Strahlen nicht geladen sind, werden sie in einem elektromagnetischen Feld nicht abgelenkt, während die Alpha- und die Beta-Strahlen in unterschiedliche Richtungen abgelenkt werden.

3. Die Emission eines Alphateilchens wandelt das emittierende Atom in das Atom eines anderen Elements um, wobei die Ordnungszahl um 2 und die Massenzahl um 4 reduziert wird. Elektronen bilden sich im Kern, wenn sich ein Neutron in ein Proton umwandelt, wodurch es zur Emission eines Betateilchens kommt und die Ordnungszahl erhöht wird. In künstlichen Radionukliden wandeln sich auch Protonen in Neutronen um, was zur Emission von Positronen führt. Gamma-Strahlung tritt auf, wenn ein Elektron der K-Schale in den Kern übergeht und ein Hüllenelektron einer äußeren Schale auf die K-Schale springt.

PK 7 . PA 2 · SQ A

LE 0 Wortschatz zur Wiederholung

attention: Aufmerksamkeit / to burn: (ver)brennen / destruction: Zerstörung / engine: Maschine; Motor / peaceful: friedlich / per cent: Prozent / to put, put, put: setzen, stellen, legen / to rely on: sich verlassen auf / weapon: Waffe

LE 1 Neue Lexik

fission	['fiʃən]	(phys.) Spaltung, Teilung
breakup	['breikʌp]	Aufbrechen, Aufspaltung
medium	['mi:djəm]	Subst. Mittel, Medium; Adj. mittel-, mittlere(r, s)
to release	[ri'li:s]	(chem., phys.) freisetzen
to decay	[di'kei]	(phys.) zerfallen
spontaneous	[spɔn'teinjəs]	spontan, selbständig, Selbst-
fissionable	['fiʃ(ə)nəbl]	spaltbar
co-worker	['kou'wə:kə]	Mitarbeiter(in)
to irradiate	[i'reidieit]	bestrahlen; beschießen
activity	[æk'tiviti]	Aktivität; Radioaktivität; Wirksamkeit
capture	['kæptʃə]	(Neutronen)Einfang
to remain	[ri'mein]	(zurück)bleiben, (übrig)bleiben
merely	['miəli]	nur, lediglich, bloß
in fact	[in 'fækt]	tatsächlich, wirklich
chain-reaction	['tʃeinri'ækʃən]	Kettenreaktion
basic	['beisik]	grundlegend, fundamental, Grund-
feature	['fi:tʃə]	charakteristischer (wichtiger) (Bestand)Teil; Grundzug, Merkmal
chance	[tʃa:ns]	Möglichkeit, Wahrscheinlichkeit
to escape	[is'keip]	entweichen, entkommen
critical	['kritikəl]	kritisch

to lower	[ˈlouə]	senken, erniedrigen
to mix	[miks]	(ver)mischen; sich mischen
to slow down	[ˈslou ˈdaun]	(ab)bremsen; verzögern
solution	[səˈlu:ʃən]	(chem., math.) Lösung

LE 2   Internationalismen

fragment	[ˈfrægmənt]	Bruchstück; Spaltprodukt; (Bruch)Teil
radiochemical	[ˈreidiouˈkemikəl]	radiochemisch
radiochemist	[ˈreidiouˈkemist]	Radiochemiker
reactor	[ri(:)ˈæktə]	Reaktor
reaction	[ri(:)ˈækʃən]	(chem.) Reaktion; Reaktion, Gegenwirkung
minimum	[ˈminiməm]	Subst. Minimum Adj. minimal, kleinster, Mindest-
graphite	[ˈgræfait]	Graphit
moderator	[ˈmodəreitə]	Bremssubstanz, Moderator

LE 3   Der dt. Ausdruck 'sowohl ... als auch' kann in folgender Weise ins Engl. übersetzt werden:
sowohl Metalle als auch Nichtmetalle = both metals and non-metals /
metals as well as non-metals

 Beantworten Sie die Fragen nach einem der beiden Muster:

T: Did Marie Curie discover polonium or radium?
S: She discovered both polonium and radium.

T: Did Marie Curie discover polonium or radium?
S: She discovered polonium as well as radium.

LE 4   Das engl. Äquivalent für 'beziehungsweise' ist *respectively*. Es steht meist hinter den beiden durch *and* verbundenen Nomen, gelegentlich auch davor: N + *and* + N, *respectively*

Direct and alternating currents have the symbols DC and AC, respectively.
Gleichstrom und Wechselstrom haben (im Englischen) die Symbole DC bzw. AC.

 Übersetzen Sie ins Engl. nach dem Muster:

T: Optische Mikroskope bzw. Elektronenmikroskope
S: Optical microscopes and electron microscopes, respectively

PK 7 · PA 2 · SQ B

LE 1 | ⊕ ⊕ | Beantworten Sie die Fragen nach dem Muster:

T: Is the power of this engine large? — size —
S: Considering its size, it is.
Die dt. Übersetzungen sind: Berücksichtigt man seine Größe, ja! / In Anbetracht seiner Größe, ja!

range of application / speed / experimental condition / our experimental results / importance

LE 2 | ⊕ ⊕ | Beantworten Sie die Fragen nach dem Muster:

T: Can alpha-particles be deflected? — close to the nucleus —
S: Yes, they can, provided they are close to the nucleus.
Die dt. Übersetzung ist: Ja, vorausgesetzt sie sind dicht beim Kern.

pass through a crystal / be ionized / potential difference / charge carrier / test charge

LE 3 | ⊕ ⊕ | Beantworten Sie die Fragen nach dem Muster:

T: How can atomic properties be explained? — methods of quantum mechanics —
S: They can be explained, using the methods of quantum mechanics.

a high potential difference / their different physical properties / wave concept / the free electron model / electric field concept

LE 4 | ⊕ ⊕ | Beantworten Sie die Fragen nach dem Muster:

T^1: In 1885 Balmer studied the line spectrum of hydrogen.
T^2: And were the line spectra of other elements also studied?
S: Following Balmer's study, the line spectra of other elements were also studied.
Die dt. Übersetzung ist: Im Anschluß an Balmers Untersuchungen wurden auch die Linienspektren anderer Elemente untersucht.

de Broglie's suggestion / Thomson's discovery / Becquerel's discovery / Bohr's paper / Chadwick's discovery

LE 5 | ⊕ ⊕ | Übersetzen Sie ins Engl. nach den Mustern:

T: mit Hilfe der Quantentheorie der Strahlung
S: using the quantum theory of radiation

T: nach der Entdeckung der Radioaktivität
S: following the discovery of radioactivity

PK 7 · PA 2 · SQ C

LE 1   Lesen Sie den folgenden Text, und beantworten Sie danach die Fragen am Ende des Textes:

Radioactivity

Radioactivity is the term applied to the spontaneous disintegration (Zerfall) of atomic nuclei. It was one of the first and most important phenomena which led to our present understanding of nuclear structure.

A discussion of radioactivity requires that mention be made of the stability of nuclei. Stable species or nuclides exist for all elements having proton numbers in the range from 1 to 83, with the exception of the elements 43 and 61 (technetium and promethium). In general, elements having even atomic numbers have two or more stable isotopes, whereas odd-numbered nuclei never have more than two.

The assumption is usually made that all possible nuclides were formed in the original atomic production processes and that those which remain at the present time do so because of some inherent stability. In general, this stability involves the neutron-proton ratio, and a number of theoretical studies have been carried out to determine the conditions for the maximum stability for nuclei. Stability may be considered from three different standpoints: relative to the size and the number of particles in the nucleus, the ratio of the neutrons and protons in the nucleus, and the ratio of the total mass-energy of the nucleus. A nucleus which is unstable with respect to its size will emit alpha particles whereas a nucleus unstable with respect to its neutron-proton ratio may emit a negative or positive electron or may capture (einfangen) an electron. If a nucleus is unstable with respect to its total energy, the excess energy may be given off as gamma radiation which is electromagnetic in nature. Alpha particles, consisting of two protons and two neutrons, are, with certain exceptions, observed to come only from larger nuclei.

Nuclei with neutron-proton ratios higher than stable nuclei eject a negative electron from the nucleus and are thus transmuted (umwandeln) into a nucleus of the next higher atomic number. If the neutron-proton ratio is low and if there exists a certain minimum mass-energy difference between the unstable nucleus having one less proton, a proton may transform into a neutron, a positive electron (positron), and a neutrino. The positron is then ejected from the nucleus. It should be mentioned also that gamma-radiation is given off following nuclear reactions. Thus a nucleus may change from an unstable to a stable form by one of several decay (Zerfall) processes. It was shown very early that the rate of radioactive decay is proportional to the amount of the radioactive material present.

1. Was wird als Radioaktivität bezeichnet? 2. Welche Elemente sind in ihrer großen Mehrheit stabil? 3. Vom Zahlenverhältnis welcher Kernteilchen hängt die Stabilität ab? 4. Unter welchen Gesichtspunkten kann Stabilität betrachtet werden? 5. Welche Arten von Instabilität bedingen

Alpha-, Beta- oder Gammastrahlung? 6. Welche Kerne emittieren Alphateilchen, Elektronen oder Positronen?

Bereiten Sie die Übersetzung des Textes *"Nuclear Fission"* (7.3.C. – 1.)
vor!

PK 7 . PA 2 · SQ D

LE 1 ⊕ ⊕ Einführung

comparis$\hat{o}$n: Vergleich / to penetrate: durchdringen / with regard to: in bezug auf,
hinsichtlich / aluminium

LE 2 ⊕ ⊕ ⊳ Hören Sie den BTV *"Comparison of Radiations"*, und
machen Sie sich Notizen!

LE 3 ⊳ Geben Sie eine kurze zusammenhängende Darstellung der wesentlichen Informationen in Dt. auf der Basis des Komplexdias!

LE 4 Give a short characterization of the three types of radioactive radiation:

– What do they consist of?
– Compare their ionizing and their penetrating powers.
– How do they differ in their electrical properties?
– How does the emission of these rays influence the emitting nuclides?

PK 7 · PA 3 · SQ A

LE 1 Mit Hilfe des Suffixes *-able* [əbl] können im Engl. Adjektive aus Verben
gebildet werden. Diese Adj. weisen folgende gemeinsamen Bedeutungskomponen-
ten auf:

1. *can(not) be* V-*ed* → (*un*)V-*able* = V-'bar'
    can   be controlled →   controllable = kontrollierbar
    can   be compared →   comparable = vergleichbar
    can(not) be detected → (un)detectable = (nicht) feststellbar
    can   be relied on →   reliable = zuverlässig

2.   *can* V   → V-*able*
      can suit → suitable = geeignet
      can vary → variable = variabel

Die zu 1. gehörenden Adj. sind zahlreicher. Das Adj. *changeable* 'veränderlich' gehört beiden Gruppen an:

      changeable → can be changed / can change

3. Das End-*e* des engl. Verbs muß erhalten bleiben, wenn es für die Aussprache wichtig ist; vergleichen Sie:

      change − changeable   aber: use − usable

LE 2   Eine ähnliche Funktion wie -*able* weist auch -*ible* [əbl] auf. Allerdings ist bei Adj. mit diesem Suffix die Beziehung zum Verb nicht immer deutlich aus der Wortform erkennbar bzw. es existiert kein vergleichbares Verb im Engl.:

(ir)reversible → can(not) be reversed   = (ir)reversibel
reproducible → can   be reproduced = reproduzierbar
permissible   → can   be permitted = zulässig
negligible   → can   be neglected = vernachlässigbar
audible   = hörbar
visible   = sichtbar

LE 3   π—0   Analysieren Sie die folgenden Ausdrücke nach dem angegebenen Muster, und nennen Sie das dt. Äquivalent:

      separable components → the components can be separated
                        = trennbar

1. measurable quantity 2. changeable radius 3. mov(e)able anode 4. rechargeable battery 5. reliable instrument 6. negligible amount 7. reproducible value 8. undistinguishable substances 9. unnoticeable change 10. reversible proess

LE 4   π—0   Zu den Adj. mit -*able* und -*ible* bestehen häufig Subst.

      Bilden Sie Adj. zu den Subst. und nennen Sie die dt. Äquivalente:
      repeatability − repeatable = Wiederholbarkeit, wiederholbar
      flexibility   − flexible   = Flexibilität, flexibel

1. reliability 2. suitability 3. visibility 4. replaceability 5. variability

PK 7 · PA 3 · SQ B

LE 1   Bei den bisher behandelten adverbialen Partizipialkonstruktionen waren deren Handlungsträger mit dem Subj. des Kernsatzes identisch, oder diese beiden Größen schlossen sich doch zumindestens nicht aus. Die Partizipien waren deshalb mit dem Kernsatz "verbunden". Hat das adverbiale Partizip einen eigenen Handlungsträger, so wird es als "unverbunden" bezeichnet. Für die Übersetzung benötigen wir die gleichen Muster wie für das "verbundene Partizip", nur daß die dt. Nebensätze nach 'da', 'als', 'nachdem', 'wobei', 'wodurch' u. a. jetzt ein vom Kernsatz verschiedenes Subj. haben.

1. Die inhaltliche Beziehung zwischen Kernsatz und "unverbundenem Partizip" kann kausal oder temporal sein und wird durch einen dt. Nebensatz mit 'da', 'als', 'nachdem' u. a. wiedergegeben:

> Chemical processes are related only to the outer shell. The nucleus remains unchanged. →
> Chemical processes being related only to the outer shell, the nucleus remains unchanged.
>
> N^1 + *being* + V^1-*ed* + ..., N^2 + V^2 + ...
>
> Da chemische Vorgänge sich nur auf die Außenschale beziehen, bleibt der Kern davon unberührt.

2. In der Mehrzahl der Fälle enthält das "unverbundene Partizip" ein Detail oder eine Untergliederung der Hauptaussage des Satzes, ohne daß eine spezifische inhaltliche Beziehung gegeben wäre. Oft wird das Subj. des Kernsatzes durch den Handlungsträger des Partizips in abgewandelter Form (z. B. als Pronomen) wiederaufgenommen.

> Organic compounds consist of a few elements. −
> The most important ones are carbon, hydrogen, oxygen and nitrogen. →
> Organic compounds consist of a few elements, the most important ones being carbon, hydrogen, oxygen and nitrogen.
> Organische Verbindungen bestehen nur aus einigen Elementen, wobei die wichtigsten Kohlenstoff, Wasserstoff, Sauerstoff und Stickstoff sind.

In einigen Fällen ist auch die Übersetzung mit Hilfe eines Relativsatzes zum Ausdruck des Teilungsverhältnisses möglich:

> Organische Verbindungen bestehen nur aus einigen Elementen, von denen die wichtigsten Kohlenstoff, Wasserstoff, Sauerstoff und Stickstoff sind.

3. Manchmal muß die Partizipialkonstruktion auch mit Hilfe eines zweiten Hauptsatzes übersetzt werden, der mit 'und' angeschlossen werden kann.

LE 2   Übersetzen Sie mit Hilfe der Muster 1.–3. aus LE 1:

1. The thermal conductivity falls when a magnetic field is applied, the effect being analogous to the fall in electrical conductivity. 2. Ordinary hydrogen gas is not made up of free hydrogen atoms, but of hydrogen molecules, each molecule being made up of two atoms. 3. There is considerable use in representing experimental data by means of equations, the correct form of them being often suggested by theoretical considerations. 4. Several methods, some of them based on spectroscopic studies and others involving the behaviour of nuclei in a magnetic field, have been devised for determining nuclear spins. 5. Nuclei with odd mass numbers, and therefore containing an odd number of nucleons have spin quantum numbers of 1/2, 3/2 etc., no value higher than 9/2 having been observed for the ground state of any stable nucleus. 6. The simplest arrangement of all crystals is that which gives cubic crystals, the atoms throughout the crystal being also arranged in little cubes.

LE 3   Als zusätzliches Zeichen der Untergliederung im Satz kann *with* vor die Partizipialkonstruktion gesetzt werden. An die Stelle des Partizips kann in der *with*-Phrase auch ein N^1 + *of* + N^2-Gefüge treten, wobei N^1 einen Vorgang bezeichnet, z. B. *discovery*. Die "*with*-Phrase" erfüllt wie das "unverbundene Partizip" unterschiedliche Funktionen und kann wie dieses in sehr verschiedener Weise ins Dt. übersetzt werden:

> Wenn ... / Bei ...
> Nachdem ... / Nach ...
> wobei / wodurch ...
> deren / dessen ... (Relativsatz)

Dagegen ist die Übersetzung durch 'mit' nur selten möglich.

LE 4   ⊓──O   Übersetzen Sie:

1. Einstein showed that under some circumstances the energy in the radiation field can be considered as concentrated in discrete quanta, with the relation between quantum energy and wave frequency given by the equation $E = h\nu$. 2. Even in the best vacuum, with the pressure reduced to 10^{-9} at or less, 1 cm³ of gas still contains more than 10^{10} molecules. 3. As an atom moves it does not carry its whole charge cloud with it; the free electrons, with their wave functions extending throughout the lattice, tend to form a background gas inside which the ions move.

LE 5   Für Zusammenfassungen, Kurzberichte und andere Mitteilungsformen der wissenschaftlichen Literatur haben sich Satztypen herausgebildet, bei denen ein Vorgang allgemeinen Charakters durch einen stereotypen Satzkern ausgedrückt wird, während die spezifischen Mitteilungselemente in nominaler Form präpositional an diesen Satzkern angeschlossen werden. Entwicklung und Funktionsweise dieser Satzstrukturen kann man sich wie folgt veranschaulichen:

> The ion-exchange behaviour of alkali metal cations was studied.
> A study of the ion-exchange behaviour of alkali metal cations was made.
> A study was made of the ion-exchange behaviour of alkali metal cations.

Die Übersetzung erfolgt meist durch eine unpersönliche Passivkonstruktion:

> Es wurde das Ionenaustauschverhalten von Alkalimetallkationen untersucht.

LE 6 Unterstreichen Sie den Satzkern "N + *be* + V-*ed* + Prep" und übersetzen Sie:

1. Measurements were made of the level of radioactivity in these specimens. 2. Particular attention is given to these problems. 3. An attempt was made to correct these data. 4. Use has been made in various ways of molecular weights in the determination of the atomic weights of the elements. 5. In calculating the nuclear binding energy, consideration must be given to the influence of the odd or even character of the number of protons and neutrons.

LE 7 ⊼—0 Übersetzen Sie nach den Mustern:

> Es wurde eine Reihe solcher Verbindungen untersucht.
> a) A study was made of a number of such compounds.
> b) A study of a number of such compounds was made.

1. Es werden verschiedene Methoden verwendet (to make use of). 2. Es werden die Ergebnisse von zwei Versuchsserien ausgewertet (to make an analysis of). 3. Es wird eine Einführung in die Tieftemperaturphysik gegeben (to give an introduction to). 4. Es wurde versucht, sehr geringe Ionenkonzentrationen nachzuweisen (to make an attempt). 5. Es wurde eine Anzahl von Substanzen untersucht, die ähnliche Eigenschaften haben (to make an investigation of). 6. Am Ende der Arbeit werden einige neu eingeführte Termini definiert (to give a definition of).

PK 7 · PA 3 · SQ C

LE 1 Übersetzen Sie:

Nuclear Fission

Nuclear Fission is the breakup of a heavy nucleus, such as that of uranium, into two medium-weight nuclei, with the release of a considerable quantity of energy. Also produced are a few neutrons, some gamma-rays, and a number of beta-particles (electrons) from the radioactive decay of the two fragments. Fission occurs spontaneously in some cases, or may be induced by bombardment of the fissionable material with neutrons, protons, or other particles.

Although fission was not discovered until 1939 it had been realized, ever since Einstein published his theory of relativity in 1905, that release of very large amounts of energy from matter was theoretically possible.

Fission is now known to have been first discovered by Enrico Fermi and his co-workers in 1934, when they irradiated many elements, including uranium, with the newly discovered neutrons. They found that a number of different beta-activities were produced from uranium, but believed that these were due to neutron capture. Later radiochemical work indicated that some of the new activities were from elements chemically similar to the much lighter elements Ba, La, etc. Fission remained unrecognized until O. Hahn and F. Strassmann, German radiochemists, showed by very careful work that these products were not merely chemically similar to lighter elements, but were in fact lighter elements. It was realized by many that a chain reaction was possible for fission, with the neutrons from each fission producing more fissions, resulting in the release of very large amounts of energy. This chain reaction is the basic feature for both nuclear reactors and nuclear weapons. If there is not enough fissionable material, or it is not arranged closely enough, no chain reaction will be possible. The fission neutrons emitted in such a situation will have too great a chance to escape from the fissionable material, or to be absorbed in nonfissionable material, to continue the chain of fissions should one fission occur.

There is thus a "critical mass", or minimum amount of fissionable material, necessary for a chain reaction in any given arrangement. For a spherical mass of metal in air, the critical mass of highly enriched (94 per cent) U^{235} or Pu^{239} metal is lower, about 16 kg. The critical mass can be lowered by mixing fissionable material with graphite or other material as a "moderator" to slow down the neutrons. The smallest critical masses are achieved by water (or heavy water) solutions of fissionable material, since H and D are most effective in slowing down neutrons.

LE 2 Übertragen Sie die wesentlichen Informationen dieses Textes in 8 – 10 Sätzen ins Engl.:

Kernspaltung

Die Spaltung eines schweren Atomkerns unter Einwirkung eines Elementarteilchens oder eines Gamma-Quants bezeichnet man als Kernspaltung. Die erste künstliche Kernreaktion erzielte Rutherford 1919, als er Stickstoff ($^{14}_{7}N$) mit den Alphastrahlen von Radium C' beschoß. Ähnliche Resultate wurden später auch beim Beschuß anderer leichter Elemente mit Alphastrahlen erzielt. So hatte man eine Möglichkeit gefunden, mit Hilfe von Alphastrahlen Kernreaktionen auszulösen.

Nach der Entdeckung des Neutrons durch den britischen Physiker Chadwick (1932) unternahmen viele Physiker Versuche, in denen sie Atomkerne mit Neutronen beschossen. Im Jahre 1934 ließ der Physiker Fermi Neutronen auf Atomkerne des schwersten natürlich vorkommenden Elements Uran treffen. Die deutschen Wissenschaftler Otto Hahn und Fritz Strassmann wiederholten die Versuche

Fermis. 1938 fanden sie nach intensiven physikalischen Versuchen, daß bei dem Beschuß der Urankerne mit Neutronen neue Atomkerne entstehen. Die Kernladungszahlen dieser Atomkerne entsprachen denen der Elemente in der Mitte des Periodischen Systems. Sie betrugen also etwa die Hälfte der Kernladungszahl des Urankerns. Die Mitarbeiterin Hahns, Lisa Meitner, fand hierfür die Erklärung: Bei der Kernspaltung zerfällt ein Atomkern in zwei, etwa gleich große Bruchstücke, die meist radioaktiv sind.

PK 7 · PA 4 · SQ A

LE 0   Wortschatz zur Wiederholung

above: oberhalb, über / broad: breit / dark: dunkel / especially: besonders / to keep, kept, kept (up): (aufrecht) (er)halten, behalten / means: Mittel, Instrument / pound: Pfund / to secure: sicherstellen, sichern

LE 1   ⊕ ⊕   Neue Lexik

interaction	[ˌintərˈækʃən]	Wechselwirkung, gegenseitige Beeinflussung
to investigate	[inˈvestigeit]	untersuchen, Untersuchungen anstellen
to yield	[jiːld]	ergeben, liefern
accurate	[ˈækjurit]	genau, sorgfältig; richtig, exakt
concerning	[kənˈsəːniŋ]	in bezug / Hinsicht auf, hinsichtlich, bezüglich
environment	[inˈvaiərənmənt]	Umgebung; Umwelt
major	[ˈmeidʒə]	größere(r,s); wichtig; wesentlich, Haupt-
to subdivide	[ˈsʌbdiˈvaid]	unterteilen, untergliedern; aufteilen
fairly	[ˈfɛəli]	ziemlich, verhältnismäßig, relativ
overlap	[ˈouvəlæp]	Überlagerung, Überlappung
to overlap	[ˌouvəˈlæp]	sich überlagern, überlappen, übergreifen
inner	[ˈinə]	innere(r, s), Innen-
irradiation	[iˌreidiˈeiʃən]	Bestrahlung, Einstrahlung
expulsion	[iksˈpʌlʃən]	Abstoßung; Entfernung
to excite	[ikˈsait]	(phys.) anregen, (el.) erregen
to absorb	[əbˈsɔːb]	absorbieren; aufnehmen
as a result of	[riˈzʌlt]	als Ergebnis; als Folge; auf Grund
excitation	[ˌeksiˈteiʃən]	Anregung, Erregung
region	[ˈriːdʒən]	Bereich, Bezirk; Zone, Gebiet

to saturate	[ˈsætʃəreit]	(ab)sättigen
analysis	[əˈnælisis]	Analyse, Untersuchung; Auswertung
organic	[ɔːˈgænik]	organisch
scope	[skoup]	Bereich, Gebiet; Spielraum
infrared	[ˈinfrəˈred)	Infrarot
microwave	[ˈmaikrouweiv]	Mikrowelle

LE 2 ⊕ ⊕ Internationalismen

spectroscopy	[spekˈtrɔskəpi]	Spektroskopie
fluorescence	[fluəˈresns]	Fluoreszenz
ultraviolet	[ˈʌltrəˈvaiəlit]	Ultraviolett; ultraviolett
complex	[ˈkɔmpleks]	komplex, zusammengesetzt; kompliziert
quantitative	[ˈkwɔntitətiv]	quantitativ
qualitative	[ˈkwɔlitətiv]	qualitativ
internuclear	[ˌintəˈnjuːkliə]	internuklear, Kern

LE 3 ⊕ ⊕ Beantworten Sie die Fragen nach dem Muster:

> T: Is this process reversible?
> S: Yes, it can be reversed.

LE 4 ⊕ ⊕ Beantworten Sie die Fragen nach dem Muster:

> T: Is this solid flexible?
> S: Yes, it has a high flexibility.

PK 7 · PA 4 · SQ B

LE 1 ⊕ ⊕ Wiederholen Sie die folgenden Ausdrücke und die entsprechenden Verben

to make use of	= to use
to make a study of	= to study
to make an analysis of	= to analyse
to take a measurement of	= to measure
to make an investigation of	= to investigate
to make a test on	= to test
to draw conclusions as to	= to conclude
to make reference to	= to refer to
to give consideration to	= to consider

LE 2 ⊕ ⊕ Beantworten Sie Fragen mit Hilfe der soeben geübten verbalen Ausdrücke nach dem Muster:

T: Did he make use of these data?
S: Yes, use was made of them.

LE 3 ⊕ ⊕ Beantworten Sie die Fragen nach dem Muster:

T: Are these data important? Will you consider them?
S: Well, I think, consideration should be given to them.

to give consideration to / to make an investigation of / to make mention of / to make reference to / to make use of

LE 4 ⊕ ⊕ Reagieren Sie nach dem Muster:

T: We need the characteristics of these substances.
  We want to study them.
S: But studies have already been made of them.

to make a study of / to take measurements of / to make tests on / to make an analysis of / to make investigations of

LE 5 ⊕ ⊕ Beantworten Sie die Fragen nach dem Muster:

T: What kind of study was made?
S: A study was made of the change in conductivity.

LE 6 ⊕ ⊕ Reagieren Sie nach dem Muster:

T: They made a study of radioactive phenomena — to give consideration to —
S: In this connection consideration must be given to the proton-neutron ratio.

PK 7 · PA 4 · SQ C

LE 1 Lesen Sie den Text und unterstreichen Sie die wichtigen Informationen. Geben Sie auf dieser Grundlage eine kurze dt. Inhaltsangabe in Stichpunkten und nach Hauptinformationen gegliedert:

Nuclear Fusion

It was realized by Einstein at the beginning of this century that mass could be transformed into energy and that the destruction of only a very small quantity of matter was a practicable source of great power. This has been put into practical use in the power reactor and is known as fission. The energy is released in the form of energetic neutrons and finally appears as heat.

Since the medium mass nuclei are the most tightly bound (i.e. have the smallest ratio of actual to nominal atomic weight), it is possible to release energy also by fusing (verschmelzen) together lighter elements. We are familiar with the immense power produced by these processes in the sun. The major problem in the peaceful application is to release energy with laboratory-size apparatus slowly and in a controlled way.

Unless (wenn nicht) their separation is very small, the nuclei of the light elements are repelled (abstoßen) from each other by electrostatic forces. Very high velocities of approach are required to overcome these electrostatic "barriers" and, if the reacting particles are in the form of a gas, this corresponds to a very high temperature. At such a temperature all the gas atoms are ionized and the mixture of ions and gas atoms is called a plasma. The electrostatic forces increase as the square (Quadrat, 2. Potenz) of the atomic number and so reactions between only the very lightest elements may be used. The reactions with probabilities sufficiently (ausreichend) high for power productions are

$$D + D \rightarrow He^3 + n + 3.25 \text{ MeV}$$

$$D + D \rightarrow T + p + 4.0 \text{ MeV}$$

$$D + T \rightarrow He^4 + n + 17.6 \text{ MeV}$$

When considering a thermonuclear reactor the energy release must be balanced against the energy required to heat the plasma, and the losses (Verlust). To achieve power balance, it is necessary also that at least about 1 per cent of the fuel is "burned" before being lost from the system. This results in the condition that the product of the density and the average lifetime of an ion must be greater than 10^{14} sec/cm^3 for the D, T reaction or 10^{16} sec/cm^3 for the D, D reaction. The problem of thermonuclear power production is therefore twofold (zweifach): to heat particles to a sufficiently high temperature, and to contain a sufficient number of them for long enough to achieve power balance.

Bereiten Sie die Übersetzung des Textes "*Spectroscopy*" (8.1.C.−1.) vor!

PK 7 · PA 4 · SQ D

LE 1 | ⊕ ⊕ | Einführung:

target nucleus: Target / acceleration: Beschleunigung

LE 2 | ⊕ ⊕ |▷| | Hören Sie den BTV "*Nuclear Reactions*" und machen Sie sich Notizen!

LE 3 ⊳ ☐ Geben Sie eine kurze zusammenhängende Darstellung der wesentlichen Informationen in Dt. auf der Basis des Komplexdias!

LE 4 Speak about nuclear fission and nuclear fusion as sources of energy:

— Why will nuclear energy play an ever increasing role?
— Compare nuclear energy with the traditional fuels (coal, oil).
— Where are nuclear power stations in the GDR?
— What do you know about international co-operation in the field of nuclear energy?

Spectroscopy and Optical Properties of Materials

PK 8 · PA 1 · SQ A

LE 1 Das Verb *to appear* tritt in physikalischen Texten in mehreren Bedeutungsvarianten und syntaktischen Strukturen auf.

1. Das Verb *to appear* dient der Bezeichnung eines subjektiven Eindrucks, den
objektive Fakten beim Beobachter hervorrufen. Dieser Tatbestand kann durch
folgende syntaktische Varianten ausgedrückt werden:

a) *It appears that ...*

> It appears that most of the positive charge is concentrated near the nucleus
> of the atom.
> Es scheint so, daß der größte Teil der positiven Ladung in der Nähe des
> Atomkerns konzentriert ist. / Offenbar ist der größte Teil der positiven
> Ladung in der Nähe des Atomkerns konzentriert.

b) $N^1 + appear + to + V + N^2 + ...$

> All K-mesons appear to have the same mass, which is 966 times greater
> than that of the electron.
> Alle K-Mesonen haben offenbar (Offenbar haben ...) die gleiche Masse,
> die 966 Mal größer ist als die Masse des Elektrons. = sichere Annahme /
> Alle K-Mesonen scheinen die gleiche Masse zu haben ... (Es scheint, als
> ob ...) = Vermutung

c) *It appears from the table | ... that ... From this appears that ...*

> It appears from the above table that the data obtained in the second
> experiment were more accurate than those of the first.
> Aus der oben angeführten Tabelle ... / Daraus ergibt sich, daß im zweiten
> Versuch genauere Werte erhalten wurden als im ersten.
> Daraus ist zu ersehen, daß ...
> Es / So zeigt sich, daß ...

2. Das Verb *to appear* dient zur Bezeichnung der objektiven Existenz einer Sache
oder Erscheinung an einem bestimmten Ort.

> In a mass spectrograph the record appears on a photographic plate.
> In Massenspektrographen erscheinen die Informationsprodukte auf einer
> photographischen Platte.
> Sie treten auf ... / sind vorhanden ...

3. Das Verb *to appear* bezeichnet den Zustand oder die Form, in der ein Gegenstand oder eine (materielle) Erscheinung auftritt.

> In the absorption spectrum of sunlight the elements appear as characteristic dark lines.
> Im Absorptionsspektrum des Sonnenlichtes treten die Elemente als charakteristische dunkle Linien auf.
> Sie erscheinen als ...

LE 2 ⊤—0 Übersetzen Sie mit Hilfe dieser Varianten:
1. In nature energy appears in many forms. 2. The data are in good agreement. This appears clearly in the table shown above. 3. When light with a continuous spectrum falls on a substance in which it is not absorbed, it appears white. 4. The whole process appears to take place in three steps. 5. The essential importance of a radiation field appears to lie in its effects upon the motion of charged particles. 6. Diffraction effects have been observed with streams of hydrogen and helium ions. It thus appears that these particles also have wave properties.

LE 3 Die inhaltliche Funktion des "verbundenen" Perfektpartizips "V-*ed*" kann durch die vorangestellte Konjunktion *as* in der Struktur *as* + V-*ed* konkretisiert werden.

1. Für "*as* + V-*ed*" gibt es mehrere Übersetzungsmöglichkeiten.

a) Es schließt sich an den Kernsatz an und bezieht sich auf den Gesamtinhalt des Kernsatzes:

> The Lorentz theory was used to explain the effect of a magnetic field in splitting spectral lines as observed by Zeeman.
> ... (so) wie dies von Zeemann beobachtet wurde.

b) Nachgestelltes "*as* + V-*ed*" kann auch durch eine verkürzte Partizipialkonstruktion wiedergegeben werden:

> The technique was used in the same way as described above.
> ... (so) wie oben beschrieben.

c) Vorangestelltes "*as* + V-*ed*" bezieht sich auf das Subj. des Kernsatzes:

> As found in nature, uranium contains three isotopic forms with mass numbers of 234, 235, and 238.
> Uran, wie es in der Natur vorkommt, besteht aus drei Isotopenformen mit den Massenzahlen 234, 235 und 238.

2. In manchen Fällen lassen sich durch "*as* + V-*ed*" eingeleitete Satzteile am besten durch feste adverbielle Wendungen bzw. präpositionale Wortgruppen wiedergeben.

> a) The temperature must be kept constant while the pressure may be varied, as required.
> Die Temperatur muß konstant gehalten werden, während der Druck entsprechend verändert werden kann.

b) Nuclear energy changes are of the order of millions of electron volts as compared with one or two electron volts for chemical reactions.
Veränderungen in der Kernenergie haben Größenordnungen von Millionen Elektronenvolt im Vergleich zu / verglichen mit ein bis zwei Elektronenvolt bei chemischen Reaktionen.

LE 4   Übersetzen Sie mit Hilfe dieser Muster:

1. As already noted, there is a magnetic moment, $1_{\mu B}$ associated with an electron's atomic quantum state. 2. No more than one electron can occupy each possible energy state, as defined by the four quantum numbers. 3. Isotopic weights as determined by the mass spectrograph and other methods, are close to whole numbers but they nearly always differ from integers by small amounts. 4. The results of the two experimental series are represented in tables as shown above. 5. The experiments were carried out using the same techniques as described by Fairhall.

PK 8 · PA 1 · SQ B

LE 1   Die Form "V-*ing*" kann präpositional als Bestimmung an ein Nomen angeschlossen werden. Die Struktur N + *of* / *for* + V-*ing* + ... wird als "attributives Gerundium" bezeichnet.

Für die Übersetzung gibt es folgende Varianten:

a) Uranium salts have the property *of* emitting rays.
Uransalze haben die Eigenschaft, Strahlen zu emittieren.

b) An ammeter is an instrument *for* measuring electric current.
Ein Amperemeter ist ein Instrument (,)
      zur Messung von elektrischem Strom /
      für die Messung von elektrischem Strom /
      um elektrischen Strom zu messen.

LE 2   Übersetzen Sie:

1. Slow neutrons have a high probability of producing fission of U^{235}. 2. The main criterion for classifying an element in one group or the other of the Periodic Table is its chemical properties, especially the nature of its oxides. 3. An electrometer is an instrument for detecting or measuring potential differences by means of the mechanical or electrostatic forces exerted between electrically charged bodies. 4. The centimeter-gram-second system of units is an absolute system for measuring physical quantities. 5. The cyclotron is an instrument developed in 1931 for the purpose of obtaining a beam of charged atomic particles travelling at high speed.

LE 3 ⇥—0 Bilden Sie Sätze mit der Struktur "N + *of* / *for* + V-*ing* + ..."
nach dem Muster:

Scientists developed a new method ...
measure — amount — ionization
... for measuring the amount of ionization.

1. analyse — structure — unknown — substance
2. measure — wavelength — spectral — line
3. investigate — property — radioactive — element
4. measure — quantity — electric — charge
5. detect — ionizing — particle — in — gas
6. distinguish — isotope — same — element

LE 4 Eine weitere substantivierte *ing*-Form kann — wie ein echtes Substantiv —
den bestimmten oder den unbestimmten Artikel, ein Demonstrativpronomen oder
ein Adj. vor sich haben und ein Substantiv mit *of* anschließen. Jedoch bilden diese
ing-Formen im Gegensatz zu den Substantiven vom Typ *building* keinen Plural.
Sie werden gelegentlich von den Gerundien unterschieden und als "Verbalsubstan-
tiv" bezeichnet. Vgl.:

by carefully learning English
by the careful learning of English

Der Gebrauch dieser *ing*-Form wird durch die zahlreichen Substantive eingeschränkt, die wie *conduction, formation, application, measurement* u. a. durch
Wortbildung aus Verben entstanden sind. Sie wird u. a. von den Verben *understand, split* (spalten) und *scatter* gebildet.

LE 5 Übersetzen Sie nach dem Muster:

The theory of atomic structure provided the basis for an understanding of
the nature of chemical reactions.
Die Theorie des Atomaufbaus lieferte die Grundlage für ein Verständnis
des Wesens chemischer Reaktionen / die Grundlage dafür, das Wesen
chemischer Reaktionen zu verstehen.

1. Rutherford's former co-worker Hans Geiger conducted extensive studies of the
scattering of alpha particles. 2. Excitation is the raising of an atom from its normal
quantum state or energy level to a higher quantum state or energy level. 3. A knowledge of the elements of mechanics is necessary for an understanding of the funda-
mentals of physics. 4. The splitting of a uranium nucleus has two important
effects: the release of energy and the release of neutrons. 5. The charged particles
formed in electrolytes by the breaking up of molecules are called ions. 6. Nuclear
fission is the splitting of an atomic nucleus into two fragments of more or less
equal mass, as a result of the capture of a bombarding neutron.

PK 8 · PA 1 · SQ C

LE 1   Übersetzen Sie:

Spectroscopy

Spectroscopy is the branch of science in which the interaction of energy between electromagnetic radiation and matter is investigated. It is one of the few branches of science which yield, directly, accurate information concerning the nature of substances in their own environment. It has been practically the only experimental method until recently for obtaining information from outer space. Its importance as a major experimental method in physics, chemistry and other sciences, can be demonstrated by the wide range of problems which can be solved with its technique.

The broad field of spectroscopy can be subdivided in various ways, e.g. according to the energy (or frequency) range of the electromagnetic radiation studied or according to the nature of the transition involved. Several processes which result in absorption or emission of energy may occur within an atom or molecule, but it is interesting to note that each process is associated with a fairly definite frequency range, with very little overlap. At very high frequencies or high energies, the transitions involve changes in the atomic nucleus and are independent of the environment of the nucleus. At slightly lower energy, inner shell electronic transitions occur. Irradiation of a material with X-rays results in expulsion of electrons from the inner shells and then emission of X-rays as the electrons return to their normal states (X-ray fluorescence).

The frequency of the radiation emitted when outer-shell electrons, which have been excited, return to their ground states depends on the element involved and is usually independent of chemical state.

Molecules absorb radiation in the far ultraviolet, ultraviolet and visible regions, as a result of the excitation of outer shell electrons. The absorption spectra in these regions are useful in studying the electronic states of small or unsaturated molecules and they are a useful means of studying unsaturated organic compounds or inorganic complex ions.

In order to indicate the broad scope of spectroscopy, some of the types of information which can be obtained and the experimental methods used for obtaining them may be indicated. Thus studies in the ultraviolet, visible, microwave and radio frequency regions have all found use in qualitative and quantitative analysis. Microwave spectroscopy, for example, provides probably the most accurate method of determining internuclear distances in certain types of molecules.

LE 2   ☛—0   Übertragen Sie die Informationen des folgenden Textes ins Engl.: Die elektromagnetischen Wellen unterscheiden sich in ihren Wellenlängen und in ihren Wirkungen. Der Wissenschaftszweig, in dem die Wechselwirkung von

elektromagnetischer Strahlung und Materie untersucht wird, wird als Spektroskopie
bezeichnet. Die spektroskopischen Verfahren liefern genaue Informationen über
die untersuchten Substanzen in einer bestimmten Umgebung. Die Spektroskopie
wird nach den Frequenzbereichen der elektromagnetischen Strahlungen unterteilt.
Die verschiedenen Vorgänge in den atomaren und molekularen Strukturen, die
zur Absorption und Emission von Energie führen, sind mit bestimmten Frequenzbereichen verbunden, die sich kaum überschneiden. Die Wechselwirkung von
elektromagnetischen Wellen mit kristallinen Materialien wird in der Kristalloptik
untersucht. Im allgemeinen wird jedoch der Begriff der Kristalloptik nur auf den
Spektralbereich des sichtbaren Lichts angewendet. Man erhält das Spektrum des
sichtbaren Lichts, indem man weißes Licht durch ein Beugungsgitter oder ein
Prisma (prism) schickt.

PK 8 · PA 2 · SQ A

LE 0   Wortschatz zur Wiederholung

engineer: Ingenieur, Techniker / to happen: (zufällig) geschehen, sich ergeben;
sich ereignen, vorfallen / history: Geschichte, Entwicklung / to prevent from:
hindern an / to stop: (+ Gerund.) aufhören, einstellen; aufhalten, unterbrechen;
(+ Inf.) (an-/inne)halten

LE 1   ⊕ ⊕   Neue Lexik

to initiate	[i'niʃieit]	einleiten, in Gang setzen, hervor-rufen
stress	[stres]	(techn.) Beanspruchung, Belastung
tube	[tju:b]	(techn.) Rohr, Röhre
to take + Zeitangabe		dauern, in Anspruch nehmen
phosphorus	['fɔsfərəs]	Phosphor
energy gap	['enədʒi 'gæp]	Energielücke, verbotene Zone
to coat	[kout]	beschichten, mit einem Überzug versehen, belegen
glow	[glou]	Glimmen; Glühen, Leuchten
mercury	['mə:kjuri]	Quecksilber
discharge	[dis'tʃa:dʒ]	(el.) Entladung
otherwise	['ʌðəwaiz]	sonst, anderenfalls
to prefer	[pri'fə:]	vorziehen, bevorzugen, bevorzugt etw. tun
to descend (to)	[di'send]	herab-, heruntersenken, herabfallen (auf)
possibility	[ˌpɔsi'biliti]	Möglichkeit

to radiate	['reidieit]	(ab)strahlen, (Strahlen) emittieren, aussenden; (Licht, Wärme etc.) ausstrahlen
infrequent	[in'fri:kwənt]	selten
except for	[ik'sept]	außer, mit Ausnahme von, bis auf
to trap	[træp]	einfangen; auffangen
eventually	[i'ventjuəli]	schließlich, endlich
thermal	['θə:məl]	thermisch, Wärme-, Thermo-
to give off		abgeben (Elektronen, Energie)
(in)coherent	[(ˌin)kou'hiərənt]	(in)kohärent
phase	[feiz]	Phase
to be out of phase		ungleichphasig sein
to stimulate	['stimjuleit]	anregen (Strahlung etc.)
abbreviation	[əˌbri:vi'eiʃən]	Abkürzung (von Wörtern etc.)
amplification	[ˌæmplifi'keiʃən]	(el.) Verstärkung

LE 2 ⊕ ⊕ Internationalismen

luminescence	[ˌlu:mi'nesns]	Lumineszenz
luminescent	[ˌlu:mi'nesnt]	lumineszierend, Lumineszenz-, Leucht-
fluorescent	[fluə'resnt]	fluoreszierend, fluoreszent, Leucht(stoff)-
activator	['æktiveitə]	Aktivator
phosphorescent	[ˌfɔsfə'resnt]	phosphoreszierend
laser	['leizə]	Laser

LE 3 ⊕ ⊕ Beantworten Sie die Fragen nach dem Muster:

T: Why is it necessary to have imperfections in the crystal of semiconductors? — conductivity
S: Because their conductivity is dependent on imperfections.

absorption — wavelength / stability — proton-neutron ratio / fluorescence — absorption of radiation / conductivity — temperature / orbit — energy level

LE 4 ⊕ ⊕ Beantworten Sie die Fragen nach dem Muster:

T: Why can the temperature of radioactive substances be neglected? — radioactivity
S: Because radioactivity is independent of temperature.

charge of the nucleus — number of neutrons / mass — attraction of the earth / magnetic field — conductor / acceleration — mass of falling bodies / frequency of the radiation — chemical state

LE 5 ⊕ ⊕ Beantworten Sie die Fragen nach dem Muster:

T: How does nuclear fission start? − neutron capture
S: It starts as the result of neutron capture.

PK 8 · PA 2 · SQ B

LE 1 ⊕ ⊕ Beantworten Sie die Fragen nach dem Muster:

T: How is it possible to determine internuclear distances?
S: There is a special method of determining these distances.

to excite atoms / to measure the wavelength / to control a nuclear reaction / to investigate organic molecules / to determine the effect

LE 2 ⊕ ⊕ Beantworten Sie die Fragen nach dem Muster:

T: Can this effect be achieved only in this way?
S: No, there are different ways of achieving this effect.

to increase the energy level / to excite crystals / to change a magnetic field / to subdivide the field / to do the analysis

LE 3 ⊕ ⊕ Reagieren Sie nach dem Muster:

T: If the energy level is too high, it has to be reduced.
S: Do you know a means for reducing the energy level?

to excite an element / to slow down neutrons / to measure diffraction / to produce high potentials / to accelerate electrons

LE 4 ⊕ ⊕ Übersetzen Sie nach dem Muster:

T: a way of releasing energy
S: eine Möglichkeit, Energie freizusetzen

PK 8 · PA 2 · SQ C

LE 1 Lesen Sie den folgenden Text und unterstreichen Sie die wichtigsten Informationen. Untergliedern Sie den Text nach Hauptinformationen und geben Sie auf dieser Grundlage eine Zusammenfassung in Dt.:

Crystal Optics

The whole field of the interaction of crystalline matter with electromagnetic radiation could be looked upon as crystal optics. More usually, the term is restricted (beschränken) to the wavelength within the visible spectrum. Within this limitation crystal optics can be divided into phenomena associated with the transmission of light through the crystal and phenomena associated with the reflection of light by an opaque (lichtundurchlässig) crystal. The latter effects, although interesting theoretically, are not so important practically as the optical transmission properties of crystalline matter. Concerning the propagation (Ausbreitung) of light through the solid, crystalline matter can be divided into two categories. In the first — the isotropic media — unpolarized light is transmitted unchanged along any wave normal (Wellenfrontnormale) direction in the crystal with a velocity that is characteristic of the material but which is independent of the direction of propagation. In such materials, the optical properties are in all respects similar to the well-known optical properties of glass and other non-crystalline substances. Only crystalline material belonging to the most symmetrical cubic system is optically isotropic.

Crystalline matter classified into one of the other six crystal system is optically anisotropic. In general, there are within an anisotropic crystal two different optical disturbances associated with each wave normal direction of propagation; these two disturbances are plane (linear) polarized perpendicular (senkrecht) to each other, and one or both of them travel with speeds dependent on the direction of propagation. Unpolarized light entering an anisotropic crystal is split into two disturbances sharing a common wave normal direction but plane polarized in perpendicular planes. Further the ray directions associated with the wave fronts are not always in the wave normal direction: this leads to the formation of two images (Abbild) of an object viewed through the anisotropic crystal, known as double refraction (Brechung). There are propagation directions, however, for which no double refraction occurs and for which unpolarized light is transmitted unchanged; these directions are called the optical axes of the crystal.

Bereiten Sie die Übersetzung des Textes *"Optical Properties of Materials"* (8.3.C. – 1.) vor!

PK 8 · PA 2 · SQ D

LE 1 | ⊕ ⊕ | Einführung

not until: erst / prism: Prisma / refraction index: Brechungsindex / to be faced with: konfrontiert werden mit

LE 2 | ⊕ ⊕ |⊃▷| | Hören Sie den BTV *"Spectroscopy"* und machen Sie sich Notizen!

11*

8.3.

LE 3 ⤳▷☐ Geben Sie eine kurze zusammenhängende Darstellung der wesentlichen Informationen in Dt. auf der Basis des Komplexdias!

LE 4 Give a summary of the text *"Crystal Optics"* (8.2.C. −1.) on the basis of the following questions:

– How can the field of crystal optics be defined?

investigation of interaction of crystalline matter with electromagnetic radiation / particularly in the range of the visible spectrum

– Which properties of crystalline matter are especially important in this respect?

optical properties in the transmission of light

– What are the two categories of crystalline matter in crystal optics?

isotropic and anisotropic media

– What are the main features of isotropic media?

unpolarized light is transmitted unchanged / velocity is characteristic of the material / optical properties similar to those of glass

– What are the main features of anisotropic media?

two different optical disturbance / one or both with speeds dependent on the direction / two images of an object seen through an anisotropic crystal due to double refraction

PK 8 · PA 3 · SQ A

LE 1 In der Fachsprache ist es mitunter notwendig, einen Gegenstand oder einen Vorgang unter dem Aspekt einer bestimmten Annahme, Hypothese oder Theorie darzustellen. Hierfür werden eine Reihe von Verben mit nachfolgendem *as* benutzt.

to regard as to consider as	betrachten als, ansehen als
to describe as to represent as to picture as	beschreiben als, darstellen als
to imagine as to think of as	sich vorstellen als
to interpret as	deuten, darstellen, interpretieren als

Diese Verben werden in zwei syntaktischen Strukturen verwendet:

a) Physicists regard   the electron   as (an)   elementary particle.
   N^1 + V + N^2 + *as* + N^3
   Physiker betrachten   das Elektron als (ein) Elementarteilchen.

b) The electron is   regarded as (an) elementary particle.
   N^2 + *be* + V-*ed as* + N^3
   Das Elektron wird   als ein Elementarteilchen betrachtet.

LE 2 Auf der Grundlage dieser auch in der dt. Übersetzung übersichtlichen Struktur haben sich zwei komplizierte Strukturen herausgebildet:

a) Physicists regard the electron

   N^1 + V + N^2 +

            as carrying a negative unit charge.
            as + V-*ing* + ...

b) The electron is regarded

   N^2 +   *be* + V-*ed* +

                 as carrying a negative unit charge.
                 as + V-*ing* + ...

Hier tritt an Stelle von ... + *as* + N → ... + *as* + V-*ing* + ...

LE 3 Es gibt folgende Übersetzungsmöglichkeiten:

1. Oft ist es zweckmäßig, ein Substantiv (Nomen) nach "V + *as*" einzufügen, auf das sich das Präsenspartizip "V-*ing*" mit den nachfolgenden Satzgliedern als Attribut beziehen kann. Das Substantiv muß eine inhaltliche Anknüpfung an den Kernsatz erlauben (verallgemeinernde Bedeutung):

   a) Physicists regard the electron as [a particle]
   carrying a negative unit charge.
   Die Physiker betrachten das Elektron als ein Teilchen,
   das eine negative Einheitsladung trägt.

   b) The electron is described as [a particle]
   carrying a negative unit charge.
   Das Elektron wird als ein Teilchen beschrieben,
   das eine negative Einheitsladung trägt.

2. Diese Struktur kann manchmal verkürzt werden, wenn sich das Präsenspartizip mit den nachfolgenden Satzgliedern durch ein erweitertes Substantiv wiedergeben läßt:

   ... as a particle carrying a negative unit charge
   ... als −   Träger einer negativen Einheitsladung

3. In einer Reihe von Fällen liefern die obigen Varianten keine brauchbare Übersetzung. Die Annahme, Darstellung usw. kann dann im Dt. ausgedrückt

werden durch:

a) Man geht von der Annahme / Vermutung / Darstellung aus, daß ... / Man nimmt an, daß ...

> Energy can be transported by electromagnetic waves and it is customary to regard the waves as containing a certain energy density.
> ... man geht von der Vorstellung aus (... nimmt an ...), daß die Wellen eine bestimmte Energiedichte haben.

b) Man stellt ... so / in der Weise dar, daß ...

> In the Bohr theory of the H atom the electron was pictured as moving in a fixed orbit of well-defined radius.
> Nach der Bohrschen Atomtheorie des H-Atoms stellt man das Elektron so / in der Weise dar, daß es sich auf einer bestimmten Bahn mit definiertem Radius bewegt.

LE 4 ☞—0 Übersetzen Sie:

1. Under certain conditions we must regard the energy of an electromagnetic wave as being concentrated in discrete photons or quanta. 2. It is convenient to regard the orbital magnetic moment of the atomic electron as resulting from its motion about the nucleus. 3. The radius of the hydrogen nucleus is difficult to define exactly, but it may be regarded as being about 1×10^{-13} cm. 4. Covalent bonding is described qualitatively as being due to the sharing of electron pairs between bonded atoms. 5. In beta-radioactivity electrons and neutrinos are emitted by the nucleus, yet the nucleus is not assumed as containing these particles.

PK 8 · PA 3 · SQ B

LE 1 Das Gerundium "V-*ing* + N" kann Subjektfunktion haben.

1. Vergleichen Sie die Satzteile, die als Subj. N^1 fungieren: "Adj + N", "N + Prep + N" und "V-*ing* + N". Im letzteren Fall ist "V-*ing*" das führende Element innerhalb der Struktur.

N^1	+	V	+	N^2
High	temperatures	accelerate	the process.	
Adj	+	N		
A rise	in temperature	accelerates	the process.	
N	+	Prep + N		
Raising	the temperature	accelerates	the process.	
V-*ing*	+	N		

2. Die Übersetzung kann meist mit Hilfe eines nominalen Gefüges oder eines 'wenn'-Satzes erfolgen.

3.   Übersetzen Sie:

1. Moving positive charge from left to right along a wire produces the same magnetic effect as the movement of negative charge at the same rate from right to left. 2. Connecting together charged conductors equalizes their potentials. 3. Developing new electronic devices is of great importance for our industry. 4. Measuring the length of a metre accurately has always been a problem to engineers. 5. Learning foreign languages effectively requires much work.

LE 2   Das Gerundium "V-*ing* + N" kann auch als (Präpositional)Objekt fungieren.

Wenn das übergeordnete Verb oder Adj. im Prädikat fest mit einer Präp. verbunden ist, muß ein unmittelbar folgendes Verb die Form "V-*ing*" haben:

> N + V / Adj + Prep + V-*ing* + N

> Fluorescence depends on absorbing radiant energy.
> X-rays are capable of ionizing gases.

Häufig gibt es folgende Entsprechungen:

> N depends on   V-*ing* = N hängt davon ab, daß ...
> N results in   V-*ing* = N führt dazu, daß ...
> N consists in   V-*ing* = N besteht darin, daß ...
> N is capable of V-*ing* = N ist dazu in der Lage, daß ... /
>   N kann ... + Inf.
> N succeeds in   V-*ing* = Es gelingt N (etw. zu tun)

Übersetzen Sie:

1. One of the industrial applications of radioisotopes depends on using them as sources of ionizing radiation. 2. Newton succeeded in calculating the force of gravity between the sun and the planets. 3. In books on classical mechanics considerable space is given to developing the more complicated mathematical methods. 4. Alpha-particles from radioactive substances are capable of reacting with most of the lighter nuclides. 5. Thomson succeeded in deflecting cathode rays by means of an electric field. 6. Alpha particles are prevented by repulsion from entering the nucleus from outside. 7. Ionization is a process by which an atom becomes electrically charged due to losing or gaining one or more of its electrons. 8. According to the generally accepted theory of valence and electron structure, atoms tend toward assuming the electron structure of the zero-valent rare gas atoms, which have only completed electron shells.

LE 3   Wenn bestimmte Verben im Prädikat stehen, muß bzw. kann ein folgender verbaler Ausdruck, der als Objekt fungiert, die Form "V-*ing*" haben: N + V + V-*ing* + ... / *to* + V + ...

> begin, start   = beginnen, anfangen
> cease, stop*)   = aufhören, beenden

continue   = fortsetzen
keep on*),⎱   = fortsetzen, (etw.) weiter (machen),
go on*)   ⎰   (etw.) ständig (machen)
prefer   = vorziehen
resist   = widerstehen, sich widersetzen

*) Nach diesen Verben muß "V-*ing*" stehen.

⊼—0 Übersetzen Sie:

1. Some materials cease giving off radiation in a very short time after the exciting Jadiation has been taken away. 2. In special cases engineers prefer using semiconductors for producing heat and cold. 3. Atoms that resist either giving up or taking in electrons must share bonding electrons.

LE 4 ⊼—0 Ergänzen Sie den folgenden Satzteil mit Hilfe des angegebenen Wortmaterials durch "V-*ing* + N + ...":

Scientists succeeded in ...

1. to determine − charge − particle 2. to develop − new − method − to study − phenomenon 3. to diffract − gamma rays − by means of − crystal 4. to calculate − ratio − between − various − proportion 5. to relate to − emission − spectrum − atomic structure

LE 5 ⊼—0 Ergänzen Sie den folgenden Satzteil mit Hilfe des angegebenen Wortmaterials durch "V-*ing* + N + ...":

This substance is capable of ...

1. to act − as − insulator 2. to initiate − interesting − process 3. to cause − many − chemical − reaction 4. to absorb − energy − and − to emit − radiation 5. to give off − electron − and − to become − ionized

PK 8 · PA 3 · SQ C

LE 1 Übersetzen Sie:

Optical Properties of Materials

Many inorganic and some organic substances can absorb energy and emit visible or near-visible radiation. Such behaviour, called luminescence, can be initiated by bombardment with photons, electrons, or positive ions, and by mechanical stress, chemical reactions, or heating. In industrially important luminescent materials absorption of ultraviolet light is followed by emission of visible light, e.g. in fluorescent lamp tubes. If the emission takes place within 10^{-8} seconds of excitation, a luminescent material is referred to as fluorescent. If the emission takes longer, the material is called phosphorescent. Controlled amounts of impurities are put into phosphors to provide localized states in the energy gap; these impurities are called activators. Thus, for example, the inside of fluorescent lamps is coated with materials which can be excited by the ultraviolet light from a mercury glow discharge. An effective activator level is one which the electron can readily enter and leave. Otherwise the electron may prefer to recombine directly, by descending to the valence band. There are two possibilities for recombination. In one, the electron descends to an excited activator level, and radiates by transition to the activator ground state. This process is infrequent at all except high free carrier transitions. In the other process the electron is first trapped in levels which do not allow transitions involving radiation. The electron is eventually thermally excited to the conduction band, and then radiates by going to an activator level.

The light emitted by fluorescent lamps or other light sources results from energy transitions from higher states to lower ones. Atoms of the same element make similar transitions and therefore give off photons of similar wavelengths. They do so, however, independent of one another and at random times. This results in the emission of incoherent radiation because it is out of phase. Since the early work of Weber and Townes on stimulated emission of electromagnetic radiation, solid-state and gas-light sources have been developed which give coherent radiation. Such light sources are called lasers, which is an abbreviation for light amplification by stimulated emission of radiation. Light beams from lasers have applications in many areas.

LE 2   Wir bereiten die Sinnübertragung vor:

    1. Bilden Sie Sätze mit den folgenden Satzteilen

a) zur Angabe des Untersuchungsgegenstandes:

a study is made of

      Many studies were made of the isotopes of uranium.
      a number of – phosphorescent materials
      numerous   – behaviour of semiconductors

an analysis is made of

      A quantitative analysis was made of the isotopic mixture,
      complicated – luminescent light
      qualitative   – radioactive materials

b) zur Angabe der Untersuchungsmethode oder -grundlage:

use is made of

      Various uses have been made of molecular weights.
      important – the emission of photons
      practical   – the luminescence of solids

c) zur Unterscheidung:

a distinction is made between

A distinction is made between conductors and non-conductors.
- different types of luminescence
- metals and non-metals

d) zur Hervorhebung:

attention is given to

Special attention was given to excitation by ultraviolet rays.
particular — intensity of fluorescent light
careful — optical behaviour of organic substances

e) zur Illustration oder zum Vergleich:

mention is made of

In this connection mention may be made of television tubes.
- should — fluorescent light tubes
- has to- — effective activator levels

2. Beachten Sie die Beziehung zwischen

result: Ergebnis, Resultat
to result from: folgen, resultieren aus; erfolgen nach
to result in: führen zu, zur Folge haben

A is the result of *B*. / *A* results from *B*. / *B* results in *A*.
Die beiden verbalen Strukturen sind jedoch aus sachlich-logischen Gründen nicht immer austauschbar, so daß u.U. *may*, *often*, *sometimes* u. a. eingeschoben werden muß.

Formen Sie die Sätze nach diesen Mustern um:
Luminescence is the result of energy absorption.
Luminescence results from energy absorption.
Energy absorption results / may result in luminescence.

1. A spectrum is the result of the dispersion of electromagnetic radiations. 2. Photon emission is the result of the transition of electrons into lower energy states. 3. Coherent radiation is the result of stimulated emission.

LE 3 Übertragen Sie ins Engl.:

Es wurde eine Reihe von Untersuchungen zum Verhalten lumineszierender Substanzen durchgeführt. Besondere Aufmerksamkeit wurde der Lumineszenz von Festkörpern gewidmet. In Festkörpern erfolgt die Emission von Photonen nach optischen Übergängen von Elektronen aus angeregten Zuständen in tiefere Energiezustände. Die Lumineszenz stellt einen Überschuß über die Temperaturstrahlung des Festkörpers dar. Sie tritt nur während oder nach der Anregung durch bestimmte Formen von Energieabsorption auf. In Abhängigkeit von der Art der Energieabsorption unterscheidet man verschiedene Typen der Lumineszenz. Es ist besonders bemerkenswert, daß Lumineszenz bei allen Arten von kristallinen Festkörpern beobachtet werden kann, außer bei Metallen. Die Lumineszenz kristalliner Substanzen wird industriell verwendet. In diesem Zusammenhang können Fernseh-bildröhren, Leuchtstoffröhren und Festkörperlaser erwähnt werden. Ferner wird die Lumineszenz für wissenschaftliche Untersuchungen genutzt; z. B. können Analysen durch Messung der Intensität des Fluoreszenzlichtes durchgeführt werden.

PK 8 · PA 4 · SQ A

LE 0 Wortschatz zur Wiederholung

to attack: angreifen / to drop: fallen (lassen) / drop: Tropfen; Abfall (z. B. in voltage drop: Spannungsabfall) / to intend: beabsichtigen / straight: gerade, gerad-linig; direkt, ununterbrochen

LE 1 ⊕ ⊕ Neue Lexik

undoubtedly	[ʌnˈdautidli]	zweifellos, ohne (jeden) Zweifel
ore	[ɔ:]	Erz
hence	[hens]	folglich, daher, deshalb, von dort, daher
to attract	[əˈtrækt]	anziehen
to magnetize	[ˈmægnitaiz]	magnetisieren
rod	[rɔd]	Stab, Stange
to acquire	[əˈkwaiə]	erwerben, erlangen, erhalten
to be suspended	[səsˈpendid]	aufgehängt sein; frei tragen; (frei) schweben (Teilchen in Flüssigkeit oder Gas)
approximately	[əˈprɔksimitli]	annähernd, angenähert, ungefähr
to be confined (to)	[kənˈfaind]	eingeschränkt, beschränkt, begrenzt, eingeengt sein (auf)
pivot(ed)	[ˈpivət(id)]	Trag-, Drehzapfen; Drehpunkt; (drehbar) gelagert; Dreh-, Schwenk-, Kipp-
momentary	[ˈmouməntəri]	momentan, augenblicklich, kurzzeitig
nearby	[ˈniəbai]	in der Nähe liegend / gelegen, nahe
afterward(s)	[ˈa:ftəwəd(z)]	später, nachher, hinterher
pure	[pjuə]	pur, rein, völlig; (chem.) rein
continuous	[kənˈtinjuəs]	ununterbrochen, stetig, kontinuier-lich; zusammenhängend, ununter-brochen

tiny	[ˈtaini]	(winzig, extrem) klein
verification	[ˌverifiˈkeiʃən]	(Nach)Prüfung, Überprüfung, Verifizierung; Nachweis
to deal (dealt, dealt) with	[di:l (delt)]	sich befassen / beschäftigen mit, zu tun haben mit; handeln von, behandeln, zum Thema haben
to set (set, set) up	[ˈset ˈʌp]	(magn. Feld etc.) errichten, aufbauen
to neglect	[niˈglekt]	vernachlässigen
(in) comparison (with)	[kəmˈpærisn]	(im) Vergleich (zu, mit)
similarity	[ˌsimiˈlæriti]	Ähnlichkeit; Gleichartigkeit
inherent	[inˈhiərənt]	zugehörig, innewohnend; Eigen-, Selbst-

LE 2 ⊕ ⊕ Internationalismen

pole	[poul]	(el., magn.) Pol
rotation	[rouˈteiʃən]	Rotation, Drehung, Umlauf(bewegung)
medium	[ˈmi:djəm]	Medium, Mittel; Medium, vermittelnder Stoff, Träger
vertical	[ˈvəːtikəl]	vertikal, senkrecht; Vertikal-, Senkrecht-; stehend

LE 3 ⊕ ⊕ Reagieren Sie nach dem Muster:

T: At this college a study was made of fluorescent materials.
S: We also intend to study fluorescent materials.

the isotopes of plutonium / excitation waves / the luminescence of solid bodies / optical transition of electrons / energy absorption by crystals

LE 4 ⊕ ⊕ Reagieren Sie nach dem Muster:

T: At this laboratory an analysis was made of the intensity of light.
S: It is interesting to note that you analysed the intensity of light.

absorption spectra / internuclear distances / inner shell transitions / properties of plasmas / behaviour of complex ions

LE 5 ⊕ ⊕ Reagieren Sie nach dem Muster:

T: In this work use was made of ultraviolet radiation.
S: I didn't know that they used ultraviolet radiation.

controlled amounts of impurities / excitation by X-rays / stimulated emission / gas-light sources / amorphous substances

LE 6 | ⊕ ⊕ | Reagieren Sie nach dem Muster:

 T: A distinction is made between phosphorescence and fluorescence.
 S: How do they distinguish between phosphorescence and fluorescence?

gamma-rays and X-rays / pi-mesons and mu-mesons / the ultraviolet and the infrared regions / ionic bonding and covalent bonding / n-type semiconductors and p-type semiconductors

LE 7 | ⊕ ⊕ | Reagieren Sie nach dem Muster:

 T: In this connection mention is made of television tubes.
 S: Why do they mention television tubes?

the effective activator level / the Compton effect / X-ray fluorescence / solid-state lasers / dislocations in crystals

PK 8 · PA 4 · SQ B

LE 1 | ⊕ ⊕ | Übersetzen Sie ins Dt.:

LE 2 | ⊕ ⊕ | Reagieren Sie auf die Frage nach dem Muster:

 T: Do you know who explained the photoelectric effect? — Einstein
 S: Didn't Einstein explain it?
 T: That's right, it was Einstein who succeeded in explaining it.

Lorentz — explain / Maxwell — discover / Hertz — discover experimentally / Moseley — determine experimentally / Urey — separate

LE 3 | ⊕ ⊕ | Beantworten Sie die Fragen nach dem Muster:

 T: What can you tell me about the effect of X-rays? — to produce ionization
 S: They are capable of producing ionization.

PK 8 · PA 4 · SQ C

LE 1 Lesen Sie den Text und unterstreichen Sie die wichtigsten Informationen. Untergliedern Sie den Text nach Hauptinformationen:

Excitons

The principal effects of imperfections in almost perfect crystals are to a large extent the result of six main types of imperfection and of the interactions between them. The six main imperfections are: (a) phonons; (b) electrons and holes; (c) excitons; (d) vacant lattice sites and interstitial atoms (Zwischengitteratom); (e) foreign atoms; (f) dislocations. Excitons are discussed below.

An exciton or excitation wave is produced when an insulator is raised to the first non-conducting excited state of its electronic system. The first electronic transition is called the first fundamental absorption band of the crystal. It is centered at 1580 Å in sodium chloride (NaCl), at 1920 Å in sodium bromide (NaBr), and at 2200 Å in potassium iodide (KJ). In silicon and germanium it lies in the near infrared. The associated absorption of light is very intense. An exciton may be thought of as the excited state of an atom or ion, with the excitation wandering from one cell of the lattice to another. If we excite one atom in a solid, the excitation will in general not remain localized on the original atom, but later there is a finite probability that any other identical atom in the solid will happen to be excited. A moving state of excitation is called an exciton.

The transmission of the excitation takes place by means of electrostatic or electromagnetic coupling between the excited atom and its neighbours. It should be noted that an excitation wave will not carry current, as there is no translation of charge. The energy of an excitation may be treated in the simplest case as the sum of the internal energy required to excite a single ion and a translational energy related to the velocity with which the excitation state moves from one atom to another.

LE 2 Geben Sie eine kurze schriftliche Zusammenfassung des Textes in Engl. auf der Basis dieser Stichpunkte:

– types of imperfection in crystals
– characterization of an exciton
– transmission of the excitation in crystals

Bereiten Sie die Übersetzung des Textes *"Magnetism"* (9.1.C. −1.) vor!

PK 8 · PA 4 · SQ D

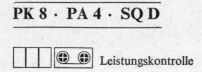 Leistungskontrolle

Phenomena of Magnetism and the Magnetic Field

PK 9 · PA 1 · SQ A

LE 1 In der Wortkombination "N^1 + Prep + N^2" werden das Grundwort N^1 und das Bestimmungswort N^2 durch die Präposition zueinander in Beziehung gesetzt.

1. Am häufigsten findet sich die Kombination "N^1 + of + N^2". In der Fachsprache der Physik unterscheidet man im wesentlichen:

    a) mass of the electron – Masse des Elektrons
    b) beam of photons   – Photonenstrahl
    c) energy of light   – Lichtenergie

Zwischen diesen Typen bestehen

1.1. Strukturunterschiede:

    a) N + Prep + the + N (im Singular)
    b) N + Prep + N (im Plural)
    c) N + Prep + N (im Singular)

1.2. Unterschiede in der Variabilität der Nomen:

    a) mass of the proton, mass of the nucleus, mass of the particle etc.; spin of the electron, movement of the electron, charge on / of the electron etc.
    b) beam of electrons, beam of X-rays, beam of photons.
    c) energy of light, energy of migration.

Im Typ a) sind das Grundwort N^1 und das Bestimmungswort N^2 beide relativ frei austauschbar. Die Typen b) und c) sind wesentlich fester gefügt und nur innerhalb enger fachsprachlicher Grenzen variabel.
Die dt. Entsprechungen der Typen b) und c) sowie, mit Ausnahmen, des Typs a) sind meist zusammengesetzte Subst. (s. 1.)
Beachten Sie: Bei *energy of light* hat die Übersetzung '(die) Energie des Lichts' keinen Terminuscharakter.

2. Strukturen des Typs 'N^1 + of + N^2' konkurrieren nicht selten mit solchen des Typs "N^2 + N^1".

    absorption of neutrons – neutron absorption
    energy of light – light energy

Die beiden Wortbildungsstrukturen entsprechen sich in der Bedeutung fast immer. Die Termini des Typs "N^2 + N^1" bilden hierbei eine wesentlich geschlossenere Bedeutungseinheit.

In ähnlicher Weise konkurrieren bei relativer Bedeutungsgleichheit in manchen Fällen auch die Strukturen "Adj + N" und "N^1 + of + N^2".

    a) fission of the nucleus   – nuclear fission
    b) energy of rotation   – rotational energy
    c) displacement of electrons – electronic displacement

Alle drei Wortbildungsstrukturen können nebeneinander existieren:

shell of electrons N^1 + of + N^2	
electron shell N^2 + N^1	Elektronenhülle
electronic shell Adj + N	

3. In der Struktur "N^1 + Prep + N^2" kommen neben *of* auch andere Präpositionen vor: *in, by, to, from, for, between, before, at, with*. Die drei Grundtypen a), b) und c) bleiben die gleichen. Die Beziehungen zwischen N^1 und N^2 werden jedoch durch die Eigenbedeutung der Präpositionen konkreter verdeutlicht. Dabei konkurrieren gelegentlich *of* und *in*.

difference in / of pressure	– Druckunterschied
increase in / of efficiency	– Erhöhung (Verbesserung) des Wirkungsgrades
bombardment by protons	– Protonenbeschuß
resistance to heat	– Hitzebeständigkeit
forces between nucleons	– Kernkräfte
limit for decay	– Zerfallsgrenze
electron at rest	– Ruheelektron
deviation from zero	– Nullabweichung
motor with series characteristic	– Motor mit Reihenschlußverhalten

LE 2   ━─0 Bilden Sie dt. Entsprechungen zu den engl. Termini. Ordnen Sie die engl. Termini den folgenden Mustern zu:

    a) N^1 + of + N^2; b) N^1 + Prep (nicht of) + N^2; c) N^2 + N^1; d) Adj + N.

1. decrease in conductivity; 2. reduction in temperature; 3. diffraction of electrons; 4. molecular motion; 5. limit of stability; 6. charge of / on the electron; 7. degree of ionization; 8. atomic rays; 9. number of atoms; 10. orbital velocity; 11. line of force; 12. difference in / of pressure; 13. electronic computer; 14. range of measurements; 15. resistance to low temperature; 16. frequency of oscillation; 17. beam of light; 18. state of equilibrium; 19. metallic oxide; 20. change of / in colour; 21. nuclear forces; 22. atom arrangement

(1) Elektronenbeugung; (2) Elektronenladung; (3) Bahngeschwindigkeit; (4) Schwingungsfrequenz; (5) Farbänderung; (6) Molekularbewegung; (7) Leitfähigkeitsabnahme; (8) Meßumfang, -bereich; (9) Atomstrahlen; (10) Gleichgewichtszustand; (11) Kernkräfte; (12) Tieftemperaturfestigkeit; (13) Atomzahl; (14) Atomanordnung; (15) Kraftlinie; (16) Stabilitätsgrenze; (17) Druckunterschied; (18) elektronische Rechenanlage; (19) Ionisationsgrad; (20) Metalloxid; (21) Lichtstrahl; (22) Temperatursenkung

PK 9 · PA 1 · SQ B

LE 1 Wir üben die Struktur: "Objekt + Infinitiv" (AcI):

Im Dt. und Engl. gibt es zwei Strukturen aus Infinitiv + Objekt, die eine ähnliche Beziehung zum Prädikat des Satzes aufweisen:

1. Die erste Struktur enthält einen einfachen Inf. ohne 'zu' bzw. *to*:

$N^1 + V^1 + N^2 + N^3 + V^2$

  Wir lassen ihn das Experiment wiederholen.

$N^1 + V^1 + N^2 + V^2 + N^3$

  We make him repeat the experiment.
  We let him repeat the experiment.

Beachten Sie, daß dt. 'lassen' hier zwei Bedeutungen hat.

2. Die zweite Struktur enthält einen Infinitiv mit 'zu' bzw. *to*:

$N^1 + V^1 + N^2 + N^3 + zu + V^2$

  Das Ergebnis veranlaßte ihn, das Experiment zu wiederholen.

$N^1 + V^1 + N^2 + to + V^2 + N^3$

  The result caused him to repeat the experiment.

3. In wissenschaftlichen Texten finden wir in der Struktur LE 1.1. die Verben *make, let, see, observe, notice* u. a. und in der Struktur LE 1.2. die Verben *allow, permit, cause, require, consider, assume, suppose, expect, find* u. a.

4. Nach einer lateinischen Konstruktion wird die Struktur "$N^2 (+ to) + V^2$" traditionell oft als "AcI" (Accusativus cum Infinitivo) bezeichnet.

5. In einer Reihe von Fällen ist im Dt. die Infinitivstruktur nicht möglich:

  We expect the value to drop below zero.
  Wir erwarten, daß der Wert unter Null fällt.

Beachten Sie: Die Übersetzung mit dem 'daß'-Satz ist auch in den Fällen LE 1.1. und LE 1.2. möglich.

LE 2 Übersetzen Sie! Da der 'daß'-Satz stets möglich ist, sollten Sie von diesem ausgehen und danach eine Vereinfachung mit Hilfe eines Inf. versuchen:

1. The difference of potential may be compared to the difference of temperature that makes heat flow through a conductor of heat. 2. Anderson found mu-mesons to have 150–210 times the mass of the electron. 3. The emission of a beta-particle causes the atomic number of the emitting nucleus to increase by 1. 4. Conductors vary widely in their ability to allow an electric charge to pass through them. 5. Isaac Newton considered the best way to explain the fact that light travels in

straight lines was to suppose it to consist of small particles or corpuscles. 6. Neutrons are slowed down by causing them to collide repeatedly with the nuclei of the atoms of the moderator.

LE 3 Der Infinitiv kann auch passivisch sein, so daß die Struktur entsteht: $N^1 + V^1 + N^2 + to + be + V^2\text{-}ed$

Spectroscopy permits the structure of molecules to be analysed.
Die Spektroskopie gestattet, die Struktur von Molekülen zu untersuchen.

Beachten Sie die Unterschiede:
1. Im dt. Satz steht das Objekt vor dem Infinitiv.
2. Dem passiven engl. Infinitiv "*to + be + V-ed*" entspricht im Dt. kein passiver Infinitiv, sondern die Form "zu + V".

LE 4 Übersetzen Sie:

1. There is a method which allows charge distributions to be calculated. 2. Numerous tests, based on characteristic physical properties, permit elements to be distinguished. 3. There are enough collisions among the nucleons to permit the conditions necessary for energy redistribution to be realized.

LE 5 ⚓—O Dagegen muß in den folgenden Sätzen die Infinitivstruktur mit Hilfe eines passiven 'daß'-Satzes übersetzt werden:

1. Since the electron-pair bonds between the individual atoms make use of all the valence electrons of the atoms, the existence of any free electron causes an electron-pair bond to the broken. 2. The separation of ions causes the cell to become polarized until the field of the electrodes is neutralized.

LE 6 Auch in anderen Fällen entspricht dem engl. passiven Infinitiv "*to + be + V-ed*" im Dt. die Form "zu + V":

The book was not to be found.
Das Buch war nicht zu finden.

Dagegen hat nach den Adjektiven *difficult, hard, easy* u. a. auch im Engl. die Form "*to + V*" passive Bedeutung:

The question is easy to answer.
Die Frage ist leicht zu beantworten.

LE 7 Übersetzen und vergleichen Sie:

1. The positive test charge is to be moved from a to b. 2. In ordinary chemical or molecular processes the change in mass is too microscopically small to be measured or even observed. 3. The new book on quantum mechanics is difficult to read. 4. Beryllium is very difficult to prepare in the pure state. 5. A technique, which is now beginning to be applied, is to study the lattice waves experimentally by means of their interaction with other radiation.

PK 9 · PA 1 · SQ C

LE 1   Übersetzen Sie:

Magnetism

The first magnetic phenomena to be observed were undoubtedly those associated with so-called "natural" magnets, which were rough fragments of an iron ore near the ancient city of Magnesia (hence the term "magnet"). These natural magnets have the property of attracting to themselves unmagnetized iron, the effect being most pronounced in certain regions of the magnet known as poles. It was found that an iron-rod after being brought near a natural magnet, would acquire and retain this property of the natural magnet; and that such a rod when freely suspended about a vertical axis would set itself approximately in the north-south direction. The study of magnetic phenomena was confined for many years to iron magnets. Not until 1819 was there shown to be any connection between electrical and magnetic phenomena. In that year Hans Christian Oerstedt (1770–1851) observed that a pivoted magnet was deflected when it was placed near a wire carrying a current. Twelve years later, Faraday found that a momentary current existed in a circuit while the current in the nearby circuit was being started and stopped. Shortly afterwards followed the discovery that the motion of a magnet toward or away from the circuit would produce the same effect.

It is believed at the present time that all so-called magnetic phenomena arise from forces between electric charges in motion. That is, moving charges exert "magnetic" forces on one another, in addition to the purely "electrical" or "electrostatic" forces given by Coulomb's law.

Since the electrons in atoms are in motion about the atomic nuclei and since each electron appears to be in continuous rotation about an axis passing through it, we can expect all atoms to exhibit magnetic effects. In fact, such is found to be the case. The possibility that the magnetic properties of matter were the result of tiny atomic currents was first suggested by Ampere in 1820. Not until recent years has the verification of these ideas been possible. As with electrostatic forces the medium in which the charges are moving has a pronounced effect on the observed magnetic forces between them.

Instead of dealing with the forces exerted on one moving charge by another it is found more convenient to assume that a moving charge sets up a magnetic field in the space around it. It is this field which then exerts a force on another charge moving through it. The magnetic field around a moving charge exists in addition to the electrostatic field which surrounds the charge whether it is in motion or not. A second charged particle in this combined field experiences a force due to the electric field whether it is in motion or at rest. The magnetic field exerts a force on it only if it is in motion.

The electric field set up by moving charges or by currents is, in many instances, so small that the electrostatic force on a moving charge can be neglected in comparison with the magnetic force.

12*

There are many similarities between electric and magnetic fields although the two are inherently different in nature and relate to entirely distinct sets of phenomena.

LE 2   Wir bereiten die Sinnübertragung vor:

Bearbeiten Sie den Text unter LE 3, so daß Sie seinen Sinngehalt sicher ins Engl. übertragen können.

Beachten Sie dabei folgende Hinweise:

1. Übersetzen Sie zunächst den Satzkern aus Subjekt und Prädikat:

Das magnetische Feld ist durch die in jedem Punkt des Raumes vorhandene magnetische Feldstärke H charakterisiert.
The magnetic field is characterized by ...

2. Zerlegen Sie mehrgliedrige Satzgefüge und Teile von Satzgefügen in selbständige Sätze:

Die Kraftwirkungen, die magnetisierte Körper aufeinander ausüben, führt man auf einen besonderen Zustand des Raumes in der Umgebung dieses Körpers zurück.

2.1. Wir lösen das Satzgefüge auf:

Magnetisierte Körper üben Kraftwirkungen (= Kräfte) aufeinander aus.
Magnetized bodies exert forces on each other.
Diese Kräfte werden auf einen besonderen Zustand ... zurückgeführt. /
Dies führt man ... zurück auf.
These forces are due to a special state. / This is due to ...
... in der Umgebung dieser Körper ...
... of the space which surrounds these bodies.
        surrounding   these bodies.
        around   these bodies.

2.2. Wir vereinfachen die Aussage:

Die Kräfte zwischen magnetisierten Körpern ...
The forces (acting) between magnetized bodies ...

2.3. Wir kombinieren die beiden Aussagen wieder:

The forces (which are) exerted by / acting between magnetized bodies are due to a special state of the space surrounding them.

3. Achten Sie auf die Mehrdeutigkeit von Wörtern und suchen Sie erst dann ein engl. Äquivalent, wenn Ihnen die inhaltliche Funktion klar ist:

3.1. Verben:

Diese Kräfte führt man auf einen besonderen Zustand ... zurück.

Das Verb 'zurückführen' bezeichnet hier die Feststellung eines Ursache-Folge-Verhältnisses, durch das ein Zustand erklärt wird. Daher sind folgende Übersetzungen möglich:

These forces are   due to   a special state ...
              are   explained by a special state ...
              can be explained by a special state ...
              are   caused   by a special state ...

3.2. Satzüberleitungen:

Damit wird die Kraft gleich dem Produkt aus Polstärke und Feldstärke.
In this way / Therefore the force is equal to the product of pole strength
and field strength.

LE 3   Übertragen Sie sinngemäß ins Engl.:

Das magnetische Feld

Die Kraftwirkungen, die magnetisierte Körper aufeinander ausüben, führt man
auf einen besonderen Zustand des Raumes in der Umgebung dieser Körper zurück.
Man sagt: In der Umgebung magnetischer Kräfte herrscht ein magnetisches Feld,
das von den magnetischen Körpern ausgeht (originate at). Das magnetische Feld
ist durch die in jedem Punkt des Raumes vorhandene magnetische Feldstärke $\vec{H}$
charakterisiert. Sie ist definiert durch die Kraft, die ein als selbständig angenom-
mener magnetischer Nordpol erfährt, der die Stärke der magnetischen Polstärke
besitzt. Damit wird die Kraft K, die auf einen Pol der Stärke P ausgeübt wird,
gleich dem Produkt aus Polstärke P und der am Ort des Pols herrschenden Feldstärke $\vec{H}$. Das Magnetfeld wird durch magnetische Feldlinien beschrieben. Die
Linien der magnetischen Feldstärke $\vec{H}$ beginnen bei einem Magneten an den
Nordpolen und enden an den Südpolen. Die Richtung der Magnetisierung $\vec{I}$ und
des magnetischen Moments $\vec{M}$ rechnet man von den Südpolen nach den Nordpolen positiv.

PK 9 · PA 2 · SQ A

LE 0   Wortschatz zur Wiederholung

aid: Hilfe / firm(ly): fest / guide: Leiter, Führer; Anleitung / to report: berichten /
to send, sent, sent: senden

LE 1   ⊕ ⊕   Neue Lexik

detection	[di'tekʃən]	Nachweis, Feststellung, Auffinden; Registrierung, Aufzeichnung
torque	[tɔːk]	Subst. Drehmoment, Richtmoment; Adj. Drehmoment-, Dreh-

coil	[kɔil]	Spule, Wendel; (techn.) Rohrschlange, -spirale
compass needle	[ˈkʌmpəs ˈniːdl]	Kompaßnadel
to align (oneself)	[əˈlain]	(sich) (aus)richten; (sich) (achsgerade) einstellen
deflection	[diˈflekʃən]	Ablenkung; (Zeiger)Ausschlag, Abweichung
measure	[ˈmeʒə]	Maß, Maßstab
sensitivity	[ˌsensiˈtiviti]	Empfindlichkeit; (Meßgerät) Genauigkeit
to wind, wound wound	[waind, waund, waund]	(auf)wickeln, umwickeln
plane	[plein]	Subst. Ebene, ebene Fläche; Adj. eben, plan
available	[əˈveiləbl]	vorhanden (sein), zur Verfügung (stehen), verfügbar (sein)
to insulate	[ˈinsjuleit]	(elektr.) isolieren
rectangular	[rekˈtæŋgjulə]	rechtwinklig, rechteckig
frame	[freim]	Rahmen, Gestell
to restore	[riˈstɔ:]	rückstellen, (auf Null) stellen, wiederherstellen
lead	[li:d]	(elektr.) (Zu)Leitung
terminal	[ˈtəminl]	Kabelende, Pol; (elektr.) Anschlußklemme
negligible	[ˈneglidʒəbl]	vernachlässigbar
thrust	[θrʌst]	Druck(kraft), Schub(kraft)
couple of forces	[ˈkʌpl]	Kräftepaar
to rotate	[rouˈteit]	rotieren, (sich) drehen; umlaufen (lassen)
suspension	[səsˈpenʃən]	Subst. Aufhängung; Adj. Hänge-, Trag-, Suspensions-
angle	[ˈæŋgl]	(math.; phys.) Winkel
to reflect	[riˈflekt]	reflektieren, (Licht etc.) zurückwerfen, spiegeln
incident	[ˈinsidənt]	einfallend, auftreffend, Einfalls-
incidence	[ˈinsidəns]	Einfallen (eines Strahles), Auftreffen (von Elektronen)

LE 2 ⊕ ⊕ Internationalismen

galvanometer	[ˌgælvəˈnɔmitə]	Galvanometer
spiral	[ˈspaiərəl]	Subst. Spirale; Adj. spiralförmig, Spiral-
horizontal	[ˌhɔriˈzɔntəl]	horizontal, waagerecht; Horizontal- Waagerecht-

LE 3 ⊕ ⊕ Beantworten Sie die Fragen nach dem Muster:

T: When we think of electrons forming a beam, what do we call this?
S: We call it a beam of electrons.

LE 4 ⊕ ⊕ Beantworten Sie die Fragen nach dem Muster:

T: When isotopes are separated in a process, what is this process called?
S: It is called separation of isotopes.

LE 5 ⊕ ⊕ Formen Sie die Sätze nach diesem Muster um:

T: Light possesses energy.
S: This energy is referred to as — the energy of light.

PK 9 · PA 2 · SQ B

LE 1 ⊕ ⊕ Beantworten Sie die Fragen nach dem Muster:

T: What does a temperature difference cause? — Heat flows. —
S: It causes heat to flow.

Electrons form a current. / The atomic number increases by 1. / Nuclei emit alpha-particles. / The mass number decreases by 4.

LE 2 ⊕ ⊕ Beantworten Sie die Fragen nach dem Muster:

T: What did Newton suppose? Light consists of particles.
S: He supposed light to consist of particles.

The electrons move about the nucleus. / Light consists of discrete quanta. / Matter consists of atoms. / Exchange forces act between the nucleons. / The electrons are at various distances from the nucleus.

LE 3 ⊕ ⊕ Beantworten Sie die Fragen nach dem Muster:

T: How are you going to calculate these values? — equation —
S: I use this equation. It permits these values to be calculated.

equation — calculate the data / method — distinguish isotopes / test — identify elements / equation — determine the size of molecules / treatment — separate isotopes

PK 9 · PA 2 · SQ C

LE 1   Lesen Sie den folgenden Text und geben Sie eine schriftliche Zusammenfassung in Engl. mit Hilfe des nachfolgenden Schemas:

Ferromagnetism

The intense response to an applied magnetic field shown by iron, nickel or cobalt
is known as ferromagnetism. Investigations at low temperatures have brought to
light a large number of similarly behaved materials, and the list is still growing.
The magnetization induced by an applied field in a ferromagnetic sample is generally related in a complex way to the specimen's shape and magnetic history, as
well as to the field strength. The basic characteristics of ferromagnetism must be
obtained from this complex picture. A significant point is that a specimen generally
remains magnetized to some extent when the field is switched off (abschalten).
This residual (Rest-) magnetization is a clear indication of the most characteristic
property of ferromagnetic materials, that is the spontaneous long-range ordering
of the directions of the magnetic moments of some of the electrons in the specimen.
A second indication that there is spontaneous ordering is the fact that the intensi-
ties of magnetization induced in soft (weich) ferromagnetic materials by a field of
a few oersteds are at least half as large as the saturation values induced by very
large fields. The magnitude of the spontaneous magnetization is most clearly
revealed by observations on single crystals. With a good single crystal it is possible
to find a crystallographic direction in which an internal field of a few oersteds
is sufficient (ausreichend) to magnetize the crystal to within a few per cent of the
saturation intensity. In other crystallographic directions, magnetization is much
less induced.

It is a short step from this demonstration of direction of easy magnetization,
or "preferred" direction, to the idea that a ferromagnetic crystal is spontaneously
magnetized to a high degree at every point, but that different regions of the crystal
are magnetized in different, but crystallographically equivalent, directions.

The complex behaviour known as ferromagnetism can thus be reduced to two
major aspects, first the occurrence and the magnitude of the spontaneous magnetization existing at every point in a crystal, and secondly the way in which this spontaneous magnetization is distributed in the form of domains (Domäne, Bereich).
The two aspects in the theory attempt to answer different kinds of question, namely:
'Why is metal A ferromagnetic while metal B is not?'
'Why is a sample of ferromagnetic metal C more easily saturated than a sample of
ferromagnetic metal D?'

The present article deals with problems of ... which is defined as ... Reference is
made to ... which revealed the existence of ... When considering the basic characteristics of ..., special mention is made of ... The most characteristic property of

ferromagnetic materials is ... Experiments made on single crystals show ... The complex behaviour of ... can be reduced to two aspects, first ..., and second ...

Bereiten Sie die Übersetzung des Textes *"The Galvanometer"* (9.3.C. – 1.) vor!

PK 9 · PA 2 · SQ D

LE 1 ⊕ ⊕ Einführung

LE 2 ⊕ ⊕ ⊱▷ Hören Sie den BTV *"The Magnetic Field"* und machen Sie sich Notizen!

LE 3 Geben Sie eine kurze zusammenhängende Darstellung der wesentlichen Informationen in Dt.!

LE 4 Speak about magnets using the following German text as a guide:

Magnete sind Körper, die die Quelle eines Magnetfeldes bilden. Jeder Magnet hat zwei Stellen, an denen die magnetische Feldstärke besonders groß ist. Diese werden als Pole bezeichnet. Man unterscheidet einen magnetisch positiven Nordpol und einen magnetisch negativen Südpol. Nordpol und Südpol ziehen einander an, während zwei Nordpole oder zwei Südpole einander abstoßen. Ein Pol allein existiert nicht. Ein Magnetfeld kann man mit einer Magnetnadel nachweisen. Sie stellt sich immer in Richtung der magnetischen Feldlinien ein. Wenn man eine Magnetnadel drehbar aufhängt, wirkt das Magnetfeld der Erde auf sie ein. Sie stellt sich ungefähr in Nord-Süd-Richtung ein. Diese Eigenschaft benutzt man im Kompaß.

PK 9 · PA 3 · SQ A

LE 1 Ähnlich wie die Fügung "$N^1 + of + N^2$" (*mass of the electron*; *energy of light*; *beam of electrons*) kann in der Fachsprache der Physik die Fügung N^2*'s* $+ N^1$, z. B. *Planck's constant*, als Terminus gebraucht werden, wobei N^2 ein Eigenname ist.

1. Die dt. Entsprechungen sind meistens

a) Adjektivableitungen des Eigennamens auf '-sche' + Nomen:

    Planck's constant   = Plancksches Wirkungsquantum

    Avogadro's number   = Avogadrosche Zahl

Viel seltener

b) Fügungen mit vorangestelltem Genitiv:

Bohr's atomic model = Bohrs Atommodell

2. Die Stabilität der Fügungen ist unterschiedlich und umfaßt:

a) feste, terminologische (nicht trennbare) Verbindungen:

Avogadro's number, Coulomb's law

b) kontextgebundene (austauschbare) Fügungen:

The concept of atomic number as given in Rutherford's atomic model was firmly established by Moseley's work on X-rays.

Die kontextgebundenen Fügungen werden wiedergegeben

a) durch vorangestellten Genitiv:

Bohr's atomic model = Bohrs Atommodell

b) durch nachgestellte präpositionale Fügung:

Moseley's work on X-rays = die Arbeiten von Moseley über Röntgen-strahlen

3. Die kontextgebundenen Fügungen konkurrieren nicht selten mit *of*-Fügungen: *Moseley's work = the work of Moseley.* Ähnlich konkurrieren Termini des Typs *Planck's constant* mit solchen des Typs *"the + N^2 + N^1" = the Boltzmann constant.*

Beachten Sie den Artikel: *the Zeeman effect.*

Die dt. Entsprechungen sind

a) wie unter 1.a): die Boltzmannsche Konstante

b) Zwei-Wort-Komposita: die Boltzmann-Konstante

LE 2 ◣━0 Nennen Sie mögliche engl. Entsprechungen:

a) das Dirac-Elektron, b) Schrödingers Wellengleichung, c) das Stokessche Gesetz, d) die Rydberg-Konstante, e) die Maxwellschen Gleichungen, f) Röntgens Arbeiten über X-Strahlen, g) der Astonsche Massenspektrograph, h) der Compton-Effekt, i) die Plancksche Theorie der Strahlung, j) die Coulomb-Energie

(a) Planck's theory of radiation, (b) the Dirac electron, (c) the work of Roentgen on X-rays, (d) the Rydberg constant, (e) Aston's mass spectrograph, (f) the Compton effect, (g) Stokes' law, (h) the Coulomb energy, (i) Schroedinger's (wave) equation, (j) Maxwell's equations

LE 3 Wir üben die Verben *achieve, acquire* und *obtain*:

1. Die Verben *acquire* und *obtain* bezeichnen beide einen Vorgang, durch den der Handlungsträger etwas erhält. In physikalischen Texten unterscheiden sie sich dadurch, daß bei *acquire* der Handlungsträger stets eine physikalische Größe (ein Elementarteilchen, ein Atom u. a.) ist, während die von *obtain* bezeichnete Handlung von einer Person durchgeführt wird. Da diese nur in wenigen Fällen genannt wird, steht *obtain* meist im Passiv:

If a valency bond is formed, the atom which gives up the electron becomes a positive ion, the one which acquires the electron becomes a negative ion.
An understanding of the physical behaviour of atomic systems was obtained with the introduction of quantum mechanics.

2. Das Verb *achieve* bezeichnet die Erreichung eines Resultats:

The gas diffusion process achieves only very slight enrichment of the lighter isotope per treatment.

Der Handlungsträger ist belebt oder unbelebt. Da auch das Obj. von *to obtain* ein Resultat bezeichnen kann (vgl. 2.2.C. – 1.), gibt es hier Überschneidungen im Gebrauch der beiden Verben.

LE 4   ⚡—0   Ergänzen Sie die Sätze:

1. An electronvolt is the energy ... by an electron when allowed to fall through a potential difference of one volt. 2. An unstable nucleus may ... stability by drawing an extranuclear electron from the K-shell into the nucleus. 3. When the number of electrons returning to the ground state is equal to the number excited, a continuous supply of light is ... 4. In principle, isotope separation may be ... by the use of any physical process in which the behaviour of the atoms depends on their mass. 5. Electrons may also ... enough energy to leave a metal, even at low temperature, if the metal is illuminated by light of short wavelength. 6. By the application of the methods of thermodynamics it is possible ... an equation for the potential difference of an electric cell under equilibrium conditions.

PK 9 · PA 3 · SQ B

LE 1   Neben der Struktur "$N^1 + V^1 + N^2 (+ to) + V^2$", in der das Objekt N^2 nur durch seine Stellung charakterisiert ist, gibt es eine ähnliche Struktur, in der vor dem Obj. N^2 die Präp. *for* steht: *for* + N + *to* + V.

Wir können folgende Arten unterscheiden:

1. Das Prädikat des Kernsatzes wird von einer Form von *be* und einem Adj. wie (*im*)*possible* oder dem Nomen *tendency* gebildet:

It is not possible for a molecule to contain less than one atom of any element.
Es ist nicht möglich, daß ein Molekül weniger als ein Atom eines beliebigen Elements enthält.

Beachten Sie: Gelegentlich ist auch eine Übersetzung mit 'für' möglich, doch empfiehlt es sich, zunächst von einem 'daß'-Satz auszugehen.

2.   Übersetzen Sie:

1. It is impossible for any two electrons in the same atom to have their four quantum numbers identical. 2. In general, there is a tendency for the electrons of different energy to behave in different ways. 3. It is possible for a conduction electron to be scattered by other electrons besides those in the same energy band. 4. In solids, atoms are so closely packed together that is difficult for two atoms to change place.

3. Die Struktur "*for* + N + *to* + V" ist relativ selbständig und gibt den Zweck an:

For inelastic scattering to occur,
the neutron energy must exceed a certain amount.
Damit es zur inelastischen Streuung kommt (kommen kann),
muß die Neutronenenergie einen bestimmten Betrag überschreiten.

4.   Übersetzen Sie: .

1. For alpha-particle emission to be detected, the detachment from the nucleus of two protons and two neutrons should require no more than approximately 23 Mev. 2. In order for the process to take place, additional energy must be supplied in the form of kinetic energy. 3. Chemical energy may be converted to electrical energy in an electric cell; in order for the conversion to be reversible, equilibrium must be retained.

5. Die Adjektive im Prädikat sind mit *too* oder mit *enough* bzw. *sufficiently* verbunden:

N^1 + *be* + *too* + Adj   + *for* + N^2 + *to* + V

N^1 + *be* + Adj + *enough*   + *for* + N^2 + *to* + V

N^1 + *be* + *sufficiently* + Adj + *for* + N^2 + *to* + V

Die Übersetzungsmuster sind:

The energy is too small for the effect to occur.
Die Energie ist zu gering, als daß der Effekt auftreten könnte / so daß der Effekt nicht auftritt (auftreten kann).
The energy is large enough / sufficiently large for the effect to occur.
Die Energie ist groß genug (hinreichend groß) für den Effekt / so daß der Effekt auftritt (auftreten kann).

6.   Übersetzen Sie:

1. If the electron concentration is small enough for the Maxwell-Boltzmann distribution function to hold true, the electron gas is said to be classical. 2. When the energy of the alpha particle is sufficiently large for it to pass through a highly charged nucleus, reactions, in which two or more nucleons are emitted, take place. 3. The thermal conductivities of impure crystals are too small for this type of phonon-scattering to be important.

LE 2 Zur Angabe des Zwecks und der Folge finden sich daneben: ... so + *that* + ... / *as* + *to* + V + ...

The various substances were analysed so as to find the weight of the element present in the molecular weight of each compound.

Die verschiedenen Substanzen wurden analysiert, um das Gewicht des Elements im Molekulargewicht jeder Verbindung festzustellen (feststellen zu können) / damit man ... feststellen konnte. / so daß man ... feststellen konnte.

1. Übersetzen Sie:

1. High-energy particles are allowed to fall on a target so as to produce a neutron beam. 2. In some cases the curves can be analysed so as to give the absorption coefficients for the individual components of radiation. 3. A nuclear explosion is achieved by bringing the fissile masses, each in itself below the critical mass, quickly together so as to make them form one supercritical mass.

2. Vergleichen Sie damit diese Strukturvariante:

1. Smaller decay constants than 10^{-20} s.$^{-1}$ will mean that radioactive disintegration is so slow as to be undetectable. 2. The concentration of impurities must not be so large as to modify the lattice constants of the solid.

LE 3 In der Struktur "N + *to* + V" bzw. "N + *to* + *be* + V-*ed*" kann der Infinitiv auch als Attribut fungieren:

Aktiv: the first scientist to discover ...
der erste Wissenschaftler, der ... entdeckte

Passiv: the results to be expected
die Resultate, die erwartet werden (können) /
die zu erwarten sind
die zu erwartenden Resultate

Übersetzen Sie:

1. Technetium was the first element to be produced artificially. 2. At the end of the eighteenth century experimenters had only permanent magnets and electrostatic machines to experiment with. 3. The particular method to be used depends to some extent on the special problem at hand. 4. An important point to note is that, in any transition process which is allowed sufficient time for completion, energy must be conserved. 5. Henry Cavendish appears to have been the first to show that the force between two equally charged bodies varies directly as the square of the charge measured on an electroscope.

PK 9 · PA 3 · SQ C

LE 1   Übersetzen Sie:

Any device used for the detection or measurement of current is called a galvano-meter, and the majority of such instruments depend for their action on the torque exerted on a coil in a magnetic field. The earliest form of galvanometer was simply a compass needle placed below the wire in which the current was to be measured. Wire and needle were both aligned in the north-south direction with no current in the wire. The deflection of the needle when a current was sent through the wire was then a measure of the current. The sensitivity of this form of galvanometer was increased by winding the wire into a coil in a vertical plane with the compass needle at its centre.

Practically all galvanometers now available, however, are of the moving coil or pivoted coil type, in which the magnet is much larger and stationary, while the coil is moving in the field of the magnet. The coil consists of insulated copper wire wound on a rectangular frame and suspended by a fine conducting wire which provides a restoring torque when the coil is deflected from its normal position and which also serves as one current lead to the coil.

The other terminal of the coil is connected to a spiral which serves as the second lead, but which exerts a negligible control on the coil. When a current is sent through the coil, horizontal and oppositely directed side-thrusts are exerted on its vertical sides, producing a couple of forces about a vertical axis through its centre. The coil rotates in the direction of this couple and eventually comes to rest in such a position that the restoring torque exerted by the suspension equals the de-flecting torque due to the side-thrust. Since light incident on a mirror is reflected at an angle of reflection equal to the angle of incidence, the angle of deflection can be observed with the aid of a beam of light reflected from a small mirror.

LE 2   Wir bereiten die Sinnübertragung vor:

Zum Ausdruck des dt. Pronomens 'man' gibt es in der engl. Fachsprache eine Reihe von Möglichkeiten, die von einer bestimmten syntaktischen Umgebung und / oder kommunikativen Funktion abhängig sind.

1. In der mündlichen Darlegung und in Lehrbüchern, die Elemente des Vortrags-stils enthalten, findet man:

a) *you*, wenn sich eine Person an einen Personenkreis wendet, ohne sich selbst einzubeziehen (z. B. Vortragender gegenüber Auditorium):

When you look at these two pictures, you will see that the two curves are identical.

b) *we*, wenn sich die mitteilende Person in den angegebenen Personenkreis ein-beziehen will (Autor und Leser; Vortragender und Zuhörer):

The spectrum of light is produced when we separate white light into a colour band.

c) *they*, bei Mitteilungen über Dritte (z. B. Vortragender über Forschungsergebnisse anderer Wissenschaftler):

> In the Soviet Union scientists have made interesting experiments with a new type of lasers. They have found that ...

2. Vor allem in der schriftsprachigen Darlegung finden sich für dt. 'man':

a) Passivkonstruktionen (und davon abhängige Partizipien):

> The osmotic pressure can be determined by Berkeley and Hartley's method.
> It has been found that the lines of the spectrum are characteristic for each element.
> The process is assumed to proceed in two steps.
> Assuming the truth of the hypothesis, it can be shown that ...

b) Gelegentlich *one*, wenn eine Aussage abstrakt formuliert wird, ohne Bezug auf eine Person oder einen Personenkreis (z. B. bei Definition von Begriffen oder bei der Formulierung von Gesetzen, Annahmen, Voraussetzungen etc.):

> Under these conditions, one might say that the two curves are nearly identical.

LE 3 Geben Sie unter Beachtung dieser Hinweise eine engl. Zusammenfassung (6–8 Sätze) der wesentlichen Informationspunkte dieses Textes! Benutzen Sie als Hilfe die nachfolgenden dt. Fragen zum Text:

Lichtspektrum

Das Spektrum des Lichtes entsteht, wenn man das weiße Licht in ein Farbband zerlegt. Wir wissen heute, daß dieses Spektrum des Lichtes nur ein kleiner Teil des gesamten elektromagnetischen Spektrums ist, das die elektromagnetischen Wellen mit den Wellenlängen von etwa 400 bis etwa 800 nm erfaßt. Diese Wellenlängen sehen wir mit den Augen als Farben. Sie bilden zusammen das weiße Licht. Man kann nun die einzelnen Wellen räumlich in einem Spektralapparat trennen nach ihren Wellenlängen. Das weiße Licht eines glühenden festen Körpers und glühender Flüssigkeiten ergibt ein kontinuierliches Spektrum, in dem alle Wellenlängen enthalten sind. In diesem Farbband kann man die Farben Rot, Orange, Gelb, Grün, Blau und Violett gut sehen und man kann mit dem bloßen Auge bis zu 160 verschiedene Farben unterscheiden. Das Linienspektrum entsteht durch das Licht von leuchtenden Gasatomen (z. B. He-Atome oder Na-Atome). Die Untersuchungen zum Linienspektrum haben noch ein weiteres wichtiges Ergebnis gehabt. Man hat festgestellt, daß die Linien des Spektrums für jedes chemische Element charakteristisch sind. Dadurch können die Elemente an ihren Linienspektren erkannt werden.

> 1. Wie entsteht das Spektrum des Lichtes? 2. In welchem Verhältnis steht das Lichtspektrum zum gesamten elektromagnetischen Spektrum? 3. In welcher Weise kann man elektromagnetische Wellen räumlich nach einzelnen Wellenlängen trennen? 4. Unter welchen Bedingungen entsteht ein

kontinuierliches Spektrum? 5. Kann der Mensch mit bloßem Auge einzelne Farben im kontinuierlichen Spektrum erkennen? 6. Wann entsteht ein Linienspektrum? 7. Welche Bedeutung hat das Linienspektrum als Methode zum Nachweis chemischer Elemente?

PK 9 · PA 4 · SQ A

LE 0   Wortschatz zur Wiederholung

gap: Spalte, Lücke / to decide: entscheiden / leaf, Pl. leaves: Blatt, Blättchen / piece: Stück / sure: sicher / to surprise: überraschen / to want: wünschen, wollen; nötig haben

LE 1   ⊕ ⊕   Neue Lexik

to regard as	[riˈgaːd]	betrachten als, ansehen als
to constitute	[ˈkɔnstitjuːt]	bilden, darstellen
to be subject to	[ˈsʌbdʒikt tə]	unterworfen sein, unterliegen
interconnection	[ˈintəkəˈnekʃən]	Zwischenverbindung, Verkettung
constraint	[kənˈstreint]	Zwangsbedingung; Beschränkung
rigid	[ˈridʒid]	starr, unbiegsam
collection	[kəˈlekʃən]	Ansammlung, Anhäufung
invariable	[inˈvɛəriəbl]	unveränderlich, gleichbleibend
suitable	[ˈsjuətəbl]	geeignet
constitution	[ˌkɔnstiˈtjuːʃən]	Zustand
to be composed of	[kəmˈpouzd]	bestehen aus, zusammengesetzt sein aus
to alter	[ˈɔːltə]	ändern, verändern
(with) reference (to)	[ˈrefrəns]	(in) Bezug (auf)
fixed	[fikst]	fest, unbeweglich
narrow	[ˈnærou]	eng, schmal
twisted	[ˈtwistid]	gekrümmt; verwunden, verschränkt
arc	[aːk]	(math., techn.) Bogen
origin	[ˈɔridʒin]	Ausgangspunkt; Nullpunkt; Ursprung, Quelle
namely	[ˈneimli]	namentlich, besonders; (bei Aufzählungen) das heißt, z. B.
taut	[tɔːt]	straff (gespannt)
string	[striŋ]	Seil; Saite
unique	[juːˈniːk]	(math.) eindeutig; einzigartig

to denote	[di'nout]	bezeichnen, kennzeichnen; angeben
finite	['fainait]	(math.) endlich (Zahl)
in turn	[in 'tə:n]	wiederum

LE 2   ⊕ ⊕   Internationalismen

coordinate	[kou'ɔ:dinit]	Koordinate
dynamic(al)	[dai'næmik(əl)]	dynamisch
configuration	[kɔnˌfigju'reiʃən]	Konfiguration; Anordnung, Struktur
curve	[kə:v]	Kurve
Eulerian	[ju:'liəriən]	Euler(i)sch
cosine	['kousain]	Kosinus

PK 9 · PA 4 · SQ B

LE 1   ⊕ ⊕   Beantworten Sie die Fragen nach dem Muster:

T: Who determined the electronic charge for the first time? — Millikan —
S: Millikan was the first to determine it.

to obtain hydrogen / to investigate radioactivity / to observe artificial radioactivity / to observe the magnetic effect of a current / to study cosmic rays

LE 2   ⊕ ⊕   Stellen Sie die Fragen und hören Sie die Antwort nach diesem Muster:

T: We are going to analyse a number of substances.
S: What kind of substances are to be analysed?
T: The substances to be analysed are of special interest for photoconductivity.

to analyse compounds / to investigate materials / to study crystals / to develop new tubes / to discuss solids

LE 3   ⊕ ⊕   Beantworten Sie die Fragen nach dem Muster:

T: Let's assume you carry out an experiment. How do you decide on the method which must be used?
S: The method to be used depends on the aim of the experiment.

LE 4   ⊕ ⊕   Beantworten Sie die Fragen nach dem Muster:

T: How are you going to analyse these substances?
S: I'm still not quite sure how to analyse them.

LE 5   ⊕ ⊕   Beantworten Sie die Fragen nach dem Muster:

T: Can a molecule contain less than two atoms?
S: It is impossible for a molecule to contain less than two atoms.

alpha-rays − to penetrate lead / atom − to emit continuous radiation / dielectric − to conduct an electric current / metallic atoms − to gain electrons / gamma-rays − to be deflected by electromagnetic fields

LE 6   ⊕ ⊕   Bestätigen Sie die Antwort nach dem Muster:

T^1: Why were these substances analysed?
T^2: I think they wanted to determine their weight.
S: Quite right, they were analysed so as to determine their weight.

suspended − determine the deflection / introduced − provide activators / pivoted − to be movable / wound into a coil − increase sensitivity / accelerated − increase energy

PK 9 · PA 4 · SQ C

LE 1   Lesen Sie den Text und geben Sie eine schriftliche Zusammenfassung in Engl. mit Hilfe des nachfolgenden Schemas:

Particle Accelerators

A particle accelerator may be defined as any device used to give kinetic energy to ions or electrons. Early X-ray and canal-ray tubes also correspond to this definition. However, the major development of most accelerators for inducing nuclear reactions has occurred since 1926. The simplest way to accelerate a particle of charge e is to let it fall through a potential difference V. Thus it acquires a kinetic energy eV. The potential drop (Potentialabfall) V can be either steady-state or time-varying. Conceptually the simplest type of machine is one in which potential drop is constant. R. J. Van de Graaff built the first electrostatic generator now associated with his name at Princeton University. This machine employs a moving charge against a potential gradient and thereby builts up the potential to a definite value. Ions characterized by an excess of electrons are obtained from a source. These negative ions are accelerated from ground potential to a positive electrode at a potential of 5 Mev. In this electrode the electrons are removed (entziehen) to give an ion of opposite sign. These positive ions, already with a kinetic energy of 5 Mev, are further accelerated back to ground potential with a final kinetic energy of 10 Mev. The first practical induction accelerator was built by D. W. Kerst at the University of Illinois in 1940, and his suggested name of "betatron" has been universally accepted. The betatron accelerates electrons in a continuous electric field and can be compared with a transformer with the secondary winding consisting of electrons circulating in an evacuated torus (Ring). The potential-drop accelerators depend upon very high voltages to produce the very high energies so that the dimensions of the machines become very large. On the other hand, the resonance accelerator uses a high-frequency voltage applied to a series of gaps through which the particles pass. The field is always in the accelerating direction as the particles cross each gap. The particles may move in a straight line (linear accelerator) or, under the influence of a magnetic field, in a circle (synchrotron or microtron) or spiral (cyclotron), passing repeatedly through the accelerating gap.

— Particle accelerators are defined as devices: to give kinetic energy to ions or electrons
— simplest way: to let a charged particle fall through a potential difference.
— A short description is given of: Van de Graaff machine / to employ a moving charge against a potential gradient / to accelerate negative or positive ions from or back to ground potential / to remove electrons
— Reference is also made to: induction accelerators ("betatron") / other types

> Bereiten Sie die Übersetzung des Textes "*The Coordinates of a Dynamical System*" (10.1.C. – 1.) vor!

PK 9 · PA 4 · SQ D

LE 1   ⊕ ⊕   Einführung
paramagnetic: paramagnetisch / diamagnetic: diamagnetisch / container: Behälter

LE 2   ⊕ ⊕ ⊃▷   Hören Sie den BTV "*Magnetic Properties*" und machen Sie sich Notizen!

LE 3   Geben Sie eine kurze zusammenhängende Darstellung der wesentlichen Informationen in Dt.!

LE 4   Speak about the relation between electricity and magnetism using the following German text as a guide:

Die Beziehung zwischen Elektrizität und Magnetismus wurde von Oerstedt entdeckt. Diese Beziehung kann durch folgendes Experiment demonstriert werden:

Eine Magnetnadel wird parallel zu einem Leiter angeordnet. Wenn elektrischer Strom durch den Leiter fließt, bewegt sich die Magnetnadel in einer bestimmten Richtung. Sie dreht sich, wenn der Strom in entgegengesetzter Richtung fließt. Die Kraftwirkung des magnetischen Feldes auf die Magnetnadel ist ein Maß für die elektrische Feldstärke. Wie die elektrische Feldstärke hat auch die magnetische Feldstärke Betrag und Richtung und ist deshalb ein Vektor. Das Magnetfeld eines stromdurchflossenen Leiters hat die gleichen Eigenschaften wie das Magnetfeld um einen magnetischen Körper. Diese Tatsache wird technisch im Elektromagneten genutzt.

Mechanics

PK 10 · PA 1 · SQ A

LE 1 Engl. dreigliedrige Mehrworttermini der Physik bauen sich auf zweigliedrigen Strukturen auf:

a) N + N   — rest mass (siehe 4.3.A.)
b) N + *of* + N   — centre of mass (siehe 9.1.A.)
c) Adj + N   — magnetic field (siehe 5.3.A.)

1. Vor diese Strukturen wird ein Nomen (Subst.) gestellt:

a) $N^3 + N^2 + N^1$ — electron rest mass
                            electron multiplier tube
b) $N^3 + N^1 + of + N^2$ — deuteron centre of mass
c) $N^2 + Adj + N^1$ — cyclotron magnetic field
                            electron linear accelerator

2. Durch Umformung der Wortfügungen a) bis c) wird die Beziehung der Einzelwörter zueinander deutlich, so daß die Bedeutung des Gesamtterminus erschlossen werden kann:

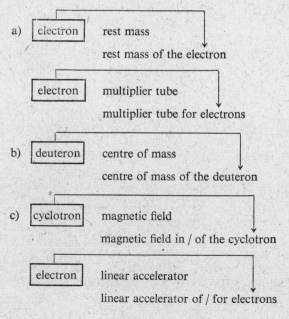

a) electron   rest mass

            rest mass of the electron

    electron   multiplier tube

            multiplier tube for electrons

b) deuteron   centre of mass

            centre of mass of the deuteron

c) cyclotron   magnetic field

            magnetic field in / of the cyclotron

    electron   linear accelerator

            linear accelerator of / for electrons

3. Gelegentlich tritt vor "N + N" oder "Adj + N" ein Determinativadjektiv, das wie N^3 in der Struktur a) fungiert:

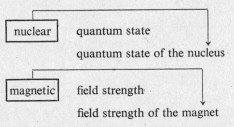

| nuclear | quantum state |
| magnetic | field strength |

quantum state of the nucleus

field strength of the magnet

4. Die dt. Entsprechungen der drei Strukturen sind:

4.1. meist dreigliedrige zusammengesetzte Substantive, deren erster Bestandteil im Singular oder Plural steht (vgl. LE 1.2.)

| electron multiplier tube | = Elektronenvervielfacher |
| charge distribution factor | = Ladungsverteilungsfaktor |

In der Struktur "Adj + N + N" kann der erste Bestandteil im Dt. ein N oder ein Adj sein, das auch getrennt vor dem zweigliedrigen Substantiv stehen kann:

magnetic field strength	= magnetische Feldstärke
	Magnetfeldstärke
linear electron accelerator	= Linearelektronenbeschleuniger

4.2. seltener zweigliedrige zusammengesetzte Substantive mit Genitivanschluß oder präpositionalem Anschluß:

| electron rest mass | = Ruhemasse des Elektrons |
| cyclotron magnetic field | = Magnetfeld des / im Zyklotron(s) |

LE 2 ☞ Finden Sie dt. Entsprechungen:

a) atomic ground state; b) electron diffraction pattern; c) electron rest energy; d) electronic band spectrum; e) electron distribution curve; f) linear particle accelerator; g) neutron chain reaction; h) atomic magnetic moment; i) sodium emission spectrum; j) neutron rate of escape

(a) Elektronenbeugungsbild, -aufnahme; (b) Neutronenkettenreaktion; (c) Elektronenbandspektrum; (d) Ruheenergie des Elektrons; (e) Linear-Teilchenbeschleuniger; (f) atomarer Grundzustand; (g) Neutronenaustrittsgeschwindigkeit; (h) Elektronenverteilungskurve; (i) Natriumemissionsspektrum; (j) magnetisches Atommoment

LE 3 Zum Gebrauch von *would* und *should*:

1. Ebenso wie *will* (vgl. 4.1.A.) kann auch *would* benutzt werden, um die Zwangsläufigkeit oder Regelmäßigkeit eines Vorganges zu unterstreichen. Im Dt. fehlt meist ein entsprechender Ausdruck:

The electric field is a vector field specifying the magnitude and direction of the electric force that would act on unit positive charge placed at any point in space.

Dagegen muß *would* mit 'wäre(n)', 'würde(n)' usw. übersetzt werden, wenn es ausdrückt, daß der Vorgang nur als Folge einer bestimmten Bedingung eintritt:

The analogy between an atom and the sun's planetary system is misleading, because the particles in the atom are electrically charged. From the electromagnetic theory, the rotating electron would follow a spiral path and eventually fall into the nucleus. Further, atomic spectra would cover a continuous range of wave lengths instead of consisting of well defined lines.

2. *should* wird in Fachtexten häufig verwendet, um auszudrücken, daß der Vorgang mit großer Wahrscheinlichkeit stattfindet bzw. eigentlich zu erwarten wäre. In dieser Funktion entspricht es dem dt. Modalverb 'müßte (eigentlich)' und 'muß':

If nuclei consist essentially of neutrons and protons, both of which have masses of almost 1, the atomic weights of all elements should be very close to whole numbers.

Nach Ausdrücken der Überraschung bleibt *should* unübersetzt:

The atomic nucleus probably cannot be strictly considered as having a definite size. It is not surprising, therefore, that different methods for determining what are really "effective" radii should give different results.

PK 10 · PA 1 · SQ B

LE 1   Bedingungsnebensatz − Hauptsatz

In wissenschaftlichen Texten werden häufig in einem Satzgefüge ein Tatbestand und seine Bedingung miteinander verbunden. Meist beginnt die Mitteilung mit der Bedingung. Neben *if* = 'wenn' / 'falls' können die Nebensätze eingeleitet werden durch:

even if / even though	= selbst wenn
if ... not / unless	= wenn ... nicht
provided / providing (that)	= vorausgesetzt (,daß)
supposing / supposed (that)	= angenommen (,daß)
in case (that)	= i(n de)m Falle (,daß)
on condition that	= unter der Bedingung, daß

LE 2   Übersetzen Sie:

1. If a piece of metal is charged, the charge will so distribute itself that the field within the metal is zero. 2. A metallic wire is characterized by the fact that, if

its temperature is kept constant, the current which it will pass is directly proportional to the voltage difference applied to its terminals. 3. If we choose a set of coordinate axes, we must specify three independent coordinates to define the position of an electron in space relative to these axes. 4. Provided radium is brought near a charged electroscope, the leaves will come together, thus showing the loss of charge. 5. Unless one knows the weight of an object and its heat capacity, in addition to its temperature, one cannot tell how much heat it contains.

LE 3   Neben den unter LE 1 genannten dt. Entsprechungen findet man im Dt. häufig Bedingungsnebensätze ohne besondere Einleitung − die sog. konjunktionslosen Konditionalsätze. Meist entsprechen ihnen im Engl. Sätze mit *if*:

Wird die Entladungsröhre bis zu 10^{-3} Torr evakuiert, so tritt Fluoreszenz auf.

If the discharge tube is evacuated down to 10^{-3} Torr, fluorescence will occur.

Beachten Sie, daß im Hauptsatz ein *will* verwendet wird, wenn es sich um konkrete realisierbare Vorgänge handelt.

LE 4   ⊶O Übersetzen Sie:

1. Sind die Ladungsträger beweglich, dann werden sie infolge der auf sie einwirkenden Kraft beschleunigt. 2. Legt man eine Spannung an einen elektrischen Leiter, dann entsteht in ihm ein elektrisches Feld, das auf die Elektronen eine Kraft ausübt. 3. Fügt man einem Halbleiter Fremdatome zu, dann erhöht sich dessen Leitfähigkeit. 4. Erhöht man die Spannung zwischen den Elektroden, dann vergrößert sich die Kraft und somit auch die Beschleunigung der Ladungsträger. 5. Wird der Druck in einer Gasentladungsröhre vermindert, so vergrößert sich der Abstand zwischen den Gasmolekülen.

LE 5   Enthält der konjunktionslose Nebensatz einen Umstand, unter dem eine Beobachtung oder Feststellung möglich ist, dann kann man statt des *if*-Satzes folgende Ausdrücke verwenden:

Looking at	= Betrachtet man / Untersucht man
Given	= Ist / Sind ... gegeben
Considering (that) / Taking ... into consideration / account	= Berücksichtigt man (, daß) / Angesichts

1.   Übersetzen Sie:

1. Looking at the periodic table, it is found that helium (He) is very much like argon (Ar), lithium (Li) like potassium (K) and so on. 2. Given a wave in which the electric field has an amplitude $\vec{E}$, it can be shown that the energy per unit volume associated with the wave is proportional to E^2. 3. In comparison with the energy released at the fission of $^{235}_{92}U$ (200 Mev), the amount obtained by the fusion of two deuterons (3.5 Mev) may appear to be small but considering the great differences in the masses involved, the proportion of energy is much greater.

2.　　　🔴 Übersetzen Sie:

1. Untersucht man eine Gasentladungsröhre, so findet man zwei einander gegen-überliegende Metallelektroden. 2. Betrachtet man die Ergebnisse unter diesem Aspekt, so ergeben sich wesentliche Unterschiede. 3. Ist eine Temperatur in der Nähe des absoluten Nullpunktes gegeben, so werden die Moleküle durch die Wärmebewegung nur wenig beeinflußt.

LE 6　　Ist die Bedingung hypothetischer Natur, so finden wir im *if*-Satz das Präterium, das hier keine Vergangenheitsbedeutung hat, und im Hauptsatz das Konditional I "*would* + V". Durch die Verwendung von *were* statt *was* in der 3. Person Sg. wird die Bedingung als nicht realisierbar gekennzeichnet:

> If the thermal vibrations of the lattice in a solid were perfectly harmonic, there would be no change of dimensions of a body on raising its tempera-ture.
> Wenn die thermischen Schwingungen eines Festkörpergitters vollständig harmonisch wären, gäbe es bei Temperaturanstieg keine Veränderung in den Abmessungen dieses Körpers.

Übersetzen Sie:

1. It was thought at one time that the nuclear mass was essentially electromagnetic in nature; if this were the case, nuclear radii would be very much smaller than they actually are. 2. According to a theory developed by Elsasser in 1934, alpha par-ticles could only exist in the nuclei of other atoms if the radius of the alpha particle were small compared with the distance between the particles in the nucleus. 3. A theory of the physical properties of solids would be practically impossible if the most stable structure for most solids were not a regular crystal lattice.

LE 7　　Ist die Bedingung irreal, da sie in der Vergangenheit nicht eingetreten ist, so enthält der *if*-Satz ein Plusquamperfekt und der Hauptsatz das Konditional II "*would* + *have* + V-*ed*":

> If the author had concentrated on a single aspect of the problem his book would have proved easier to read.
> Wenn der Verfasser sich auf einen einzigen Aspekt des Problems konzen-triert hätte, wäre sein Buch leichter lesbar gewesen.

Übersetzen Sie:

1. If Dalton had known the molecular weight of water to be 18, it would have been clear that its formula could not be HO, as he thought. 2. It would have simplified many things if Franklin had assumed that glass became negatively electrified when rubbed. 3. If a modern scientific textbook had fallen into the hands of a physicist two hundred years ago, it would have speeded up the development of physics by several generations.

PK 10 · PA 1 · SQ C

LE 1   Übersetzen Sie:

The Coordinates of a Dynamical System

Any material system is regarded from the dynamical point of view as constituted of a number of particles, subject to interconnexions and constraints of various kinds, a rigid body being regarded as a collection of particles, which are kept at invariable distances from each other by means of suitable reactions.

When the constitution of such a system (i.e. the shape, size, and mass of the various parts of which it is composed, and the constraints which act on them) is given, its configuration at any time can be specified in terms of a certain number of quantities which vary when the configuration is altered, and which will be called the coordinates of the system; thus, the position of a single free particle in space is completely defined by its three rectangular coordinates (x, y, z) with reference to some fixed set of axes; the position of a single particle which is constrained to move in a fixed narrow tube, which has the form of a twisted curve in space, is completely specified by one coordinate, namely the distance measured along the arc of the tube to the particle from some fixed point in the tube which is taken as the origin; the position of a rigid body, one of whose points is fixed, is completely determined by three coordinates, namely the three Eulerian angles Θ, Φ, Ψ. The position of two particles which are connected by a taut inextensible string can be defined by five coordinates, namely the three rectangular coordinates of one of the particles and two of the direction-cosines of the string (since, when these five quantities are known, the position of the second particle is uniquely determined); and so on. We shall generally denote by n the number of coordinates required to specify the configuration of a system, and shall suppose the systems considered to be such that 'n' is finite. The coordinates will generally be denoted by $q_1, q_2, \ldots q_n$. If the system contains moving constraints (e.g. if it consists of a particle which is constrained to be in contact with a surface which in turn is made to rotate with constant angular velocity round a fixed axis), it may be necessary to specify the time t in addition to the coordinates $q_1, q_2, \ldots q_n$, in order to define completely a configuration of the system.

LE 2   ▼──0 Drücken Sie die vorgegebenen Sachverhalte in Englisch mit Hilfe von *if, provided, assuming* u. a. aus:

Ein Körper kann sich nicht bewegen.

Bedingung: Drei nicht auf der gleichen Linie befindliche Punkte sind fest.

If three points of a body which are not in the same straight line are fixed, it is unable to move.

1. Ein Körper ist im Zustand der Bewegung.
Bedingung: Er ändert im Laufe der Zeit seine Lage im Raum.

2. Jeder Körper bleibt im Zustand der Ruhe oder Bewegung.
Bedingung: Er wird nicht durch auf ihn ausgeübte Kräfte gezwungen, seinen Zustand zu ändern.

3. Wir können die Bewegung eines Körpers beschreiben.
Voraussetzung: Wir haben einen Bezugspunkt.

4. Wir wählen einen Körper als Bezugspunkt für die Bewegung.
Annahme: Dieser Körper bewegt sich nicht.

5. Eine Bewegung heißt Translation.
Bedingung: Die Wege, die die einzelnen Punkte eines Körpers relativ zum Bezugssystem zurücklegen, sind einander parallel und kongruent.

6. Eine Bewegung heißt Rotation.
Bedingung: Eine gerade Linie, die als Achse bezeichnet wird, behält bei der Bewegung des Körpers dieselbe Lage bei.

7. Die Bewegung eines Körpers ist vollständig bestimmt.
Bedingung: Der Ort jedes seiner Punkte ist zu jedem Zeitpunkt bestimmt.

PK 10 · PA 2 · SQ A

LE 1 ⊕ ⊕ Neue Lexik

terrestrial	[ti'restriəl]	terrestrisch, Erd-
reference	['refrəns]	Subst. Verweis, Bezug, Hinweis; Quellennachweis; Adj. Bezugs-, Vergleichs-; Nachschlage-
path	[paːθ]	Bahn, Flugbahn; Weg; Strecke; Verlauf
to describe	[dis'kraib]	beschreiben, darstellen; (einen Kreis etc.) beschreiben
circumstance(s)	['səːkəmstəns(iz)]	Umstand (Umstände); (Sach)-Lage; Sachverhalt, Verhältnisse
projection	[prə'dʒekʃən]	Projektion
circumstances of projection		hier: Anfangsbedingungen
acceleration	[æk͵selə'reiʃən]	Beschleunigung
gravity	['græviti]	Schwere; Schwerkraft
sufficient	[sə'fiʃənt]	ausreichend, genügend
to enable	[i'neibl]	(etw.) möglich machen, ermöglichen; (jmdn.) befähigen (zu), es (jmdn.) möglich machen

simplicity	[sim'plisiti]	Einfachheit, Unkompliziertheit; Klarheit
thread	[θred]	Faden
slack	[slæk]	locker, schlaff, lose
instant	['instənt]	Zeitpunkt, Moment, Augenblick
instantaneous	[ˌinstən'teinjəs]	augenblicklich, Augenblicks-; momentan, Momentan-; unverzögert
to superpose	['sjupəpouz]	überlagern
to compound	[kəm'paund]	(zu einem Ganzen) zusammensetzen
immediate	[i'mi:djət]	unmittelbar, direkt; sofort
throughout	[θru:'aut]	hindurch, während; überall in, durch ... gesamt
mode	[moud]	Art (und Weise); Methode; Typ; Form
to state	[steit]	angeben; erklären, darstellen; (verbal) feststellen
statement	['steitmənt]	Angabe; Darstellung, Feststellung
mutual	['mju:tjuəl]	gegen-, wechselseitig; gemeinsam
truth	[tru:θ]	Richtigkeit; Wahrheit

LE 2 ⊕ ⊕ Internationalismen

extreme	[iks'tri:m]	extreme, Extrem-, äußere(r, s), höchste(r, s), sehr groß, hoch, Hoch-
resultant	[ri'zʌltənt]	Subst. Resultierende, Resultante; Adj. resultierend
to generalise	['dʒenərəlaiz]	generalisieren, verallgemeinern
cosmic	['kɔsmik]	kosmisch
universal	[ˌju:ni'və:səl]	universal, universell, Universal-; Mehrfach-; Mehrzweck-

LE 3 ⊕ ⊕ Beantworten Sie die Fragen nach dem Muster:

T: As far as I know Rutherford was a pupil of Thomson's. Didn't he continué Thomson's research in the atomic structure?

S: You are right, Rutherford in his turn did also important research in this field.

PK 10 · PA 2 · SQ B

LE 1 ⊕ ⊕ Beantworten Sie die Fragen nach dem Muster:

    T: Supposing you wish to describe motion, what do you need? – a point
    of reference
    S: If one describes motion, one needs a point of reference.

test charge / zero potential / constitution / constraints / three coordinates

LE 2 ⊕ ⊕ Beantworten Sie die Fragen nach dem Muster:

    T: Will the experiment be possible without an increase in voltage?
    S: The experiment won't be possible unless the voltage is increased.

increase in energy / decrease in temperature / specifying the initial values / altering
the configuration / having enough test samples

LE 3 ⊕ ⊕ Beantworten Sie die Fragen nach dem Muster:

    T^1: Can germanium conduct a current?
    T^2: I do think so, if its crystals are not perfect.
    S: Oh yes, it can, provided its crystals are not perfect.

LE 4 ⊕ ⊕ Beantworten Sie die Fragen nach dem Muster:

    T: Are you going to mention this study?
    S: It would perhaps be better if I mentioned it.

read the paper / refer to that book / describe the experiment in detail / calculate
the values again / compare the values with other results

LE 5 ⊕ ⊕ Beantworten Sie die Fragen nach dem Muster:

    T: Why didn't you read this book? It contains useful information.
    S: Of course I would have read the book if I had known it.

use a method / consider a hypothesis / refer to a study / mention the experiments /
prefer this technique

PK 10 · PA 2 · SQ C

LE 1 Lesen Sie den Text und geben Sie eine engl. Zusammenfassung auf der Grundlage der nachstehend aufgeführten Fragen:

Definition and Description of Particles

The simplest mechanical system is one which may be represented in the mathematical scheme of mechanics by a point. Such a system is called a particle. How good a representation this is for a particular system can be determined only when we come to consider a more complicated representation of the system and can estimate the effects due to features neglected in the particle treatment. Intuitively it is plausible that it will be a good approximation for a given body provided that this body is small compared with its distance from other bodies and provided that the motion of the body as a whole is only slightly affected (beeinflussen) by its internal motion. Thus a particle is a body whose internal motion is irrelevant to its motion as a whole, so that it may be represented by a mass point having no extension (Ausdehnung) in space. A particle is described when its position in space is given and when the values of certain parameters such as mass, electric charge, and magnetic moment are given. By our definition of a particle, these parameters must have constant values because they describe the internal constitution of the particle. If these parameters do vary with time, we are not dealing with a simple particle. The position of a particle may, of course, vary with time.

We may specify the position of a single particle in space by giving its distance from each of three mutually perpendicular planes. These three numbers are called the cartesian coordinates of the particle. Since three mutually perpendicular planes meet in three mutually perpendicular lines, we may also consider the cartesian coordinates of a particle as the displacements in the directions of these three lines needed to move the particle from the point of intersection (Schnittpunkt) of the three lines to its actual position.

The coordinate system introduced in this way plays the role of the observer of the particle in the mathematical scheme. The very complex relationship between the particle and the observer which is to be described mathematically is reduced to the relationship of a point to a set of coordinates. In this way we tend to almost forget the observer entirely. In quantum mechanics and relativity theory the role of the observer himself is much more important.

1. What is described? (A description is given of ...) 2. Under what condition is this a good representation of a mechanical system? 3. As what is the particle defined? 4. How can the position of a particle be specified? 5. What is the coordinate system compared with? (A comparison is made between ...) 6. What is mentioned in this connection? (In this connection mention is made of ...)

Bereiten Sie die Übersetzung des Textes *"The Laws of Motion"* (10.3.C. – 1.) vor!

PK 10 · PA 2 · SQ D

LE 1 ⊕ ⊕ Einführung

LE 2 ⊕ ⊕ ⊐▷ ☐ Hören Sie den BTV *"The Reference System"* und machen Sie sich Notizen!

LE 3 Geben Sie eine schriftliche Zusammenfassung der wesentlichen Informationen in Dt.!

LE 4 Illustrate the following statements by an example of your own:

– A body may be simultaneously "at rest" and "in motion" because positions and motions are relative matters.
– A body is "at rest" if its coordinates with respect to a chosen reference system are not changing.
– The exact location of the reference system must be specified.

PK 10 · PA 3 · SQ A

LE 1 Dreigliedrige Mehrworttermini können einerseits durch Voranstellung eines Nomens (N) vor zweigliedrige Strukturen entstehen (vgl. 10.1.A.):

    a) electron rest mass   rest mass of the electron

    <u>N + · N + N</u>

    b) deuteron centre of mass   centre of mass of the deuteron

    <u>N + · N + of + N</u>

    c) cyclotron magnetic field   magnetic field of the cyclotron

    <u>N + · Adj + N</u>

1. Andererseits können aus den gleichen zweigliedrigen Strukturen durch Anfügen eines Nomens dreigliedrige Termini gebildet werden:

    a) ion trap magnet

    <u>N + N · + N</u>

    b) rate of climb indicator

    <u>N + of + N · + N</u>

c) black body cavity

Adj + N · + N

2. Eine Umformung verdeutlicht die Beziehung der Einzelwörter und kann die Erschließung der Terminusbedeutung ermöglichen. Besondere Beachtung verlangt "N + N + N", wie in *electron rest mass* und *neutron current density*, wegen der formalen Gleichheit der beiden Strukturmuster:

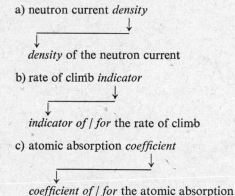

a) neutron current *density*

density of the neutron current

b) rate of climb *indicator*

indicator of | for the rate of climb

c) atomic absorption *coefficient*

coefficient of | for the atomic absorption

3. Die dt. Entsprechungen sind, wie bei LE 1,

a) vor allem dreigliedrige zusammengesetzte Substantive, deren erste und / oder zweite Glieder im Sg. oder Pl. stehen:

neutron current density   Neutronenstromdichte
rate of climb indicator   Steiggeschwindigkeitsmesser
Diese engl. Termini entsprechen weitgehend dem Aufbau der dt. Termini.

b) seltener zweigliedrige Strukturen mit Genitivanschluß oder präpositionalem Anschluß:

ion trap magnet   Magnet für Ionenfalle
total energy change   Änderung der Gesamtenergie

Der Wechsel von *total energy change* und *change of total energy* zeigt, daß vor allem diese Fügungen im Engl. wie im Dt. kontextgebunden sein können und keinen Terminuscharakter haben.

4. In Strukturen des Typs

atomic absorption coefficient   atomarer Absorptionskoeffizient

ist die dt. Entsprechung "Adj + N's + N" zu einem nur schwer gliederbaren Ausdruck verschmolzen, wohingegen

nuclear resonance spectrometer   Kernresonanzspektrometer

mit dt. "N + N + N" für engl. "Adj + N + N" deutlich gliederbar ist.

LE 2 ⊼—0 Suchen Sie dt. Entsprechungen:

a) data transmission system b) black body radiation c) cathode potential fall d) center of mass system e) electron tube tester f) atomic mass unit g) range of speed regulation h) charge carrier diffusion i) nuclear charge number j) thermal insulation material

(a) Schwarz(körper)strahlung (b) atomare Masseneinheit (c) Massenmittelpunkt-system (d) Kernladungszahl (e) Katoden(spannungsab)fall (f) Drehzahlregel-bereich / Regelung des Drehzahlregelbereichs (g) Röhrenprüfgerät (h) Datenüber-tragungssystem (i) Ladungsträgerdiffusion (j) Wärmeisolierstoff

PK 10 · PA 3 · SQ B

LE 1 Adverbien sind Angaben über die Art und Weise, den Grad oder andere Umstände, die Zustands- und Eigenschaftsbezeichnungen, Vorgänge und Sach-verhalte ergänzen oder modifizieren. Ein Teil von ihnen sind ursprünglich, wie *now* und *soon*. In anderen Fällen erfüllen mehrgliedrige Ausdrücke wie *in addition* adverbiale Funktion. Eine besondere Schwierigkeit stellen die Adverbien dar, die mit Hilfe von *-ly* von Adjektiven gebildet werden. Sie werden verwendet:

1. Zur Modifikation von attributiven Adjektiven und Partizipien, d. h. von Zu-stands- und Eigenschaftsbezeichnungen:

   a relatively large distance, the currently accepted view, a slowly decreasing pressure

2. Zur Modifikation verbaler Vorgänge:

   The earth is commonly used as a reference body at zero potential.

3. Zur Modifikation der Gesamtmitteilung des Satzes:

   Finally, the detailed study of charged particles led to the formulation of quantum mechanics.

LE 2 Die auf *-ly* endenden Adverbien haben unterschiedliche ·Entsprechungen im Dt.:

1. In den meisten Fällen ist die dt. Entsprechung endungslos:

   opposite direction   entgegengesetzte Richtung
   oppositely directed force · entgegengesetzt gerichtete Kraft

Beachten Sie jedoch, daß im Dt. auch das adjektivische Prädikativum endungslos ist:

   Die Anwendung dieser Methode scheint möglich.
   The application of this method seems possible.

Darum muß nach *become*, *seem*, *appear* und *consider* geprüft werden, ob eine Eigenschaft (*what*?) oder die Art des Vorgangs (*how*?) mitgeteilt wird:

> He considered the application of this method (as / to be) possible. →
> The application of this method is possible.
> He considered the application of this method carefully.
> He considered it in a careful way.

2. In einigen Fällen ist das Adverb im Dt. durch die Endung '-weise' gekennzeichnet. Eine ähnliche Funktion hat der Ausdruck 'in ... Hinsicht':

> A gas made up of neutral atoms is normally an insulator.
> Beta-rays are more penetrating than alpha-rays but they are less active photographically.

LE 3 ☛─0 Bilden Sie aus den Vorgaben Ausdrücke der Struktur "Adv + Adj / V-*ed* / V-*ing* + N":

1. A particle with a positive charge. 2. This charge is so small that it is sufficient for this purpose. 3. These observations were qualitative to a large extent. 4. These isotopes occur in nature. 5. The material has a high radioactivity.

LE 4 Die Stellung des Adverbs wird bestimmt durch die Satzstruktur und durch seinen Mitteilungswert. Bei hohem Mitteilungswert bzw. bei nachfolgender Erläuterung steht es meist am Ende.

> Übersetzen und vergleichen sie:
> 1.   N + *be* + Adv + Adj
>
>   N + *be* + Adj + Adv

1. The potential energy concept is particularly useful when we come to consider electrical circuits. 2. A given quantity of positive charge can be neutralised by an equal quantity of negative charge; such a neutralisation is possible electrically. 3. A test body is assumed to have a charge sufficiently small so that its presence will not alter the position of other charges as it is moved about.

2.   N + *be* + Adv + V-*ed*

     N + *be* + V-*ed* + Adv

1. The electrons in the inner shells are tightly bound to the nucleus. 2. Mesons are currently assumed to supply the force which holds the nucleons together. 3. Matter can be classified electrically into two categories, according to whether electrical forces will produce moving charges or not. 4. The term "enriched" is applied to fissile material in which the proportion of a certain desirable isotope has been artificially raised above the level of its abundance.

3.   N + Adv + V (+ Prep + N)

     N + V + Adv (+ Prep + N)

1. A molecule is the smallest part of a substance that can exist separately and still retain its chemical properties. 2. In a nuclear reactor the velocity of neutrons is reduced by causing them to collide repeatedly with the nuclei of the atoms of a moderator without being captured by the latter. 3. Nuclear isomers are rare among the naturally radioactive elements but occur frequently among artificial radio-isotopes. 4. The Geiger-Müller counter consists essentially of a tube containing air at low pressure and two electrodes, between which a critical potential difference is maintained.

4. $N^1 + Adv + V + N^2$

        $N^1 + V + N^2 + Adv$.

1. In order to compute electrical changes, it is not necessary for us to know whether conductors actually carry positive or negative charges in motion. 2. When the excess of neutrons over the protons becomes too great, the nucleus has a tendency to convert a neutron internally into a proton to re-establish the proper ratio required for stability. 3. If several charges are present, the resultant force exerted on some one charge may be found through adding the forces exerted by the separate charges vectorially.

5. Beachten Sie die Stellung des Adverbs bei Modalverben und Hilfsverben:

$$\text{This effect} \begin{matrix} \text{has} \\ \text{can} \end{matrix} \textit{occasionally} \begin{matrix} \text{been} \\ \text{be} \end{matrix} \text{seen.}$$

LE 5   ⊓—0 Setzen Sie Adverbien ein:

1. The emission of gamma-rays occurs in close association with the emission of alpha- and beta-particles (usual). 2. At high voltage differences, a spark may jump through the air from one sphere to the other (sufficient). 3. A cyclotron is an apparatus for the nuclear bombardment of elements by accelerated particles (high). 4. Aston's dark space is the narrow dark region of the discharge in a vacuum tube which can be seen between cathode glow and cathode (occasional). 5. An electron tube is evacuated to such a degree that its electrical characteristics are due to electron emission (essential).

LE 6   ⊓—0 Übersetzen Sie:

Um die Position eines Teilchens eindeutig zu bestimmen, brauchen wir ein Bezugs-system. Die Position des Teilchens im Raum kann vollständig definiert werden mit Hilfe seiner drei rechtwinkligen Koordinaten. Die Zahl der benötigten Koordi-naten wird gewöhnlich mit "n" angegeben. Die Zahl der Koordinaten ändert sich natürlich, wenn Zwangsbedingungen berücksichtigt werden müssen. Auch bei der Betrachtung größerer sich bewegender Objekte beginnt man normalerweise mit der Untersuchung eines sich frei im Vakuum bewegenden Teilchens.

LE 1 Übersetzen Sie:

The Laws of Motion

Considering the motion of terrestrial objects, and taking the earth as the frame of reference, it is natural to begin by investigating the motion of a very small material body, or particle as we shall call it, when moving in vacuo and entirely unconnected with surrounding objects. The paths described by such a particle under various circumstances of projection may be observed and the acceleration of the particle at any point of any particular observed path may be calculated. It is found that for all the paths the acceleration is of constant amount, and is always directed vertically downwards. This acceleration is known as gravity, and is generally denoted by the letter g. The knowledge of this experimental fact is theoretically sufficient to enable us to calculate the path of any free terrestrial particle in vacuo, when the circumstances of its projection are known. The case of motion which is next in simplicity is that of two particles which are connected together by an extremely light inextensible thread, and are free to move in vacuo at the earth's surface. So long as the thread is slack, each particle moves with the acceleration gravity, just as if the other were not present. But when the thread is taut, the two particles influence each other's motion. We can now as before observe the path of one of the particles, and hence calculate the acceleration by which at any instant its motion is being modified. In this way, we arrive at the experimental fact that this acceleration can be represented at any instant by the resultant of two vectors, of which one represents the acceleration g and the other is directed along the instantaneous position of the thread.

The influence of one particle on the motion of the other consists therefore in superposing on the acceleration due to gravity another acceleration, which acts along the line joining the particles and which is compounded with gravity according to the vectorial law of composition of accelerations. Denoting the particles by A and B, we can at any instant calculate, from the observed paths, the magnitudes of the accelerations f_1 and f_2, thus exerted by B on A and by A on B respectively; and this calculation immediately yields the result that the ratio of f_1 to f_2 does not vary throughout the motion. On investigating the motions which result from various modes of projection, at various temperatures etc., we are led to the conclusion that this ratio is an invariable physical constant of the pair of bodies A and B.

On consideration of the motion of more complex systems it is found that the experimental laws just stated can be generalised so as to form a complete basis for all dynamics, whether terrestrial or cosmic. This generalised statement is as follows: If any set of mutually connected particles are in motion, the acceleration with which any one particle moves is the resultant of the acceleration with which it would move if perfectly free, and accelerations directed along the lines joining it to the other particles which constrain its motion. The evidence for the truth of this statement is to be found in the universal agreement of the calculations based on it.

LE 2   Wir bereiten die Sinnübertragung vor.

1.   ◀─○ Übersetzen Sie:

elektrisch geladenes Teilchen; eindeutig bestimmte Position; völlig falsche Annahme; mikroskopisch kleine Dimension; unendlich großer Wert

2.   ◀─○ Suchen Sie Möglichkeiten, die folgenden Mitteilungen dt. und engl. auszudrücken. Beachten Sie dabei folgende Varianten:

(1) to describe correctly   – to give / supply a correct description
(2) to explain adequately   – to give a(n) adequate / satisfactory explanation
(3) to define sufficiently   – to give / provide a sufficient definition
(4) outside the domain,   – outside their original domain
    for which they were
    originally developed
(5) to prove / show   – to prove / show by experiment
    experimentally

1. Durch die klassische Mechanik wurde es möglich, die Bewegungen der Planeten und aller Objekte auf der Erde unter dem Einfluß der Gravitation zu beschreiben. 2. Die Wirkungsweise mechanischer Maschinen fand eine befriedigende Erklärung. 3. Die klassische Mechanik kann die Rotation und Schwingung großer Körper zureichend definieren. 4. Die Gesetze der klassischen Mechanik können nicht außerhalb des Gebietes, für das sie ursprünglich entwickelt wurden, angewendet werden. 5. Es ist experimentell nachgewiesen worden, daß Raum und Zeit nicht voneinander unabhängig sind.

LE 3   Legen Sie in 8 bis 10 engl. Sätzen dar, warum die klassische Mechanik durch die Relativitätstheorie und die Quantentheorie ergänzt werden mußte. Benutzen Sie dafür Informationen aus dem folgenden Text:

Durch die klassische Mechanik wurde es möglich, die Bewegung der Planeten und aller Objekte auf der Erde unter dem Einfluß der Gravitation richtig zu beschreiben. Auch die Wirkungsweise mechanischer Maschinen, die Rotation und Schwingung großer Objekte und viele andere Erscheinungen fanden in der klassischen Mechanik eine befriedigende Erklärung. Es zeigt sich jedoch, daß die Newtonschen Gleichungen außerhalb des Bereiches, für den sie ursprünglich entwickelt wurden, nicht mehr gültig sind. Die klassische Mechanik bedarf im Gebiet hoher Geschwindigkeiten der Ergänzung durch die Relativitätstheorie und im Bereich atomarer Dimensionen durch die Quantentheorie. Die Newtonsche Mechanik benutzte ein Konzept von Raum und Zeit, nach dem die Zeit nicht von den Ortskoordinaten abhängig ist. Es ist jedoch inzwischen experimentell nachgewiesen worden, daß Raum und Zeit nicht voneinander unabhängig sind. Ferner kann sich kein Körper schneller bewegen als die Lichtgeschwindigkeit, und bei der Annäherung an die Lichtgeschwindigkeit wird seine Masse unendlich groß. Schließlich können wir mit der klassischen Mechanik nicht die Bewegung der Nukleonen im Kern beschreiben, da bei Bewegungen in mikroskopischen Dimensionen der Wellencharakter der Materie eine entscheidende Rolle spielt.

PK 10 · PA 4 · SQ A

LE 1 ⊕ ⊕ Neue Lexik

apparatus	[ˌæpəˈreitəs]	Apparatur, Gerät(e); System
device	[diˈvais]	Gerät, Apparat; Vorrichtung
investigation	[inˌvestiˈgeiʃən]	Untersuchung; Prüfung
to count	[kaunt]	zählen
chamber	[ˈtʃeimbə]	Kammer, (abgeschlossener) Raum
to insert (into)	[inˈsə:t]	einsetzen, einfügen (in); einführen, (hin)einstecken
to multiply	[ˈmʌltiplai]	multiplizieren, malnehmen
to extract a root	[iksˈtrækt]	(math.) eine Wurzel ziehen
to identify	[aiˈdentifai]	identifizieren, erkennen; nachweisen, feststellen
to register	[ˈredʒistə]	registrieren; (automatisch) anzeigen; aufzeichnen, erfassen
to solidify	[sɔˈlidifai]	(sich) verfestigen, erstarren, fest werden
gaseous	[ˈgeizjəs]	gasförmig, Gas-
to melt	[melt]	schmelzen
zero	[ˈziərou]	Null (Zahl, Zeichen); Nullpunkt; Ausgangspunkt, Ursprung
freezing point	[ˈfri:ziŋ ...]	Gefrierpunkt
to boil	[bɔil]	kochen, sieden
boiling point		Siedepunkt
to evaporate	[iˈvæpəreit]	verdampfen / verdunsten (lassen); eindampfen
vapour	[ˈveipə]	Dampf; Gas; Rauch
to remove	[riˈmu:v]	beseitigen, entfernen; entziehen (Energie etc).
to condense	[kənˈdens]	kondensieren; verdichten
to add	[æd]	(math.) addieren; hinzufügen, -setzen

scale	[skeil]	Skala, Gradeinteilung; Maßstab; Maß, Umfang
to differentiate	[ˌdifəˈrenʃieit]	differenzieren, unterscheiden, trennen
vessel	[ˈvesl]	Gefäß, Behälter
to affect	[əˈfekt]	(ein)wirken auf, beeinflussen, beeinträchtigen
monitoring	[ˈmɔnitəriŋ]	Überwachung, Kontrolle

LE 2 ⊕ ⊕ Internationalismen

thermometer	[θəˈmɔmitə]	Thermometer
parabolic	[ˌpærəˈbɔlik]	parabolisch
proportional	[prəˈpɔːʃənl]	proportional, Proportional-

PK 10 · PA 4 · SQ B

LE 1 ⊕ ⊕ Übersetzen Sie ins Engl. nach dem Muster:

T: positiv geladen   S: positively charged

LE 2 ⊕ ⊕ Übersetzen Sie ins Engl. nach dem Muster:

T: Wir untersuchten den Vorgang genau.
S: We studied the process closely.

LE 3 ⊕ ⊕ Übersetzen Sie ins Engl. nach dem Muster:

T: Die Konfiguration wurde genau untersucht.
S: The configuration was closely investigated.

LE 4 ⊕ ⊕ Beantworten Sie die Fragen nach dem Muster:

T: Has the deuteron a positive or a negative charge?
S: The deuteron is positively charged.

LE 5 ⊕ ⊕ Stellen Sie die Fragen nach dem Muster:

T: I think, the book contains a careful consideration of this problem.
S: Would you really say that the author considered it carefully?

careful treatment / sufficient explanation / clear discussion / correct description / unique definition

LE 6 ⊕ ⊕ Beantworten Sie die Fragen nach dem Muster:

T: Do these coordinates determine the position of the particle uniquely?
S: Yes, the position is uniquely determined.

LE 7 ⊕ ⊕ Stellen Sie Fragen nach dem Muster:

T: For this experiment we need a narrow tube. − comparative
S: Isn't this tube comparatively narrow?

PK 10 · PA 4 · SQ C

LE 1 Lesen Sie den Text und geben Sie eine engl. Zusammenfassung auf der Grundlage der Instruktion am Ende des Textes:

Beachten Sie, daß *unity* in phys. Fachtexten meist 'eins' bedeutet!

The kinematical quantity velocity is a vector quantity. Constancy of a velocity therefore implies (implizieren) motion with unchanging speed in a straight line. On the other hand, a change in velocity may mean either a change in speed or a change in direction or a change in both speed and direction simultaneously. All changes in velocity may be collectively expressed by a single vector equation. If we let $\vec{u}$ and v be the velocities of a particle at the beginning and end, respectively, of a given time interval, then the change in velocity during this interval will be given by the vector expression $\vec{v} - \vec{u}$, in which no limitation is imposed (auferlegen) upon the way in which the velocity may change. That this velocity change is a vector quantity is evident.

Acceleration has been defined as the quantity which expresses the change in velocity in a unit interval of time. If we divide the vector $\vec{v} - \vec{u}$ by the time (a scalar quantity) in which change occurred, we still have a vector expressing the change of velocity but whose magnitude has been changed, unless the particular value of the time interval happened to be unity. In general, then, we may define the average acceleration over a given time interval by the equation $\vec{w} = \dfrac{\vec{v} - \vec{u}}{t}$ in which the vector $\vec{w}$ shall be used to represent the acceleration, and t the time interval. This equation is general and includes all possible changes of the velocity. The rate of change of the velocity need not be constant. This possibility necessitates (erfordern) the inclusion of the term "average" in the above definition. When the variations in the acceleration are small or a knowledge of them is not important for the particular consideration, average acceleration may provide all of the information which is needed. There are many considerations, however, which require a knowledge of the exact value of the particle or at definite time instants. We shall use the term instantaneous acceleration to describe the value of the acceleration at any given position or instant. Instantaneous acceleration may be defined in the following manner. Let the change in the velocity during a small interval of time Δt be expressed by the vector $\Delta \vec{v}$. The average rate of change of the velocity in the time interval Δt is therefore $\Delta \vec{v}/\Delta t$. If the time interval approaches zero as a limit, the value of the ratio $\Delta \vec{v}/\Delta t$ at the limit will be the acceleration at the instant selected. Using the notation of calculus, we may express the instantaneous acceleration as follows:

$$\vec{w} = \frac{d\vec{v}}{dt} = \lim_{\Delta t \to 0} \frac{\Delta \vec{v}}{\Delta t}$$

Summary: The present paper deals with problems of ...
- Start with a short definition of the term vector.
- Give a definition of the term "acceleration".
- Explain why the term "average" should be included in this definition.
- Refer to the term "instantaneous acceleration" and state what it is used for!

Bereiten Sie die Übersetzung des Textes "*Aspects of X-Ray Spectroscopy*" (11.1.C. −1.) vor!

PK 10 · PA 4 · SQ D

LE 1   ⊕ ⊕   Einführung

small g: klein g / capital M: groß M

LE 2   ⊕ ⊕ ⊳   Hören Sie den BTV "*Gravitation*" und machen Sie sich Notizen!

LE 3   Geben Sie eine schriftliche Zusammenfassung der wesentlichen Informationen in Dt.!

LE 4   Give an example for this statement:

Every object attracts every other object with a force directly proportional to the product of the masses of the objects and inversely as the square of the distance between them. If m_1 is the mass of one object, m_2 the mass of the other, d the distance between them, then the gravitational force

$$F = \frac{km_1m_2}{d^2},$$

where k is a constant. For objects on or near the earth, the mass of the earth is very much greater than an object, and so the gravitational force between them makes the object "fall" towards the earth. The acceleration as it does this is called the acceleration due to gravity.

Trends in Modern Physics

PK 11 · PA 1 · SQ A

LE 1   Wir beschreiben die Zustandsänderung von Stoffen:

Substances occur in different *states of aggregation*. So, they may be either *solid*, *liquid* or *gaseous*. Water, for example, is normally a liquid. When water *solidifies*, it is called ice. The point at which ice *melts*, or water solidifies, is called the *freezing point* of water. The fixed point at which pure water *boils* is called the *boiling point* of water. At this point water evaporates so rapidly that it turns into steam. – All substances can be transformed from the *liquid state* into the *gaseous state* or into *vapour*, when energy is added to them. Conversely, when energy is removed from a gaseous state it finally *condenses* and turns into a liquid. We talk of a vapour only if the liquid state can exist at room temperature, whereas a gas needs cooling in order to *liquefy*.

Changes in the state of aggregation of a substance such as those described for water occur at certain fixed points. Thus, a substance is said to melt or evaporate at a definite *temperature*. Temperature is the degree of hotness or coldness measured on some given scale. In measuring temperatures, different *temperature scales* are used. The best known temperature scale is the *Celsius scale* (also called *centigrade scale*). So temperatures are given in degrees, for example 0° or 100°, with the abbreviation C., indicating the Celsius scale.

LE 2   Benutzen Sie LE 1 als Grundlage für eine sinngemäße engl. Darstellung der folgenden Fakten:

Die Temperatur beschreibt den Wärmezustand eines Stoffes. Die Erhöhung der Temperatur ist möglich, wenn man dem Körper Energie zuführt. Dann bewegen sich die den Körper aufbauenden Moleküle schneller. Man sagt, die kinetische Energie der Moleküle des Körpers hat sich erhöht. Zur Messung der Temperatur wurden verschiedene Temperaturskalen aufgestellt. Am häufigsten wird die Temperaturskala benutzt, die 1742 von dem schwedischen Physiker A. Celsius vorgeschlagen wurde. Die Celsiusskala basiert auf dem Temperaturverhalten von reinem Wasser. Die Temperatur t, bei der Eis schmilzt bzw. Wasser erstarrt, wird als Nullpunkt bezeichnet. Die Temperatur, bei der reines Wasser bei einem Luftdruck von 760 Torr siedet, d. h. verdampft, wird die Bezeichnung 100° gegeben. Zwischen diesen Festpunkten wird die Celsiusskala in gleiche Teile eingeteilt, die als Grade Celsius bezeichnet werden. Für die Messung von Temperaturen unterhalb des Gefrierpunktes bzw. Siedepunktes von Wasser wird die Skala weitergeführt. Die Temperaturen unterhalb 0° erhalten ein Minuszeichen. Die Angabe des Luftdrucks ist notwendig, weil Veränderungen des Aggregatzustandes eines S toffes von der Temperatur und vom Druck abhängig sind.

PK 11 · PA 1 · SQ B

LE 1   Wir geben den Zweck an (vgl. 6.1.B.):

What is the instrument / device / apparatus used for?
It is used for the investigation of ...

> for investigating ...
> in investigating ...
> (in order) to investigate ...

LE 2   Read the text and answer the following questions:

What is the ionization chamber / proportional counter / Geiger-Müller counter used for?
One of the oldest, but still most widely used, types of detector employs a gas-filled chamber. Depending on the mode of operation of this chamber, the detector type is known either as an ionization chamber, a proportional counter, or a Geiger-Müller (G-M) tube. The ionization chamber is an apparatus for measuring the amount of ionization produced by radioactivity in air or some other gaseous medium. It finds wide-scale use, for example, in monitoring radiation for personnel protection. Proportional counters are useful as counting devices and for energy measurements. Geiger-Müller counters are widely used for counting electrons where a large discharge pulse is triggered by a very small ionization. However, they cannot be used for differentiating between radiation types or for measuring the energy of the particles which trigger the discharge.

LE 3   Wir geben an, wie die Analyse durchgeführt wird:

> Particle rays are studied / detected / identified ...
> by means of
> with the help of nuclear instruments / using Wilson's cloud chamber.

The analysis is performed / carried out ...
by passing rays through the vessel /
by counting the discharges (automatically) /
by registering the impulses (automatically) /
by measuring the ionization current at the electrodes.

LE 4   Charakterisieren Sie in Engl. die folgenden Verfahren nach dem Muster:

> Zweck: Untersuchung der Strahlungsintensität radioaktiver Substanzen
> Mittel: Elektroskop
> Verfahren: Man läßt die Strahlung durch das im Instrument enthaltene Gas hindurchtreten und registriert die Geschwindigkeit der Entladung, die von der Anzahl der durch die Strahlung erzeugten Ionen abhängt.

Radioactive substances can be investigated by means of an electroscope in order to establish their radiation intensity. The analysis is carried out by passing rays from the radioactive substance through the gas contained in the device and registering the speed of the discharge (which is) dependent on the number of ions produced by the radiation.

1. Zweck: Messung der durch Radioaktivität verursachten Ionisation
Mittel: Ionisationskammer
Verfahren: Die durch die Radioaktivität erzeugten Ionen werden von den Elektroden angezogen. Der Ionisationsstrom wird gemessen.

2. Zweck: Nachweis und Zählung ionisierender Teilchen
Mittel: Geiger-Müller-Zählrohr
Verfahren: Die von einem eindringenden Korpuskularteilchen gebildeten Ionen werden durch die angelegte Spannung beschleunigt und rufen eine kurze Entladung hervor; diese Entladungen werden gezählt.

3. Zweck: Informationen über Elementarteilchen erhalten
Mittel: Wilsonsche Nebelkammer
Verfahren: Man läßt Elektronen, Protonen und Alphateilchen durch die Kammer hindurchgehen. Dabei werden die Gasmoleküle ionisiert und dienen als Kondensationskerne (condensation nuclei).

LE 5   Lesen Sie den Text und beantworten Sie die Fragen:
  1. Why was a discharge passed through the vessel?
  2. How was a narrow stream of positive rays obtained?
  3. How were the rays deflected?
  4. How was it possible to obtain a photographic picture of the parabolic curves?
  5. What can positive-ray analysis be used for?

In the course of his extended studies of positive rays, J. J. Thomson made in 1912 an interesting observation which was related to the existence of isotopes of stable elements. If a beam of positive rays contains particles of different masses they will be differentiated in such a manner that all the particles with the same mass, or, more correctly, all having the same e/m value will fall on one parabolic curve. An electric discharge was passed through a vessel containing the experimental gas at suitable low pressure. A narrow stream of positive rays was obtained, using an aluminium cathode connected to a tube. After passing through electric and magnetic fields arranged so as to give deflections at right angles to one another, the positive rays were allowed to fall on a photographic plate. On development, the latter showed a series of parabolic lines, each corresponding to a definite value of the charge-to-mass ratio (e/m) of atomic and molecular particles present in the positive rays. A method of positive-ray analysis is thus available for detecting the presence of, and even for identifying, atomic and molecular particles whose masses differ from each other.

LE 6 ☛—O Geben Sie den Inhalt des folgenden Textes sinngemäß in Engl. wieder:

Alle Isotope lassen sich trennen. Zur Isotopentrennung gibt es verschiedene Verfahren, die auf den unterschiedlichen Eigenschaften der Isotope beruhen. Das älteste und bekannteste Gerät zur Isotopentrennung ist der Massenspektrograph, der bereits 1919 von dem britischen Physiker Aston entwickelt wurde. Durch eine Kombination von elektrischen und magnetischen Feldern gelingt es, Kanalstrahlen (canal rays) so abzulenken, daß Ionen gleicher Massenzahl und gleicher elektrischer Ladung im selben Punkt einer photographischen Platte auftreffen. Die Fokussierung läßt sich erreichen durch ein elektrisches Feld und durch ein zu diesem und der Bewegungsrichtung der Teilchen senkrechtes magnetisches Feld. Da im Massenspektrograph Teilchen mit gleicher elektrischer Ladung in einem Punkt einer photographischen Platte fokussiert werden, wenn sie gleiche Massen haben, und da die Schwärzung (blackening) an dieser Stelle der Anzahl der aufgetroffenen Teilchen proportional ist, können alle Isotope und die Häufigkeit ihres Vorkommens bestimmt werden.

PK 11 · PA 1 · SQ C

LE 1 Übersetzen Sie mit Hilfe des Wörterbuches:

Aspects of the X-Ray Spectroscopy of Solids

When an atom is brought into close proximity to other atoms as in compound molecules or in solids X-ray phenomena involving only ionization in an inner shell are little affected, but those involving also the atomic exterior are considerably modified. A number of cases have been studied, but only a partial understanding has been achieved. Details tend to be obscured by the great natural breadth of X-ray lines, especially if the wavelength is less than 5 Å.

In a solid, the outermost atomic electrons come to be associated with the entire solid rather than with individual atoms, and essentially continuous bands of electronic states may be supposed to replace the discrete atomic states so far as these electrons are concerned.

The simplest case is that of the alkali metals. Here the set of electronic states for the valence electrons in their individual atoms is replaced in the crystal by a band of electronic states 5–20 ev wide in energy. Displacement of an electron within this band, or from this into another band, is associated in simple cases with an equal change in the crystal energy. In the alkali metals, however, the number of valence electrons is only sufficient to fill the valence band half full, the remainder of the band being normally empty. In general, X-ray spectra are related primarily to the inner atomic structure. But, as can be seen, certain finer features of X-ray spectra involve in their explanation a consideration of the outer part of the atom, or even, in a solid or liquid, of the surrounding material.

PK 11 · PA 2 · SQ A

LE 1 ⊕ ⊕ Neue Lexik

ordinary	[ˈɔːdnəri]	gewöhnlich, normal, üblich
reply	[riˈplai]	Antwort
proposal	[prəˈpouzəl]	Vorschlag
successful	[səkˈsesful]	erfolgreich, mit Erfolg
to report	[riˈpɔːt]	berichten
recent	[ˈriːsnt]	vor kurzem, unlängst (geschehen, entstanden), nicht lange zurückliegend; neu; modern
to concern	[kənˈsəːn]	betreffen, sich beziehen auf, an(be)langen
to be concerned with		sich beschäftigen mit, befaßt sein mit, zu tun haben mit
findings	[ˈfaindiŋs]	(Untersuchungs)Ergebnisse
view	[vjuː]	Ansicht, Meinung
precise	[priˈsais]	genau, präzise; Präzisions-, Fein-
review	[riˈvju(ː)]	Bericht; Übersicht; Überblick(sartikel); Buchbesprechung, Rezension
issue	[ˈisjuː]	Herausgabe, Veröffentlichung; Ausgabe, Auflage
complete	[kəmˈpliːt]	ganz, gesamt; vollständig
in / with regard to /	[riˈgɑːd]	in Hinsicht auf, hinsichtlich,
regarding		in bezug auf
to conclude	[kənˈkluːd]	folgern, schließen, eine Schlußfolgerung ziehen; beenden, (ab)schließen
to point out	[pɔint]	hervorheben, unterstreichen
to derive (from)	[diˈraiv]	(chem., math.) ableiten (aus)
to prove	[pruːv]	beweisen, nachweisen; sich erweisen als
to proceed	[prəˈsiːd]	fortfahren, weiterführen; vorgehen, verfahren; verlaufen, vonstatten gehen
to verify	[ˈverifai]	verifizieren, nachprüfen
to confirm	[kənˈfəːm]	bestätigen, bekräftigen
valid	[ˈvælid]	gültig, zutreffend; wirksam; stichhaltig
evident	[ˈevidənt]	klar (ersichtlich), offenbar
operation	[ˌɔpəˈreiʃən]	(math.) Operation, Rechnungsverfahren, -art; Arbeitsvorgang, Verfahren, Arbeitsstufe

LE 2 ⊕ ⊕ Internationalismen

journal	[ˈdʒəːnl]	(Fach)Zeitschrift, Journal
author	[ˈɔːθə]	Autor, Verfasser
passage	[ˈpæsidʒ]	Abschnitt, Passage
diameter	[daiˈæmitə]	Durchmesser, Diameter

LE 3 ⊕ ⊕ Hören und üben Sie mathematische Ausdrücke*):

Decimal point:

5.02 *five point 0 two*

INDEX:

x_1 *x subscript one*

Relation signs:

$a = b$	*a is equal to b | a equals b | a is equivalent to b*
$b > a$	*b is greater than a*
$c \gg a$	*c is much greater than a*
$a < b$	*a is less than b*
$a \ll c$	*a is much less than c*
$P \geqq Q$	*p is greater than or equal to Q*
$M \approx 4$	*The atomic weight of helium is approximately equal to four*
$a \subset b$	*a is (directly) proportional to b*

ADDITION: sum

$a + b = c$ *a plus b is equal to c*

SUBTRACTION: difference

$c - b = a$ *c minus b is equal to a*

MULTIPLICATION: factor, product

$a \times b = c$ *a times b is equal to c*

DIVISION: numerator, denominator, quotient, fraction

$a : b = c/$ *a divided by b is equal to c \|*

$\dfrac{a}{b} = c$ *a over b is equal to c*

NATURAL LOGARITHM of a number

ROOTS AND POWERS: to extract a root

$\sqrt{x}$ *square root of x*

$\sqrt[3]{x}$ *cube root of x*

---

*) Vgl. dazu: Städtler/Städtler, Englisch. Symbolik und Fachausdrücke. Mathematik · Physik · Chemie, Leipzig 1969, wonach diese Auswahl getroffen wurde.

$\sqrt[n]{x}$ *n-th root of x*
a^2 *a squared*
a^3 *a cubed*
a^n *a to the n-th (power)*

PK 11 · PA 2 · SQ B

LE 1   ⊕ ⊕   Üben Sie den folgenden Dialog:

T: Generally speaking, any substance may occur in three states of aggregation.
S: That's true, but (normally) a substance occurs only in one state.
T: Of course, under ordinary conditions a substance is either a solid, a liquid, or a gas. What are examples you can think of?
S: Examples I can think of are air, metals and so on.

1. either a conductor or an insulator / copper, wood 2. they are distinguished into pulse- and non-pulse type instruments / Geiger-Müller tube, proportional counter 3. only some are used as sources of nuclear energy / uranium 235, plutonium 4. there are exceptions / sodium and cobalt 5. there are exceptions / deuterium and tritium

LE 2   ⊕ ⊕   Üben Sie den folgenden Dialog:

T: He set up a new theory for explaining this phenomenon.
S: Is there already some (experimental) evidence for this (theory / ...) / that it is correct / successful?
T: To answer your question / In reply to your question, there is some evidence obtained by means of a semiconductor radiation detector / ...

LE 3   ⊕ ⊕   Üben Sie den folgenden Dialog:

S: We published a study on
   semiconducting compounds / non-equilibrium statistics / geophysical problems
   We reported on new results in
   solid state physics / crystal optics / semiconductor physics.
T: Did your paper also contain new experimental evidence?
S: To answer your question, we obtained some evidence by means of crystal growing / by means of lasers / by carrying out new measurements / by nuclear resonance measurements / by deriving a system of equations.
T: Thank you very much for that interesting information.

PK 11 · PA 2 · SQ C

LE 1   Lesen Sie mit Hilfe des Wörterbuches:

Laser

A laser is a device which generates a beam of light. The light from a laser is very much more intense than light from other sources and, in addition, possesses the property of coherence which ordinary light beams do not possess.

An electron which has been lifted to an upper energy level will normally, after a short interval of time, spontaneously fall to a lower level with the emission of a photon of definite frequency v. If, while the electron is still in the upper level, a photon of exactly this frequency is incident upon the atom, the electron may be stimulated to fall to the lower level at the instant the external photon passes. The external photon is not absorbed or affected in any way, but passes on. In falling to the lower level the electron will lose energy, and this energy is emitted from the atom as a photon of frequency v, the same frequency as that of the external photon. Further, this photon travels in the same direction as, and is in phase with, the external photon which stimulated its fall. This is the phenomenon of stimulated emission of radiation, and the action of the laser is completely dependent upon it.

When a beam of monochromatic light passes through a transparent medium its intensity is reduced. This is due to a reduction in the number of photons in the beam. It is possible, however, to create an abnormal condition of the medium so that a monochromatic beam of light actually increases its intensity as it travels through the medium. Three different types of transition will take place, if a beam is made to pass through the medium:

(a) Some of the photons in the incident beam will be absorbed and cause electrons to be lifted from the lower level to the upper level. This process will cause a reduction in the intensity of the beam.

(b) Some of the photons in the incident beam will stimulate electrons to fall from the upper to the lower level, with the emission of another photon of the same frequency, the stimulating photon passing on unaffected. Since the stimulated photon travels in the same direction as the stimulating photon, this process causes an increase in the intensity of the beam.

(c) Some electrons will spontaneously fall from the upper to the lower level with the emission of a photon. These photons are emitted randomly in all directions and, since only a small proportion will travel in the same direction as the incident beam, their contribution to the intensity of the beam can be neglected.

It is readily seen that, if the beam is to increase in intensity as it passes through the medium, the stimulated emission of photons must exceed the absorption of photons.

The number of upward transitions is proportional to the number of electrons in the lower level. The number of downward transitions is proportional to the number of electrons in the upper level. Therefore, for stimulated emission to exceed absorption, there must be more electrons in the upper level than in the lower level. Under normal conditions of thermal equilibrium, there are always more electrons in a lower level than in an upper level. The reversal of this condition needed for light amplification is called an "inverted population".

LE 2 Geben Sie eine Zusammenfassung in Engl. auf der Grundlage der folgenden Wendungen:

- The paper deals with / is concerned with / reports on ...
- First(ly) a short definition is given of / the author gives a short definition of ...
- I should mention here / the author mentions that light from a laser ...
- The following passage from the paper describes (in detail) the phenomenon of stimulated emission of radiation.
- I can only mention here that ...
- The author then goes on to discuss the passage of a beam of monochromatic light through a transparent medium.
- Three cases are distinguished ...
- With regard to the first case ...
- To take the second case ...
- Regarding the third case ...
- Concluding his paper / In conclusion the author points out / underlines that ...

   Bereiten Sie die Übersetzung des Textes "*Plasma Physics*" (11.3.C. −1.) vor!

PK 11 · PA 2 · SQ D

LE 1   ⊕ ⊕ Einführender Dialog:

fundamental / elucidation, illumination: Erhellung, Aufklärung / to originate: entstehen / aim: Ziel / hybrid / to adopt: übernehmen / contribution to: Beitrag zu

LE 2   ⊕ ⊕ Hören Sie den TV "*Physics and other Sciences*" und machen Sie sich Notizen!

LE 3 Give a summary of this text in English and think of additional examples!

You may use: As far as I have understood ... / I believe the author pointed out that ... / In listening to this paper I was struck by the fact that ... / With regard to this point ... / I would like to state that ... / I would like to / cannot comment on ... (but) I can give some information ... / I would like to mention here ... / It is my opinion ... / I might add that ...

LE 4 Speak about instruments and methods used in physical research, e.g.

– techniques used in semiconductor physics
– the application of isotopes
– the function and design of nuclear instruments

PK 11 · PA 3 · SQ A

LE 1 Wir geben mathematische Verfahren an

		by substituting the variable for a
	derived	by inserting the values into the expression
X is		by dividing A by B
	obtained	by multiplying A by B
		by extracting y

LE 2 Erläutern Sie in Engl.:

1. Mass-energy equivalence principle:

$$E = mc^2; \qquad m = \frac{E}{c^2}$$

where E is the energy, m the mass and c the speed of light in vacuo.

2. The mean free path between colliding molecules is inversely proportional to the molecular diameter:

$$L = \frac{1}{nd^2 \sqrt{2}}$$

where n is the number of molecules per cm^2, and d the diameter of the molecules.

LE 3 Wir geben Nachweisverfahren an

What is the purpose of this investigation / examination / study?

We $\begin{cases} \text{detect} \\ \text{identify} \\ \text{prove} \\ \text{calculate} \end{cases}$ $\begin{array}{l} A \text{ in } B. \\ A \text{ present in } B. \\ \text{that } A \text{ has the property } B. \\ A \text{ from } B. \end{array}$

The substance under investigation / under study / under examination / we studied

is characterised by
is recognised by / through ... as
is recognised $\begin{cases} \text{to consist of} \\ \text{to be made up of} \\ \text{to be composed of} \end{cases}$

is found {to behave / to act
is calculated {to be / as

LE 4   Stellen Sie Nachweisverfahren im Engl. dar:

1. Radioaktive Substanzen können nachgewiesen werden in ...

da sie {gekennzeichnet sind durch / erkennbar sind an

unterschiedliche (*n*/*r*) {chemische(n) Eigenschaften. / Rückstoßgeschwindigkeiten. / Strahlungsintensität.

2. Es kann nachgewiesen werden,

daß ein Material {radioaktive Substanzen enthält, / aus radioaktiven Substanzen besteht,

weil die letzteren {Strahlen emittieren. / Wirkungen auf andere Substanzen ausüben.

LE 5   Wir weisen die Richtigkeit einer Hypothese nach

In the course of a(n) examination / (experimental) study / investigation

we {assume / suppose}   that X is A.
postulate   that A is (in)finite / discrete ...
conclude   that X is A.
{set up / suggest}   a hypothesis which implies ...
proceed   from the {assumption ... / hypothesis ...}

As a result of our examination / investigation / study

the hypothesis is {verified / confirmed /

the hypothesis is found {to be true ... / valid for ... / to hold (good) for ...

Our examination / investigation / study

results in the {verification of ... / confirmation of ...

The {verification / confirmation} of ... was achieved by ...

LE 6 ᴨ—0 Stellen Sie in Engl. dar, wie die Hypothese von den Leitungselektronen nachgewiesen wurde:

Im Verlauf der Untersuchung der Elektroneneigenschaften wurde die Hypothese aufgestellt, daß bewegliche Elektronen die Grundlage der Leitung in Metallen sind. Die Bestätigung dieser Hypothese erbrachte der Physiker Tolman. Er ging von der Annahme aus, daß Elektronen infolge ihrer Masse einer Trägheitswirkung (effect of inertia) unterliegen und sich in der ursprünglichen Bewegungsrichtung weiterbewegen müßten. Das müßte dann einen Spannungsstoß (voltage pulse) verursachen. Im Ergebnis einer experimentellen Untersuchung gelang T. der Nachweis dieses Spannungsstoßes. Aus dem Spannungsstoß konnte die spezifische Ladung des Elektrons berechnet werden. Da man die gleichen Werte wie bei Elektronen im Vakuum erhielt, waren frei bewegliche Elektronen als Ursache der metallischen Leitung nachgewiesen.

LE 7 Stellen Sie in Engl. dar, wie Maxwells Annahme der Existenz elektromagnetischer Wellen nachgewiesen wurde:

Auf der Grundlage der experimentellen Untersuchungen Faradays über die Felder postulierte Maxwell das Vorhandensein elektromagnetischer Wellen, mit denen eine Übertragung elektromagnetischer Energie verbunden sein müsse. Darüberhinaus kam er zu der Folgerung, daß auch das Licht eine solche elektromagnetische Wellenerscheinung sei. Bereits im Jahre 1862 hatte der Physiker Feddersen nachgewiesen, daß der elektrische Funke (spark) keine einfache, nur in einer Richtung vor sich gehende Entladungserscheinung sei. Aus dieser Entdeckung ergab sich die Möglichkeit, nach den elektromagnetischen Wellen zu suchen. Heinrich Hertz gelang es, mit elektrischen Funken die Richtigkeit der Maxwellschen Annahme durch das Experiment nachzuweisen. Durch weitere Experimente konnte Hertz später zeigen, daß die von ihm gefundenen elektromagnetischen Wellen neben der Reflexion noch weitere Eigenschaften des Lichts, wie Brechung und Interferenz, zeigen. Damit war auch die zweite Annahme Maxwells bestätigt.

PK 11 · PA 3 · SQ B

LE 1 Wir begründen

Why   can A be used for B?
        A can be used for B because it contains C.
Since   A contains C,   it can be used for B.
        A contains C.,
Therefore it can be used for B.
        A can be used for B because of C.

LE 2   Vergleichen Sie die Angabe des Grundes nach *as* und *for* mit anderen Funktionen dieser Funktionswörter:

1. As there are large numbers of electrons always available, a positron does not exist for any appreciable time. 2. As the neutron approaches the nucleus, attractive forces begin to operate and the neutron may be captured. 3. Nowadays the particle aspect of X-rays is very evident, for we often measure the intensity of an X-ray beam by actually counting the quanta by a Geiger counter. 4. The fact that most solids are diamagnetic is a consequence of the strong tendency for electrons to form closed shells.

LE 3   🖛—0 Verbinden Sie die folgenden Aussagenpaare durch die Angabe des Grundes:

1. Most radioelements are available in very small amounts only. Their separation is usually performed in the presence of carriers. 2. Gamma rays are highly dangerous. They have a long range and a high penetration power. 3. Gamma rays produce secondary ionization. They can be detected in the cloud chamber. 4. Most of the volume of an atom is just empty space. Alpha particles are able to penetrate matter.

LE 4   Wir folgern bzw. ziehen einen Schluß

1. Daraus ist zu ersehen / ergibt sich, daß ...

So / Thus / Hence $\begin{cases} \text{it can be seen} \\ \text{it is evident} \\ \text{it is apparent} \\ \text{it is clear} \end{cases}$ (from this) that ...

2. Wir ziehen daraus den Schluß / Daraus folgt, daß ...

From this we can conclude that ...
From this it can be concluded that ...
It follows from this that ...

LE 5   Wie kann man im Engl. die Beziehungen des Grundes und / oder der Folge bzw. der Schlußfolgerung zwischen den vorgegebenen Sachverhalten ausdrücken:

Im vorliegenden Fall sind alle Elektronen am Aufbau des Kristallgitters beteiligt. Es sind keine freien Elektronen vorhanden.

Since / As in the present case, all electrons are used in forming the crystal lattice, there are no free electrons, because ...
There are no free electrons, because ...

In the present case, all electrons are used in forming the crystal lattice. So, it is clear / It is clear from this that / Hence there are no free electrons.

Beachten Sie, daß nicht alle Sachverhalte beide Mitteilungen zulassen!

1. Die Vakuumröhre besitzt zwei Elektroden. Man bezeichnet sie als Diode.
2. Leuchtende Stoffe ergeben im Gaszustand Linienspektren. Diese Atome strahlen Energie ganz bestimmter Frequenzen aus. 3. Magnetische und elektrische Felder bedürfen nicht eines stofflichen Trägers. Die elektromagnetischen Wellen breiten sich auch im Vakuum aus. 4. Die Elektronen geben einen Teil ihrer kinetischen Energie an die Gitterbestandteile ab. Das Metall erwärmt sich (Stromwärme). 5. Die Protonen stoßen einander ab wegen ihrer gleichen positiven Ladung und Gravitationskräfte reichen nicht aus, um die Stabilität zu erklären. Es müssen besondere Kernkräfte existieren, die bei geringster Reichweite außerordentlich groß sind. 6. Ein Teil der radioaktiven Strahlung erfährt durch ein starkes Magnetfeld eine geringe, aber deutliche Ablenkung, die der Ablenkung der Elektronen entgegengesetzt ist. Dieser Teil muß aus positiv geladenen Teilchen bestehen.

PK 11 · PA 3 · SQ C

LE 1   Übersetzen Sie mit Hilfe des Wörterbuches:

Plasma Physics

A plasma may be defined as a gas composed of charged particles — free electrons and ions. In addition to possessing the general properties of an ordinary gas, a plasma, being an electrically conducting fluid, can be acted upon by electromagnetic fields. In fact, the plasma itself can be the source of electromagnetic fields — fields arising from the collective motions of the plasma particles. For this reason, plasmas, particularly when in the presence of a magnetic field, exhibit complex dynamical behaviour that sets the plasma state apart from all other forms of matter (solids, liquids, and ordinary gases). The unusual properties of this "fourth state of matter" are of intrinsic scientific interest, and elucidation of them could lead to technological developments of far-reaching importance. Among these is the achievement of the controlled release of nuclear-fusion energy, which would be of profound importance in the future. Modern plasma physics owes its origin to three older disciplines — gas-discharge physics, astrophysics, and geophysics. Gas discharge constituted an important subfield of physics from 1900 to 1930. However, gases involved in these studies were typically only slightly ionized and at low temperatures, and thus were dominated by surface effects and atomic processes. Collective effects were usually unimportant and received little attention. Nevertheless, it was in a gas discharge that Langmuir, in 1927, made the pioneering discovery of electrostatic plasma oscillations that initiated modern plasma physics. Early developments relating to plasma effects and to the underlying question of charged-particle dynamics also arose from astrophysics and geophysics. The theories of radio propagation through the ionosphere and of the motion of cosmic-ray particles in the earth's magnetic field are early examples. It was in the 1950's, however, that a rapid growth in plasma physics began. The stimulation for this growth came from the scientifically challenging goal of controlled fusion, promising an inexhaustible source of safe nuclear power. Another major influence in the recent growth of plasma physics has been the emphasis on space research. As a result, modern plasma physics has emerged as a well-defined scientific field of study.

PK 11 · PA 4 · SQ A

LE 1 ⊕ ⊕ Neue Lexik

foundation	[faun'deiʃən]	Grundlage, Basis
course	[kɔ:s]	Studium (university course); Reihe (von aufeinanderfolgenden Dingen); Kurs (language course); Studienjahr
extended secondary school		Erweiterte Oberschule
admission (to)	[əd'miʃən]	Zulassung (z. B. zum Studium)
subject	['sʌbdʒikt]	(Studien)Fach; Gegenstand (z. B. einer Diskussion)
instruction	[in'strʌkʃən]	Unterricht; Anweisung; Hinweise
additional	[ə'diʃənəl]	zusätzlich, weitere(r, s); Zusatz-
current	['kʌrənt]	gegenwärtig; modern; laufend
to cover	['kʌvə]	umfassen (Thematik)
topic	['tɔpik]	Thema, (Gesprächs)Gegenstand; Fach(gebiet)
to be designed (+ to + Inf.)	[di'zaind]	bestimmt sein für, sollen; den Zweck haben
career	[kə'riə]	berufliche Laufbahn, Beruf
lecture	['lektʃə]	Vorlesung
curriculum	[kə'rikjələm]	Studien-, Lehrprogramm
regular	['regjulə]	regelmäßig (aufgebaut); regelmäßig
staff	[stɑ:f]	Lehrkörper (Universität u. ä.); Belegschaft (Betrieb)
individual	[ˌindi'vidjuəl]	individuell, persönlich; einzeln
tutorial	[tju(:)'tɔ:riəl]	(Fach)Konsultation (an Bildungsinstitutionen)
term	[tə:m]	Semester; Begriff
adviser	[əd'vaizə]	Berater, Betreuer
guidance	['gaidəns]	Führung, Leitung; Beratung, Betreuung

to examine	[ig'zæmin]	prüfen (Examen); (nach)prüfen, untersuchen
oral	['ɔːrəl]	mündlich
to take into account	[ə'kaunt]	berücksichtigen; in Betracht ziehen
mark	[mɑːk]	(Bewertungs)Note; Zeichen, Kennzeichen
thesis	['θiːsis]	Dissertation; (Diplom)Arbeit
to summarize	['sʌməraiz]	zusammenfassen; (zusammenfassend) darstellen

LE 2 ⊕ ⊕ Internationalismen

institution	[ˌinsti'tjuːʃən]	Institution, Einrichtung
academic	[ˌækə'demik]	akademisch; Universitäts-, Studien-
specialization	[ˌspeʃəlai'zeiʃən]	Spezialisierung; Spezialfach
seminar	['seminɑː]	Seminar; Übung
laboratory	[lə'bɔrətəri]	Labor(atorium)

LE 3 ⊕ ⊕ Hören und üben Sie mathematische Ausdrücke:

Linear equation, quadratic equation
parenthesis, -es: ( )
brackets: [ ]
brace(s): { }

$$d^2 \frac{y}{dx^2} + \left(\frac{dy}{dx}\right) + xy = 0$$

ANALYSIS:

$y = f(x)$	*y equals f of x*
$y = \sin x$	*y equals sine x*
$y = \cos x$	*y equals cos x*
$y = \tan x$	*y equals tan x*
$y = \cot x$	*y equals cot x*

INTERVALS AND LIMITS:

$\lim\limits_{x \to x_1} f(x) = L$	*the limit of f of x as x tends to x one is capital L*
$\lim\limits_{x \to x_0} f(x) \uparrow f(x_0)$	*the limit of f of x as x tends to x nought is not equal to f of x nought*
$\lim\limits_{n \to \infty} a_n = 0$	*the limit of a sub n is zero as n tends to infinity*

DIFFERENTIAL CALCULUS:

| $\dfrac{dx}{dy}$ | dx by dy |
| $(\sin x)' = \cos X$ | *the first derivative of sine x is cos x* |

INTEGRAL CALCULUS:

$\int$	integral sign
$f(x)$	integrand
x	variable of integration

GREEK ALPHABET:

$A\ \alpha$	alpha	['ælfə]	$N\ \nu$	nu	[nju:]
$B\ \beta$	beta	['bi:tə]	$\Xi\ \xi$	xi	[ksai]
$\Gamma\ \gamma$	gamma	['gæmə]	$O\ o$	omicron	[o'maikrən]
$\Delta\ \delta$	delta	['deltə]	$\Pi\ \pi$	pi	[pai]
$E\ \varepsilon$	epsilon	[ep'sailən]	$P\ \varrho$	rho	[rou]
$Z\ \zeta$	zeta	['zi:tə]	$\Sigma\ \sigma$	sigma	['sigmə]
$H\ \eta$	eta	['i:tə]	$T\ \tau$	tau	[tɔ:]
$\Theta\ \vartheta$	theta	['θi:tə]	$Y\ \upsilon$	upsilon	[ju:p'sailən]
$I\ \iota$	iota	[ai'outə]	$\Phi\ \varphi$	phi	[fai]
$K\ \varkappa$	kappa	['kæpə]	$X\ \chi$	chi	[kai]
$\Lambda\ \lambda$	lambda	['læmdə]	$\Psi\ \psi$	psi	[sai]
$M\ \mu$	mu	[mju:]	$\Omega\ \omega$	omega	['oumigə]

PK 11 · PA 4 · SQ B

LE 1   ⊕ ⊕   Üben Sie den folgenden Dialog:

T: I'd like to ask you a question concerning this paper. What does it deal with / report on / is it concerned with?

S: The paper deals with / ... problems of semiconductor physics / plasma physics / superconductors / lasers / quantum mechanics

T: How does the author start?

S: First(ly) / In the first passage(s) / In the first part the author gives a short definition of semiconductors / ...

T: How does the author then go on? Does he discuss the application of semiconductors in industry? / ...?

S: That's right. He then goes on / also discusses their application in industry / ...

LE 2   ⊕ ⊕   Üben Sie den folgenden Dialog:

T: I'd like to know / I wonder whether you're familiar with current trends in plasma physics / ...

S: Well, the other day I read a report which summarized current trends in plasma physics / ...

T: Do you happen to know / Have you any idea how the academy contributes to research in this field?

S: Your question is difficult to answer. /
I can only give some information about the work in our department / research team. /
I regret to have / Unfortunately I have no information about this. / I've no idea. /
I'm not familiar with these things. /
As far as I know they concentrate on problems of ...

LE 3 ⊕ ⊕ Üben Sie den folgenden Dialog:

T: I've got a review / ... of current trends in solid-state physics. Are you interested in it / ...?

S: It might be of some interest / ... for my present study. Does the author also refer to / report on / comment on / deal with / consider special problems?

T: Well, at the end of the review / ... the author sums up / ... problems which have not been solved yet.

S: It seems to me that I should at least read this summary / ... May I have this review / ...?

T: Of course you may. The summary / ... is on page 53.

PK 11 · PA 4 · SQ C

LE 1 Lesen Sie mit Hilfe des Wörterbuches:

Superconductors

Superconductors are metals which, when cooled below a certain very low temperature, suddenly lose all trace of electrical resistance. The temperature at which resistance disappears is called the transition temperature, and is different for each metal. Not all metals become superconducting; about half the metallic elements and a large number of alloys have been found to become superconducting at various temperatures below about 20 K. For example, niobium-zirconium alloy becomes superconducting below about 12 K, pure niobium metal below about 12 K, pure niobium metal below about 9.5 K, aluminium below 1.2 K, but iron and gold retain their resistance to the lowest temperatures at which measurements have been made.

The current in a metal is, of course, carried by electrons moving through the material, and it turns out that a superconductor will only carry a resistanceless current if the average momentum of the electrons is less than a certain value. If the current is increased so that the electrons have more than this momentum, superconductivity is destroyed and the metal reverts to its normal resistive state. The maximum current that a superconductor can carry and yet remain resistanceless is called its critical current. Every piece of superconducting metal has therefore a critical current which cannot be exceeded if the wire is to remain resistanceless. The critical current decreases as the temperature is raised and falls to zero at the metal's transition temperature.

We speak of superconductors and not perfect conductors, and there is some significance in this distinction, because superconductors have an additional property that a merely resistanceless conductor would not have. A metal in the superconducting state has the peculiar feature that it does not permit any magnetic flux to exist in the body of the material. When a magnetic field is applied to a superconductor, resistanceless currents begin to flow on the surface, and these circulate in such a manner that they create within the material a magnetic field which is everywhere equal and opposite to the applied field. Consequently within the bulk of the metal the magnetic induction, and hence the magnetic flux, are both zero. We say, therefore, that a superconductor is "perfectly diamagnetic". If we lower the temperature in the presence of a weak magnetic field, all flux is suddenly expelled from the metal when its temperature falls below the transition temperature. It can be seen that this behaviour is quite different from that of a perfect conductor. As the field strength is increased, the circulating surface currents which annul the magnetic flux within the material must also increase. Eventually, however, the critical current is reached, and when this happens superconductivity is destroyed, the metal reverts to the normal state and the magnetic flux of the applied field penetrates into the material. The magnetic field strength at which superconductivity is destroyed is called the "critical magnetic field". We see therefore that a superconductor has two possible states: the superconducting state which is resistanceless and diamagnetic, and the normal state which is exactly like a normal metal.

LE 2   Geben Sie eine Zusammenfassung in Engl. auf der Grundlage der folgenden Wendungen:

This is a review of / a report which summarizes / sums up current trends / problems / research work in ...
In the first part / passage(s) / By way of introduction a definition is given of ...
Comparing conduction in normal conductors and superconductors, the distinction is made that ...
The author points out that we speak of superconductors and not perfect conductors / that we use the term ... and not ...
At the end of the survey, the author gives again the main characteristics / criteria / features / properties of the possible states which are characteristic for ...

Bereiten Sie die Übersetzung des Textes *"University Course of Physics Studies"* (12.1.C. – 1.) vor!

PK 11 · PA 4 · SQ D

LE 1 ⊕ ⊕ Einführender Dialog:

indispensable: unentbehrlich / to be engaged in: sich beschäftigen mit / to meet the needs: den Bedürfnissen entsprechen / equipment: Ausrüstung

LE 2 Hören Sie den TV "*Physics and Technology*" und machen Sie sich Notizen!

LE 3 Give a summary of this text in English and comment on

- the influence of discoveries in physics on modern industry
- the constant need for research workers in physics to develop new devices and instruments
- the application of new research tools and techniques in industry.

LE 4 Speak about current trends in physics, e.g.

- the development of semiconductors
- the promise of plasmas
- the advantages of superconductors

University Courses and Co-operation in Research

PK 12 · PA 1 · SQ A

LE 1 Die dt. Präp. 'bei' spielt für die Angabe gleichzeitiger Vorgänge, für Quellen- und Wertangaben sowie für verschiedene Arten der Zuordnung eine wichtige Rolle, da sie eine kurze Ausdrucksweise ermöglicht. Die engl. Äquivalente sind:

1. Zeitliche Beziehung: Handelt es sich um einen Zeitpunkt, so nehmen wir *on*, während bei einem Zeitraum *in* vorgezogen wird:

> *On* the formation of atoms energy is liberated.
> *In* studying the properties of electrons, the results of a diffraction experiment may be described in terms of waves.

Engl. *in* kann stets Verwendung finden, wenn statt dt. 'bei' auch 'während' gesagt werden könnte:

$$\frac{in}{during} \text{ the experiment} = \frac{beim}{während\ des} \text{ Experiment(s)}$$

Einige Ausdrücke werden fast immer mit *on* verwendet:

on closer examination = bei näherer Untersuchung
on heating = beim Erwärmen
on melting = beim Schmelzen

2. Beim Verweis auf ein Buch bzw. auf einen Autor finden wir engl. *in*:

> A description of this method can be found *in* Kittel.

3. Werte auf einer Skala werden mit *at* angeschlossen:

> The substance melts *at* 150°C.

4. Die Zuordnung von Eigenschaften bzw. Verhaltensweisen zu Größen erfolgt durch *for*, die Zuordnung zu gleichzeitig stattfindenden Vorgängen durch *with*:

> *For* elements of low atomic weight, the atomic number is approximately half the mass number.
> *With* an increase in temperature, the conductance of metals decreases.

5. Verben oder Nomen können sich fest mit bestimmten Präp. bzw. präpositionalen Ausdrücken verbinden:

> A periodic character may be *observed with* many physical and chemical properties.
> This theory cannot be *applied in the case of* liquids.
> This is not *the case with* hydrogen.

6. In einigen Fällen entspricht dem engl. präpositionalen Ausdruck nur gelegentlich die dt. Präp. 'bei':

     with regard to = in bezug auf / hinsichtlich / 'bei'

LE 2   Gehen Sie bei der Übertragung der folgenden Texte, in denen 'bei' in verschiedenen Funktionen verwendet wird, in folgenden Schritten vor:

a) Der Kern der Aussage wird in Engl. formuliert.
b) Neben- oder untergeordnete Mitteilungspunkte werden dem bereits formulierten Sachverhalt hinzugefügt bzw. in ihn eingefügt oder in einem selbständigen Satz zum Ausdruck gebracht.
c) Die Sätze werden durch Zusätze und Überleitungen miteinander verknüpft.

    Beispiel:

1. Das Kristallgitter von Festkörpern kann in vielen Fällen als ein regelmäßiges Muster harter Bälle — der Atome — angesehen werden. 2. Bei näherer Untersuchung stellt man jedoch fest, daß eine derartige vollkommene Kristallstruktur nicht existiert, sondern daß alle Festkörper Störstellen aufweisen. 3. Auch wenn nur wenige Störstellen auftreten, sind diese bei der Untersuchung der Eigenschaften von großer Bedeutung. 4. Solche Eigenschaften sind z. B. das Verhalten unter mechanischem Druck oder bei Temperaturanstieg. 5. Bei den elektrischen Eigenschaften der Festkörper ist die Art der Störung von besonderer Bedeutung.

(1a) The crystal lattice of solids can be regarded / considered / thought of as a
     regular pattern of hard balls   →
(1b) ... of hard balls, i.e. (of) atoms.
(2a) Such a perfect crystal does not exist.   →
(2b) All solids show / have / exhibit defects.   →
     It is found that all solids ...   →
(2c) On closer examination, however, it is found that ... but ...
(3a) There are only few defects.   →
     These are very important / of great importance.   →
(3b) in / for the investigation of properties / in / for investigating properties /
     when the properties are investigated.   →
(3c) Even if there are only ... these are ... in / for ...
(4a) Such properties are e.g. the behaviour under mechanical stress or in the case
     of temperature increase / when the temperature is increased.
(5a) The kind of defect is particularly important.   →
(5b) For / In the case of the electrical properties of solids, the kind of defect is ...

LE 3   Übertragen Sie sinngemäß ins Engl.:

Die Festkörperphysik beschäftigt sich mit den verschiedenen physikalischen Eigenschaften der Festkörper, besonders der kristallinen Stoffe. Bei der Untersuchung dieser Eigenschaften kommt eine Vielzahl unterschiedlicher experimenteller Verfahren zur Anwendung. Bei der theoretischen Deutung der experimentellen Ergebnisse macht man sowohl von Prinzipien der klassischen Mechanik als auch von denjenigen der Quantenmechanik Gebrauch.

LE 4 Übertragen Sie sinngemäß ins Engl.:

Bei Halbleitern ist die Leitfähigkeit stark von der Temperatur abhängig. Im Gegensatz zu den Metallen nimmt die Leitfähigkeit bei wachsender Temperatur zu, da eine Energiezufuhr dazu führt, daß Elektronen ihren Platz im Kristallgitter verlassen. Diese Energiezufuhr kann erfolgen durch Erhöhung der Temperatur, durch Lichteinstrahlung oder durch Anlegen einer Spannung, aber bereits bei Zimmertemperatur sind genügend Elektronen aus ihren Bindungen gelöst, so daß eine Leitung nachgewiesen werden kann. Fügt man einem Halbleiter drei- oder fünfwertige Fremdatome zu, dann erhöht sich dessen Leitfähigkeit stark. Bei dreiwertigen Fremdatomen erhält man überwiegend eine Elektronenleitung, während bei fünfwertigen Fremdatomen überwiegend eine Löcherleitung beobachtet wird.

PK 12 · PA 1 · SQ B

LE 1 Lesen und ergänzen Sie den Text.
Beantworten Sie die abschließenden Fragen:

University Entrance Requirements

The "Abitur" is required for university entrance. This is a certificate obtained on passing the final examination of the extended secondary school. Apart from the extended secondary school there are other opportunities for obtaining this cerficate. I obtained my "Abitur" in ... / ... year(s) ago.

What are the university entrance requirements in the GDR?
How did you fulfil these requirements?

Beachten Sie den Unterschied zwischen *Present Tense* und *Past Tense*!

LE 2 Lesen und ergänzen Sie den Text.

Beantworten Sie die abschließenden Fragen:

University Admission:

I was admitted to university in ... / ... year(s) ago. Before I took up studies, I had worked as ... / had been to ... / had finished ... I was in ... / worked as ... for ... year(s). Now I have been a student of physics since ... / for ...

What had you done before you were admitted to university?
For how long did you do that / were you there?
Since when have you been a student of physics?

Beachten Sie den Unterschied zwischen *Past Tense, Present Perfect* und *Past Perfect*!

LE 3 Lesen und ergänzen Sie den Text!
Beantworten Sie die abschließenden Fragen:

Course Structure

I've been studying physics since ... / for ... year(s). I'm in my ... academic year. While we're following the lecture in ..., we're being introduced to the fundamental problems of ... Seminars are also being held on these subjects. Furthermore, we're attending laboratory classes to familiarize ourselves with experimental techniques. Individual tutorials may be given when we're working in the laboratory.

> In which academic year are you now? How long have you been studying? Which lectures, seminars and classes are you attending at present? Are these seminars associated with the lectures? Are there also special courses being held?
> Are you taking part in laboratory classes? What are you learning there? Are there tutorials being given?

Beachten Sie den Unterschied zwischen *Simple Form* and *Expanded Form*!

LE 4 Lesen und ergänzen Sie den Text!
Beantworten Sie die abschließenden Fragen:

Degree and Examination

At the end of my studies I'll have to take examinations and to submit a thesis. This thesis will be based on a research project carried out during the final year. If I finish my studies successfully, I'll obtain the degree of "Diplomphysiker". The degree will be awarded on the results of the examination and of the thesis. The final mark will also include an assessment of my coursework. After I've obtained my degree, I'll work as ... / in ...

> When will you take your final examinations? What kind of examination will you have to pass, oral or written, or both?
> Will you also have to submit a paper?
> What will you do after you have obtained your degree?

Beachten Sie den Gebrauch des *Future Tense*!

PK 12 · PA 1 · SQ C

LE 1 Übersetzen Sie mit Hilfe des Wörterbuches:

University Course of Physics Studies

Physics is the most basic of the natural sciences and the foundation for many of the developments in other fields of science and engineering. Students admitted to a university course of physics studies will be required to have obtained the "Abitur" at an extended secondary school or at an institution providing the qualification required for university admission. On entry, students are expected to have a good working knowledge of their school subjects.

The purpose of the first and second academic years is to lay a firm foundation for specialization in the following years of the course. This will also include foreign language instruction in Russian and a second language, usually English. Additionally, special courses in these languages are available. The third- and fourth-year curriculum provides a broad education in current physics thought and modern techniques. The different courses cover all the important topics of physics and are designed to provide a firm foundation upon which a professional physicist can build his or her career, be it in industry, teaching or fundamental research. Included in the curriculum are such topics as electromagnetic theory, mathematics for physicists, low-temperature physics, solid-state physics, thermodynamics, quantum mechanics, optics, crystallography, spectroscopy, experimentation, Marxism-Leninism.

Associated with each lecture course are regular seminar periods at which problems can be discussed. Students are allocated to staff tutors and individual tutorials may be held. In the physical sciences tutorial teaching takes place during periods of laboratory work. The laboratory classes and practical courses are designed to familiarize students with a range of experimental techniques. In the laboratory students spend two terms on a project of a research nature.

The university attaches great importance to regular contact between staff and students outside the student-teacher relationship, especially during a student's first year. Groups of students are therefore assigned to an adviser, to whom they may turn for help and guidance relating both to their academic work and to their personal affairs. Advisers are members of the academic staff.

Every student will be examined at the end of the course in subjects covering the essential fields of physics. In the oral examinations, coursework done by the students may be taken into account and an assessment of this may form part of the final mark. The degree of "Diplomphysiker" is awarded on the results of these examinations and on the basis of a thesis summarizing the results of the final-year project.

LE 2   Beantworten Sie diesen Brief in Engl.:

Dear Andrea(s),

You will remember that we met in Prague almost two years ago when we both were on a trip through Czechoslovakia. We found that we were both interested in physics problems and intended to study the subject. I've been meaning to write to you for a long time but somehow I couldn't make up my mind to do it. Have you already started your studies? As for me, I've been studying physics at the University of Essex for about a year. It is one of seven new universities established in the early 1960's. So it is a fairly modern institution which differs considerably from the old universities at Oxford and Cambridge and from the provincial universities of the 19th century (the "red-brick" universities) and from London University (the largest in Britain, as you may know). We've got no faculties or colleges but a number of departments such as History, Mathematics, Physics and so on which are organised in four large groups called "Schools of Study". One of them is the "School of Physical Studies", which also includes chemistry, electronic engineering, computer engineering etc. All undergraduates (you will know that this is a student studying for a first degree) follow a "scheme of study" (or "curriculum" as it is called elsewhere). This scheme of study leads to an honours degree, that is, a first degree based on a single subject. The degree is called "Bachelor of Arts" or "Bachelor of Science" according to the School of Study. Schemes in Physical Sciences lead of course to B.Sc. degrees. Our honours degree courses include a fairly broad introductory section (the "first year scheme") and a more specialised section. Degree schemes normally involve three years' study of a chosen subject, whereas in your country it is four or five years, as far as I know. Is this really true? At the same time we seem to have more specialisation. Applied Physics, Theoretical Physics and Chemical Physics in addition to Physics form separate schemes, although many of the courses overlap. There are already some differences in the entrance requirements, which lay down the subjects you must have passed at General Certificate of Education "Ordinary" and "Advanced" Levels for a particular course. It would be interesting to hear something about the entrance requirements in your country and of course about your "scheme of study" or curriculum, particularly which subjects are available to you. Have you already some idea about what you will specialise in or where you would like to work later on? I hope it won't take you as long to answer this letter as it took me to write it.

I'm looking forward to your reply.

My best wishes to you,

John

PK 12 · PA 2 · SQ A

LE 1 Neue Lexik

textbook	[ˈtekstbuk]	Lehrbuch
account	[əˈkaunt]	Bericht, Darstellung
acquaintance (with)	[əˈkweintəns]	Bekanntschaft (mit)
intermediate	[ˌintəˈmi:djət]	zwischenliegend; Zwischen-, Mittel-
to aim (at)	[eim]	(ab)zielen (auf)
to emphasize	[ˈemfəsaiz]	hervorheben, betonen
to avoid	[əˈvɔid]	vermeiden
to present	[priˈzent]	darstellen
undergraduate	[ˌʌndəˈgrædjuit]	Student (ohne akad. Grad)
to be devoted to	[diˈvoutid]	gewidmet sein; behandeln (Buch, Thema etc.)

thorough	[ˈθʌrə]	genau, gründlich
collaborator	[kəˈlæbəreitə]	Mitarbeiter
item	[ˈaitem]	Gegenstand, Einzelheit; (Gesprächs-, Verhandlungs-) Punkt
overall	[ˌouvərˈɔ:l]	Gesamt-, Total-
validity	[vəˈliditi]	Gültigkeit (eines Gesetzes etc.)
to assess	[əˈses]	einschätzen, beurteilen
survey	[ˈsə:vei]	Übersicht, Überblick
primary	[ˈpraiməri]	ursprünglich; primär, Primär-
sole	[soul]	einzig, alleinig, Allein-
valuable	[ˈvæljuəbl]	wertvoll
outline	[ˈautlain]	Umriß, Überblick; Abriß, Grundzüge
reference book	[ˈrefrəns ...]	Nachschlagewerk
significance	[sigˈnifikəns]	Bedeutung; Signifikanz
guide	[gaid]	Leitfaden, Handbuch, Einführung; (leitendes) Prinzip, Richtschnur
brief	[bri:f]	kurz (gefaßt)
report	[riˈpɔ:t]	Bericht; Meldung

LE 2 ⊕ ⊕ Internationalismen

relevant	[ˈrelivənt]	relevant, einschlägig, sachdienlich
explicit	[iksˈplisit]	explizit, deutlich, ausdrücklich
abstract	[ˈæbstrækt]	Adj. abstrakt; Subst. (Inhalts-) Referat; Auszug
monograph	[ˈmɔnəgra:f]	Monographie

LE 3 ⊕ ⊕ Beantworten Sie die Fragen nach dem Muster:

T: What is the melting point of mercury?
S: Mercury melts at −39°C.

Cu, 1083°C. / H_2O, 100°C. / Fe, 1537°C. / Hg, 2497°C. / Al, 659°C.

LE 4 ⊕ ⊕ Hören Sie den folgenden engl. Kurztext. Achten Sie besonders auf die Präpositionen!

LE 5 ⊕ ⊕ Übersetzen Sie die folgenden dt. Sätze. Achten Sie besonders auf die Präpositionen!

PK 12 · PA 2 · SQ B

LE 1   ⊕ ⊕   Üben Sie den folgenden Dialog:

T: Did you attend the lecture / conference yesterday?

S: No, I didn't. While the lecture was being held, I was taking part in a(nother) meeting / conference / I was attending a(nother) lecture / seminar. Was it interesting?

T: On the whole it was, Perhaps it will be repeated. / Summing it up, the papers read there were interesting. Perhaps they will be published.

S: I doubt   whether it will be repeated. /
It's hardly likely /
It's most unlikely that they will be published.

LE 2   ⊕ ⊕   Üben Sie den folgenden Dialog:

T: How long have you been studying physics / ...?

S: I've been studying physics / ... for one year / since last September.

T: And will you have to take an examination this year / ...?

S: Yes, we were told that we would have to take an examination.

LE 3   ⊕ ⊕   Üben Sie den folgenden Dialog:

T[1]: The only thing a physicist needs is theoretical knowledge. / ...

S: I can't agree with you. My point is that theoretical knowledge / ... is not enough / (not) necessary.

T[2]: I quite agree with you. There's one more thing to be noted. A thorough training in the laboratory is necessary when you're going to work in industry / ...

S: And many of us will go to industry / ...

PK 12 · PA 2 · SQ C

LE 1   Lesen Sie mit Hilfe des Wörterbuches und bereiten Sie eine Diskussion vor zu dem Thema *"Scientific Research and Postgraduate Work"*:

Joint Institute for Nuclear Research

The name of the new town of Dubna has been constantly in the pages of the world's newspapers and magazines in the past few years. It is the home of the Joint Institute for Nuclear Research, an international scientific centre. For a large number of experiments in nuclear physics extremely complicated, accurate and powerful devices are needed. Their construction involves considerable investment. This is possible only if development has reached a high level in the allied branches of science and industry, i.e. mechanics, optics, radio and electrical engineering, high vacuum technique, superlow temperature technique, and many others. That is why not only large universities and institutes but even a number of highly developed industrial countries encounter insuperable difficulties in this field. To be successful, experiments in nuclear physics must, as a rule, be carried out on a large scale. Hence the co-operation of hundreds of scientists, engineers and technicians is needed. Theoretical research in nuclear physics has to be just as extensive. On the basis of experimental data and a great number of extremely complicated mathematical calculations, hundreds of theoreticians all over the world strive to elucidate as fully as possible problems resulting from experiments. For all these reasons, it becomes necessary to combine the efforts of the scientists of many countries. Proceeding from the necessity to further the development of modern nuclear physics, the Soviet Government proposed the foundation of an international research centre and handed over to the new Joint Institute the former Institute of Nuclear Problems and the Electrophysical Laboratory of the Soviet Academy of Sciences. The Charter defines the legal status of the Joint Institute as that of an international organisation. The main purposes of the Institute are defined in its charter: "All the activities of the Institute shall contribute to the use of atomic energy for peaceful aims only and for the benefit of all mankind."

The basic programme of the Institute comprises: "... ensuring joint theoretical and experimental research in nuclear physics by the scientists of the member states;

"promoting the development of nuclear physics in the member states by exchanging experience and results in theoretical and experimental research;

"maintaining contact with national and international research and other institutions involved in the development of nuclear physics and in finding new possibilities for the peaceful uses of atomic energy."

The Scientific Council is responsible for the research activities of the Institute. It examines and approves plans for research work, considers the completion of the plans of research work and of separate investigations and considers other problems relevant to the scientific activities of the Institute.

The Institute is headed by an Executive Board elected by the representatives of the member states. The Director is elected for a term of three years. He is Chairman of the Scientific Council. The laboratories of the Institute are organised so as to embrace in their scientific activities the whole range of modern nuclear physics.

Co-operation between scientists from the member states goes far beyond the joint work at Dubna. The Joint Institute performs important functions in co-ordinating the work of scientific organisations in the member states. Conferences are periodically held at Dubna on various problems of nuclear physics. At these conferences scientists read papers on the work that is being done at the Joint Institute and in the member states, outline the programme for further investigations, and speak of their own research projects. The papers of the Institute are published in scientific periodicals, and an exchange of preprints has been organised. In return, the Institute receives a great number of preprints from foreign scientists.

Bereiten Sie die Übersetzung des Textes *"The Position of Theoretical Physics"* (12.3.C. – 1.) vor!

PK 12 · PA 2 · SQ D

LE 1 ⊕ ⊕ Listen to the biography of John Bernal

crystallography / to appoint: berufen, ernennen / lecturer: Dozent / in recognition of: in Anerkennung / to elect: wählen / health: Gesundheit(szustand)/ editorial board: Redaktionskollegium

LE 2 Speak about John Bernal's life and work:

1901 born in Ireland; 1919 student in Cambridge; 1927 lecturer at Cambridge; 1937 Fellow of the Royal Society; 1938 Professor of Physics at London University; 1941–45 Scientific Adviser to the British Government; 1958–65 President of the World Peace Council

LE 3 Speak about the life of a famous physicist, for example, about Frédéric Joliot-Curie:

geb. 1900; entdeckt zusammen mit seiner Frau Irène, Tochter Marie Curies, die künstliche Radioaktivität (1933); entdeckt Positronenemission und Annihilationsstrahlung (1934); erhält zusammen mit seiner Frau den Nobelpreis (1935); 1946 Hoher Kommissar Frankreichs für Atomenergie, später aus politischen Gründen entlassen, errichtet 1948 den ersten französischen Kernreaktor; wird 1949 zum Präsidenten des Weltfriedensrates gewählt; stirbt 1958 an den Folgen einer Strahlenkrankheit (radiation disease)

PK 12 · PA 3 · SQ A

LE 1 Im naturwissenschaftlichen Englisch können Substantive, die ursprünglich nur qualitative Bedeutung haben, wie

ionization	Ionisierung
application	Anwendung, Verwendung

oder Mengen- bzw. Kollektivbezeichnungen, die keine Pluralform annehmen können, wie

work	Arbeit
information	Information(en)
knowledge	Wissen, Kenntnisse

im Gegensatz zum Dt. im allgemeinen nur dann mit quantitativer Bedeutung gebraucht werden, wenn sie zusätzlich charakterisiert werden. Diese quantifizierende Funktion übernehmen meist die folgenden Substantive:

the extent of application / automation / ionization
    — 'Umfang', Maß, Grad
the amount of work / energy / knowledge
    — 'Menge', Maß, Grad
the level of intelligence / co-operation / radioactivity
    — 'Niveau', Grad, Umfang
the range of application / co-operation / automation
    — 'Bereich', Maß, Grad
the degree of automation / intelligence / ionization
    — 'Grad', Maß

In gleicher Funktion kann *much* in der Bedeutung 'viele, ein großer Teil' verwendet werden.
Im Dt. wird die Funktion der Grad- bzw. Maßangabe häufig entweder durch den Plural übernommen, z. B. 'umfangreiche Kenntnisse' = *much knowledge*, oder ergibt sich lediglich aus dem Kontext, z. B. 'Intelligenz' (= Intelligenzgrad) = *degree of intelligence.*
Innerhalb der Grad- bzw. Maßangabe kann wiederum eine Differenzierung erreicht werden, wenn dem quantifizierenden Substantiv ein Adjektiv zugeordnet wird:

The article contains a great amount of information.
Der Artikel enthält zahlreiche Informationen.

LE 2   Einige quantifizierende Substantive bilden Wortgruppen zur Angabe des Grades bzw. des (Aus)Maßes:

to a large extent	im hohen Grade / Maß
to a high degree	in großem Umfang, beträchtlich
to a certain extent	bis zu / in einem gewissen Grade
to such an extent that	bis zu einem solchen Grade, daß
in an (hitherto) unknown degree	in einem (bisher) unbekannten Maße

LE 3   ⊪—0   Vervollständigen Sie die Sätze:

1. A great ... of work has still to be done in this field. 2. Only metals, especially heavy metals, can stop X-rays ... 3. This method increases the ... application of this material in industry. 4. The ... of automation in many industries has been

considerably increased. 5. New power-stations are being built to incrase the ... of electrical energy that is needed in industry. 6. Experiments were carried out to test the ... of radioactivity. 7. Niels Bohr was one of the greatest contributors to nuclear science, whose studies are ... responsible for the controlled release of nuclear energy. 8. The ... of co-operation between these two countries has been increased. 9. Space flights have considerably increased the ... of technical knowledge. 10. This technique may be used to determine the ... of ionization of the gas.

LE 4   ⚷—0 Übertragen Sie sinngemäß ins Engl.

Achten Sie auf die quantitativen Angaben:

Die Zusammenarbeit zwischen der Akademie der Wissenschaften und der Industrie ist in den letzten Jahren ständig vertieft worden. Ein wichtiges Gebiet dieser Zusammenarbeit ist die Elektronik. Die Entwicklung und Produktion elektronischer Bauelemente (electronic components) ist im hohen Maße auf Ergebnisse der Grundlagenforschung angewiesen. Seit 1960 werden viele Arbeiten auf dem Gebiet der Halbleiterphysik durchgeführt. Daneben sind es Forschungen zu den Grundlagen und der Technologie optoelektronischer Bauelemente, die im Mittelpunkt der Kooperation stehen. Um den Einsatz dieser Geräte erhöhen zu können, werden außer dem Silizium weitere Materialien benötigt, darunter besonders Verbindungen aus Elementen der III. und IV. Gruppe des Periodischen Systems. Ein weiteres Gebiet der Zusammenarbeit ist die energetische Basis, von deren Erweiterung die wirtschaftliche Entwicklung in hohem Maße abhängt. Die in den letzten Jahren errichteten Kernkraftwerke erhöhten die der Industrie zur Verfügung stehende Energiemenge. Zur Zeit werden Untersuchungen durchgeführt, um neue Meßverfahren zu entwickeln und um durch Rationalisierung der Betriebsführung (management) von Reaktoren den Auslastungsgrad der Anlagen zu erhöhen. Als letztes Beispiel für die Zusammenarbeit der Akademie mit der Industrie soll erwähnt werden, daß die Automation von Produktionsprozessen beträchtlich erhöht werden konnte.

PK 12 · PA 3 · SQ B

LE 1   Beantworten Sie die Fragen:

International Scientific Co-operation

Why is it necessary to develop international co-operation in physics?
What do you know about the Joint Institute for Nuclear Research?

LE 2   Lesen Sie den Text.

Beantworten Sie die Fragen:

Information through Conferences and Periodicals

Conferences are meetings for discussion and the exchange of views. Many conferences on scientific problems are held every year. They are attended by scientists interested in these problems. They may read papers or present short communications. These may later be published in periodicals. Sometimes the papers are exchanged as preprints or reprints.

What do you know about scientific conferences?
Can you give examples for periodicals in physics?

LE 3   Lesen Sie den Text.

Beantworten Sie die Fragen:

Research Work and Academic Degrees

A thesis submitted for the degree of a "Diplomphysiker" or of a "Dr. rer. nat." it based on a particular research project. Normally it forms part of the research work carried out at a university department of physics, at an academy institute, or in an industrial research laboratory. Some doctoral theses are prepared at international research institutions such as that at Dubna.

What are the main fields of physics research in the GDR?
Which research problems receive special attention at the physics department of this university?
What do you know about the way in which your department takes part in international co-operation?

PK 12 · PA 3 · SQ C

LE 1   Übersetzen Sie mit Hilfe des Wörterbuches:

The Position of Theoretical Physics

Theoretical physics deals with the concepts, and the relations between them, that are useful for organizing the experimental information of physics quantitatively. Theoretical physics proceeds on many different levels. Concepts that are applicable in the description of a few experiments are considered in phenomenological investigations. Concepts applicable to a general type of physical phenomena are considered in the formulation of laws of nature. Concepts of very broad applicability are considered in the formulation of general principles of physics. Sometimes the emphasis in theoretical physics is on inductive thinking in search of concepts useful for describing known experimental information. At other times the emphasis is on deductive reasoning, starting from accepted concepts to suggest new relevant experiments and to predict their results. In still others the emphasis is on the construction of models that isolate from complex physical phenomena certain specific characteristics.

Theoretical physics covers all physical phenomena. The history of physics is the history of the continuous interplay between theoretical developments and experimental advances. Through centuries of intimate contact, theoretical physics and mathematics have interacted strongly, to their mutual benefit. Theoretical physics uses the concepts of mathematics to formulate descriptions of natural phenomena. Mathematics, in turn, is stimulated by the problems posed by physics. Physics is an experimental science, which means that the principles and relationships developed by the theorists must stand the test of experiments. The theoretical physicist is thus distinguished from the mathematician, who invents and manipulates mathematical formalism for its own sake without constraint imposed by the realities of nature.

When one considers its breadth as a science and the extent of its applications, physics is remarkable for its high degree of unity. Concern for the simplest and most fundamental laws of nature inherently lends unity, because the generality of these laws provides a common foundation for all of physics. Responsibility of maintaining this unity falls increasingly to the theoretical physicist. The techniques available to him are often widely applicable throughout physics, and it is thus possible for him to work effectively on a variety of topics.

PK 12 · PA 4 · SQ A

LE 1   ⊕ ⊕   Beantworten Sie die Fragen nach dem Muster:

> T: Didn't Roentgen discover the X-rays while he was experimenting with the so-called Crookes' tube?
> S: Quite so. He discovered them during an experiment.

experiment / conference / study / stay abroad / lecture

LE 2   ⊕ ⊕   Beantworten Sie die Fragen nach dem Muster:

> T: Are both protons and neutrons charged?
> S: Quite the contrary. Only protons are charged, whereas neutrons are not charged.

alpha-rays, gamma-rays — cause strong ionization / metals, semiconductors — have free electrons / heavy hydrogen, ordinary hydrogen — contain a neutron / alpha-rays, gamma-rays — corpuscular rays / emission of alpha-rays, of beta-rays — decrease the atomic number

LE 3 [⊕ ⊕] Üben Sie den folgenden Dialog:

T: You seem to know our foreign guest. Did you meet him during the last international conference? / ...?
S: You're right. We met each other while we were at that conference. / ...
T: So you're colleagues? / ...?
S: Not quite. I'm a biophysicist, whereas he's a biologist. / working on problems
   of semiconductors − crystallography / studied physics − mechanics / was admitted in (Jahreszahl) − one year later / in the first academic year − in the second
   year / working on ... − working on ...

PK 12 · PA 4 · SQ B

LE 1 [⊕ ⊕] Üben Sie den folgenden Dialog:

T: I'd like to ask a question concerning your recent studies in this field? / ...?
S: My recent studies concerned problems of solid-state physics / semiconductor
   physics / some semiconducting compounds / certain problems of optics / plasma
   physics / ...
T: How do your results agree with the findings published in the Journal of Physics
   last month? / ...?
S: Our results agreed quite well with these findings. (not so well / remarkably well /
   to a large extent / considerably)
T: This leads me on to another question. Would you say that new experimental
   techniques should be developed in this field? / ...?
S: In my view / In our experience / I think / I feel / It seems to me
   a great deal of work is still necessary (to be done) / some major difficulties remain to be solved. / the present methods are (not) precise enough. / the problems are not quite understood.

LE 2 [⊕ ⊕] Üben Sie den folgenden Dialog:

T: I would like to hear your opinion / ... of this method / ... Is it reliable? / ...?
S: In my opinion / My opinion is that it is (not) reliable / ...
T: You know that others do not share your opinion / ... How do you explain
   this?
S: I've no explanation to offer.
T: Is it possible that their experimental conditions / ... were not quite the same?
S: Their experimental conditions / ... may have been different.
T: So this remains to be elucidated.

PK 12 · PA 4 · SQ C

LE 1   Lesen Sie mit Hilfe des Wörterbuches:

Classification of Physics Literature

There is a large variety of books which can be used by students of physics in the course of their studies. They can be classified according to the scope of problems they deal with and the readers for whom they are intended. Introductory texts for the first-year course will give a first comprehensive treatment of physics problems. Other textbooks may cover at an intermediate level the physics of a particular field or provide an account of the theory required for the understanding of a definite subject. Sometimes a special problem such as the whole range of modern methods for the analysis of materials is treated in one volume. Broadly speaking, the following types of scientific literature may be distinguished:

(1) University textbooks provide an up-to-date treatment of the principles and experimental aspects of some branch of physics, together with an elementary account of the underlying theory. They are comprehensive introductions which are mostly designed to meet the requirements of degree courses and include sufficient relevant scientific information to make the book self-contained and equally suited for use by the student working alone. Normally the author explicitly states that "the book assumes only a knowledge of elementary quantum mechanics" or that "acquaintance with elementary quantum mechanics is assumed". If the problems are treated at an intermediate level, physical explanations are widely used, whereas the mathematical standard is set no higher than necessary. Usually, problems are given at the end of each chapter or throughout the text, with sketched solutions at the end of the book. To give an example, a textbook may introduce quantum mechanics to students who are unfamiliar with it and develop it to a stage useful for research. The first part will contain the basic theory. If the book aims to emphasize application, mathematical details are avoided and difficult theorems stated without proof. The second part will contain examples of application to a wide range of physical phenomena and present a collection of results helpful in solving problems. Special textbooks are concerned with applying mathematics to physics and engineering problems. Mention should be made of the so-called "physics series" normally intended for undergraduates which provide a coherent set of short textbooks that together cover all the material required for a degree course in physics. They prepare students for the study of more advanced or specialised texts. New editions of textbooks, which are published regularly, take account of recent developments and provide new data.

(2) Monographs are larger studies devoted to the thorough treatment of a particular item of research. They may deal entirely with experimental researches carried out by the writers and their collaborators or colleagues, or they may summarize the progress made over the past years in this field. In doing this, they may

treat important aspects of the field in historical perspective to give an overall view as well as a knowledge of its present state. Problems of current interest receive special attention. Others provide introductions to topics of present interest or deal exclusively with recent work on the development and application of theories. Comparison of the implications of theoretical models with experimental data enables the range of validity to be assessed and often suggests how they may be improved. Studies of this kind are also found useful by specialists for the survey they provide of the subject as a whole. In addition, there are books which are written with the sole aim of making a survey of a given subject by concentrating on its essential aspects. Necessary mathematical ideas and methods are introduced and developed as an integral part of the exposition. Although primarily intended for research in the given field, it will usually also be valuable to workers in related fields, as well as to final-year undergraduates. In this connection reference should be made to the "Studies in Physics" series providing outlines of modern research for graduate students and for scientists at any stage of their careers who want to inform themselves of a newly developing field of general interest. The topics are covered in a manner that is intermediate between a review article and a proper monograph.

(3) Handbooks or Reference Books are mostly arranged like an encyclopedia. Each entry describes in a few paragraphs the physical significance of one topic, and is followed by a detailed bibliography and sometimes a commentary on the sources of further information. Such handbooks are invaluable to all students and teachers whenever they feel the need for a qualitative explanation of any aspect of physics.

(4) Periodicals are devoted to the publication of advances in physics. In order to permit quick orientation, each article is introduced by an abstract. An informative abstract presents the conceptual content of an article. Summarizing the essential ideas in an article, the informative abstract should show the meaningful, coherent relationship between the author's ideas and arguments. Review articles, reports and the like cannot readily be summarized and hence require indicative abstracts which serve primarily as descriptive guides. An indicative abstract tells briefly what an article is about, what significant subjects it includes, and what its scope is.

Schlüssel

1.1. B. – 6.

1. were arranged by M. 2. have been studied 3. is determined by the total number 4. is produced by power-stations 5. were not found in nature 6. has been studied since about 1900.

1.2. C. – 1.

1. are determined 2. be obtained 3. be obtained / created 4. was discovered 5. are called 6. have been used 7. be found / obtained

1.2. C. – 3.

1. The isotopes of an element have different mass numbers. 2. This element occurs in various compounds. 3. There are many compounds of the same element with different properties. 4. The different properties of the elements depend on their structure. 5. Oxygen forms compounds with various elements.

1.2. C. – 4.

1. distinguished 2. differ 3. differs 4. differ 5. vary 6. varies 7. distinguished 8. distinguish

1.3. B. – 7.

1. The young scientist was offered ... 2. He was shown ... by ... 3. The new element wa given ... 4. Newly produced substances are often given names that ... 5. The students wer shown ... 6. We were shown ...

1.4. C. – 1.

1. proportion 2. ratio 3. proportion 4. proportion 5. proportion 6. relation / ratio 7. proportion 8. relation

1.4. C. – 2.

1. The neutron was discovered by C. in 1932. 2. The nucleus of deuterium is made up of a proton and a neutron. 3. The radioactive isotope of hydrogen is called tritium. 4. Isotopes of the same chemical element cannot be separated chemically / by chemical means. 5. Up to now 105 chemical elements have been found. 6. Almost the total mass of the atom is contained in the atomic nucleus. 7. The electron was discovered already in 1897 by J. J. T., while the proton and the neutron were discovered much later. 8. New radioactive isotopes of chemical elements are formed in nuclear reactions.

2.1. A. – 1.

1. up to 20 grams 2. up to 105 3. down to 70° 4. down to 6 kg

2.1. B. – 3.

1. The mass number of radon was found to be 222. 2. R. is known to have discovered the proton. 3. The mass of the atom is now known to be mainly contained in the nucleus. 4. Most elements have been found to consist of two or more isotopes. 5. Heavy hydrogen is known to have the atomic number 1 and the mass number 2.

2.1. B. – 4.

1. It is now believed that the universe is made up of certain elementary particles. 2. It could not be shown that the hydrogen isotope of mass number 3 occurs in natural hydrogen. 3. It was found that lithium is formed when deuterium is bombarded with neutrons.

4. In former years it was believed that the nucleus in heavier atoms also contains electrons. 5. It was recognized that isotopes have the same chemical properties with the exception of those of hydrogen.

2.2. C.—1.

1 b/a; 2 e/b; 3 f/a/c; 4 b/a; 5 a; 6 a; 7 f/d/c; 8 a/d;

2.2. C.—2.

1. It has been found that there are about 300 different stable isotopes in nature. 2. Today it is known that the atomic number is determined by the number of protons in the atomic nucleus. 3. In former years the separation of isotopes was only considered as evidence for their existence. 4. In order to define the extent of separation, the initial state has to be considered. 5. In both experiments the application / use of this method had / gave the same results. 6. The discovery of this radioactive element is / can be considered as a great success. 7. With the exception of 22 pure elements all the other elements are mixtures of different types / kinds of atom(s) with the same nuclear charge but different masses. 8. It was established / found that the percentage of a given isotope in a mixture of isotopes gradually decreased down to 0.03 %. / The percentage of a given isotope ... was found to decrease gradually down to 0.03 %.

2.3. A.—1.

1 a; 2 b/a; 3 b; 4 c/b; 5 c; 6 a/d; 7 a/e; 8 b/c;

2.4. C.—1.

1 b; 2 a; 3 a; 4 b; 5 c;

2.4. C.—2.

1. Radioactive isotopes can be produced if neutrons are made / permitted to fall on / strike particular elements. 2. R. is known to have discovered the proton in 1920. 3. Isotopes can be distinguished on the basis of their different masses. 4. The artificial uranium isotope 239 is formed when / if slow neutrons are permitted / made to fall on uranium 238. 5. 200 years ago it was found that water is composed of hydrogen and oxygen and is thus a compound and not an element / ... water was found to be composed of :... 6. On the basis of their electrical properties elements and compounds can be classified as conductors and insulators. 7. Since metals contain free electrons they are used as material for wires. 8. Conduction processes in ionized gases and liquids differ from those in solids.

3.1. B.—2.

1. different kinds of atoms called isotopes 2. properties of a natural isotope contained in any quantity of the element 3. the nucleus of a deuterium atom called a deuteron 4. the two isotopes contained in neon 5. the charge carried by a single electron

3.1. B.—4.

1. nuclei occurring in nature 2. table of atomic weights consisting of 3. electrical forces acting on ions 4. a substance containing free electrons 5. alpha-particles moving through gases

3.1. B.—5.

1. atomic nuclei containing 2. the properties distinguishing 3. the first transuranic element called neptunium 5. hydrogen ion consisting

3.1. B.—6.

1. a gas which is made up of 2. nuclei that / which contain 3. any system that / which consists of 4. the free electrons that / which move about 5. matter which is contained

3.1. B. — 7.

1. only atoms of non-metals containing 2. the charge of the electron determined by M. 3. their structure formed by 4. deuterium having mass number 2

3.1. C. — 2.

1. In many chemical compounds there are atoms connected with each other by an electron pair. 2. A technique for the separation of substances called / known as ion exchange, is often used in industry. 3. Metals are solids in which the atoms are very close to each other. 4. There are metals which rarely occur / rarely occurring in nature but have / having important technical applications. 5. In a wire connected to a circuit electrons will flow in one direction.

3.3. A. — 4.

  d/c; 2 a; 3 a; 4 b; 5 b; 6 a;

3.3. B. — 2.

1. isotope separation achieved by 2. The signs of electrical charge chosen by F. 3. the alpha-particles discovered by R. 4. uranium enriched in 5. theory established by H.

3.3. B. — 3.

1. the charge which is carried by 2. a particle which was discovered by C. D. A. 3. types of atoms which were found 4. the force which is exerted 5. scientists who were / had been invited 6. a charge that is placed

3.3. B. — 6.

1. a separation factor much higher than 2. the electric strength due to 3. the work neces sary to move 4. a positive charge equal to 5. a mass less than 6. the potential due to

3.3. B. — 7.

1. the number of neutrons present in 2. the positive charge carried by 3. the theory of the hydrogen atom established by N. B. 4. one method for the separation of isotopes developed by G. H. 5. the number of molecules contained in

3.3. C. — 2.

1. Electric forces act between (those) bodies having an excess of electrons or protons 2. Electrons flowing in a positive direction / to the positive side form a negative current 3. The nucleus carries the positive charge contained in the atom. 4. Physical quantities such as mass and charge are scalars that can only be defined by means of one number. 5. Alpha-particles and deuterons are considered as elementary particles because of their important role in nuclear reactions.

3.3. C. — 3.

Every charge is surrounded by a field which extends / extending theoretically to infinity. Every charge (which is) placed into such a field experiences a force. The electric field strength can be defined in terms of / by means of the force (which is) experienced by an electric unit charge in this field. The force exerted on a positive charge acts in the direction of the electric field. The field strength caused by a single charge is / can be calculated on the basis of Coulomb's law.

4.1. A. — 4.

1. ziemlich 2. und nicht / statt als 3. und nicht 4. (an)statt 5. statt dessen 6. vielmehr

4.1. B. — 6.

a)=(g); b)=(d); c)=(a); d)=(e); e)=(c); f)=(f); g)=(b)

4.1. C. – 2.

1. It was possible to support the equation established by de B. experimentally. 2. It was shown by M. that there is a definite relation(ship) between the work done and the heat produced. 3. The experiments carried out in 1927 showed for the first time that electrons behave like / as waves. 4. The results obtained show that this formula does not correspond to the experimental data. 5. Crystals can be used to diffract rays which consist of / consisting of atoms or molecules.

4.1. C. – 3.

Quantum mechanics was developed by H. and B. and, at the same time, by S. It describes the wave properties and the particle properties of the electrons in a consistent theory. / It is a consistent theory which ... It had already been suggested by de B. in 1924 that the dual nature established for light could be a property of all matter. The experiments carried out by D. and G. in 1927 showed for the first time that electrons can behave as waves. Evidence for the wave properties of atomic and molecular rays was obtained by experiments carried out in 1932.

4.3. A. – 4.

1. exhibit 2. reveal 3. exhibit 4. reveal 5. exhibit / display 6. reveal

4.3. B. – 5.

1. The separation of isotopes the chemical properties of which ... 2. Electrons the mass of which ... 3. X-rays the properties of which ... 4. ... Goldstein, whose book on classical mechanics is well known, ... 5. ... isotopes the proportion of which in any given quantity ...

4.3. B. – 8.

1. ... isotopes two of which are stable 2. These students, some of whom I know ... 3. ... radioactive elements, some of which occur ... 4. ... in various ways the simplest of which ... 5. ... radioactive isotopes, only five of which have ...

4.3. C. – 2.

1. The element lead has nine isotopes, five of which are radioactive. 2. Protons are elementary particles, all of which have / carry a positive charge. 3. The data obtained experimentally are in good agreement with the theoretical results calculated by means of the de Broglie equation. 4. The diffraction effect observed in experiments will only occur under definite conditions. 5. E. established the photon theory, which in a (certain) sense is a revival of Newton's idea / concept of light.

4.3. C. – 3.

Light is an electromagnetic radiation of definite / certain wavelengths, only part of which are visible to the human eye. Light has all the properties which are also shown / exhibited by all the other electromagnetic waves. The theory established by H. and F. explained lihgt as a wave phenomenon. M., who recognized the electromagnetic nature of light, developed the electromagnetic wave theory of light. The idea / concept established by P. and E. that light consists of smallest corpuscles — so-called photons or light quanta — is in a (certain) sense a revival of the corpuscle / particle theory which had already been established / suggested by N. in 1704. Modern theory, however, combines / connects the (typical) wave properties with the emission and absorption of light, both of which show the quantum nature of light.

5.1. A. – 2.

1. zurückgehen auf / verursacht werden durch 2. auf Grund 3. zurückzuführen auf / bedingt sein durch 4. die Folge sein von 5. infolge

5.1. B.—2.
1. ... the forces they exert ... 2. ... the force acting ... 3. ... atomic structure containing ...
4. ... with energy divided by Planck's constant ... 5. The heaviest stable element we know ...
6. ... the wave theory based on Maxwell's equation.

5.1. C.—2.
1. The results of the tests made in the present experiment were similar to those in / of
former studies. 2. The crystal (line) structure of most inorganic substances differs from
those of other substances. 3. For crystal analysis a method is used which is due to M. v. L.
4. The lattice structure of natural crystals is never so regular as that of an ideal crystal.

5.1. C.—3.
it was possible to show that crystalline substances exhibit a lattice made up of / consisting of atoms, molecules or ions. The structure of almost all inorganic substances differs
from that of other substances because the atoms of the former do not combine to form
molecules. A crystal consists of a three-dimensional periodic arrangement / array of atomic (structural) units. The type of crystal lattice of the particular substance is caused
by / due to the size of the atoms and the forces acting between them. The structure of
naturally occurring crystals / natural crystals, however, differs from that of the ideal
crystal, because the pattern does not repeat itself quite regularly, due to / owing to
vacant sites, dislocations etc.
    Direct evidence for the structure of crystals was obtained in 1912 / not ... until 1912
by means of a method due to M. v. L. He suggested to study the crystal lattice by means
of X-rays. The diffraction pattern (thus) obtained / obtained in this way revealed the wave
nature of the X-rays and the lattice structure of crystalline substances. The diffraction
patterns obtained later on for electrons and slow neutrons were similar to those caused /
produced by X-rays.

5.3. A.—2.
1. umfassen / verbunden sein mit 2. umfassen 3. von Bedeutung sein / wichtig sein / zusammenhängen mit 4. zur Folge haben / mit sich bringen 5. beteiligt sein an 6. mit sich
bringen

5.3. B.—3.
1. ... electrons moving through ... 2. ... the mechanical work done ... 3. — 4. The energy
required ... 5. The amount of energy lost in the production of ... 6. ... positive ions of
the substance the gas consists of 7. —

5.3. B.—4.
1. Many scientific developments, a number of which are due to ... 2. ... into two parts
having opposite electrical charges. 3. Several methods involving the behaviour of nuclei ...
4. ... of two or more simpler particles held together by some type of force.

5.3. C.—2.
1. The conductivity of semiconductors is due to conduction electrons or holes. 2. Conduction in metals is different from that in gases. 3. The motion of free electrons in metals is
similar to that of particles in gases. 4. On the basis of / According to their electrical behaviour substances can (generally) be divided / distinguished into two groups — conductors and non-conductors. 5. The conductivity of semiconductors can be explained by
means of / on the basis of / in terms of the band model.

6.1. A. — 2.

a) having a high energy, = (i); b) transported over a long distance, = (b); c) acting over a long range, = (j); d) at high temperature, = (e); e) showing slow motion, = (d); f) having high energy, = (l); g) having a high power, = (h); h) operating / working over a long distance, = (a); i) studying low temperature (phenomena), = (c); j) carried out / made at low pressure, = (f); k) working at low frequency, = (g); l) of high frequency, = (k)

6.1. B. — 7.

1. ... to make discoveries by using the electron theory. 2. ... a new method for introducing impurities. 3. ... in one of its orbits without having the same nuclear charge. 4. ... by emitting ... 5. ... without having ... 6. ... a sodium ion by losing an electron.

6.1. C. — 2.

1. The electrical conductivity of metals can be decreased by raising / increasing their temperature. 2. Semiconductors are used for solving many technical problems. 3. Theoretical problems cannot be solved without following certain general rules. 4. Electronegative elements can complete / fill their shells by taking up an electron. 5. Rutherford made experiments with alpha-particles for studying the structure of the atom.

6.1. C. — 3.

Semiconductors are substances which differ in their electrical properties from metals and insulators. They differ from metals, because / In contrast to metals their conductivity is increased by raising their temperature. Furthermore, a higher conductivity can be obtained by increasing the energy in the semiconductor crystal by means of light- or X-rays. Because of this effect semiconductors are used in thermometers and for measuring light. In a semiconductor all electrons are part of the crystal lattice / are involved / used / in forming the crystal lattice. By introducing energy electrons are detached / ejected from their bonds. A particularly strong increase in / of conductivity is obtained by introducing foreign atoms with / having an odd number of valency electrons. The free electrons or holes (thus) produced can be used for conduction.

6.3. B. — 5.

1. By / On applying heat to a material ... 2. ... for obtaining heat and cold. 3. On losing or gaining electrons, atoms ... 4. ... in passing through a magnetic field. 5. After establishing / having established the exclusion principle ...

6.3. B. — 6.

1. for separating the isotopes of an element; for determining the extent of ionization; for / in establishing the structure of unknown substances. 2. in / by studying the conductivity of this liquid; on / by / after increasing the amount of heat during the reaction; by / in passing X-rays through a magnetic field. 3. by / on comparing the data of various experiments; by / in passing electrons through a crystal; by / in studying the effect of an electric current on a magnet. 4. without / before raising the temperature of the substance; by applying a low potential difference only; without losing some energy in the form of heat.

6.3. C. — 2.

After introducing / having introduced the concept of the energy quantum, P. was able to explain black-body radiation. 2. After introducing a foreign atom the semiconductor crystal has / shows / exhibits a conduction electron or a hole. 3. Before considering / studying / dealing with special problems of semiconductors, we / one must know the most important relations between crystal structure and conductivity. 4. In passing / moving through gases alpha-particles may collide with an atomic nucleus. 5. In / On increasing the temperature the conductivity of the semiconductors increases / rises, while that of metals decreases.

7.1. A. – 2.

a) = (h); b) = (a); c) = (c); d) = (e); e) = (b); f) = (d); g) = (f); h) = (g)

7.1. B. – 5.

1. Eine wärmere Flüssigkeit bewegt sich durch eine kältere hindurch, wobei sie Wärme mit sich führt / unter Mitführung von Wärme. 2. Freie Elektronen lagern sich an benachbarte Atome an, wobei sie diese durch Zusammenstoß / bei Zusammenstößen ionisieren und in negative Ionen umwandeln. / Dabei ionisieren ... 3. Das Ionisierungspotential wird / ist definiert als die Energie, die für die Ablösung eines Elektrons von einem im Grundzustand befindlichen Atom oder Molekül benötigt wird, wobei das dabei entstehende Ion in seinem niedrigsten Energiezustand verbleibt. 4. Bestimmte radioaktive Atome emittieren Positronen / senden P. aus, wodurch sich ihre Ordnungszahl um eins verringert, ihre Massenzahl jedoch unverändert bleibt. 5. Die klassische Theorie der freien Elektronen lieferte einen Wert für die elektrische Leitfähigkeit, wobei man davon ausging, daß die Zahl der freien Elektronen gleich der Zahl der Atome ist.

7.3. A. – 3.

1. The quantity can be measured. meßbar 2. The radius can be changed. veränderlich 3. The anode can be moved. beweglich 4. The battery can be recharged. wiederaufladbar 5. The instrument can be relied on. verläßlich 6. The amount can be neglected. vernachlässigbar, kann vernachlässigt werden 7. The value can be reproduced. reproduzierbar 8. The substance cannot be distinguished. nicht unterscheidbar 9. The change cannot be noticed. nicht feststellbar 10. The process can be reversed. reversibel.

7.3. A. – 4.

1. reliable; verläßlich / Zuverlässigkeit 2. suitable; geeignet / Eignung 3. visible; sichtbar / Sichtbarkeit 4. replaceable; ersetzbar / Ersetzbarkeit 5. variable; variabel / Variabilität

7.3. B. – 4.

1. E. zeigte, daß unter bestimmten Bedingungen die Energie im Strahlungsfeld als in diskreten Quanten konzentriert angesehen werden muß, wobei die Beziehung zwischen Energiequant und Wellenfrequenz durch die Gleichung $E = h\nu$ geliefert wird. 2. Selbst im besten Vakuum, bei dem / in dem / dessen Druck auf 10^{-9} at und weniger verringert worden ist, enthält ein 1 cm³ Gas immer noch mehr als 10^{10} Moleküle. 3. Ein Atom führt bei seiner Bewegung nicht die ganze Ladungswolke mit sich; vielmehr haben die freien Elektronen die Tendenz ein Untergrundgas zu bilden, in dem sich die Ionen bewegen. Dabei erstrecken sich die Wellenfunktionen der freien Elektronen durch das ganze Gitter.

7.3. B. – 7.

1. Use was made of various methods. 2. An analysis was made of the results of two experimental series. 3. An introduction to low-temperature physics is given. / An introduction is given to ... 4. An attempt was made to detect very small ion concentrations. 5. An investigation was made of a number of substances which have similar properties. 6. At the end of the study / paper a definition of new(ly introduced) terms is given. / ... a definition is given of ...

8.1. A. – 2.

1. auftreten 2. sich zeigen, sich ergeben 3. auftreten / erscheinen 4. offenbar (stattfinden) 5. scheinen / offenbar (liegen) 6. offenbar (haben)

8.1. B. – 3.

1. for analysing the structure of unknown substances. 2. for measuring the wavelength of spectral lines. 3. for investigating the properties of radioactive elements. 4. for measuring the quantity of electric charge. 5. for detecting ionizing particles in a gas. 6. for distinguishing isotopes of the same element.

8.1. C. – 2.

The electromagnetic waves differ in their wavelengths and in their effects. The branch of science studying / investigating the interaction between electromagnetic radiation and matter is called spectroscopy. The spectroscopic methods / techniques yield accurate information on the investigated substances in a definite environment. (The field of) Spectroscopy is subdivided on the basis of / according to the frequency ranges of electromagnetic radiation. The various processes in atomic and molecular substances resulting in / leading to the absorption and emission of energy are associated with definite frequency ranges which hardly overlap / with little or no overlap. The interaction of electromagnetic waves with crystalline materials is investigated / studied in crystal optics. In general, however, the term "crystal" optics is used only for / applied only to the spectrum of visible light. The spectrum of visible light is obtained by passing white light through a diffraction lattice or through a prism.

8.3. A. – 4.

1. Unter bestimmten Bedingungen müssen wir davon ausgehen, daß die Energie einer elektromagnetischen Welle in diskreten Photonen oder Quanten konzentriert ist. 2. Es ist zweckmäßig, das magnetische Bahnmoment des im Atom befindlichen Elektrons als eine Größe anzusehen, die sich aus dessen Bewegung um den Kern ergibt. 3. Der Radius des Wasserstoffkerns ist schwer genau zu definieren, aber er kann mit ungefähr $1 \cdot 10^{-13}$ cm angenommen werden. 4. Die kovalente Bindung wird qualitativ als das Ergebnis der gleichzeitigen Zugehörigkeit eines Elektronenpaares zu den in Bindung stehenden Atomen beschrieben. 5. Obwohl bei der Beta-Radioaktivität Elektronen und Neutrinos vom Kern emittiert werden, nimmt man nicht an, daß letzterer diese Teilchen enthält.

8.3. B. – 3.

1. Einige Materialien hören kurze Zeit nach der Entfernung der anregenden Strahlung ihrerseits auf, Strahlen auszusenden. 2. In besonderen Fällen gibt man in der Technik Halbleitern für die Erzeugung von Wärme und Kälte den Vorzug. 3. Atome, die weder Elektronen abgeben noch Elektronen aufnehmen, müssen paarige Valenzelektronen haben.

8.3. B. – 4.

1. determining the charge of the particle. 2. developing a new method to study / for studying this phenomenon 3. diffracting gamma rays by means of crystals 4. calculating the ratio between the various proportions 5. relating the emission of the spectrum to the atomic structure

8.3. B. – 5.

1. acting as an insulator 2. initiating an interesting process 3. causing many chemical reactions 4. absorbing energy and emitting radiation 5. giving off an electron and becoming ionized

9.1. A. – 2.

1. = 7b; 2. = 22b; 3. = 1a; 4. = 6d; 5. = 16a; 6. = 2a/b; 7. = 19a; 8. = 9d; 9. = 13a; 10. 3d; 11. = 15a; 12. = 17a/b; 13. = 18d; 14. = 8a; 15. = 12b; 16. = 4a; 17. = 21a; 18. = 10a; 19. = 20d; 20. = 5a/b; 21. = 11d; 22. = 14c

9.1. B. − 5.

1. Da die Elektronenbindungen zwischen den einzelnen Atomen alle Valenzelektronen der Atome einbeziehen, führt bereits das Vorhandensein eines einzigen freien Elektrons dazu, daß eine Elektronenpaarbindung zerstört ist. 2. Die Ionentrennung bewirkt, daß das Element so lange polarisiert wird, bis das Feld um die Elektroden neutralisiert ist.

9.3. A. − 2.

a) = (b); b) = (i); c) = (g); d) = (d); e) = (j); f) = (c); g) = (e); h) = (f); i) = (a); j) = (h).

9.3. A. − 4.

1. acquire 2. acquire 3. obtain 4. achieve / obtain 5. acquire 6. obtain

10.1. A. − 2.

a) = (f); b) = (a); c) = (d); d) = (c); e) = (h); f) = (e); g) = (b); h) = (j); i) = (i); j) = (g).

10.1. B. − 4.

1. If the charge carriers are movable / mobile they will be accelerated by the force exerted / acting on them. 2. If a voltage is applied to an electric conductor, an electric field will be formed / produced which exerts a force on the electrons. 3. If foreign atoms are introduced into a semiconductor, its conductivity will be increased. 4. If the voltage between the electrodes is increased, the force will also increase and hence the acceleration of the charge carriers. 5. If the pressure in a gas discharge tube is decreased / reduced, the distance between the gas molecules will also decrease.

10.1. B. − 5.2.

1. Looking at a gas discharge tube, we find two metal electrodes which are opposite to each other. 2. Considering the results from this aspect, essential differences are found. 3. Given a temperature near absolute zero, the molecules are only little influenced by heat motion.

10.1. C. − 2.

1. If a body changes its position in space with time, it is in the state of motion. 2. A body stays / remains in the state of rest or motion, unless it is caused to change its state by forces exerted / acting on it. 3. Provided we have a point of reference, we can describe the motion of a body. 4. We choose / select / take a body as point of reference, assuming / supposing that the body itself does not move. 5. A motion is called translation if / on condition that the paths which the individual points of a body travel relative to the reference system are parallel to and congruent with each other. 6. A motion is called rotation, if a straight line called axis keeps the same position when in motion. 7. The motion of a body is completely determined, if the position of each of its points is determined at each time.

10.3. A. − 2.

a) = (h); b) = (a); c) = (e); d) = (c); e) = (g); f) = (b); g) = (f); h) = (i); i) = (d); j) = (j).

10.3. B. − 3.

1. a positively charged particle 2. a sufficiently small charge 3. largely qualitative observations 4. naturally occurring isotopes 5. a highly radioactive material

10.3. B. − 5.

1. usually occurs 2. At sufficiently high voltage differences 3. by highly accelerated particles 4. which can occasionally be seen 5. are essentially due to electron emission

10.3. B. − 6.

In order to determine the position of a particle uniquely, we need a reference system. The position of the particle in space can be completely determined by means of / with the help of its three rectangular coordinates. The number of the coordinates required is usually given as "n". The number of coordinates will, of course, change, if constraints have to be considered. Also when / in observing larger moving objects we would normally start with the investigation of a particle which is freely movable / mobile in vacuo.

10.3. C. − 2.1.

electrically charged particle; uniquely determined position; totally wrong assumption; microscopically small dimension; infinitely large value

10.3. C. − 2.2.

1. Classical mechanics made it possible to describe the motions of the planets and of any object on the earth under the influence of gravity correctly / to give / supply / a correct description of the motions ... / By means of classical mechanics it became possible to give ... 2. The operation of mechanical machines was explained adequately. / An adequate / satisfactory explanation was given of the operation ... 3. Classical mechanics defined the rotation and oscillation of large bodies sufficiently / ... gave / provided a sufficient definition of the rotation ... 4. The laws of classical mechanics cannot be applied / do not apply outside the domain, for which they were originally developed / outside their original domain. 5. It was proved / established experimentally / Experimental evidence / proof was obtained that space and time are not independent of each other.

11.1. B. − 6.

All isotopes can be separated. There are various methods for the separation of isotopes which depend on the different properties of the isotope. The oldest and best known device / apparatus for the separation of isotopes is the mass spectrograph which was already developed / devised in 1919 by the British physicist A. By combining electric and magnetic fields it is possible to deflect canal rays in such a way that ions of / with / having the same mass number and the same electric charge hit / strike upon the same point of a photographic plate. Focussing / This can be achieved by means of an electric field and a magnetic field which is (arranged) perpendicular (both) to the electric field and to the direction in which the particle moves. Since in the mass spectrograph particles carrying the same electric charge are focussed in one point of a photographic plate, in case they have the same mass, and since the blackening at this point is proportional to the number of incident particles, it is possible to determine the isotopes and their relative abundance.

11.3. A. − 6.

In the course of the study of electronic properties, the hypothesis was established / it was suggested that movable electrons are the basis for the conduction in metals. Confirmation of this hypothesis was achieved / obtained by the physicist T. He proceeded from the assumption / He assumed that electrons are subject to the effect of inertia owing to their mass and therefore should continue to move in the original direction. This should then cause a voltage pulse. As the result of an experimental investigation T. succeeded in providing evidence for this voltage pulse. From this he was able to calculate the specific charge on the electron. Since the same values were obtained for electrons in vacuo, evidence had been provided for the fact that freely movable electrons were the cause of / the basis for metallic conduction. / ... it had been proved / established that metallic conduction was due to / caused by freely movable electrons.

11.3. B. – 3.

1. Since / As most radioelements are available ... 2. ... because they have a long range and a high penetration power / because of their long range and their high penetration power. 3. Since / As gamma rays produce secondary ionization ... 4. Since / As most of the volume of an atom ...

12.3. A. – 3.

1. amount 2. to a large extent 3. range 4. level / extent 5. amount 6. degree / level 7. to a high degree 8. level / extent 9. amount 10. degree

12.3. A. – 4.

Over recent years the extent of co-operation between the Academy and the industry has been continuously increased. Electronics is an important field of this co-operation, because basic research is to a high degree necessary for the production and development of electronic components. Since 1960 much work has been done in the field of semiconductor physics. Another main field of co-operation involves research on the fundamental principles and the technology of optoelectronic components. In order to increase the range of application of these devices, materials other than silicon are required, particularly compounds of the third and fourth group of the Periodic Table. Another / A third field of co-operation concerns the power industry, because economic development will depend to a high on its extension / because its extension is an essential condition for economic development / the extension of which is ... The Power stations built in recent years increased the amount of electric power available to industry. At present investigations are carried out for developing new measuring techniques and for increasing the degree of utilization of reactor capacity by the rationalization of management. As a final example it may be mentioned that as a result of the co-operation between the Academy and the industry it has been possible to increase the level / degree of automation of production processes considerably.

Alphabetisches Wörterverzeichnis

A

abbreviation Abkürzung (von Wörtern etc.) (8.2.A.)
about (bei Zahlen- u. Maßangaben) etwa, ungefähr (1.1.A.)
above über, oberhalb (1.2.A.)
to absorb absorbieren; aufnehmen (7.4.A.)
absorption Absorption; Aufnahme (6.2.A.)
abstract Adj. abstrakt; Subst. (Inhalts)-Referat; Auszug (12.2.A,)
abundance (Vorkommens)Häufigkeit (1.2.A.)
abundant häufig (vorkommend) (1.2.A.)
academic akademisch; Universitäts-, Studien- (11.4.A.)
to accelerate beschleunigen (4.2.A.)
to accompany begleiten, eine Begleiterscheinung sein (6.2.A.)
account Bericht, Darstellung (12.2.A.)
to account for erklären (1.3.B.)
accurate genau, sorgfältig; richtig, exakt (7.4.A.)
acquaintance (with) Bekanntschaft (mit) (12.2.A.)
to acquire erwerben, erlangen, erhalten (8.4.A.)
to act on (ein)wirken auf; angreifen (2.4.A.)
activator Aktivator (8.2.A.)
activity Aktivität, Radioaktivität; Wirksamkeit (7.2.A.)
actual wirklich, real; eigentlich (4.4.A.)
to adapt to anpassen an; einrichten für (11.4.D.)
to add (math.) addieren; hinzufügen, -setzen (10.4.A.)
addition Addition (11.2.A.)
in addition to zusätzlich zu, außer (11.4.A.)
additional zusätzlich, weitere(r/s), Zusatz- (11.4.A,)
admission (to) Zulassung (z. B. zum Studium) (11.4.A.)
to adopt übernehmen (11.2.D.)
adviser Berater, Betreuer (11.4.A.)

to affect (ein)wirken auf, beeinflussen; beeinträchtigen (10.4.A.)
afterward(s): später, nachher, hinterher (8.4.A.)
aim Ziel; Zweck, Absicht (11.2.D.)
to aim (at) (ab)zielen (auf) (12.2.A.)
to align (oneself) (sich) (aus)richten; (sich) (achsgerade) einstellen (9.2.A.)
alkali Alkali, Alkali- (5.4.A.)
all the rest alle übrigen, der Rest (1.2.A.)
allowable erlaubt, zulässig (6.2.A.)
to allow for berücksichtigen (1.3.B.)
to alter ändern, verändern (9.4.A.)
amorphous amorph (5.4.A.)
amplification (elektr.) Verstärkung (3.1.A.)
amplifier Verstärker (3.1.A.)
analysis Analyse (3.4.A.); Untersuchung; Auswertung (7.4.A.); (math.) Analysis (11.4.A.)
analytical analytisch (4.4.A.)
angle (math., phys.) Winkel (9.2.A.)
angular Dreh-, Winkel- (6.2.A.)
apparatus Apparatur, Gerät(e); System (10.4.A.)
apparent offenbar, offensichtlich; scheinbar; anscheinend (4.2.A.)
to appear scheinen; erscheinen als (8.1.A.)
application Anwendung, Verwendung, Gebrauch, Verwendungszweck (2.2.A.)
to apply (to) anwenden (auf), verwenden (für); anlegen (an); ausüben (auf); gelten für (2.4.A.)
to appoint berufen, ernennen (11.2.D.)
to approximate sich nähern, nahekommen, nähern (4.4.A.)
approximately annähernd, angenähert, ungefähr (8.4.A.)
approximation Annäherung, Näherung (5.4.A.)
arc (math., techn.) Bogen (9.4.A.)
to arise from entstehen aus, die Folge sein von, sich ergeben aus (5.2.A.)
array Ordnung, Anordnung, Reihe (4.4.A.)
artificial künstlich; synthetisch (1.2.A.)
as wenn, in dem Maße, wie (1.2.A.)

aspect Aspekt, Gesichtspunkt, Hinsicht
(3.4.A.)
to assess einschätzen, beurteilen (12.2.A.)
to assume annehmen, vermuten (2.2.A.)
assumption Annahme, Vermutung;
Voraussetzung (5.4.A.)
as well as sowohl als auch (7.2.A.)
atom Atom (1.1.A.)
atomic atomar, Atom- (1.1.A.)
atomic model Atommodell (5.3.A.)
atomic number Ordnungszahl (eines
Elements) (1.1.A.)
atom model Atommodell (4.3.A.)
to attach to beimessen, zurechnen;
befestigen an, verbinden mit (2.2.A.)
to attempt (abstr.) versuchen (3.4.A.)
to attract (gel. Teilchen etc.) anziehen
(8.4.A.)
attraction Anziehung (5.4.A.)
attractive force Anziehungskraft (3.2.D.)
author Autor, Verfasser (11.2.A.)
available vorhanden (sein), zur Verfügung
stehen, verfügbar (sein) (9.2.A.)
to avoid (Schwierigkeit) umgehen (3.4.A.);
(ver)meiden (12.2.A.)
axis Achse (6.2.A.)

B

band theory Bandtheorie (6.2.D.)
basic grundlegend, fundamental, Grund-
(7.2.A.)
on the basis of auf der Grundlage von,
auf Grund von, ausgehend von; entsprechend, nach (1.2.A.)
beam (Leit-, Richt)Strahl, Strahlenbündel
(4.2.A.)
to behave sich verhalten; funktionieren
(3.4.A.)
behaviour Verhalten (4.2.A.)
to belong to gehören zu (4.4.A.)
billion (US Engl.) Milliarde (1.2.A.)
to bind, bound, bound (ver)binden;
zusammenfügen (2.4.A.)
binding energy Bindungsenergie (2.2.D.)
to boil kochen, sieden (10.4.A.)
boiling point Siedepunkt (10.4.A.)
to bombard beschießen (2.3.B.)
bond (chem.) Bindung (5.2.A.)
bonding Bindung(en) (5.2.D.)

both ... and sowohl ... als auch (7.2.A.)
brace geschweifte Klammer (11.4.A.)
bracket eckige Klammer (11.4.A.)
breakup Aufbrechen, Aufspaltung (7.2.A.)
brief kurz (gefaßt) (12.2.A.)

C

to calculate berechnen (3.2.A.)
capture (Neutronen)Einfang (7.2.A.)
carbon Kohlenstoff (5.2.A.)
career berufliche Laufbahn, Beruf
(11.4.A.)
carrier Träger; (elektr.) Träger(welle)
(3.4.A.)
to cease aufhören (8.3.B.)
cell Zelle (4.4.A.)
century Jahrhundert (6.4.A.)
certain gewiß, bestimmt (2.2.A.)
chain-reaction Kettenreaktion (7.2.A.)
chamber Kammer, (abgeschlossener)
Raum (10.4.A.)
chance Möglichkeit, Wahrscheinlichkeit
(7.2.A.)
change Veränderung, Wechsel (3.1.A.)
characteristics Charakteristik; (phys.,
chem.) Kenndaten, -ziffern (6.4.A.)
charge (elektr.) Ladung (1.4.A.)
to charge laden (Batterie etc.) (2.4.A.)
charge exchange Ladungsausgleich
(4.3.A.)
chemical chemisch (1.1.A.)
by chemical means auf chemischem Wege,
chemisch (1.4.A.)
chemist Chemiker (1.4.A.)
chief Haupt-, hauptsächlich; Ober-,
Höchst- (6.4.A.)
chloride Chlorid (5.4.A.)
chlorine Chlor (2.2.A.)
to choose, chose, chosen wählen (3.2.A.)
circuit Stromkreis; Kreislauf (2.4.A.)
circular rund, kreisförmig, Kreis- (6.2.A.)
classification (Ein)Ordnung, Klassifizie-
rung (3.1.A.)
to classify (ein)ordnen, einteilen, klassi-
fizieren (2.4.A.)
close nahe, dicht, benachbart (2.4.A.)
to close (ab-, ein-, zu)schließen, ver-
schließen (5.4.A.)
cloud Wolke (2.4.A.)

to coat beschichten, mit einem Überzug versehen, belegen (8.2.A.)

coil Spule, Wendel; (techn.) Rohrschlange, -spirale (9.2.A.)

coincidence Übereinstimmung, Koinzidenz (4.4.A.)

collaborator Mitarbeiter (12.2.A.)

collection Ansammlung, Anhäufung (9.4.A.)

to collide zusammenstoßen (4.1.A.)

collision Zusammenstoß, Stoß, Zusammenprall (2.4.A.)

combination Verbindung, Vereinigung; Kombination (1.1.A.)

common gemeinsam; häufig; üblich (1.2.A.)

(in) comparison (with) (im) Vergleich (zu/mit) (8.4.A.)

compass needle Kompaßnadel (9.2.A.)

complete ganz, gesamt; vollständig (9.2.A.)

to complete vervollständigen, ergänzen; (Elektronenschale) auffüllen (5.4.A.)

complex komplex, zusammengesetzt; kompliziert (7.4.A.)

to be composed of bestehen aus, zusammengesetzt sein aus (9.4.A.)

compound chemische Verbindung (1.1.A.)

concentration Konzentration, Konzentrierung, Anreicherung (2.2.A.)

concept Begriff, Vorstellung (2.2.A.)

to concern betreffen, sich beziehen auf, anbelangen (9.2.A.)

to be concerned with sich beschäftigen mit, befaßt sein mit, zu tun haben mit (9.2.A.)

concerning in bezug/ Hinsicht auf, hinsichtlich, bezüglich (7.4.A.)

to conclude folgern, schließen, eine Schlußfolgerung ziehen; beenden, (ab)schließen (9.2.A.)

conclusion (logischer) Schluß, Schlußfolgerung (3.4.A.)

to condense kondensieren, verdichten (10.4.A.)

to conduct leiten (Strom) (2.4.A.)

conduction (Strom)Leitung (2.4.A.)

conduction band Leitungsband (5.2.A.)

conductivity Leitfähigkeit (El., Wärme) (5.2.A.)

conductor (el.) Leiter (2.4.A.)

configuration Konfiguration; Anordnung, Struktur (9.4.A.)

to be confined (to) eingeschränkt, beschränkt, begrenzt, eingeengt sein (auf) (8.4.A.)

to confirm bestätigen, bekräftigen (9.2.A.)

consequently daher, deshalb, infolgedessen, folglich (4.2.A.)

to consider betrachten (als), ansehen (als) (1.4.A.)

considerable erheblich, beträchtlich, ziemlich (2.2.A.)

consideration Betrachtung, Darstellung (3.1.A.)

constant Subst. Konstante; Adj. konstant (3.4.A.)

constituent Subst. Bestandteil, Komponente; Adj. einen Teil bildend oder ausmachend (6.4.A.)

to constitute bilden, darstellen (9.4.A.)

constitution Zustand (9.4.A.)

constraint Zwangsbedingung; Beschränkung (9.4.A.)

to contain enthalten (1.4.A.)

continuous kontinuierlich, stetig (4.2.D.); ununterbrochen; zusammenhängend (8.4.A.)

contribution to Beitrag zu (11.2.D.)

convenient zweckmäßig, praktisch, geeignet (3.2.A.)

converse gegenteilig, umgekehrt (3.4.A.)

coordinate Koordinate (9.4.A.)

corpuscle Korpuskel, klein(st)es Teilchen (3.4.A.)

to correspond (to) (etwas) entsprechen, äquivalent sein (3.4.A.)

cosine Kosinus (9.4.A.)

to count zählen (10.4.A.)

couple of forces Kräftepaar (9.2.A.)

course Studium (*university course*); Reihe (von aufeinanderfolgenden Dingen); Kurs (*language course*); Studienjahr (9.4.A.)

covalent kovalent, Kovalenz- (5.2.A.)

to cover umfassen (Thematik) (9.4.A.)

co-worker Mitarbeiter(in) (7.2.A.)

criterion Kriterium (3.4.A.)

critical kritisch (7.2.A.)

crystal Kristall (3.4.A.)

crystalline kristallin(isch); Kristall- (5.2.A.)

crystallography Kristallografie (12.2.D.)
cube Kubus, Würfel, Hexaeder, Kubik-
zahl (5.2.A.)
cube root Kubikwurzel (11.2.A.)
cubic kubisch, würfelförmig; Kubik-,
Raum- (5.2.A.)
current Strom (3.2.D.); Adj. gegenwärtig,
modern; laufend (11.4.A.)
curriculum Studien-, Lehrprogramm
(11.4.A.)
curve (9.4.A.)

D

data (Pl.) Daten, Angaben, Werte
(1.4.A.); ungebr.: datum (Sg.)
to deal (dealt, dealt) with behandeln,
sich beschäftigen mit (1.3.B.); zu tun
haben mit; handeln von, zum Thema
haben (8.4.A.)
to decay (phys.) zerfallen (7.2.A.)
decimal point Dezimalstelle (11.2.A.)
decrease Verringerung, Senkung, Abfall
(3.1.A.)
to decrease abnehmen, sich verringern,
fallen; senken, erniedrigen (1.2.A.)
to define definieren, bestimmen (2.2.A.)
definite bestimmt; eindeutig, genau
(1.1.A.)
definition Definition (3.2.A.)
to deflect ablenken (Strahl etc.) (6.4.A.)
deflection Ablenkung; (Zeiger)Ausschlag,
Abweichung (9.2.A.)
to deliver liefern (Energie etc.), abgeben
(5.2.A.)
denominator (math.) Nenner (11.2.A.)
to denote bezeichnen, kennzeichnen;
angeben (9.4.A.)
density Dichte (3.4.A.)
derivative Ableitung (11.4.A.)
to derive (from) (chem., math.) ableiten
(aus) (11.2.A.)
to descend (to) herab-, heruntersenken,
herabfallen (auf) (8.2.A.)
to be designed (+ to + Inf.) bestimmt sein
für, sollen; den Zweck haben (11.4.A.)
to detach ablösen, (ab-, los)trennen,
loslösen (5.4.A.)
to detect nachweisen; feststellen (3.2.A.)

detection Nachweis, Feststellung, Auf-
finden; Registrierung, Aufzeichnung
(9.2.A.)
to determine bestimmen (1.1.A.)
device Gerät, Apparat, Vorrichtung
(10.4.A.)
to devise (Versuchsanordung) entwickeln;
ausdenken, erfinden (3.4.A.)
to be devoted to gewidmet sein, behandeln
(Buch, Thema etc) (12.2.A.)
diamagnetic diamagnetisch (9.4.D.)
diameter Durchmesser, Diameter (11.2.A.)
diamond Diamant (5.2.A.)
dielectric Dielektrikum (3.4.D.)
dielectric strength Durchschlagsfestigkeit
(3.4.D.)
dielectric breakdown Durchschlag (3.4.D.)
to differ (from) sich unterscheiden (von)
(1.1.A.)
differential calculus Differentialrechnung
(11.4.A.)
to differentiate differenzieren, unterscheiden, trennen (10.4.A.)
differentiation Differenzierung (3.4.A.)
to diffract (phys.) beugen (3.4.A.)
diffraction (phys.) Beugung, Diffraktion
(4.2.A.)
dimensional dimensional (4.4.A.)
directed gerichtet (5.4.A.)
discharge Entladung (8.2.A.)
to discover entdecken; feststellen (1.2.A.)
discovery Entdeckung; Auffindung (6.4.A.)
discrete diskret (6.2.A.)
to discuss diskutieren, besprechen,
erörtern (4.4.A.)
dislocation Dislokation (4.4.A.)
to disperse zerlegen (4.1.A.)
dispersion Zerlegung (4.1.A.)
to display zeigen; aufweisen; zum Ausdruck kommen (4.3.A.)
to dissipate (sich) zerstreuen; verloren-
gehen, dissipieren (3.4.A.)
distinct eindeutig; charakteristisch,
ausgeprägt (1.4.A.)
to distinguish (etwas) unterscheiden (1.1.B.)
to distort verzerren (4.2.A.)
distribution Verteilung (6.2.A.)
disturbance Störung; Wellen- (5.2.A.)
division Teilung (4.1.A.); Division
(11.2.A.)

double doppelt, zweifach, Doppel-; das Doppelte, Zweifache (1.4.A.)
down to bis zu (2.1.A.)
dual zweifach, doppelt; Doppel- (3.4.A.)
dynamic(al) dynamisch (9.4.A.)
dyne Dyn (3.2.A.)

E

earth's crust Erdrinde (1.2.A.)
editorial board Redaktionskollegium (12.2.D.)
effect Effekt, Einwirkung, Einfluß; Ergebnis, Resultat (4.2.A.)
either ... or entweder ... oder (1.1.A.)
to eject ausstoßen, emittieren (5.2.A.)
to elect wählen (12.2.D.)
electromagnetic elektromagnetisch (6.4.A.)
electronegative elektronegativ (5.4.A.)
electronegativity Elektronegativität (5.4.A.)
electropositive elektropositiv (5.4.A.)
electrostatic elektrostatisch (3.2.A.)
electrostatics Elektrostatik (3.2.A.)
element (chem. etc.) Element (1.1.A.)
elementary Element-, Elementar- (5.3,A.)
elliptic elliptisch (6.2.A.)
elucidation Aufklärung, Erläuterung (11.2.D.)
to emphasize hervorheben, betonen (12.2.A.)
empty leer (6.2.D.)
energy gap Energielücke; verbotene Zone (8.2.A.)
to be engaged in sich beschäftigen mit (11.4.D.)
to enrich anreichern, konzentrieren (2.2.A.)
entire gesamt, ganz, vollständig; Gesamt- (3.4.A.)
environment Umgebung; Umwelt (7.4.A.)
equal gleich (in bezug auf etw.), gleichartig (2.1.A.)
to equal gleich sein (2.1.A.)
equation Gleichung (3.4.A.)
equilibrium Gleichgewicht (5.4.A.)
equipment (techn.) Ausrüstung (11.4.D.)
equivalent Subst. Äquivalent, gleichwertiger Betrag, gleichwertige Menge; Adj. äquivalent, gleichwertig; Äquivalent- (4.2.A.)

to escape entweichen, entkommen (7.2.A.)
essential (unbedingt) notwendig, erforderlich, wesentlich; wichtig, bedeutend (6.2.A.)
to establish feststellen; aufstellen; beweisen (2.4.C.)
Eulerian Euler(i)sch (9.4.A.)
to evaporate verdampfen/verdunsten (lassen); eindampfen (10.4.A.)
even if/even so selbst wenn (10.1.B.)
even number gerade Zahl (1.2.A.)
eventually schließlich, endlich (8.2.A.)
evidence Beweis, Nachweis; Beweismaterial (2.2.A.)
evident klar (ersichtlich), offenbar (11.2.A.)
examination Untersuchung, Prüfung (4.2.A.)
to examine prüfen (Examen); (nach-)prüfen, untersuchen (11.4.A.)
except (for) außer, mit Ausnahme von, bis auf (8.2.A.)
exception Ausnahme (1.4.A.)
excess Überschuß, Übermaß (2.4.A.)
exchange Austausch (2.4.A.)
excitation Anregung; Erregung (7.4.A.)
to excite anregen, erregen (6.2.A.)
exclusion Ausschließung, Ausschluß (6.2.A.)
to exert ausüben (3.2.A.)
to exhibit zeigen, aufweisen (4.2.A.)
to exist existieren, vorhanden sein, (da)sein, sich finden (5.2.A.)
existence Existenz, Vorhandensein (2.2.A.)
to experience erfahren (3.2.A.)
experimental experimentell; Experimental-, Versuchs- (3.4.A.)
explanation Erklärung, Erläuterung; Aufklärung (6.2.A.)
explicit explizit; deutlich; ausdrücklich (12.2.A.)
expulsion Abstoßung; Entfernung (7.4.A.)
to extend sich erstrecken, sich ausdehnen, reichen (3.2.A.)
extended secondary school Erweiterte Oberschule (11.4.A.)
extent Ausmaß, Umfang, Grad (2.2.A.)
to extract a root (math.) Wurzel ziehen, radizieren (10.4.A.)
extranuclear außerhalb des Kerns (befindlich) (1.4.A.)

F

in fact tatsächlich, wirklich (7.2.A.)
factor (mitwirkender) Umstand, Wirkgröße (2.2.A.); (math.) Faktor (11.2.A.)
to fail + Infinitiv: Ausdruck der Verneinung (4.4.A.)
fairly ziemlich, verhältnismäßig, relativ (7.4.A.)
to fall fallen; auftreffen (2.3.B.)
to favour bevorzugen, begünstigen, erleichtern (5.4.A.)
feature charakteristischer (wichtiger) (Bestand)Teil; Grundzug; Merkmal (7.2.A.)
field Feld (3.2.A.)
findings (Untersuchungs)Ergebnisse (11.2.A.)
finite (math.) endlich (Zahl) (8.4.A.)
fission (phys.) Spaltung, Teilung (7.2.A.)
fissionable spaltbar (7.2.A.)
fixed fest, unbeweglich; ortsfest (9.4.A.)
flexibility Flexibilität (7.3.A.)
flexible flexibel (7.3.A.)
flow Fluß, Strömung, Strom (3.1.A.)
to flow fließen (Strom, Flüssigkeit); strömen (2.4.A.)
fluorescence Fluoreszenz (7.4.A.)
fluorescent fluoreszierend, fluoreszent, Leucht(stoff)- (8.2.A.)
to forbid, forbade, forbidden verbieten (6.2.D.)
forbidden gap verbotene Zone (6.2.D.)
force Kraft; Stärke (2.4.A.)
to force zwingen (zu) (3.4.A.)
form Form, Gestalt (1.4.A.)
to form bilden; sich bilden (1.1.A.)
formation Bildung (3.1.A.)
formula (math., chem.) Formel (3.4.A.)
foundation Grundlage, Basis (11.4.A.)
fraction Anteil; Bruchteil; Fraktion (2.2.A.); (math.) Bruch (11.2.A.)
fragment Bruchstück; Spaltprodukt; (Bruch)Teil (7.2.A.)
frame Rahmen; Gestell (9.2.A.)
freezing point Gefrierpunkt (10.4.A.)
frequency (phys.) Frequenz, Schwingungszahl; (math.) Häufigkeit (3.4.A.)

G

to gain gewinnen; aufnehmen (6.2.A.)
gallium Gallium (5.2.A.)
galvanometer Galvanometer (9.2.A.)
gap (Energie)Lücke (6.2.D.)
gaseous gasförmig, Gas- (9.4.A.)
geometrical geometrisch (4.4.A.)
germanium Germanium (5.2.A.)
given bestimmt, gegeben, beliebig (1.1.A.)
to give off abgeben (Elektronen, Energie) (8.2.A.)
glow Glimmen, Glühen, Leuchten (8.2.A.)
gold Gold (1.1.A.)
gradual(ly) allmählich (1.2.A.)
graphite Graphit (7.2.A.)
ground state Grundzustand (4.4.A.)
guidance Führung, Leitung; Beratung, Betreuung (9.4.A.)
guide Leitfaden, Handbuch, Einführung; (leitendes) Prinzip, Richtschnur (12.2.A.)

H

halogen Halogen (5.4.A.)
health Gesundheit(szustand) (12.2.D.)
heavy (Gewicht) schwer (1.2.A.)
hence folglich, daher, deshalb, von dort (8.4.A.)
horizontal horizontal, waagerecht; Horizontal-, Waagerecht- (9.2.A.)
hybrid Hybrid, Misch- (11.2.D.)
hydrogen Wasserstoff (1.2.A.)
hypothesis Hypothese (3.4.A.)

I

ideal ideal, uneigentlich (4.4.A.)
idealized idealisiert (4.4.A.)
identical (genau) gleich, identisch (1.4.A.)
to identify identifizieren; nachweisen; bestimmen (6.4.A.); erkennen; feststellen (10.4.A.)
i.e. (id est), meist **that is** das heißt (1.4.A.)
illumination Aufhellung; Aufklärung (11.2.D.)
to imagine sich vorstellen (3.2.A.)

to imagine as sich vorstellen als (8.3.A.)
imperfection Störung; Störstelle, Fehlstelle (5.2.A.)
impurity Verunreinigung; Störstelle (5.2.A.)
incidence Einfallen (eines Strahles), Auftreffen (von Elektronen) (9.2.A.)
incident einfallend, auftreffend, Einfalls- (9.2.A.)
including einschließlich, darunter (1.4.A.)
(in)coherent (in)kohärent (8.2.A.)
increase Anstieg, Erhöhung (3.1.A.)
index Index (3.4.A.)
to indicate (an)zeigen; angeben; hinweisen, hindeuten (auf) (4.2.A.)
indispensable to unerläßlich für (11.4.D.)
individual einzeln, Einzel-; verschieden (6.4.A.); individuell, persönlich (11.4.A.)
to induce induzieren; hervorrufen, bewirken, auslösen (6.4.A.)
to infer (from) schließen, folgern, herleiten (aus) (3.2.A.)
infinity unendliche Menge oder Größe; das Unendliche (3.2.A.)
to infinity bis ins Unendliche (3.2.A.)
infrared Infrarot (7.4.A.)
infrequent selten (8.2.A.)
inherent zugehörig, innewohnend; Eigen-, Selbst- (8.4.A.)
initial anfänglich, Anfangs-, Ausgangs- (2.2.A.)
to initiate einleiten, in Gang setzen, hervorrufen (8.2.A.)
inner innere(r,s), Innen- (7.4.A.)
to insert (into) einsetzen, einfügen (in); einführen, (hin)einstecken (10.4.A.)
(in)stability (In)Stabilität, (Un)Beständigkeit (6.4.A.)
institution Institution, Einrichtung (11.4.A.)
instruction Unterricht; Anweisung; Hinweise (11.4.A.)
to insulate (elektr.) isolieren (9.2.A.)
insulator Isolator, Nichtleiter (2.4.A.)
integral calculus Integralrechnung (11.4.A.)
integral number ganze Zahl (1.1.A.)
intensity Stärke; Intensität (3.2.A.)
interaction Wechselwirkung (4.4.D.); gegenseitige Beeinflussung (7.4.A.)
interconnection Zwischenverbindung, Verkettung (9.4.A.)
interest in Interesse an (2.2.A.)
internuclear internuklear, Kern- (7.4.A.)

intermediate zwischenliegend; Zwischen-, Mittel- (12.2.A.)
to interpret (as) interpretieren, auffassen (als) (3.4.A.)
interpretation Interpretation, (Aus)Deutung, Erklärung (3.4.A.)
interval Intervall (11.4.A.)
to introduce into einführen, hineinbringen in (5.2.A.)
invariable unveränderlich, gleichbleibend (9.4.A.)
inversion Umkehrung (4.2.A.)
to invert umkehren (4.2.A.)
to investigate untersuchen, Untersuchungen anstellen (7.4.A.)
investigation Untersuchung; Prüfung (10.4.A.)
to involve einbeziehen, einschließen; von Bedeutung sein, eine Rolle spielen (4.2.A.)
ion Ion (2.4.A.)
to ionize ionisieren (2.4.A.)
to irradiate bestrahlen; exponieren; beschießen (7.2.A.)
irradiation Bestrahlung, Einstrahlung (7.4.A.)
isolated isoliert (4.2.D.)
isotope Isotop (1.1.A.)
isotopic Isotopen- (1.4.A.)
issue Herausgabe, Veröffentlichung; Ausgabe, Auflage (9.2.A.)
item Gegenstand, Einzelheit; (Gesprächs-, Verhandlungs)Punkt (12.2.A.)

J

journal (Fach)Zeitschrift, Journal (11.2.A.)

K

kinetic kinetisch (3.4.A.)

L

laboratory Labor(atorium) (11.4.A.)
laser Laser (8.2.A.)
latter letztere(r,s) (6.4.A.)
lattice Gitter (4.4.A.)

lead Blei (1.2.A.)
lead (elektr.) (Zu)Leitung (9.2.A.)
lecture Vorlesung (11.4.A.)
lecturer Dozent (12.2.D.)
length Länge, z. B. in wave-length (3.4.A.)
level Niveau, Höhe, Ebene, Stufe (5.2.A.)
likewise auch, ebenfalls, gleichfalls, desgleichen (5.4.A.)
limit Limes, Grenzwert (11.4.A.)
linear linear (11.4.A.)
liquid Subst. Flüssigkeit, Adj. flüssig (2.4.A.)
localized lokalisiert; ortsgebunden (5.2.A.)
logarithm Logarithmus (11.2.A.)
to look upon as ansehen, betrachten als (1.3.B.)
to lower senken, erniedrigen (7.2.A.)
luminescence Lumineszenz (8.2.A.)
luminescent lumineszierend, Lumineszenz-, Leucht- (8.2.A.)

M

to be made up of bestehen aus, gebildet werden aus (1.1.A.)
magnet Magnet (4.2.A.)
to magnetize magnetisieren (8.4.A.)
magnitude Betrag, (zahlenmäßig ausdrückbare) Größe (3.2.A.)
major größere(r,s); wichtig; wesentlich, Haupt- (7.4.A.)
manner Art, Weise, Art und Weise (5.4.A.)
mark (Bewertungs)Note; Zeichen, Kennzeichen (11.4.A.)
mass Masse (1.1.A.)
mass defect Massendefekt (2.2.D.)
mass spectrograph Massenspektrograf (1.4.D.)
massive massehaltig, Masse- (6.4.A.)
material materiell (1.1.A.)
matter Materie, Stoff (2.4.A.)
maximum Maximum (3.4.A.)
by means of mittels, mit Hilfe von, durch (2.2.A.)
measure Maß, Maßstab (9.2.A.)
to measure messen (3.1.A.)
measurement Messung (3.1.A.)
mechanical mechanisch (6.4.A.)
mechanics Mechanik (3.4.A.)

medium Medium (3.4.A.); Subst. Mittel, Adj. mittel-, Mittel-, mittlere(r,s) (7.2.A.); vermittelnder Stoff, Träger (8.4.A.)
to melt schmelzen (10.4.A.)
mercury Quecksilber (8.2.A.)
merely nur, lediglich, bloß (7.2.A.)
metal Metall (2.4.A.)
microwave Mikrowelle (7.4.A.)
minimum Minimum (3.4.A.); Adj. minimal, kleinste(r,s), Mindest- (7.2.A.)
to mix (ver)mischen; sich mischen (7.2.A.)
mixture Mischung, Gemisch (1.4.A.)
moderator Bremssubstanz, Moderator (7.2.A.)
to modify modifizieren, abändern, abwandeln (6.2.A.)
molecular molekular; Molekular- (3.4.A.)
molecule Molekül (2.4.A.)
momentary momentan, augenblicklich, kurzzeitig (8.4.A.)
momentum (phys.) Impuls, Bewegungsgröße (3.4.A.)
monitoring Überwachung, Kontrolle (10.4.A.)
monograph Monographie (12.2.A.)
motion Bewegung (2.4.A.)
multiple Subst. (das) Vielfache; Adj. Vielfach-, Mehrfach-, Mehr- (6.2.A.)
multiplication Multiplikation (11.2.A.)
to multiply multiplizieren (10.4.A.)

N

namely namentlich, besonders; (bei Aufzählungen) das heißt, z. B. (9.4.A.)
narrow eng, schmal (9.4.A.)
nature Natur (1.2.A.); Charakter, (Eigen)-Art (3.4.A.)
nearby in der Nähe liegend/gelegen, nahe (8.4.A.)
negative negativ, Negativ- (1.4.A.)
to neglect vernachlässigen (8.4.A.)
negligible vernachlässigbar (9.2.A.)
neon Neon (2.2.A.)
net Rest-; Gesamt-, total; Nutz-; Netto- (5.2.C.)
neutral neutral (el. etc.) (2.4.A.)
neutron Neutron (1.1 A.)
nickel Nickel (4.2.A.)
to note feststellen, bemerken (1.4.A.)

nuclear nuklear, Kern-, Nuklear- (1.4.A.)
nucleon Nukleon (1.2.D.)
nuclide Nuklid (6.4.A.)
nucleus, nuclei (Plural) Kern (z. B. Atomkern) (1.1.A.)
numerator (math.) Zähler (11.2.A.)
numerical zahlenmäßig, numerisch (phys. oder math.) (3.2.A.)

O

observation Beobachtung (7.4.D.)
to observe beobachten, verfolgen; feststellen (4.2.A.)
to obtain erhalten, bekommen, erzielen (1.2.A.)
to occur vorkommen (1.2.A.)
odd number ungerade Zahl (1.2.A.)
operation (math.) Operation, Rechnungsverfahren, -art; Arbeitsvorgang, Verfahren, Arbeitsstufe (11.2.A.)
opposite entgegengesetzt (3.2.A.)
oral mündlich (11.4.A.)
ordinary gewöhnlich, normal, üblich (11.2.A.)
ore Erz (8.4.A.)
organic organisch (7.4.A.)
origin Ausgangspunkt; Nullpunkt; Ursprung, Quelle (9.4.A.)
original Original-, original, ursprünglich (6.2.A.)
to originate entstehen (11.2.D.)
to oscillate oszillieren, schwingen (4.4.A.)
otherwise sonst, andernfalls (8.2.A.)
outer Außen-, äußere(r,s); äußerste(r,s) (5.4.A.)
outline Umriß (8.2.D.); Überblick; Abriß, Grundzüge (12.2.A.)
overall Gesamt-, Total- (12.2.A.)
overlap Überlagerung, Überlappung (7.4.A.)
to overlap sich überlagern, überlappen, (7.4.A.)
owing to auf Grund, infolge, durch (5.1.A.)
oxygen Sauerstoff (1.1.A.)

P

parabolic parabolisch (10.4.A.)
paramagnetic paramagnetisch (9.4.D.)
parenthesis, -es runde Klammer (11.4.A.)
partial teilweise, partiell; Teil-, Partial- (2.2.A.)
particular besondere(r,s), speziell, bestimmt, einzeln, jeweilig (2.3.A.)
to pass hindurchtreten (lassen); hindurchschicken (4.2.A.)
passage Abschnitt, Passage (11.2.A.)
pattern Muster; Struktur; Schema; System (4.2.A.)
to penetrate durchdringen, eindringen in (4.4.A.)
penetrating power Durchdringungsvermögen (7.2.D.)
percentage Prozentsatz, Anteil (1.4.A.)
perfect vollkommen, perfekt, ideal, fehlerfrei (5.2.A.)
periodic table Periodensystem (der Elemente) (1.4.A.)
to permit Ausdruck des Zulassens (lassen) (2.3.B.)
phase Phase (8.2.A.)
to be out of phase (phys.) ungleichphasig sein (8.2.A.)
phenomenon Phänomen (3.4.A.)
phosphorescent phosphoreszierend (8.2.A.)
phosphorus Phosphor (8.2.A.)
photographic photographisch (4.2.A.)
physicist Physiker (1.4.A.)
pivot(ed) Trag-, Drehzapfen; Drehpunkt; (drehbar) gelagert; Dreh-, Schwenk-, Kipp- (8.4.A.)
to place anordnen; setzen, stellen, legen; bringen (3.2.A.)
plane Subst. Ebene, ebene Fläche, Adj. eben, plan (9.2.A.)
point Punkt (3.2.A.)
to point out hervorheben, unterstreichen (11.2.A.)
pole (elektr., magn.) Pol (8.4.A.)
positive positiv, Positiv- (1.4.A.)
to possess besitzen, haben (6.2.A.)
possibility Möglichkeit (8.2.A.)
potential Subst. Potential, Adj. potentiell (4.2.A.)
potential difference Potentialdifferenz (3.2.D.)

power (math.) Potenz (11.2.A.)
precise genau, präzise; Präzisions-, Fein-
(11.2.A.)
predominant vorwiegend, vorherrschend
(5.4.A.)
to prefer vorziehen, bevorzugen, bevorzugt
etwas tun (8.2.A.)
present vorliegend; zur Debatte stehend
(2.4.A.)
to be present vorhanden sein; anwesend
sein, vorliegen (2.2.A.)
to present darstellen (12.2.A.)
present-day gegenwärtig, heutig; modern
(6.4.A.)
primary ursprünglich; primär, Primär-
(12.2.A.)
probability Wahrscheinlichkeit (3.4.A.)
probable wahrscheinlich; vermutlich,
mutmaßlich (6.2.A.)
to proceed fortfahren, weiterführen; vor-
gehen, verfahren; verlaufen, vonstatten
gehen (11.2.A.)
product (math.) Produkt (11.2.A.)
progressive progressiv; Folge- (5.3.A.)
pronounced ausgeprägt, deutlich, klar
(6.4.A.)
proof Beweis, Nachweis (4.2.A.)
property Eigenschaft (1.2.A.)
proportion Verhältnis, Proportion; Menge,
Anteil (1.1.A.)
proportional proportional, Proportional-
(10.4.A.)
proposal Vorschlag (11.2.A.)
to propose vorschlagen (6.2.A.)
proton Proton (1.1.A.)
to prove beweisen, nachweisen; sich er-
weisen als (11.2.A.)
provided/providing (that) vorausgesetzt
(, daß) (10.1.B.)
pure pur, völlig; (chem.) rein (8.4.A.)
purpose Zweck, Ziel (2.2.A.)

Q

quadratic quadratisch (11.4.A.)
qualitative qualitativ (7.4.A.)
quantitative quantitativ (7.4.A.)
quantity Menge, Masse, Betrag, Quantität,
Größe (1.4.A.)

quantization Quantelung (6.2.A.)
quantum Quant (6.2.A.)
quotient Quotient (11.2.A.)

R

to radiate (ab)strahlen, (Strahlen) emittieren, aussenden, (Licht, Wärme etc.)
ausstrahlen (8.2.A.)
radiation Strahlung, Strahlen (6.2.A.)
radioactive radioaktiv (1.2.A.)
radioactivity Radioaktivität (6.4.A.)
radiochemical radiochemisch (7.2.A.)
radiochemist Radiochemiker (7.2.A.)
radius Radius (3.4.A.)
random zufällig, Zufalls-; ungeordnet;
regellos, wahllos (5.4.A.)
range Raum, Bereich, Gebiet (4.4.A.)
rare selten (2.4.A.)
rather ziemlich; eher, vielmehr; statt dessen
(4.2.C.)
rather than anstatt; und nicht (4.2.A.)
ratio (quantitatives) Verhältnis, Zahlenverhältnis (1.2.A.)
ray (phys.) Strahl (3.4.A.)
reaction (chem.) Reaktion; Gegenwirkung
(7.2.A.)
reactor Reaktor (7.2.A.)
readily leicht (5.1.A.)
real real, tatsächlich, wirklich (4.4.A.)
rearrangement Umlagerung, Umgruppie-
rung, Umstellung (6.4.A.)
recent vor kurzem, unlängst (entstanden,
geschehen etc.) (6.4.A.); neu; modern
(11.2.A.)
in recognition of in Anerkennung (12.2.D.)
to recognize erkennen (1.4.A.)
recoil Rückstoß (4.4.D.)
rectangular rechtwinklig, rechteckig (9.2.A.)
to refer to verweisen auf (1.3.B.)
to refer to as bezeichnen als (1.3.B.)
(with) reference (to) (in) Bezug (auf) (9.4.A.)
reference system Bezugssystem (10.2.D.)
reference book Nachschlagewerk (12.2.A.)
to reflect reflektieren, (Licht etc.) zurück-
werfen, spiegeln (9.2.A.)
reflection (phys.) Reflexion, Reflektierung
(4.2.A.)
to regard as betrachten als, ansehen als
(9.4.A.)

in/with regard to in Hinsicht auf, hinsichtlich, in bezug auf (11.2.A.)

region Bereich, Bezirk; Zone, Gebiet (7.4.A.)

to register registrieren; (automatisch) anzeigen; aufzeichnen, erfassen (10.4.A.)

regular regelmäßig (aufgebaut) (4.4.A.); gleichmäßig (11.4.A.)

to relate to in Zusammenhang (Beziehung, Verbindung) bringen, verbinden; sich beziehen, Bezug haben, in Verbindung (Beziehung) stehen (zu, mit) (5.4.A.)

relation Beziehung oder Verhältnis zwischen zwei oder mehr Größen (1.3.A.)

relative relativ; verhältnismäßig (1.2.A.)

to release (chem., phys.) freisetzen (7.2.A.)

relevant relevant, einschlägig, sachdienlich (12.2.A.)

reliable zuverlässig (7.3.A.)

to remain (zurück)bleiben, (übrig)bleiben (7.2.A.)

to remove beseitigen, entfernen; entziehen (Energie etc.) (9.4.B.)

reply Antwort (11.2.A.)

report Bericht, Meldung (12.2.A.)

to report berichten (11.2.A.)

repulsive abstoßend, Abstoßungs- (5.4.A.)

repulsive force Abstoßungskraft (3.2.D.)

to require erfordern, verlangen; nötig, erforderlich sein (5.2.A.)

with respect to in bezug auf, hinsichtlich (5.2.A.)

respectively (nachgestellt) beziehungsweise (6.4.A.)

in response to als Reaktion auf (2.4.A.)

rest Subst. Ruhe; Rest, Adj. Ruhe-; Rest- (6.4.A.)

to restore rückstellen, (auf Null) stellen; wiederherstellen (9.2.A.)

as a result of als Ergebnis; als Folge; auf Grund (7.4.A.)

to result in führen zu, zur Folge haben (2.2.A.)

to result from sich ergeben aus, resultieren aus, zurückzuführen sein auf (5.2.A.)

resulting resultierend, sich ergebend, entstehend (4.2.A.)

to retain behalten, beibehalten (5.4.A.)

to reveal zeigen; aufdecken, enthüllen; sichtbar machen (4.3.A.)

reversible reversibel (7.3.A.)

review Bericht; Übersicht; Überblick(sartikel); Buchbesprechung, Rezension (11.2.A.)

revival Wiederaufleben, Erneuerung (2.2.A.)

rigid starr, unbiegsam (9.4.A.)

rod Stab, Stange (8.4.A.)

root (math.) Wurzel (11.2.A.)

rotation Rotation, Drehung, Umlauf(bewegung) (8.4.A.)

to rotate rotieren, (sich) drehen; umlaufen (lassen) (9.2.A.)

rough (ly) ungefähr, etwa (1.1.A.)

rule Regel, Normalfall (1.4.A.)

S

same (völlig) gleich, identisch (2.1.A.)

to saturate (ab)sättigen (7.4.A.)

scale Skala, Gradeinteilung; Maßstab; Maß, Umfang (10.4.A.)

to scatter streuen (4.4.D.)

scatter (ing) Streuung, Streubereich (4.2.A.)

scope Bereich, Gebiet; (Spiel)Raum (7.4.A.)

semiconductor Halbleiter (5.2.A.)

seminar Seminar; Übung (11.4.A.)

sense Sinn, Bedeutung; Hinsicht (4.4.A.)

sensitivity Empfindlichkeit; (Meßgerät) Genauigkeit (9.2.A.)

to separate trennen, teilen (1.4.A.)

separation Trennung, Teilung (2.2.A.)

series Reihe, Serie; Reihenfolge (6.4.A.)

set (Zahlen)Reihe, System, (Zahlen)Menge (4.4.A.)

to set (set, set) up (magn. Feld etc.) errichten, aufbauen (8.4.A.)

shape Gestalt, Form (4.4.A.)

to share gemeinsam haben, anteilig besitzen (5.2.A.)

sharing Subst. vom Verb to share (5.2.A.)

sheet Platte; Scheibe (4.2.A.)

shell Schale; Hülle (5.4.A.)

sign Vorzeichen; Zeichen (2.4.A.)

significance Wichtigkeit; Sinn (5.2.A.); Bedeutung; Signifikanz (12.2.A.)

silicon Silizium (5.2.A.)

similar ähnlich (2.1.A.)

similarity Ähnlichkeit, Gleichartigkeit (8.4.A.)

simple einfach, nicht zusammengesetzt (4.4.A.)

site Stelle, Ort, Lage, Platz (z. B. im Gitter) (4.4.A.)

size Größe, Format, Ausdehnung (4.4.A.)

slight (ly) leicht, schnell (5.1.A.)

to slow down (ab)bremsen; verzögern (7.2.A.)

sodium Natrium (5.4.A.)

sole einzig, alleinig, Allein- (12.2.A.)

solid Subst. Festkörper, Adj. fest (2.4.A.)

to solidify (sich) verfestigen, erstarren, fest werden (10.4.A.)

solution (chem., math.) Lösung (7.2.A.)

some (bei Zahlwörtern) ungefähr, etwa, einige (1.2.A.)

specialization Spezialisierung; Spezialfach (11.4.A.)

to specify (genau) angeben, bestimmen, spezifizieren (3.2.A.)

specimen Muster, Probe (4.4.A.)

spectacular groß(artig), hervorragend (2.2.A.)

spectral spektral, Spektral- (6.2.A.)

spectroscopy Spektroskopie (7.4.A.)

spectrum Spektrum; Frequenzband (6.2.A.)

spherical kugelförmig, Kugel- (5.4.A.)

spin Spin, Eigendrehimpuls (6.2.A.)

spiral Subst. Spirale, Adj. spiralförmig, Spiral- (9.2.A.)

spontaneous spontan, selbständig, Selbst- (7.2.A.)

square root Quadratwurzel (11.2.A.)

stable stabil, beständig, fest (1.1.A.)

staff Lehrkörper (Universität u. ä.); Belegschaft (Betrieb) (11.4.A.)

standard Standard-, Normal-; typisch (3.2.A.)

stationary stationär; ruhend, Ruhe-; ortsfest (6.2.A.)

to stimulate anregen (Strahlung etc.) (8.2.A.)

straight gerade (4.2.D.)

stream Strom, Strahl (4.2.A.)

stress (techn.) Beanspruchung, Belastung (8.2.A.)

to strike (struck, struck) auftreffen auf (2.3.B.)

string Seil; Saite (9.4.A.)

structure Struktur, Aufbau (1.1.A.)

to subdivide unterteilen, untergliedern; aufteilen (7.4.A.)

to be subject to unterworfen sein, unterliegen (9.4.A.)

subscript tiefgestellter Index (11.2.A.)

to substitute for ersetzen durch, austauschen gegen (5.2.A.)

subtraction Subtraktion (11.2.A.)

success Erfolg (2.2.A.)

successful erfolgreich, mit Erfolg (11.2.A.)

such as wie zum Beispiel (2.2.A.)

sufficient ausreichend, zureichend (9.3.B.)

to suggest vorschlagen, anregen; (als sicher) annehmen (2.4.A.)

suitable geeignet (9.4.A.)

to summarize zusammenfassen; (zusammenfassend) darlegen (11.4.A.)

to superpose überlagern (10.2.A.)

to support (unter)stützen, aufrecht(er)halten (3.4.A.)

to suppose annehmen, vermuten (2.2.A.)

supposing/supposed (that) angenommen (, daß) (10.1.B.)

to surround umgeben (3.2.A.)

survey Übersicht, Überblick (12.2.A.)

to be suspended aufgehängt sein; frei tragen; (frei) schweben (Teilchen in Flüssigkeit/Gas) (8.4.A.)

suspension Subst. Aufhängung, Adj. Hänge-, Trag-, Suspensions- (9.2.A.)

T

to take into account/consideration berücksichtigen, erwägen (10.1.B.); in Betracht ziehen (11.4.A.)

to take up aufnehmen (5.4.A.)

to take + Zeitangabe: dauern, in Anspruch nehmen (8.2.A.)

target Ziel (7.4.D.)

taut straff (gespannt) (9.4.A.)

to tend (to + Inf.) tendieren, neigen, eine Tendenz (Neigung) haben; streben nach (5.4.A.)

tendency Tendenz, Neigung, Richtung (5.4.A.)

term Term (3.4.A.); Terminus, Begriff (6.2.A.); Semester (11.4.A.)

terminal Kabelende, Pol; (elektr.) Anschlußklemme (9.2.A.)

in terms of mit Hilfe (von) (3.2.A.)
textbook Lehrbuch (12.2.A.)
the ... the je ... desto (6.4.A.)
then damals (6.4.A.)
theoretical theoretisch (3.2.A.)
thermal thermisch, Wärme-, Thermo-
(8.2.A.)
thermometer Thermometer (10.4.A.)
thesis Dissertation; (Diplom)Arbeit
(11.4.A.)
thin dünn (4.2.A.)
to think of as sich denken, ansehen als,
halten für (1.3.B.)
thorough genau, gründlich (12.2.A.)
thrust Druck(kraft), Schub(kraft) (9.2.A.)
thus so, somit, demzufolge (1.1.A.)
tight fest, festgefügt; eng, dicht (5.2.A.)
tiny (winzig, extrem) klein (8.4.A.)
tool Mittel; Werkzeug (11.4.D.)
topic Thema, (Gesprächs)Gegenstand;
Fach(gebiet) (11.4.A.)
torque Subst. Drehmoment, Richtmoment;
Adj. Drehmoment-, Dreh- (9.2.A.)
total ganz, gesamt, total (1.1.A.)
to transform umformen (3.1.A.)
transformation Umformung (3.1.A.)
transition Übergang (6.2.A.)
translation Translokation (4.4.A.)
transmission Übertragung (3.4.A.)
to transmit übertragen (3.4.A.)
transuranic elements Transurane (1.2.A.)
to trap einfangen; auffangen (8.2.A.)
to travel sich fortbewegen, wandern
(6.4.A.)
treatment Bearbeitung(sverfahren);
Behandlung (2.2.A.)
to be true of gelten, richtig sein für (3.4.A.)
tube (techn.) Rohr, Röhre (8.2.A.)
in turn wiederum (9.4.A.)
tutorial (Fach)Konsultation (an Bildungs-
institut.) (11.4.A.)
twisted gekrümmt; gewunden, verschränkt
(9.4.A.)

U

ultraviolet Ultraviolett; ultraviolett
(7.4.A.)
undergraduate Student (ohne Universitäts-
grad) (12.2.A.)

undoubtedly zweifellos, ohne (jeden)
Zweifel (8.4.A.)
unique (math.) eindeutig; einzigartig
(9.4.A.)
unit (Maß)Einheit (3.2.A.)
universe Universum, Weltall, Kosmos
(1.1.A.)
unless wenn ... nicht (10.1.B.)
up to bis zu (1.4.A.)
usual(ly) gewöhnlich; meistens (1.2.A.)

V

vacant leer, unbesetzt, frei, Leer- (4.4.A.)
in vacuo im Vakuum (3.2.A.)
vacuum Vakuum (3.2.A.)
valence, valency Wertigkeit, Valenz (5.2.A.)
valid gültig, zutreffend; wirksam; stich-
haltig (11.2.A.)
validity Gültigkeit (eines Gesetzes etc.)
(12.2.A.)
valuable wertvoll (12.2.A.)
value Wert; Betrag (4.2.A.)
vapour Dampf; Gas; Rauch (10.4.A.)
variable variabel (7.3.A.)
to vary sich unterscheiden, abweichen
(1.1.A.); schwanken, variieren (1.1.B.)
vector Vektor (3.2.A.)
velocity Geschwindigkeit (4.2.A.)
verification (Nach)Prüfung, Überprüfung,
Verifizierung; Nachweis (8.4.A.)
to verify verifizieren, nachprüfen (11.2.A.)
vertical vertikal, senkrecht; Vertikal-,
Senkrecht-; stehend (8.4.A.)
vessel Gefäß, Behälter (10.4.A.)
vice versa umgekehrt (1.2.A.)
view Ansicht, Meinung (11.2.A.)
visible sichtbar (4.2.A.)
volt Volt (4.2.A.)
volume Volumen (3.4.A.)

W

wavelength Wellenlänge (4.3.A.)
wave-like wellenähnlich (6.4.A.)
wave-packet Wellenpaket (3.4.A.)
weak schwach (Kraft etc.) (5.4.A.)
weight Gewicht (1.1.A.)